THE SANKHYA APHORISMS OF KAPILA

THE SANKHYA APHORISMS OF KAPILA

WITH

Illustrative Extracts from the Commentaries.

Translated by

JAMES R. BALLANTYNE, LL.D.

Third Edition

GYAN

Published by

GYAN

Gyan Publishing House
5, Ansari Road
Daryaganj, New Delhi-110002
Phone: 011-47034999, 9811692060
E-mail: books@gyanbooks.com

Distribution Network
gyanbooks.com
India, USA, Canada, UK, Australia, France

ISBN : 978-81-212-9962-6 (PB)
First Published, 1885

2nd Impression 2021

Printed at: Gyan Press, Delhi.

The
Sankhya Aphorisms of Kapila
Translated by: James R. Ballantyne

THE

SÁNKHYA APHORISMS

OF

KAPILA,

WITH

Illustrative Extracts from the Commentaries.

TRANSLATED BY

JAMES R. BALLANTYNE, LL.D.,

LATE PRINCIPAL OF THE BENARES COLLEGE.

THIRD EDITION.

LONDON:
TRÜBNER & CO., LUDGATE HILL.
1885.

ADVERTISEMENT.

THE present work, both in its Sanskrit portion and in its English, is an amended reprint of three volumes,[1] published in India, which have already become very scarce. An abridged form of those volumes,[2] which subsequently

---

[1] Their titles here follow:

"The Aphorisms of the Sánkhya Philosophy of Kapila, with Illustrative Extracts from the Commentaries. [Book I.] Printed for the use of the Benares College, by order of Govt. N. W. P. Allahabad: Printed at the Presbyterian Mission Press. Rev. L. G. HAY, *Sup't.* 1852."

"The Aphorisms of the Sánkhya Philosophy, by Kapila, with Illustrative Extracts from the Commentary. Books II., III., & IV. In Sanskrit and English. Printed for the use of the Benares College, by order of Govt. N. W. P. (1st Edition, 550 *Copies:—Price* 12 *annas.*) Allahabad: Printed at the Presbyterian Mission Press. Rev. L. G. HAY, *Superintendent.* 1854."

"The Aphorisms of the Sánkhya Philosophy, by Kapila, with Illustrative Extracts from the Commentary by Vijnána-Bhikshu. Books V. & VI. Sanskrit and English. Translated by James R. Ballantyne, LL.D., Principal of the Govt. College, Benares. Printed for the use of the Benares College, by order of Govt. N. W. P. (1st Edition, 550 *Copies:—Price* 12 *annas.*) Allahabad: Printed at the Presbyterian Mission Press. Rev. L. G. HAY, *Sup't.* 1856."

[2] Occupying Fasciculi 32 and 81 of the New Series of the *Bibliotheca Indica,* issued in 1862 and 1865. The proof-sheets of only 32 pages of the whole, from the beginning, were read by Dr. Ballantyne; the rest, by Professor Cowell.

The title of the abridged form runs: "The Sánkhya Aphorisms of Kapila, with Extracts from Vijnána Bhiks[h]u's Commentary," &c. But this is a misrepresentation, as regards Book I., which takes up 63 pages out of the total of 175. The expository matter in that Book is derived, very largely, from other commentators than Vijnána.

appeared, contains nothing of the Sanskrit original but the Aphorisms.

While, in the following pages, all the corrections obtainable from the abridgment have been turned to account, an immense number of improved readings have been taken from another source. Three several times I carefully read Dr. Ballantyne's translation in as many different copies of it; entering suggestions, in the second copy, without reference to those which had been entered in the first, and similarly making independent suggestions in my third copy. All these[1] were, on various occasions, submitted to Dr. Ballantyne; and such of them as did not meet his approval were crossed through. The residue, many more than a thousand, have been embodied

---

Vedánti Mahádeva mainly supplies it at the outset, and, towards the end, well nigh exclusively, Aniruddha. Some share of it, however, will not be traced; it having been furnished by one of Dr. Ballantyne's pandits, whom I have repeatedly seen in the very act, as by his own acknowledgment, of preparing his elucidations.

[1] Many of them, especially in Books II.—VI., rest on readings of the original preferable to those which had been accepted.

Though not fully published till 1856, my edition of the *Sánkhya-pravachana-bháshya*, its preface alone excepted, was in print as early as 1853; and Dr. Ballantyne had a copy of it. A few arbitrarily chosen words apart, his text, after Book I., is borrowed from it throughout, but with no mention of the fact. My advice was unheeded, that he should profit by the copious emendations which I had amassed and digested from better manuscripts than those to which I at first had access. Greatly to his disservice, he would not be induced even to look at them. It faring the same with my typographical corrections, he has, here and there, reproduced errors, more or less gross, which might easily have been avoided. See, for specimens, pp. 197, 288, 357, 373, 374, 381, 390.

in the ensuing sheets, but are not indicated,[1] as successively introduced. The renderings proposed in the footnotes are, for the most part, from among those which have recently occurred to me as eligible.

That Dr. Ballantyne had any thought of reissuing, in whatever form, the volumes mentioned at the beginning of this Advertisement, I was unaware, till some years after he had made over the abridgment of them to Professor Cowell, for publication.[2] Otherwise, I should have placed at his disposal the materials towards improvement of his second edition, which, at the cost of no slight drudgery, are here made available.

The Sánkhya Aphorisms, in all the known commentaries on them, are exhibited word for word. The variants, now given, of the Aphorisms, afforded by accessible productions of that character, have been drawn from the works, of which only one has yet been printed, about to be specified :[3]

I. The *Sánkhya-pravachana-bháshya,* by Vijnána Bhikshu. Revelant particulars I have given elsewhere. My oldest MS. of it was transcribed in 1654.

---

[1] Nor has attention been topically directed to sundry blemishes of idiom which have been removed; as, for example, by the substitution of 'unless' for 'without,' of 'in time' for 'through time,' of 'presently' for 'just,' and of 'between the two' for 'between both.'

[2] "At the time of his departure from India, in 1860, Dr. Ballantyne left with me the MS. of his revised translation of the Sánkhya Aphorisms." "Notice," in the *Bibliotheca Indica,* New Series, No. 81.

[3] For details respecting these commentaries and their authors, see my *Contribution towards an Index to the Bibliography of the Indian Philosophical Systems,* or my Preface to the *Sánkhya-sára.*

II. The *Kápila - sánkhya - pravachana - sútra-vṛitti,* by Aniruddha. Of this I have consulted, besides a MS. copied in 1818, formerly the property of Dr. Ballantyne, one which I procured to be copied, in 1855, from an old MS. without date.[1]

III. The *Laghu-sánkhya-sútra-vṛitti,* by Nágeśa. Of this I have two MSS., both undated. One of them is entire; but the other is defective by the three first Books.

IV. The *Sánkhya-pravachana-sútra-vṛitti-sára,* by Vedánti Mahádeva. Here, again, only one of two MSS. which I possess is complete. The other, which breaks off in the midst of the comment on Book II., Aph. 15, is, in places, freely interpolated from No. I. Neither of them has a date.

Nearly all my longer annotations, and some of the shorter, were scrutinized, while in the rough, by the learned Professor Cowell, but for whose searching criticisms, which cannot be valued too highly, they would, in several instances, have been far less accurate than they now are.

F. H.

MARLESFORD, SUFFOLK,
Aug. 28, 1884.

---

[1] I once had a second copy of this very rare work, bearing no date, but most venerable in appearance. Like many of my manuscript treasures, it was lent, and never found its way back to me.

PREFACE.

THE great body of Hindu Philosophy is based upon six sets of very concise Aphorisms. Without a commentary, the Aphorisms are scarcely intelligible; they being designed, not so much to communicate the doctrine of the particular school, as to aid, by the briefest possible suggestions, the memory of him to whom the doctrine shall have been already communicated. To this end they are admirably adapted; and, this being their end, the obscurity which must needs attach to them, in the eyes of the uninstructed, is not chargeable upon them as a fault.

For various reasons it is desirable that there should be an accurate translation of the Aphorisms, with so much of gloss as may be required to render them intelligible. A class of pandits in the Benares Sanskrit College having been induced to learn English, it is contemplated that a version of the Aphorisms, brought out in successive portions, shall be submitted to the criticism of these men, and, through them, of other learned Bráhmans, so that any errors in the version may have the best chance of being discovered and rectified. The employment of such a version as a class-book is designed to subserve, further, the attempt to determine accurately the aspect of the philosophical terminology of the East, as regards that of the West.

These pages, now submitted to the criticism of the pandits who read English, are to be regarded as proof-sheets awaiting correction. They invite discussion.

J. R. B.

BENARES COLLEGE,
5th January, 1852.

THE

SÁNKHYA APHORISMS

OF

KAPILA.

BOOK I.

a. Salutation to the illustrious sage, Kapila![1]

b. Well, the great sage, Kapila, desirous of raising the world [from the Slough of Despond in which he found it sunk], perceiving that the knowledge of the *excellence* of any fruit, through the desire [which this excites] for the fruit, is a cause of people's betaking themselves to the means [adapted to the attainment of the fruit], declares [as follows] the excellence of the fruit [which he would urge our striving to obtain]:[2]

अथ त्रिविधदुःखात्यन्तनिवृत्तिरत्यन्तपुरुषार्थः ॥ १ ॥

The subject proposed. *Aph.* 1. Well, the complete cessation of pain [which is] of three kinds is the complete end of man.

---

[1] श्रीकपिलमुनये नमः ॥

[2] अथ जगदुद्दिधीर्षुर्महामुनिः कपिलः फलसौन्दर्यज्ञानस्य फलेच्छाद्वारा साधनप्रवृत्तौ कारणत्वं पश्यन्फलसौन्दर्यमाह ॥

a. The word 'well' serves as a benediction;[1] [the particle *atha* being regarded as an auspicious one].

b. By saying that the complete cessation of pain, which is of three kinds,—viz., (1) due to one's self (*ádhyátmika*), (2) due to products of the elements (*ádhibhautika*), and (3) due to supernatural causes (*ádhidaivika*),—is the *complete* end of man, he means to say that it is the *chief* end of man, among the four human aims, [viz., merit, wealth, pleasure, and *liberation* (see *Sáhitya-darpaṇa*, § 2)];[2] because the three are transitory, whereas liberation is *not* transitory: such is the state of the case.

A question whether the end may not be attained by ordinary means.

c. But then, let it *be* that the above-mentioned cessation [of all the three kinds of pain] is the complete end of man; still, what reason is there for betaking one's self to a doctrinal system which is the cause of a knowledge of the truth, in the shape of the knowledge of the difference between Nature and Soul, when there are *easy* remedies for bodily pains, viz., drugs, &c., and remedies for mental pains, viz., beautiful women and delicate food, &c., and remedies for pains due to products of the elements, viz., the residing in impregnable localities, &c., as is enjoined in the institutes of polity, and remedies for pains due to supernatural causes, viz., gems [such as possess marvellous prophylactic properties], and spells, and herbs of mighty

---

[1] अथ शब्दो मङ्गलार्थः ॥

[2] त्रिविधस्याध्यात्मिकाधिभौतिकाधिदैविकरूपस्य दुःखस्यात्यन्तनिवृत्तिरत्यन्तपुरुषार्थश्चतुर्षु पुरुषार्थेषु मध्ये श्रेष्ठः पुरुषार्थ इत्यर्थस्त्रयाणां क्षयित्वान्मोक्षस्याक्षयित्वादिति भावः ॥

power, &c.; and when [on the other hand], since it is hard to get one to grapple with that very difficult knowledge of truth which can be perfected only by the toil of many successive births, it must be still *more* hard to get one to betake himself to the doctrinal system [which treats of the knowledge in question]? Therefore [i.e., seeing that this may be asked] he declares [as follows]:[1]

न दृष्टात्तत्सिद्धिर्निवृत्तेरप्यनुवृत्तिदर्शनात्[2] ॥ २ ॥

The end is not to be attained by ordinary means.

Aph. 2. The effectuation of this [complete cessation of pain] is not [to be expected] by means of the visible [such as wealth, &c.]; for we see [on the loss of wealth, &c.,] the restoration [of the misery and evil,] after [its temporary] cessation.

---

[1] नन्वस्तूक्तनिवृत्तिरत्यन्तपुरुषार्थस्तथापि सत्त्वपुरुषान्यताख्यातिरूपतत्त्वज्ञानहेतुशास्त्रप्रवृत्तौ को हेतुः शारीरदुःखनिवर्तकानामौषधादीनां मानसदुःखनिवर्तकानां वरस्त्रीमिष्टान्नादीनमाधिभौतिकदुःखनिवर्तकानां नीतिशास्त्रोपदिष्टनिरत्ययस्थानाध्यासनादीनामाधिदैविकदुःखनिवर्तकानां मणिमन्त्रमहौषधादीनां सुकराणां सत्त्वेनानेकजन्मपरंपरायाससाध्ये तत्त्वज्ञानेऽतिदुष्करे प्रवृत्तेर्दुर्लभत्वेन शास्त्रप्रवृत्तेर्दुर्लभतरत्वादत आह ॥

[2] Instead of निवृत्तेः, the reading of Aniruddha, and of most MSS., Vijnána has, to the same effect, निवृत्ते· *Ed.*

a. 'The visible,' in the shape of the drugs, &c., above-mentioned[1] [§ 1. *c.*].

b. 'The effectuation of this,' i.e., the effectuation of the complete cessation of pain.[2]

c. *Why* is it not [to be thus effected]? Because, after the cessation (the cessation of *pain* is understood), we see its restoration, the springing up again of pain in general,[3] [from whichever of its three sources (§ 1. *b.*)].

d. The state of the matter is this: not by the expedients above-mentioned is there such a removal of pain, that no pain arises thereafter; for, when, by this or that expedient, this or that pain has been destroyed, we see other pains springing up. Therefore, though it be *not* easy [§1. *c.*], the knowledge of truth [as a complete remedy] *is* to be desired.[4]

e. But then, grant that *future* pain is not debarred by drugs, &c., [employed to remove *present* pain], still, by

---

[1] दृष्टादुक्तौषधादिरूपात् ॥

[2] तत्सिद्धेर्दुःखात्यन्तनिवृत्तिसिद्धेः ॥

[3] न भवति कुतः। निवृत्तेर्दुःखनिवृत्तेरनन्तरमिति शेषोऽनुवृत्तिदर्शनाद्दुःखजातीयोत्पत्तिदर्शनात्।

[4] अयं भावो नोक्तैरुपायैर्दुःखानुत्पत्तिविशिष्टा दुःखनिवृत्तिर्भवति तत्तदुपायैस्तत्तद्दुःखेषु नष्टेष्वपि दुःखान्तरोत्पत्तिदर्शनात्। तस्मादसुकरत्वेऽपि तत्त्वज्ञानमेषितव्यमिति ॥

again and again obviating it [as often as it presents itself], there may be the cessation of *future* pain, also. This doubt he states [as follows] :[1]

प्रात्यहिकक्षुत्प्रतीकारवत्तत्प्रतीकारचेष्टनात्पुरुषार्थत्वम् ॥ ३ ॥

The question whether the end may not be attained by the recurrent use of ordinary means.

Aph. 3. [Let us consider the doubt] that the soul's desire [the cessation of pain, may result] from exertions for the obviation [of pain], as is the case with the obviation of daily hunger.

a. When pain shall arise [let us suppose one to argue], then it is to be obviated; and thus there is the soul's desire, the cessation of pain; just as one should eat, when there is hunger; and thus there is the soul's desire of the eater, viz., the cessation of hunger. In regard to this [doubt] he states the recognized decision :[2]

सर्वासंभवात्संभवेऽपि सत्त्वासंभवाद्धेयः[3] प्रमाणकुशलैः ॥ ४ ॥

---

[1] ननु मा भूदौषधादिभिर्भाविदुःखनिवृत्तिस्तथापि पुनः पुनः प्रतीकारकरणे तु भाविदुःखनिवृत्तिरपि स्यादिति शङ्कते।

[2] यदा दुःखमुत्पत्स्यते तदा तत्प्रतिकर्तव्यं तथा च दुःखनिवृत्तिः पुरुषार्थो यथा यदा क्षुत्तदा भोक्तव्यं भुञ्जानस्य क्षुन्निवृत्तिः पुरुषार्थ इति सिद्धान्तयति ॥

[3] The more ordinary reading of MSS., and that of Aniruddha, is सत्ता°, 'excellence,' not सत्त्वा°, with Vijnána. *Ed.*

This suggestion negatived.

Aph. 4. This [method of palliatives (§3)] is to be rejected by those who are versed in evidence; because it is not everywhere possible [to employ it at all], and because, even if this *were* possible, there would be an impossibility as regards [ensuring] the perfect fitness [of the agents employed].

a. For there are not physicians, &c., in every place and at all times; and [to rely on physicians, &c., would not be advisable], even if there were the possibility,—i.e., even if these *were* [always at hand], since physicians are not *perfect* [in their art];—for pain cannot with certainty be got rid of by means of physicians, &c., with their drugs, &c. Moreover, when corporeal pain has departed, there may still be that which is *mental*, &c.; so that there is not [under such circumstances], in every respect, liberation from pain. For these reasons, *such* a soul's aim [as that which contents itself with temporary palliatives] is to be rejected by those who are versed in evidence,[1] [i.e., who are acquainted with authoritative treatises].

b. He mentions another proof[2] [of his assertion]:

---

[1] नहि सर्वस्मिन्देशे सर्वस्मिन्काले वैद्यादयः सन्ति संभवेऽपि सत्त्वेऽपि वैद्यादीनां सत्त्वाभावान्नहि वैद्यादिभिरप्यवश्यमौषधादिना दुःखं हातुं शक्यते। किं च शारीरदुःखापगमे मानसादेस्तस्य संभव इति न सर्वथा दुःखाद्विमोक्षः। तस्मात्प्रमाणकुशलैरीदृग्विधपुरुषार्थो हेय इति ॥

[2] युक्त्यन्तरमाह ॥

उत्कर्षादपि मोक्षस्य सर्वोत्कर्षश्रुतेः ॥ ५ ॥

Scriptural evidence in favour of this view.

Aph. 5. Also [an inferior method ought not to be adopted,] because of the preeminence of Liberation [as proved] by the text [of Scripture declaratory] of its pre-eminence above all else.

a. One ought not to endeavour after the removal of this or that pain by these and those expedients [§ 1. *c.*]; since Liberation (*moksha*), by being eternal, is transcendent as a remover of all pains. Moreover, one ought to endeavour only after the knowledge of truth, which is the means thereof [i.e., of Liberation]; because the Scripture tells its pre-eminence above all [other objects of endeavour], in the text: 'There is nothing beyond the gaining of Soul,[1] [with the utter exclusion of pain].'

b. But then [it may be suggested], when you say *liberation,* we understand you to mean from *bondage.* And is that bondage essential? Or is it adventitious? In the former case, it is incapable of destruction; if it come under the latter head, it will perish of itself, [like any other adventitious and, therefore, transitory thing]. What have we to do with your 'knowledge of truth,' then? To this he replies [as follows]:[2]

---

[1] न तैस्तैरुपायैस्तत्तद्दुःखोच्छेदे यतितव्यं मोक्षस्य नित्यत्वेन सर्वदुःखोच्छेदरूपत्वेनोत्कर्षात्। आत्मलाभात्परं न विद्यत इति सर्वोत्कर्षश्रुतेरपि तत्साधने तत्त्वज्ञान एव यतितव्यम् ॥

[2] ननु मोक्ष इत्युक्ते बन्धादिति प्रतीयते। स च

अविशेषश्चोभयोः ॥ ६ ॥

An objection met.

Aph. 6. And there is no difference between the two.

a. There is no difference in the applicability of liberation, on either of the suppositions, that the bondage is essential, and that it is adventitious, [supposing it were either (see § 19. *b.*)]. That is to say, we can tell both how the bondage takes place, and how the liberation takes place.[1]

b. Now, with the view of demonstrating [the real nature of] Bondage and Liberation, he declares, exclusively, in the first place, the objections to Bondage's being *essential*[2] [§ 5. *b.*]:

न स्वभावतो बद्धस्य मोक्षसाधनोपदेशविधिः ॥ ७ ॥

Liberation must be possible; else the means would not have been enjoined.

Aph. 7. There would be no rule in the enjoining of means for the liberation of one bound *essentially.*

बन्धः किं स्वाभाविक उतागन्तुकः। आद्ये नाशायोगोऽन्त्ये चेत्स्वत एव नङ्क्ष्यति। किं तत्त्वज्ञानेनेत्यत आह ॥

[1] उभयोर्बन्धस्य स्वाभाविकागन्तुकत्वयोर्मोक्षस्योपादेयत्वेऽविशेषः। यथा बन्धस्योपपत्तिर्यथा च मोक्षस्य तथा वयं वक्तुं शक्नुम इत्यर्थः ॥

[2] अथ बन्धमोक्षयोरुपपत्त्यर्थमादौ तावत्स्वाभाविकत्वे बन्धस्य दूषणान्याह ॥

a. Since Liberation has been stated [§ 1] to result from the complete cessation of pain, [it follows that] Bondage is the junction of pain; and this is not *essential* in man. For, if that were the case, then there would be no rule, i.e., no fitness, in the Scriptural or legal injunction of means for liberation: such is what must be supplied, [to complete the aphorism]. Because, to explain our meaning [by an illustration], *fire* cannot be liberated from its *heat*, which is essential to it; since that which is *essential* exists as long as the substance exists.[1]

b. And it has been declared in the Divine Song [the *Íśwara-gítá,*]: 'If the soul were essentially foul, or impure, or changeable, then its liberation could not take place even through hundreds of successive births.'[2]

c. [Since some one may be disposed to say] '*Grant* that there is no fitness [in the Scriptural and legal injunctions, (§ 7. *a.*)], what have we to do with *that?*' Therefore he declares [as follows]:[3]

---

[1] दुःखात्यन्तनिवृत्तेर्मोक्षत्वाद्बन्धो दुःखयोगः स च पुरुषे न स्वाभाविकः। तथा सति मोक्षाय साधनोपदेशस्य श्रौतस्य स्मार्तस्य च विधिरनुष्ठानं न घटत इति शेषः। न ह्यग्नेः स्वाभाविकादौष्ण्यान्मोक्षः संभवति स्वाभाविकस्य यावद्द्रव्यभावित्वादिति भावः।

[2] उक्तं चेश्वरगीतायाम्। यद्यात्मा मलिनोऽस्वच्छो विकारी स्यात्स्वभावतः। नहि तस्य भवेन्मुक्तिर्जन्मान्तरशतैरपीति॥

[3] भवत्वननुष्ठानं किमेतावतेत्यत आह॥

स्वभावस्यानपायित्वादननुष्ठानलक्षणमप्रा-
माण्यम् ॥ ८ ॥

Scripture would be nugatory, if pain were inevitable.

Aph. 8. Since an essential nature is imperishable, unauthoritativeness, betokened by impracticableness, [would be chargeable against the Scripture, if pain were essential to humanity].

a. That is to say: since the essential nature of anything is imperishable, i. e., endures as long as the thing itself, it would follow [on the supposition that pain is essential to humanity], that, since Liberation is *impossible*, the Scripture which enjoins the means for its attainment is a false authority, inasmuch as it is impracticable[1] [in its injunctions. And this is out of the question; Scripture being assumed, here, as in all the others of the six systems, to be an exact measure of truth].

b. But then [some one may say], let it *be* an injunction [to use means for the attainment of an unattainable object], on the mere strength of Scripture;[2] [and, since Scripture is an unquestionable authority, we may be excused from asking or answering the question, *why* the injunction is given]. To this he replies [as follows]:

नाशक्योपदेशविधिरुपदिष्टेऽप्यनुपदेशः ॥ ९ ॥

---

[1] स्वभावस्यानपायित्वाद्यावद्द्रव्यभावित्वान्मोक्षासंभवेन तत्साधनोपदेशश्रुतेरननुष्ठानलक्षणमप्रामाण्यं स्यादित्यर्थः ॥

[2] ननु श्रुतिबलादेवानुष्ठानं स्यात्तत्राह ॥

An impracticable injunction is no rule.

Aph. 9. There is no rule, where something impossible is enjoined: though it *be* enjoined, it is no injunction.

a. There can be no fitness, or propriety, in an injunction with a view to an impossible fruit; seeing that, though something be enjoined, or ordered [to be effected] by means that are impracticable, this is no injunction at all, but only the *semblance* of an injunction; because it stands to reason, that not even the *Veda* can make one see sense in an absurdity: such is the meaning.[1]

b. Here he comes upon a doubt:[2]

शुक्लपटवद्बीजवच्चेत् ॥ १० ॥

A doubt whether the essential be not removable.

Aph. 10. If [some one says] as in the case of white cloth, or of a seed, [something essential may be not irremovable, then he will find his answer in the next aphorism].

a. But then [the doubter is supposed to argue], the destruction even of what is essential [in spite of what is stated under § 7] *is* seen; as, for example, the essential whiteness of white cloth is removed by dyeing, and the essential power of germination in a seed is removed by

---

[1] अशक्याय फलायोपदेशस्य विधिरनुष्ठानं न संभवति यत उपदिष्टे विहितेऽप्यशक्योपायेनोपदेश एव न भवति किं तूपदेशाभास एव बाधितमर्थं वेदोऽपि न बोधयतीति न्यायादित्यर्थः ॥

[2] अत्र शङ्कते ।

fire. Therefore, according to the analogy of the white cloth and the seed, it is possible that there should be the removal of the bondage of the soul, even though it *were* essential. So, too, there may be [without any impropriety] the enjoinment of the means thereof. Well, *if* [any one argues thus], such is the meaning[1] [of the aphorism, to which he proceeds to reply].

b. He declares[2] [the real state of the case, with reference to the doubt just raised]:

शक्त्युद्भवानुद्भवाभ्यां नाशक्योपदेशः ॥ ११ ॥

Decision that an essential property may be hidden, but not removed.

Aph. 11. Since both perceptibleness and [subsequent] non-perceptibleness may belong to some power [which is indestructible], it is not something *impracticable* that is enjoined, [when one is directed to render some indestructible power imperceptible].

a. In regard even to the two examples above-mentioned [§ 10], people do not give an injunction for [the positive destruction of] something essential, which is indestructible [§ 8]. Why [do we say this]? Because, in these two

---

[1] ननु स्वाभाविकस्याप्यपायो दृश्यते यथा शुक्लपटस्य स्वाभाविकं शौक्ल्यं रागेणापनीयते यथा च बीजस्य स्वाभाविक्यङ्कुरशक्तिरग्निनापनीयते । अतः शुक्लपटवद्बीजवच्च स्वाभाविकस्यापि बन्धस्यापायः पुरुषे संभवतीति । तद्वदेव तत्साधनोपदेशः स्यादिति चेदित्यर्थः ॥

[2] समाधत्ते ॥

instances of the perceptibleness and non-perceptibleness of a power [the powers, namely, of appearing white and of germinating (see § 10. *a.*)], there are merely the manifestation and [afterwards] the *hiding* of the whiteness, &c., but not the *removal* of the whiteness, or of the power of germination; because, that is to say, the whiteness of the dyed cloth and the germinating power of the roasted seed can again be brought out by the processes of the bleacher, &c., [in the case of the dyed cloth], and by the will of the *Yogí*, [the possessor of supernatural powers, in the case of the roasted seed], &c.[1]

b. Having thus disproved the notion that bondage is *essential* [to man], wishing to disprove also the notion that it is the result of some [adherent] *cause*, he rejects the [various supposable] causes, viz., Time, &c.:[2]

---

[1] उक्तदृष्टान्तयोरप्यशक्याय स्वाभाविकायोपदेशो लोकानां न भवति। कुतः। शक्त्युद्भवानुद्भवाभ्यां दृष्टान्तद्वये शुक्लत्वादेराविर्भावतिरोभावावेव भवतो न तु शौक्ल्यस्याङ्कुरशक्तेश्चापायः। रजकादिव्यापारैर्योगिसंकल्पादिभिश्च रक्तपटभृष्टबीजयोः पुनः शौक्ल्यस्याङ्कुरशक्तेश्चाविर्भावादिति भावः॥

[2] एवं बन्धस्य स्वाभाविकत्वं निराकृत्य नैमित्तिकत्वमपि निराकरिष्यन्निमित्तानि कालादीनि निराकरोति॥

न कालयोगतो व्यापिनो नित्यस्य सर्वसं-
बन्धात् ॥ १२ ॥

Time, which applies to all, cannot be the cause of the bondage of a part.

Aph. 12. Not from connexion with *time* [does bondage befall the soul]; because this, all-pervading and eternal, is [eternally] associated with *all*, [and not with those alone who are in bondage].

a. The bondage of man is not caused by *time;* because [if that were the case,] there could be no such separation as that of the *liberated* and *unliberated;* because time, which applies to everything, and is eternal, is at all times associated with all men,[1] [and must, therefore, bring *all* into bondage, if any].

न देशयोगतोऽप्यस्मात् ॥ १३ ॥

Place, for the same reason, cannot be the cause.

Aph. 13. Nor [does bondage arise] from connexion with *place*, either, for the same [reason].

a. That is to say: bondage does not arise from connexion with *place*. Why? 'For the same reason,' i.e., for that stated in the preceding aphorism, viz., that, since it [viz., place] is connected with *all* men, whether liberated

---

[1] न कालनिमित्तकः पुरुषस्य बन्धो व्यापिनो नित्यस्य कालस्य सर्वैः पुरुषैः सर्वकालावच्छेदेन संबन्धान्मुक्तामुक्तव्यवस्थानुपपत्तेः ॥

or not liberated, bondage would [in *that* case] befall the *liberated*, also.[1]

नावस्थातो देहधर्मत्वात्तस्याः ॥ १४ ॥

The soul is not kept in bondage by its being conditioned.

Aph. 14. Nor [does the bondage of the soul arise] from its being conditioned [by its standing among circumstances that clog it by limiting it]; because *that* is the fact in regard to [not the soul, but] the *body*.

a. By 'condition' we mean the being in the shape of a sort of association. The bondage [of the soul] does not arise from *that;* because *that* is the property of the *body* [and not of the soul]; because, that is to say, bondage might befall even the liberated [which is impossible], if that which is the fact in regard to another could occasion the bondage of one quite different.[2]

b. But then [some one might say], *let* this conditioned state belong to the soul. On this point [to prevent mistakes], he declares:[3]

---

[1] देशयोगतोऽपि न बन्धः । कुतः । अस्मात्पूर्वसूत्रोक्तान्मुक्तामुक्तसर्वपुरुषसंबन्धान्मुक्तस्यापि बन्धापत्तेरित्यर्थः ॥

[2] अवस्था संघातविशेषरूपता । ततो न बन्धस्तस्या देहधर्मत्वादन्यधर्मस्य साक्षादन्यबन्धकत्वे मुक्तस्यापि बन्धापत्तेरिति भावः ॥

[3] ननु पुरुषस्यैवावस्था स्यात्तत्राह ॥

असङ्गोऽयं पुरुष इति ॥ १५ ॥

The soul is absolute.

Aph. 15. Because this soul is [unassociated with any conditions or circumstances that could serve as its bonds, it is] absolute.

a. The word *iti* here shows that it [i.e., the assertion conveyed in the aphorism] is a *reason;* the construction with the preceding aphorism being this, that, *since* the soul is unassociated, it belongs only to the body to be conditioned.[1]

न कर्मणान्यधर्मत्वादतिप्रसक्तेश्च[2]॥ १६ ॥

The fruit of works belongs not to the soul.

Aph. 16. Nor [does the bondage of soul arise] from any work; because [works are] the property of another [viz., the mind], and because it [the bondage] would be eternal,[3] [if the case were as you imagine].

---

[1] इतिर्हेतौ पुरुषस्यासङ्गत्वादवस्थाया देहमात्रधर्मत्वमिति पूर्वसूत्रेणान्वयः ॥

[2] The commentator Aniruddha omits the final word, च. *Ed.*

[3] Professor Wilson's Dictionary erroneously gives 'uninterrupted continuance' as one of the definitions of *atiprasanga*; and that definition, in all probability, suggested 'eternal' to the translator, who here had to do with *atiprasakti*. Near the end of *a*, in the next page but one, *atiprasanga* is rendered 'undue result.' For the synonymous *atiprasakti* and *atiprasanga*, respectively, see Aph. 53, with the comment on it, and the comment on Aph. 151, of this Book.

Colebrooke, on various occasions, represents one or other of these terms by 'wrest,' 'straining a rule,' 'room for misconstruction,' &c. As technicalities, they generally signify 'illegitimately extended application' of a canon, notion, or the like. *Ed.*

a. That is to say: moreover, the bondage of the soul does not arise from any work, whether enjoined or forbidden; because works are the property of another, i.e., not the property of the soul [but of the mind]. And, if, through a property of another, the bondage of one quite distinct could take place, then bondage might befall even the liberated [1], [through some acts of some one else].

b. But then [some one may say], this objection does not apply, if we hold that bondage may arise from the acts of the *associate* [2] [viz., the mental organ]: so, with allusion to this, he states another reason, 'and because it would be eternal,' i.e., because bondage, in the shape of connexion with pain, would occur [where it does not,] even in such cases as the universal dissolution [3] [of the phenomenal universe, including the mental organ, but *not* the soul].

A doubt whether the bondage, also, belongs not to something else than the soul.

c. But then [some one may say], if that be the case, then let the bondage, too, in the shape of connexion with pain, belong [not to the *soul*, but] to the *mind* alone, in accordance with the principle that it have the same locus as the works [to which it is due]; and, since it is an established point that pain is an affection

---

[1] न विहितनिषिद्धकर्मणापि पुरुषस्य बन्धः कर्मणोऽन्यधर्मत्वादनात्मधर्मत्वादित्यर्थः । अन्यधर्मेण साक्षादन्यस्य बन्धे च मुक्तस्यापि बन्धापत्तेः ॥

[2] *Upádhi*, for which see p. 53, 1, *infra*. *Ed.*

[3] ननु स्वोपाधिकर्मणा बन्धाङ्गीकारे नायं दोष इत्याशयेन हेत्वन्तरमाहातिप्रसक्तेश्चेति प्रलयादावपि दुःखयोगरूपबन्धापत्तेश्चेत्यर्थः ॥

of the *mind*, why is bondage [i.e., connexion with pain] assumed of the *soul*, also? With reference to this doubt, he declares [as follows]:[1]

विचित्रभोगानुपपत्तिरन्यधर्मत्वे ॥ १७ ॥

Why it is to the soul that the bondage must belong.

Aph. 17. If it were the property of any other, then there could not be diverse experience.

a. If bondage, in the shape of connexion with pain, were the property of another, i.e., a property of the *mind*, there could be no such thing as diverse experience; there could be no such different experience as one man's experiencing pain, and another man's not: [for, it must be remembered, it is not in point of *mind*, but of *soul*, that men are held, by Kapila, to be numerically different]. Therefore, it must be admitted that pain is connected with the soul, also. And this [pain that belongs to the soul] is in the shape merely of a *reflexion* of the pain [that attaches to its attendant organism]; and this reflexion is of its *own* attendant [organism] only; so that there is no undue result[2] [deducible from our theory].

---

[1] नन्वेवं दुःखयोगरूपोऽपि बन्धः कर्मसामानाधिकरण्यानुरोधेन चित्तस्यैवास्तु दुःखस्य चित्तधर्मतायाः सिद्धत्वाच्च किमर्थं पुरुषस्यापि कल्प्यते बन्ध इत्याशङ्कायामाह ॥

[2] दुःखयोगरूपबन्धस्यान्यधर्मत्वे चित्तधर्मत्वे विचित्रभोगानुपपत्तिः कश्चिदेव दुःखभोक्ता कश्चिन्नेति विचित्रभोगानुपपत्तिः । अतः पुरुषेऽपि

b. He rejects also the notion that Nature (*prakṛiti*) is *directly* the cause of bondage:[1]

प्रकृतिनिबन्धनाच्चेन्न तस्या अपि[2] पारतन्त्र्यम्॥१८॥

Nature is not the immediate cause of the soul's bondage.

Aph. 18. If [you say that the soul's bondage arises] from Nature, as its cause, [then I say] 'no;' [because] that, also, is a dependent thing.

a. But then [some one may say], let bondage result from *Nature*, as its cause. If you say so, I say 'no;' because that, also, i.e., Nature, also, is dependent on the *conjunction* which is to be mentioned in the next aphorism; because, if it [Nature] were to occasion bondage, even *without* that [conjunction which is next to be mentioned], then bondage would occur even in such cases as the universal dissolution,[3] [when soul is altogether disconnected from the phenomenal].

दुःखयोगः स्वीकार्यः। स च दुःखप्रतिबिम्बरूप एव प्रतिबिम्बश्च स्वोपाधेरेव भवतीति नातिप्रसङ्ग इति॥

1 साक्षात्प्रकृतिनिमित्तकत्वमपि बन्धस्यापाकरोति॥

2 Here and in the comment, I have corrected तस्यापि. *Ed.*

3 ननु प्रकृतिनिमित्ताद्बन्धो भवत्विति चेन्न यतस्तस्या अपि प्रकृतेरप्युत्तरसूत्रे वक्ष्यमाणसंयोगपारतन्त्र्यं तेन विनापि बन्धकत्वे प्रलयादावपि बन्धप्रसङ्गात्॥

b. If the reading [in the aphorism] be *nibandhaná*[1] [in the 1st case, and not in the 5th], then the construction will be as follows: 'If [you say that] the bondage is caused by Nature,' &c.[2]

c. Therefore, since Nature can be the cause of bondage, only as depending on something else [i.e., on the conjunction to be mentioned in the next aphorism], through this very sort of conjunction [it follows that] the bondage is *reflexional*, like the heat of water due to the conjunction of fire;[3] [water being held to be essentially cold, and to *seem* hot only while the heat continues in conjunction with it].

d. He establishes his own tenet, while engaged on this point, in the very middle[4] [of his criticisms on erroneous notions in regard to the matter; for there are more to come]:

न नित्यशुद्धबुद्धमुक्तस्वभावस्य तद्योगस्तद्योगादृते[5] ॥ १९ ॥

---

[1] This is the lection preferred by Aniruddha and his followers. *Ed.*

[2] निबन्धना चेदिति पाठे प्रकृतिनिबन्धना बद्धता चेदिति योज्यम् ॥

[3] अतो यत्परतन्त्रा प्रकृतिर्बन्धकारणं भवेत्तस्मादेव संयोगविशेषादौपाधिको बन्धोऽग्निसंयोगाज्जलौष्ण्यवदिति ॥

[4] स्वसिद्धान्तममुनैव प्रसङ्गेनान्तराल एवावधारयति ॥

[5] Here follows, in the first edition, the particle तु, for which no authority has been discovered. The word translating it I have retained, but bracketed. *Ed.*

What really is the relation of its bondage to the soul.

Aph. 19. [But] not without the conjunction thereof [i.e., of Nature] is there the connexion of that [i.e., of pain] with that [viz., the soul,] which is ever essentially a pure and free intelligence.

a. Therefore,[1] without the conjunction thereof, i.e., without the conjunction of Nature, there is not, to the soul, any connexion with that, i.e., any connexion with bondage; but, moreover, just through that [connexion with Nature] does bondage take place.[2]

b. In order to suggest the fact that the bondage [of the soul] is reflexional [and not inherent in it, either essentially or adventitiously], he makes use of the indirect expression with a double negative, ['not without']. For, if bondage were produced by the conjunction [of the soul] with Nature, as colour is produced by heating [in the case of a jar of black clay, which becomes red in the baking], then, just like that, it would continue even after disjunction therefrom; [as the red colour remains in the jar, after the fire of the brick-kiln has been extinguished, whereas the red colour occasioned in a crystal vase by a China-rose, while it occurs *not without* the China-rose, ceases, on the removal thereof]. Hence, as bondage ceases, on the disjunction [of the soul] from Nature, the bondage is merely reflexional, and neither essential [§ 5. *b.*] nor adventitious[3] [§ 11. *b.*].

---

[1] The Sanskrit word thus rendered was inadvertently omitted in the first edition. Vijnána here supplies the comment. *Ed.*

[2] तस्मात्तद्योगादृते प्रकृतिसंयोगं विना न पुरुषस्य तद्योगो बन्धसंपर्कोऽस्ति । अपि तु तत एव बन्धः ॥

[3] बन्धस्यौपाधिकत्वलाभाय नञ्द्वयेन वक्रोक्तिः ।

c. In order that there may not be such an error as that of the Vaiśeshikas, viz., [the opinion that there is] an absolutely real conjunction [of the soul] with pain, he says 'which is ever,' &c. [§ 19]. That is to say: as the connexion of *colour* with essentially pure crystal does not take place without the conjunction of the China-rose [the hue of which, seen athwart the crystal, seems to belong to the crystal], just so the connexion of *pain* with the soul, ever essentially pure, &c., could not take place without the conjunction of some accidental associate; that is to say, pain, &c., cannot arise *spontaneously*,[1] [any more than a red colour can arise spontaneously in the crystal which is essentially pure].

d. This has been declared, in the *Saura*, as follows: 'As the pure crystal is regarded, by people, as red, in consequence of the proximity of something [as a China-rose]

यदि हि बन्धः पाकजरूपवत्प्रकृतिसंयोगजन्यः स्यात्तदा तद्वदेव तद्वियोगेऽप्यनुवर्तेत। अतः प्रकृतिवियोगे बन्धाभावादौपाधिक एव बन्धो न तु स्वाभाविको नैमित्तिको वेति॥

[1] वैशेषिकाणामिव पारमार्थिको दुःखयोग इति भ्रमो मा भूदित्येतदर्थं नित्येत्यादि। यथा स्वभावशुद्धस्फटिकस्य रागो न जपायोगं विना घटते तथैव नित्यशुद्धादिस्वभावस्य पुरुषस्योपाधिसंयोगं विना दुःखसंयोगो न घटते स्वतो दुःखाद्यसंभवादित्यर्थः॥

that lends its colour, in like manner the supreme soul[1] [is regarded as being affected by pain].'

e. In that [aphorism, 19], the perpetual purity means the being ever devoid of merit and demerit; the perpetual intelligence means the consisting of uninterrupted thought; and the perpetual liberatedness means the being ever dissociated from *real* pain: that is to say, the connexion with pain in the shape of a *reflexion* is not a real bondage,[2] [any more than the reflexion of the China-rose is a real stain in the crystal].

f. And so the maker of the aphorism means, that the cause of its bondage is just a particular *conjunction* [§ 19.*c.*]. And now enough as to that point.[3]

g. Now he rejects [§ 18.*d.*] certain causes of [the soul's] bondage, preferred by others:[4]

---

[1] तदुक्तं सौरे। यथा हि केवलो रक्तः स्फटिको लक्ष्यते जनैः। रञ्जकाद्युपधानेन तद्वत्परमपूरुष इति॥

[2] तत्र नित्यशुद्धत्वं सदापुण्यपापशून्यत्वं नित्यबुद्धत्वमलुप्तचिद्रूपत्वं नित्यमुक्तत्वं सदापारमार्थिकदुःखायुक्तत्वं प्रतिबिम्बरूपदुःखयोगस्त्वपारमार्थिको बन्ध इति भावः॥

[3] तथा च संयोगविशेष एवात्र बन्धहेतुतया सूत्रकृदभिप्रेत इत्यलम्॥

[4] इदानीमन्याभिप्रेतान्बन्धहेतून्निरस्यति॥

नाविद्यातोऽप्यवस्तुना बन्धायेागात् ॥ २० ॥

The Vedántic tenet on this point disputed.

Aph. 20. Not from Ignorance, too, [does the soul's bondage arise]; because that which is not a reality is not adapted to binding.

a. The word 'too' is used with reference to the previously mentioned 'Time,' &c.,[1] [§ 12, which had been rejected, as causes of the bondage, antecedently to the statement, in §19, of the received cause].

b. Neither, too, does [the soul's] union with bondage result directly from 'Ignorance,' as is the opinion of those who assert non-duality [or the existence of no reality save one (see *Vedánta-sára*, § 20. *b.*)]; because, since their 'Ignorance' is not a real thing, it is not fit to bind; because, that is to say, the binding of any one with a rope merely *dreamt* of was never witnessed.[2]

c. But, if 'Ignorance' *be* a reality [as some assert], then he declares [as follows]:[3]

वस्तुत्वे सिद्धान्तहानिः ॥ २१ ॥

The Vedánti cannot evade the objection, without stultifying himself.

Aph. 21. If it ['Ignorance'] *be* [asserted, by you, to be] a reality, then there is an abandonment of the [Vedántic] tenet, [by you who profess to follow the Vedánta].

---

[1] अपिशब्दः पूर्वोक्तकालाद्यपेक्षया ॥

[2] अविद्यातोऽपि न साक्षाद्बन्धयोगोऽद्वैतवादिनां तेषामविद्याया अप्यवस्तुत्वेन तया बन्धानौचित्यान्नहि स्वाप्नरज्ज्वा बन्धनं दृष्टमित्यर्थः ॥

[3] अविद्याया वस्तुत्वे त्वाह ॥

a. That is to say: and, if you agree that 'Ignorance' *is* a reality, then you abandon your own implied dogma [see Nyáya Aphorisms I., § 31] of the unreality of 'Ignorance;'[1] [and so you stultify yourself].

b. He states another objection:[2]

विजातीयद्वैतापत्तिश्च ॥ २२ ॥

The Vedántí cannot evade the objection, without conceding a duality.

Aph. 22. And [if you assume 'Ignorance' to be a reality, then] there would be a *duality*, through [there being] something of a different kind [from soul; which you asserters of *non-duality* cannot contemplate allowing].

a. That is to say: if 'Ignorance' is real and without a beginning, then it is eternal, and coordinate with Soul: if [therefore] it be *not* soul, then there is a duality, through [there being] something of a different kind [from soul; and this the Vedántís cannot intend to establish]; because these followers of the *Vedánta*, asserting *non-duality*, hold that there is neither a duality through there being something of the same kind [with soul], nor through there being something of a different kind.[3]

---

[1] यदि चाविद्याया वस्तुत्वं स्वीक्रियते तदा स्वाभ्युपगतस्याविद्यानृतत्वस्य हानिरित्यर्थः ॥

[2] दूषणान्तरमाह ॥

[3] यद्यविद्या वस्तुभूतानादिस्तदा नित्यात्मतुल्या। अनात्मत्वे विजातीयद्वैतत्वम्। ते हि वेदान्तिनोऽद्वैतवादिनः सजातीयविजातीयद्वैताभावं मन्यन्त इति ॥

b. He ponders a doubt :[1]

विरुद्धोभयरूपा चेत् ॥ २३ ॥

The Vedánti must not allege that 'Ignorance' is at once real and unreal.

Aph. 23. If [the Vedántí alleges, regarding 'Ignorance,' that] it is in the shape of both these opposites, [then we shall say 'no,' for the reason to be assigned in the next aphorism].

a. The meaning is: if [the Vedántí says that] 'Ignorance' is not *real*,—else there would be a duality through [there being] something of a different kind [from soul, which a follower of the Vedánta cannot allow],—and, moreover, it is not *unreal*, because we experience its effects; but it is in the shape of something at once real and unreal,[2] [like Plato's ὂν καὶ μὴ ὄν: (see *Vedánta-sára*, § 21)].

न तादृक्पदार्थाप्रतीतेः ॥ २४ ॥

There is no such thing as a thing at once real and unreal.

Aph. 24. [To the suggestion that 'Ignorance' is at once real and unreal, we say] 'no;' because no such thing is known [as is at once real and unreal.]

a. That is to say: it is not right to say that 'Ignorance' is at once real and unreal. The reason of this he states in the words 'because no such thing,' &c.; because any such thing as is at once real and unreal is not known.

---

[1] शङ्कते ॥

[2] अविद्या न सती येन विजातीयद्वैतापत्ति-र्नाप्यसती कार्योपलम्भात्किं तु सदसद्रूपा चेदि-त्यर्थः ॥

For, in the case of a dispute, it is necessary that there should be an *example* of the thing [i. e. (see Nyáya Aphorisms, I., § 25), a case in which all parties are agreed that the property in dispute is really present]; and, as regards *your* opinion, such is not to be found; [for, where is there anything in regard to which both parties are agreed that it is at once real and unreal, as they are agreed that fire is to be met with on the culinary hearth?]: such is the import.[1]

b. Again he ponders a doubt:[2]

न वयं षट्पदार्थवादिनो वैशेषिकादिवत् ॥ २५ ॥

A question whether the Vedánti is bound to avoid self-contradiction.

Aph. 25. [Possibly the Vedántí may remonstrate] '*We* are not asserters of any Six Categories, like the *Vaiśeshikas* and others.'

a. 'We are not asserters of a definite set of categories [like the *Vaiśeshikas*, who arrange all things under six heads, and the *Naiyáyikas*, who arrange them under sixteen]. Therefore, we hold that there *is* such a thing, unknown though it be [to people in general], as 'Ignorance' which is at once real and unreal, or [if you prefer it], which differs at once from the real and the unreal [see

---

[1] सदसद्रूपाविद्येति न युक्तमित्यर्थः। तत्र हेतुमाह तादृगिति सदसद्रूपस्य कस्यचिदपि पदार्थस्याप्रतीतेः। विवादास्पदे हि वस्तुनि दृष्टान्त आवश्यकः स च भवन्नयेऽप्रसिद्ध इति भावः॥

[2] पुनः शङ्कते॥

Vedánta-sára, § 21]; because this is established by proofs,'[1] [Scriptural or otherwise, which are satisfactory to *us*, although they may not comply with all the technical requisitions of Gotama's scheme of argumentative exposition (see Nyáya Aphorisms, I., § 35)].

b. By the expression [in the aphorism] 'and others' are meant the *Naiyáyikas*; for the *Naiyáyika* is an asserter of sixteen categories[2] [see Nyáya Aphorisms, I., § 1].

c. He confutes[3] [this pretence of evading the objection, by disallowing the categories of the Nyáya]:

अनियतत्वेऽपि नायौक्तिकस्य संग्रहोऽन्यथा बालोन्मत्तादिसमत्वम् ॥ २६ ॥

The self-contradictory is altogether inadmissible.

Aph. 26. Even although this be not compulsory [that the categories be six, or sixteen], there is no acceptance of the inconsistent; else we come to the level of children, and madmen, and the like.

a. Let there be [accepted] no system of categories [such as that of the Vaiśeshika, § 25]; still, since *being* and *not-being* are contradictory, it is impossible for disciples to

---

[1] न वयं नियतपदार्थवादिनः । अतोऽप्रतीतोऽपि सदसदात्मकः सदसद्विलक्षणो वाविद्यापदार्थ इत्यङ्गीकुर्मो मानसिद्धत्वात् ॥

[2] आदिपदान्नैयायिकः स हि षोडसपदार्थवादीति ॥

[3] परिहरति ॥

admit, merely on Your Worship's assertion, a thing at once real and unreal, which is inconsistent, contrary to all fitness: otherwise, we might as well accept also the self-contradictory assertions of children and the like: such is the meaning.[1]

b. Certain heretics [deniers of the authority of the Vedas] assert that there exist external objects of momentary duration [individually; each being, however, replaced by its facsimile the next instant, so that the uninterrupted series of productions becomes something equivalent to continuous duration], and that by the influence[2] of these the bondage of the soul [is occasioned]. This he objects to, [as follows]:[3]

---

[1] पदार्थनियमो मास्तु तथापि भावाभावविरोधेनायौक्तिकस्य युक्तिविरुद्धस्य सदसदात्मकपदार्थस्य संग्रहो भवद्वचनमात्राच्छिष्याणां न संभवति। अन्यथा बालकाद्युक्तस्याप्ययौक्तिकस्य संग्रहः स्यादित्यर्थः ॥

[2] *Vásaná*, a term which Dr. Ballantyne has rendered variously, in divers passages of the present work, and also elsewhere. It is well defined, in Prof. Benfey's *Sanskrit-English Dictionary:* 'An impression remaining unconsciously in the mind, from past actions, etc., and, by the resulting merit or demerit, producing pleasure or pain.' *Ed.*

[3] केचिन्नास्तिका आहुः सन्ति बाह्यविषयाः क्षणिकास्तेषां वासनया जीवस्य बन्ध इति तद्दूषयति ॥

नानादिविषयोपरागनिमित्तकोऽप्यस्य[1] ॥ २७ ॥

The heretical theory of a succession of momentary objects from all eternity, as causing the soul's bondage, rejected.

Aph. 27. [The bondage] thereof, moreover, is not caused by any influence of objects from all eternity.

a. 'Thereof,' i.e., of the soul. An eternal influence of objects, an influence of objects the effect of which, in the shape of a continued stream, has had no commencement,—not by *this*, either, is it possible that the bondage [of the soul] has been occasioned: such is the meaning.[2]

b. He states the reason of this [impossibility]:[3]

न बाह्याभ्यन्तरयोरुपरज्योपरञ्जकभावोऽपि[4] देशव्यवधानात्स्रुघ्नस्थपाटलिपुत्रस्थयोरिव[5] ॥ २८ ॥

---

[1] Instead of -निमित्तकः, Aniruddha has the substantially equivalent -निमित्तः. *Ed.*

[2] अस्यात्मनः । अनादिविषयोपरागः प्रवाहरूपेणानादिकार्या विषयवासना तन्निमित्तकोऽपि बन्धो न संभवतीत्यर्थः ॥

[3] अत्र हेतुमाह ॥

[4] Dr. Ballantyne had, most probably by mere oversight, the unauthorized बाह्यान्तर°, which I have corrected. The reading उपरज्य°, here followed, is, perhaps, that of Aniruddha. उपरञ्ज्य° is the form of the word recognized by Vijnána; and I know of no manuscript warrant for the alteration of it seen in the following page, 1,—an extract from his commentary. It is, further, a regular derivative, which the other is not, if it is not even unjustified by grammatical prescription. *Ed.*

[5] Aniruddha has -भेद°, 'division,' in place of -व्यवधान°, 'separation.' *Ed.*

A thing cannot act where it is not.

Aph. 28. Also [in my opinion, as well as in yours, apparently], between the external and the internal there is not the relation of influenced and influencer; because there is a local separation; as there is between him that stays at Srughna and him that stays at Páṭaliputra.

a. In the opinion of these [persons whose theory we are at present objecting to], the soul is circumscribed, residing entirely within the body; and that which is thus *within* cannot stand in the relation of the influenced and the influencer, as regards an *external* object. Why? Because they are separated in regard to place; like two persons the one of whom remains in Srughna and the other in Páṭaliputra: such is the meaning. Because the affection which we call 'influence' (*vásaná*) is seen only when there is conjunction, such as that of madder and the cloth to which it gives its colour], or that of flowers and the flower-basket[1] [to which they impart their odour.]

b. By the word 'also' the absence of conjunction [between the soul and objects (see § 15)], &c., which he himself holds, is connected[2] [with the matter of the present aphorism].

---

[1] तन्मते परिच्छिन्नो देहान्तरस्थ एवात्मा तस्याभ्यन्तरस्य न बाह्यविषयेण सहोपरज्योपरञ्जकभावोऽपि संभवति। कुतः। स्रुघ्नस्थपाटलिपुत्रस्थयोरिव देशव्यवधानादित्यर्थः। संयोगे सत्येव हि वासनाख्य उपरागो दृष्टो यथा मञ्जिष्ठावस्त्रयोर्यथा वा पुष्पपुटकयोरिति॥

[2] अपिशब्देन स्वमते संयोगाभावादिः समुच्चीयते॥

c. Srughna and Páṭaliputra [Palibothra, or Patna] are two several places far apart.[1]

d. But then [these heretics may reply], 'The influence of objects [on the soul] may be asserted, because there *is* a contact with the object; inasmuch as the soul, according to *us*, goes to the place of the object, just as the senses, according to Your Worship.' Therefore he declares [as follows]:

द्वयोरेकदेशलब्धोपरागान्न व्यवस्था ॥ २९ ॥

On the heretical view, the free soul would be equally liable to bondage.

Aph. 29. [It is impossible that the soul's bondage should arise] from an influence received in the same place [where the object is; because, in that case], there would be no distinction between the two, [the bond and the free].

a. To complete the sense, we must supply as follows: 'It is impossible that the bondage should arise from an influence received in one and the same place with the object.' Why? Because there would be no distinction between the two, the soul bound and the soul free; because bondage would [in that case] befall the liberated soul, also; [the free soul, according to this hypothesis, being just as likely to come across objects as any other]: such is the meaning.[3]

---

[1] स्रुघ्नपाटलिपुत्त्रौ विप्रकृष्टदेशविशेषौ ॥

[2] ननु भवतामिन्द्रियाणामिवास्माकमात्मनो विषयदेशगमनाद्विषयसंयोगेन विषयोपरागो वक्तव्यः । तत्राह ॥

[3] एकस्मिन्विषयदेशे लब्धादुपरागाद्बन्धो न

b. Here he ponders a doubt:[1]

अदृष्टवशाच्चेत् ॥ ३० ॥

The heretic's attempted defence.

Aph. 30. If [the heretic, wishing to save his theory, suggests that a difference between the two cases (see § 29) *does* exist] in virtue of the *unseen,* [i.e., of merit and demerit, then he will find his answer in the next aphorism].

a. That is to say, [the heretic may argue]: 'But then, granting that they [the free soul and the bound] are alike in respect of their coming into contact with objects, when they become conjoined with them in one and the same locality; yet the *reception of the influence* may result merely from the force of the *unseen,* [i.e., from the merit and demerit of this or that soul; the soul that is liberated alike from merit and demerit being able to encounter, with impunity, the object that would enchain one differently circumstanced]': if[2] [*this* be urged, then we look forward].

a. This he disputes,[3] [as follows]:

न द्वयोरेककालायोगादुपकार्योपकारक-
भावः ॥ ३१ ॥

संभवतीति शेषः। कुतः। यस्माद्द्वयोर्बद्धमुक्तात्मनोर्न व्यवस्था मुक्तस्यापि बन्धापत्तेरित्यर्थः ॥

[1] अत्र शङ्कते ॥

[2] नन्वेकदेशसंबन्धेन विषयसंयोगसाम्येऽप्यदृष्टवशादेवोपरागलाभ इति चेदित्यर्थः ॥

[3] परिहरति ॥

Each back must bear its own burden.

Aph. 31. They cannot stand in the relation of deserver and bestower, since the two do not belong to one and the same time.

a. Since, in thy opinion, the agent and the patient are distinct, and do not belong to the same time [believing, as thou heretically dost, not only that *objects* (see § 26. *b.*) momentarily perish and are replaced, but that the duration of *souls*, also, is of a like description], there is positively no such relation [between the soul at one time and its successor at another] as that of deserver and bestower [or transmitter of its merits or demerits]; because it is impossible that there should be an influence of objects [§ 27] taking effect on a patient [say, the soul of to-day], occasioned by the 'unseen' [merit or demerit] belonging to an agent [say, the soul of yesterday, which, on the hypothesis in question, is a numerically different individual]: such is the meaning.[1]

b. He ponders a doubt:[2]

पुत्रकर्मवदिति चेत् ॥ ३२ ॥

Whether merit may, or may not, be imputed.

Aph. 32. If [the heretic suggests that] the case is like that of the ceremonies in regard to a son, [then he will find his reply by looking forward].

a. But then [the heretic, admitting the principle that

---

[1] तव मते कर्तृभोक्त्रोर्भेदादेककालासंबन्धाच्च नैवोपकार्योपकारकभावे नहि कर्तृनिष्ठादृष्टेन भोक्तृनिष्ठो विषयोपरागः संभवतीत्यर्थः ॥

[2] शङ्कते ॥

the merit or demerit of an act belongs entirely to the agent, may urge that], as the son is benefited by ceremonies in regard to a son, such as that [ceremony (see Colebrooke's 'Hindú Law,' Vol. III., p. 104) celebrated] in anticipation of conception, which [no doubt] belongs to the *father* [who performs the ceremonies, to propitiate the gods], in like manner there may be an influence of objects on the experiencer [say, the soul of to-day], through the 'unseen' [merit or demerit] that belongs even to a different subject [say, the soul of yesterday]: such is the meaning[1] [of the heretic].

b. He refutes this, by showing that the illustration is not a fact:[2]

नास्ति हि तत्र स्थिर एक आत्मा यो गर्भाधानादिना[3] संस्क्रियेत[4] ॥ ३३ ॥

This will not help the heretic's argument.

Aph. 33. [Your illustration proves nothing;] for, in that case, there is no one permanent soul which could be consecrated by the ceremonies in anticipation of conception, &c.

a. 'In that case,' i.e., on thy theory, too, the benefit of

---

[1] ननु यथा पितृनिष्ठेन गर्भाधानादिना पुत्रकर्मणा पुत्रस्योपकारो भवति तद्वद्यधिकरणेनैवादृष्टेन भोक्तुर्विषयोपरागः स्यादित्यर्थः ॥

[2] दृष्टान्तासिद्ध्या परिहरति ॥

[3] Aniruddha has गर्भाधानादिकर्मणा; and Dr. Ballantyne's rendering suits it. *Ed.*

[4] A common reading, but inferior, is संस्क्रियते. *Ed.*

the son, by [means of the performance of][1] the ceremonies in anticipation of conception, &c., could not take place; 'for,' i.e., because, on that theory, there is not one [self-identical] soul, continuing from the [time of] conception to birth, which could be consecrated [by the ceremonies in question], so as to be a fit subject for the duties that pertain to the time subsequent to birth [such as the investiture with the sacred thread, for which the young Bráhman would not be a fit subject, if the ceremonies in anticipation of his conception had been omitted]: and thus your illustration is not a real one,[2] [on your *own* theory: it is not a thing that you can assert as a fact].

b. And, according to *my* theory, also, your illustration is not a fact; seeing that it *is* possible that the benefit to the son should arise from the 'unseen' [merit] deposited in the son by means of the ceremony regarding the son: for it is an implied tenet [of my school], that it [the soul] is permanent [in its self-identity]; and there is the injunction[3] [of Manu, (Ch. II., v. 26), with regard to the ceremonies in question, which proceeds on the same grounds].

---

1 The brackets are of my inserting. *Ed.*

2 तत्र त्वन्मते गर्भाधानादिकर्मणापि पुत्रस्योपकारो न घटते हि यस्मात्तत्र गर्भाधानमारभ्य जन्मपर्यन्तस्थाय्येक आत्मा नास्ति यो जन्मोत्तरकालीनकर्माधिकारार्थं संस्क्रियेतेति तथा च दृष्टान्तासिद्धिः ॥

3 अस्मन्मतेऽपि स्थैर्याभ्युपगमाद्वचनाच्च पुत्रकर्मणा पुत्रनिष्ठादृष्टोत्पत्तेः पुत्रोपकारसंभवाद्दृष्टान्तस्यासिद्धिरित्यर्थः ॥

c. Some other heretic may encounter us, on the strength of [the argument here next stated, viz.,] 'But then, since *bondage,* also, [like everything else] is momentary, let this bondage have nothing determinate for its cause, or *nothing at all* for its cause,'[1] [which view of matters is propounded in the next aphorism]:

स्थिरकार्यासिद्धेः क्षणिकत्वम् ॥ ३४ ॥

Whether bondage may not be momentary, and so require no cause.

Aph. 34. Since there is no such thing as a permanent result [on the heretical view], the momentariness [of bondage, also, is to be admitted].

a. 'Of bondage': this must be supplied, [to complete the aphorism].[2]

b. And thus the point relied on is, that it [i.e., bondage] have no cause at all. And so this is the application [of the argument, viz.]:

(1) Bondage, &c., is momentary;

(2) Because it exists,

(3) [Everything that exists is momentary,] as the apex of the lamp-flame, or the like.[3]

---

[1] ननु बन्धस्यापि क्षणिकत्वादनियतकारणकोऽभावकारणको वा बन्धोऽस्त्वित्याशयेनापरो नास्तिकः प्रत्यवतिष्ठते ॥

[2] बन्धस्येति शेषः ॥

[3] तथा चाकारणक एवास्त्वित्याशयः । तथा चायं प्रयोगो बन्धादिकं क्षणिकं सत्त्वाद्दीपशिखादिवदिति ॥

c. And [continues the heretic,] this [reason, viz., 'existence'] does not extend *unduly*[1] [as you may object,] to the case of a jar, or the like; because *that,* also [in my opinion], is like the subject in dispute, [in being momentary]. This [in fact] is precisely what is asserted in the expression, 'since there is *no such thing* as a permanent result'[2] [§ 34].

d. He objects[3] [to this heretical view]:

न प्रत्यभिज्ञाबाधात् ॥ ३५ ॥

The fact of recognition proves that things are not momentary.

Aph. 35. No, [things are *not* momentary in their duration]; for the absurdity of this is proved by *recognition.*

a. That is to say: nothing is momentary; because the absurdity of its being momentary follows from the opposite argument [to that under § 34. *b.*], taken from such facts of recognition as, 'what I saw, that same do I touch,' [an argument which may be stated as follows], viz.:

(1) Bondage, &c., is permanent;

(2) Because it exists,

---

[1] *Vyabhichára* is the expression here paraphrased. In this work and others, the translator has given it many meanings; and so has Colebrooke, who renders it, in various contexts, by 'contradiction,' 'derogation,' 'failure,' 'impossibility,' 'unoperativeness,' &c. As a logical technicality, it denotes the presentation of the reason, or middle term, unaccompanied by the major term. *Ed.*

[2] न च घटादौ व्यभिचारस्तस्यापि पक्षसमत्वात् । एतदेवोक्तं स्थिरकार्यासिद्धेरित्यनेन ॥

[3] दूषयति ॥

(3) [Everything that exists is permanent,] as a jar, or the like.[1]

श्रुतिन्यायविरोधाच्च ॥ ३६ ॥

That things are momentary is contradicted by Scripture and reasoning.

Aph. 36. And [things are not momentary;] because this is contradicted by Scripture and by reasoning.

a. That is to say: nothing is momentary; because the general principle, that the whole world, consisting of effects and causes, is momentary, is contradicted by such texts as this, viz., '[All] this, O ingenuous one, was antecedently existing,' and by such Scriptural and other arguments as this, viz., 'How should what exists proceed from the non-existent?'[2]

दृष्टान्तासिद्धेश्च ॥ ३७ ॥

The heretic's illustration is not a truth.

Aph. 37. And [we reject the argument of this heretic;] because his instance is not a fact.

---

[1] न कस्यापि क्षणिकत्वं यदद्राक्षं तदेवाहं स्पृशामीत्यादिप्रत्यभिज्ञानुगृहीतेन बन्धाधिकं स्थिरं सत्त्वाद्घटादिवदिति प्रत्यनुमानेन क्षणिकत्वस्य बाधादित्यर्थः ॥

[2] सदेव सौम्येदमग्र आसीदित्यादिश्रुतिभिः कथमसतः सज्जायेतेत्यादिश्रौतादियुक्तिभिश्च कार्यकारणात्मकाखिलप्रपञ्चे क्षणिकत्वानुमानस्य विरोधान्न क्षणिकत्वं कस्यापीत्यर्थः ॥

a. That is to say: the general principle of the momentariness [of all things] is denied; because this momentary character does not [in fact] belong to the apex of the lamp-flame, &c., the instance [on which thou, heretic, dost ground thy generalization, (§ 34. *b.*)]. Moreover, thou quite errest in regard to momentariness, in that instance, from not taking account of the minute and numerous instants [really included in a duration which seems to thee momentary]: such is the import.[1]

If things were momentary, there could be no relation of cause and effect.

b. Moreover, if the momentary duration, &c., [of things] be asserted, then there can be no such thing as the relation of cause and effect, in the case of the earth and the jar, and the like. And you must not say that there *is* no such thing as that [relation of cause and effect]; because it is proved to be a reality by the fact that, otherwise, there would be no such thing as the efforts of him who desires an effect, [and who, therefore, sets in operation the causes adapted to its production]. With reference to this, he declares [as follows]:[2]

युगपज्जायमानयोर्न कार्यकारणभावः ॥ ३८ ॥

---

[1] दृष्टान्ते दीपशिखादौ क्षणिकत्वस्यासिद्धेर्न क्षणिकत्वानुमानमित्यर्थः। किं च सूक्ष्मानेकक्षणानाकलनेन क्षणिकत्वभ्रम एव तच्च तवेति भावः॥

[2] किं च क्षणिकत्ववादे मृद्घटादिस्थले कार्यकारणभावो नोपपद्यते। न च नास्त्येव स इति वाच्यं कार्यार्थिनः प्रवृत्त्यन्यथानुपपत्त्या तत्सिद्धेरित्यभिप्रेत्याह॥

The causal relation is not between things that arise simultaneously.

Aph. 38. It is not between two things coming simultaneously into existence, that the relation of cause and effect exists.

a. Let us ask, does the relation of product and [material] cause exist between the earth and the jar, as *simultaneously* coming into [their supposed momentary] existence, or as successive? Not the first; because there is nothing to lead to such an inference, and because we should not [in that case] find the man, who wants a jar, operating with earth, &c., [with a view to the jar's *subsequent* production]. Neither is it the last; in regard to which he declares [as follows]:[1]

पूर्वापाय उत्तरायोगात् ॥ ३९ ॥

A product cannot survive its substantial cause.

Aph. 39. Because, when the antecedent departs, the consequent is unfit [to arise, and survive it].

a. The relation of cause and effect is, further, inconsistent with the theory of the momentary duration of things; because, at the time when the antecedent, i. e., the cause, departs, the consequent, i.e., the product, is 'unfit,' i.e., is not competent to arise; because, that is to say, a product is cognized only by its inhering in [and being substantially identical with, however formally different from,] its

---

[1] किं मृद्घटयोर्युगपज्जायमानयोः कार्यकारणभावः किं वा क्रमिकयोः। नाद्यो विनिगमकाभावाद्घटार्थिनो मृदादिप्रवृत्त्यनुपपत्तेश्च। नान्त्य इत्याह ॥

substantial cause,[1] [and is incapable, therefore, of surviving it].

b. With reference to this same [topic, viz., the] substantial cause, he mentions another [the converse] objection[2] [to the theory of the momentary duration of things]:

तद्भावे तदयोगादुभयव्यभिचारादपि न ॥ ४० ॥

The coexistence of substance and product is impossible, if things be momentary.

Aph. 40. Moreover, not [on the theory of the momentary duration of things, can there be such a relation as that of cause and effect]; because, while the one [the antecedent] exists, the other [the consequent] is incompatible, because the two keep always asunder.[3]

a. To complete [the aphorism], we must say, 'moreover, [on the theory objected to], there can be no such relation as that of cause and effect; because, at the time when the antecedent exists, the consequent cannot coexist with it, the two being mutually exclusive.'[4] The two suggesters of the relation of cause and effect, in product and sub

---

[1] पूर्वस्य कारणस्यापायकाले उत्तरस्य कार्यस्यायोगादुत्पत्त्यनौचित्यादपि न क्षणिकत्ववादे संभवति कार्यकारणभाव उपादानकारणानुगततयैव कार्यानुभवादित्यर्थः ॥

[2] उपादानकारणमधिकृत्यैव दूषणान्तरमाह ॥

[3] For *vyabhichára*, the word used in the original, see 1, at p. 38, *supra*. *Ed.*

[4] Here again occurs, in the Sanskrit, the term *vyabhichára*. *Ed.*

stance,[1] are (1) this concomitancy of affirmatives, that, while the product exists, the substance thereof exists, and (2) this concomitancy of negatives,[2] that, when the substance no longer exists, the product no longer exists: and these two [conditions, on *your* theory] cannot be; because, since things [in your opinion,] are momentary in their duration, the two [viz., the substance and the product], inasmuch as they are antecedent and consequent,[3] belong to opposite times,[4] [and cannot, therefore, coexist; for the product, according to you, does not come into existence until its substance has perished, which is contrary to the nature of the causal relation just defined].

b. But then, [the heretic may say, do not let the *co-existence* of substance and product be insisted upon, as indispensable to the causal relation between the two, but] 'let the nature of a cause belong to the substantial cause,

---

[1] I have inserted the words 'in product and substance.' *Ed.*

[2] The original dual of 'concomitancy of affirmatives' and 'concomitancy of negatives' is *anwayavyatirekau.* For other English equivalents of this term, occurring in the singular number, see Book VI., Aph. 15 and 63. *Ed.*

[3] 'Antecedent and consequent' renders *kramika*, translated 'successive' in Aph. 38, *a*, at p. 41, *supra.* *Ed.*

[4] पूर्वस्य भावकाल उत्तरस्यासंबन्धादुभयव्यभि-
चारादपि न कार्यकारणभाव इति शेषः। यदो-
पादेयं तदोपादानं यदोपादानाभावस्तदोपादेया-
भाव इत्यन्वयव्यतिरेकौ उपादेयोपादानयोः का-
र्यकारणभावग्राहकौ तौ च क्षणिकत्वेन क्रमिक-
योस्तयोर्विरुद्धकालत्वान्न संभवतः॥

as it belongs to the *instrumental* cause, in respect merely of its *antecedence*.' To this he replies:[1]

पूर्वभावमात्रे न नियमः ॥ ४१ ॥

Antecedence to the product does not distinguish the Matter from the Instrument.

Aph. 41. If there were merely *antecedence*, then there would be no determination [of a substantial or material cause, as distinguished from an instrumental cause].

a. And it could not be determined that this was the *substance* [of this or that product], on the granting of nothing more than its *antecedence* [to the product]; because antecedence constitutes no distinction between it and the *instrumental* causes; for, [as we need scarcely remind you], that there *is* a distinction between instrumental and substantial causes, the whole world is agreed: such is the meaning.[2]

The question whether anything exists besides Thought.

b. Other heretics say: 'Since nothing [really] exists, except *Thought*, neither does *Bondage*; just as the things of a dream [have no real exist-

---

[1] ननु निमित्तकारणस्येवोपादानस्यापि पूर्वभावमात्रेणैव कारणतास्त्विति तत्राह ॥

[2] पूर्वभावमात्राभ्युपगमे चेदमेवोपादानमिति नियमो न स्यान्निमित्तकारणानामपि पूर्वभावाविशेषादीदृगेव हि निमित्तोपादानयोर्विभागः सर्वलोकसिद्ध इत्यर्थः ॥

ence]. Therefore it has *no* cause; for it is absolutely *false*.' He rejects the opinion of these[1] [heretics]:

न विज्ञानमात्रं बाह्यप्रतीतेः ॥ ४२ ॥

We have the evidence of Intuition for the External, as well as for the Internal.

Aph. 42. Not Thought alone exists; because there is the intuition of the external.

a. That is to say: the *reality* is not *Thought* alone; because external objects, also, are proved to exist, just as Thought is, by intuition.[2]

b. But then [these heretics may rejoin], 'From the example of intuitive perception in *dreams* [see Butler's 'Analogy,' Part I., Ch. I.], we find this [your supposed evidence of objective reality] to exist, even in the *absence* of objects!' To this he replies:[3]

तदभावे तदभावाच्छून्यं तर्हि ॥ ४३ ॥

The denial of the external amounts to Nihilism.

Aph. 43. Then, since, if the one does not exist, the other does not exist, there is a void, [i.e., nothing exists at all].

---

1 अपरे नास्तिका आहुः। विज्ञानातिरिक्तवस्त्वभावेन बन्धोऽपि स्वप्नपदार्थवत्। अतोऽत्यन्तमिथ्यात्वेन न तत्र कारणमस्तीति तन्मतमपाकरोति ॥

2 न विज्ञानमात्रं तत्त्वं बाह्यार्थानामपि विज्ञानवत्प्रतीतिसिद्धत्वादित्यर्थः ॥

3 ननु स्वप्नप्रतीतिदृष्टान्तेन विषयाभावेऽपि तदुपपत्तिरिति। तत्राह ॥

a. That is to say: if external things do not exist, then a mere *void* offers itself. Why? Because, if the external does not exist, then *thought* does not exist; for it is *intuition* that proves the objective: and, if the intuition of the external did not establish the objective, then the intuition of *thought*, also, would not establish [the existence of] thought.[1]

b. 'Then *let* the reality be a mere void; and, therefore, the searching for the cause of Bondage is unfitting, *just because a void is all:*' with such a proposal [as recorded in the next aphorism] does [some one who may claim the title of] the very crest-gem of the heretics rise up in opposition:[2]

शून्यं तत्त्वं भावो विनश्यति वस्तुधर्मत्वाद्विनाशस्य ॥ ४४ ॥

The heretic goes the length of asserting sheer Nihilism.

Aph. 44. The reality is a void: what is perishes; because to perish is the habit of things.

a. The void alone [says this prince of heretics, or the fact that nothing exists at all] is the reality, [or the only

---

[1] तर्हि बाह्याभावे शून्यं प्रसज्येत । कुतः । बाह्याभावे विज्ञानाभावात्प्रतीतिर्हि विषयसाधिका बाह्यप्रतीतिश्चेन्न विषयं साधयेद्विज्ञानप्रतीतिरपि न विज्ञानं साधयेदिति भावः ॥

[2] अस्तु तर्हि शून्यमेव तत्त्वमतश्च बन्धकारणान्वेषणमयुक्तं तुच्छत्वादिति नास्तिकशिरोमणिः प्रत्यवतिष्ठते ॥

truth]. Since everything that exists perishes, and that which is perishable is false, as is a dream, therefore, as of all things the beginnings and endings are merely nonentities, Bondage, &c., in the midst [of any beginning and ending], has merely a momentary existence,—is phenomenal, and not real. Therefore, *who* can be bound by *what?* This [question] is what we rest upon. The reason assigned for the perishableness of whatever exists is, 'because to perish is the habit of things;' because to perish is the *very nature* of things: but nothing continues, after quitting its own *nature;* [so that nothing could continue, if it *ceased* to perish]: such is the meaning.[1]

b. He rejects[2] [this heretical view]:

अपवादमात्रमबुद्धानाम् ॥ ४५ ॥

Nihilism denied; as the indiscerptible is indestructible.

Aph. 45. This is a mere counter-assertion of unintelligent persons.

a. 'Of unintelligent persons,' i.e., of blockheads, this is 'a mere counter-assertion,' i.e., a mere *idle* counter-assertion, that a thing must needs be perishable, *because it*

---

[1] शून्यमेव तत्त्वम् । यतः सर्वो ऽपि भावो विनश्यति यश्च विनाशी स मिथ्या स्वप्नवदतः सर्ववस्तूनामाद्यन्तयोरभावमात्रत्वान्मध्ये क्षणिकसत्त्वं सांवृत्तिकं न पारमार्थिकं बन्धादि। ततः किं केन बध्येत इत्याशयः । भावानां विनाशित्वे हेतुर्वस्तुधर्मत्वाद्विनाशस्येति विनाशस्य वस्तुस्वभावत्वात्स्वभावं तु विहाय न पदार्थस्तिष्ठतीत्यर्थः ॥

[2] परिहरति ॥

exists; [and such an assertion is idle,] because things that are not made up of parts, since there is no cause of the destruction of such things, cannot perish.[1]

b. [But] what need of many words? It is not the fact, that even *products* perish; [for] just as, by the cognition that 'the jar is old' [we mean that it has passed from the condition of new to that of old], so, too, by such a cognition as this, that 'the jar has passed away,' it is settled only that the jar, or the like, *is in the condition* of having passed away.[2]

c. He states another objection[3] [to the heretical view]:

उभयपक्षसमानक्षेमत्वादयमपि[4]॥ ४६ ॥

Nihilism is open to the same objections as both the Momentary and the Ideal theories.

Aph. 46. Moreover, this [nihilistic theory is not a right one]; because it has the same fortune as both the views [which were confuted just before].

---

[1] अबुद्धानां मूढानामपवादमात्रं भावत्वाद्विनाशित्वमिति मिथ्यापवाद एव नाशकारणाभावेन निरवयवद्रव्याणां नाशासंभवात् ॥

[2] किं बहुना। कार्याणामपि न विनाशसिद्धिः। घटो जीर्ण इति प्रत्ययेनेव घटोऽतीत इत्यादिप्रत्ययेनापि घटादेरतीताख्याया अवस्थाया एव सिद्धेः ॥

[3] दूषणान्तरमाह ॥

[4] Aniruddha, according to the MSS. which I have seen, reads -क्षेमाद°. *Ed.*

a. This view, moreover [§ 44], is not a good one; because it has the same fortune as, i. e., is open to similar reasons for rejection as, the theory that external things are momentary [§ 26. *b*.], and as the theory that nothing exists besides Thought [§ 41. *b*]. The reason for the rejection of the theory that things are momentary in their duration, viz. [as stated in § 35], the fact of *recognition*, &c., [which is, at least, as little consistent with Nihilism as it is with the momentary duration of things], and the reason for the rejection of the theory that nothing exists besides Thought, viz. [as stated in § 42], the intuition of the external, &c., apply equally here [in the case of Nihilism]: such is the import.[1]

b. Moreover, as for the opinion which is accepted by these [heretics], viz., '*Let the mere void* [of absolute nonentity] be the soul's aim [and *summum bonum*], since herein consist at once the cessation of pain [which cannot continue, when there is absolutely *nothing*], and also the means thereof [since there can be no further means required for the removal of anything, if it be settled that the thing positively does not exist],' this, too, can hardly be: so he declares [as follows]:[2]

---

[1] क्षणिकबाह्यपक्षेण विज्ञानमात्रपक्षेण सह समानक्षेमत्वात्तुल्यनिरसनहेतुकत्वादयमपि पक्षो न सम्यक्। क्षणिकपक्षनिरासहेतुः प्रत्यभिज्ञादिर्विज्ञानपक्षनिरासहेतुर्बाह्यप्रतीत्यादिश्चात्रापि समान इति भावः ॥

[2] यदपि दुःखनिवृत्तिरूपतया तत्साधनतया च शून्यस्यैवास्तु पुरुषार्थत्वमिति तैर्मन्यते तदपि दुर्घटमित्याह ॥

अपुरुषार्थत्वमुभयथा ॥ ४७ ॥

The soul's aim is not annihilation.

Aph. 47. In neither way [whether as a means, or as an end,] is this [annihilation] the soul's aim.

a. 'Let the void [of mere nonentity] be the soul's aim, whether as consisting in the cessation of pain, or as presenting the means for the cessation of pain,' [says the heretic. And this cannot be; because the [whole] world agrees, that the aim of the soul consists in the joys, &c., that shall abide *in it;* that is to say, because [*they* hold, while] *you* do not hold, that there is a *permanent* soul, [(see § 33) in respect of which the liberation or beatification would be possible, or even predicable].[1]

b. Now [certain] other things, also, entertained, as causes of [the soul's] bondage, by [imperfectly instructed] believers, remaining over and above those [proposed by unbelievers, and] already rejected, are to be set aside:[2]

न गतिविशेषात् ॥ ४८ ॥

It is by no movement that the soul gets into bondage.

Aph. 48. Not from any kind of motion [such as its entrance into a body, does the soul's bondage result].

---

[1] दुःखनिवृत्तिरूपतया दुःखनिवृत्तिसाधनतया वा शून्यस्य पुरुषार्थत्वं स्यात्। तच्च न घटते स्वनिष्ठत्वेनैव सुखादीनां लोके पुरुषार्थत्वावगमात्स्थिरस्य पुरुषस्यानङ्गीकारादित्यर्थः ॥

[2] इदानीं पूर्वनिरस्तावशिष्टान्यास्तिकसंभाव्यान्यप्यन्यानि बन्धकारणानि निरस्यन्ते ॥

a. 'Bondage' [required to complete the aphorism] is understood from the topic[1] [of discussion].

b. The meaning is, that the soul's bondage, moreover, does not result from any sort of *motion*, in the shape, for instance, of its entrance into a body.[2]

c. He states a reason for this:[3]

निष्क्रियस्य तदसंभवात् ॥ ४९ ॥

What is all-pervading does not change place.

Aph. 49. Because this is impossible for what is inactive, [or, in other words, without motion].

a. That is to say: because this is impossible, i.e., *motion* is impossible, in the case of the soul, which is inactive, [because] all-pervading, [and, therefore, incapable of changing its place].[4]

b. But then [the objector may say], 'Since, in the books of Scripture and of law, we hear of its *going* and *coming* into this world and the other world, let soul be [not all-pervading, as you allege, but] merely limited [in its extent]: and to this effect, also, is the text, 'Of the size

---

[1] प्रकरणाद्बन्धो लभ्यते ॥

[2] गतिविशेषाच्छरीरप्रवेशादिरूपादपि पुरुषस्य न बन्ध इत्यर्थः ॥

[3] अत्र हेतुमाह ॥

[4] निष्क्रियस्य विभोः पुरुषस्य तदसंभवाद्गत्यसंभवादित्यर्थः ॥

of the thumb is the soul, the inner spirit,' and the like:[1] [but] this conjecture he repels:[2]

मूर्त्तत्वाद्घटादिवत्समानधर्मापत्तावपसिद्धान्तः॥५०॥

Were the soul limited, it might be perishable.

Aph. 50. [We cannot admit that the soul is other than all-pervading; because] by its being limited, since it would come under the same conditions as jars, &c., there would be a contradiction to our tenet [of its imperishableness].

a. That is to say: and, if the soul were admitted to be, like a jar, or the like, limited, i.e. circumscribed [in dimension], then, since it would resemble a jar, or the like, in being made up of parts, and [hence] in being perishable, &c., this would be contrary to our settled principle,[3] [that the soul is imperishable].

b. He now justifies the text [see § 49. *b.*] referring to the *motion*[4] [of the soul, by showing that the motion is not really of the soul, but of an accessory]:

---

[1] *Śwetáśwatara Upanishad*, iii., 13. *Ed.*

[2] ननु श्रुतिस्मृत्योरिहलोकपरलोकगमनागमनश्रवणात्पुरुषस्य परिच्छिन्नत्वमेवास्तु तथा च श्रुतिरङ्गुष्ठमात्रः पुरुषोऽन्तरात्मेत्यादिरित्याशङ्कामपाकरोति ॥

[3] यदि च घटादिवत्पुमान्मूर्त्तः परिच्छिन्नः स्वीक्रियते तदा सावयवत्वविनाशित्वादिना घटादिसमानधर्मापत्तावपसिद्धान्तः स्यादित्यर्थः ॥

[4] गतिश्रुतिमुपपादयति ॥

गतिश्रुतिरप्युपाधियोगादाकाशवत् ॥ ५१ ॥

Soul moves not, any more than Space.

Aph. 51. The text regarding the *motion* [of the soul], moreover, is [applicable, only] because of the junction of an *attendant*;[1] as in the case of the Ether [or *Space*, which moves not, though we talk of the space enclosed in a jar, as moving with the jar].

a. Since there are such proofs of the soul's unlimitedness, as the declaration that 'It is eternal, omnipresent, permanent,'[2] the text[3] regarding its *motion* is to be explained as having reference to a movement pertaining [not to the soul, but] to an attendant; for there is the text, 'As the Ether [or space] included in a jar, when the jar is removed, [in this case] the *jar* may be removed, but not the space; and in like manner is the soul, which is like the sky, [incapable of being moved]';[4] and because we may conclude that the motion [erroneously supposed to belong to the soul (49. *b.*),] belongs to *Nature* [see *Vedánta Aphorisms*, Part I., §4. *l.*], from such maxims[3] as this, that '*Nature* does the works the fruits of which are blissful or baneful;

---

1 *Upádhi*; often, below, 'investment' and 'adjunct.' *Ed.*

2 *Bhagavad-gítá*, ii., 24. *Ed.*

3 'Text' and 'maxim' are here meant to represent *śruti* and *smṛiti*, taken in their more limited senses. Elsewhere the translator has, for the same terms, in wider acceptations, 'books of Scripture and of law,' &c. The first is 'revealed law,' the Vedas; the second, 'memorial law,' or a code of such law, as the *Mánava*, and also any composition of a man reputed to be inspired. Both are held to have originated from a superhuman source; but only the former is regarded as preserving the very words of revelation. *Ed.*

4 The anacoluthism observable in the translation follows that of the original, with reference to which see the *Indische Studien*, vol. ii., p. 61.

and it is wilful *Nature* that, in the three worlds, reaps these': such is the import.[1][2]

b. It has already been denied [§ 16] that the bondage [of the soul] is occasioned by works, in the shape either of enjoined or of forbidden actions. Now he declares that the bondage, moreover, does not arise from the 'unseen' [merit or demerit] resulting therefrom:[3]

न कर्मणाप्यतद्धर्मत्वात् ॥ ५२ ॥

The bondage of the soul is no result of any merit or demerit.

Aph. 52. Nor, moreover, [does the bondage of the soul result from the merit or demerit arising] from works; because these belong not thereto.

a. That is to say: the bondage of the soul does not arise directly from the 'unseen' [merit or demerit] occa-

---

[1] नित्यः सर्वगतः स्थाणुरित्यादिना प्रमाणेनात्मनोऽपरिच्छिन्नत्वे गतिश्रुतिरौपाधिकगतिपरा व्याख्येया। घटसंवृतमाकाशं नीयमाने घटे यथा। घटो नीयेत नाकाशं तद्वज्जीवो नभोपमः। इति श्रुतेः। प्रकृतिः कुरुते कर्म शुभाशुभफलात्मकम्। प्रकृतिश्च तदश्नाति त्रिषु लोकेषु कामगा। इत्यादिस्मृत्या गतेः प्रकृतिनिष्ठत्वावगमाच्चेति भावः॥

[2] For another rendering, see my translation of the *Rational Refutation*, &c., p. 57. *Ed.*

[3] पूर्वं विहितनिषिद्धव्यापाररूपेण कर्मणा बन्धो निराकृतः। इदानीं तज्जन्यादृष्टेनापि न बन्ध इत्याह॥

sioned by works.[1] Why? Because this is no property thereof, i.e., because this [merit or demerit (see § 16. *a.*)] is no property of the soul.[2]

b. But then [some one may say], '*Let* it be that the bondage resulting from the 'unseen,' i.e., the merit [or demerit] even of another, should attach to a different person;' whereupon he declares [as follows]:[3]

अतिप्रसक्तिरन्यधर्मत्वे ॥ ५३ ॥[4]

Else, bondage might cling even to the emancipated.

Aph. 53. If the case were otherwise [than as I say], then it [the bondage of the soul] might extend unduly, [even to the emancipated].

a. That is to say: if the case were otherwise, if bondage and its cause were under other conditions [than we have declared them to be], then there might be an undue extension; bondage would befall even the emancipated,[5] [for the same reasons as those stated under § 16. *a.*].

---

[1] Dr. Ballantyne should have taken 'unseen' and 'works' as in apposition, and should have made the former explanatory of the latter. Clearer than his original, and yielding substantially his sense, is the gloss of Vedánti Mahádeva: कर्मणा तज्जन्यादृष्टेनापि न पुंसः साक्षाद्बन्धः । *Ed.*

[2] कर्मणादृष्टेनापि साक्षान्न पुरुषस्य बन्धः । कुतः । अतद्धर्मत्वात्पुरुषधर्मत्वाभावादित्यर्थः ॥

[3] नन्वन्यधर्मेणाप्यदृष्टेनान्यस्य बन्धः स्यात्तत्राह ॥

[4] Aniruddha transposes Aphorisms 53 and 54. *Ed.*

[5] अन्यधर्मत्वे बन्धतत्कारणयोरन्यधर्मत्वेऽतिप्रसक्तिर्मुक्तस्यापि बन्धापत्तिरित्यर्थः ॥

b. What need of so much [prolixity]? He states a general objection why the bondage of soul cannot result from any one or other [of these causes], beginning with its essence [see § 6. *b.*], and ending with its [supposed] works [see § 16]; inasmuch as it is contrary to Scripture,[1] [that any one of these should be the cause]:

निर्गुणादिश्रुतिविरोधश्चेति ॥ ५४ ॥

A single text of Scripture upsets, equally, all the heretical notions of the soul's relation to bondage.

Aph. 54. And this [opinion, that the bondage of the soul arises from any of these causes alleged by the heretics,] is contrary to such texts as the one that declares it [the soul] to be without qualities: and so much for that point.

a. And, if the bondage of the soul arose from any one or other of those [supposed causes already treated of,] among which its essential character [§ 6. *b.*] is the first, this would be contradictory to such texts as, 'Witness, intelligent, alone, and without the [three] qualities [is the soul:'[2] such is the meaning.[3]

b. The expression 'and so much for that point' means,

---

[1] किं बहुना । स्वभावादिकर्मान्तैरन्येन वा केनापि पुरुषस्य बन्धोत्पत्तिर्न घटते श्रुतिविरोधादिति साधारणं बाधकमाह ॥

[2] *Śwetáśwatara Upanishad*, vi., 11. *Ed.*

[3] स्वभावाद्यन्यतमेन पुरुषस्य बन्धोत्पत्तौ साक्षी चेता केवलो निर्गुणश्चेत्यादिश्रुतिविरोधश्चेत्यर्थः ॥

that the investigation of the cause of the bondage [of the soul] here closes.[1]

c. The case, then, stands thus: since [all] other [theories] are overthrown by the declaratory aphorisms, 'There would be no fitness in the enjoining' [see § 7], &c., it is ascertained that the immediate cause of the bondage [of the soul] is just the conjunction of Nature and of the soul.[2]

d. But then, in that case, [some one may say], this conjunction of Nature and of the soul [§ 54. *c.*], whether it be essential, or adventitiously caused by Time or something else [§ 5. *b.*], must occasion the bondage even of the *emancipated.* Having pondered this doubt, he disposes of it [as follows]:[3]

तद्योगोऽप्यविवेकान्न[4] समानत्वम् ॥ ५५ ॥

How the true cause of bondage affects not the emancipated.

Aph. 55. Moreover, the conjunction thereof does not, through non-discrimination, take place [in the case of the emancipated]; nor is there a parity,

---

[1] इतिशब्दो बन्धहेतुपरीक्षासमाप्तौ ॥

[2] तदेवं न स्वभावतो बद्धस्येत्यादिना प्रदर्शकेनेतरप्रतिषेधतः प्रकृतिपुरुषसंयोग एव साक्षाद्बन्धहेतुरवधारितः ॥

[3] ननु तत्र प्रकृतिपुरुषसंयोगोऽपि स्वाभाविकत्वे कालादिनिमित्तकत्वे वा मुक्तस्यापि बन्धापादक इत्याशङ्क्य समाधत्ते ॥

[4] तद्योगे, the reading which I find in MSS. of Aniruddha, seems to be indefensible. *Ed.*

[in this respect, between the emancipated and the unemancipated].

a. 'The conjunction thereof,' i.e., the conjunction of Nature and of the soul; this conjunction, moreover, does not take place again 'through non-discrimination,' i.e., through the want of a discrimination [between Nature and soul] in the emancipated, [who *do* discriminate, and who thus avoid the conjunction which others, failing to discriminate, incur, and thus fall into bondage]: such is the meaning. And thus the emancipated and the bound are *not* on a level, [under the circumstances stated at § 54. *c.*]: such is the import.[1]

[विपर्ययाद्बन्धः[2] ॥ ५६ ॥

The true cause of bondage, in other words, non-discrimination.

Aph. 56. Bondage arises from the error [of not discriminating between Nature and soul].

a. Having thus declared the cause of that [bondage]

---

[1] तद्योगः प्रकृतिपुरुषसंयोगो ऽप्यविवेकान्मुक्ते ऽविवेकाभावान्न पुनः संयोगो भवतीत्यर्थः । तथा च न मुक्तबद्धसाम्यमित्याशयः ॥

[2] These words, a bad reading of the 24th Aphorism of Book III., were pointed out, by me, as having, with the sentence of comment attached to them, no place here; and Dr. Ballantyne, when he republished the Sánkhya Aphorisms in the *Bibliotheca Indica*, omitted them. Hence the brackets now inserted, and my alteration of the numbering of the Aphorisms throughout the remainder of Book I. *Ed.*

which is to be got rid of, he declares the means of getting rid of it :[1]]

नियतकारणात्तदुच्छित्तिर्ध्वान्तवत् ॥ ५६ ॥

Non-discrimination is removable by discrimination alone.

Aph. 56. The removal of it is to be effected by the necessary means, just like darkness.

a. The necessary means, established throughout the world, in such cases as 'shell-silver' [i.e., a pearl-oyster-shell mistaken for silver], viz., the *immediacy* of discrimination, by *this* alone is 'its removal,' i.e., the removal of the non-discrimination [between Nature and soul], to be effected, and not by *works*, or the like: such is the meaning: just as darkness, the dark, is removed by light alone,[2] [and by no other means].

b. 'But then [some one may say], if merely the non-discrimination of Nature and soul be, through the conjunction [of the two, consequent on the want of discrimination], the cause of bondage, and if merely the discrimination of the two be the cause of liberation, then there would be liberation, even while there remained the conceit of [one's possessing] a body, &c.; and this is contrary to Scripture,

---

[[1] एवं हेयहेतुं प्रतिपाद्य हानोपायं प्रतिपादयति ॥]

[2] शुक्तिरजतादिस्थले लोकसिद्धं यन्नियतं कारणं विवेकसाक्षात्कारस्तत एव तदुच्छित्तिरविवेकोच्छित्तिर्न कर्मादिभिरित्यर्थो यथा ध्वान्तमन्धकारः प्रकाशेनैव नश्यति ॥

to the institutes of law, and to sound reasoning.' To this he replies :[1]

प्रधानाविवेकादन्याविवेकस्य तद्धाने हानम् ॥५७॥

The discrimination of Nature, as other than soul, involves all discrimination.

Aph. 57. Since the non-discrimination of other things [from soul] results from the non-discrimination of *Nature* [from soul], the cessation of this will take place, on the cessation of that [from which it results].

a. By reason of the non-discrimination of *Nature* from the soul, what non-discrimination of *other* things there *is*, such as the non-discrimination of the *understanding* [as something other than the soul], *this* necessarily ceases, on the cessation of the non-discrimination of Nature ; because, when the non-discrimination of the understanding, for example, [as something other than soul,] does occur, it is *based* on the non-discrimination [from soul] of that cause to which there is none antecedent [viz., Nature]; since the non-discrimination of an *effect* [and the 'understanding' is an effect or product of Nature,] is, itself, an effect,[2] [and will, of course, cease, with the cessation of its cause].

---

[1] ननु प्रकृतिपुरुषाविवेक एव चेत्संयोगद्वारा बन्धहेतुस्तयोर्विवेक एव मोक्षहेतुस्तर्हि देहाद्यभिमानसत्त्वेऽपि मोक्षः स्यात्तच्च श्रुतिस्मृतिन्यायविरुद्धमिति । तत्राह ॥

[2] पुरुषे प्रधानाविवेकात्कारणाद्योऽन्याविवेको बुद्ध्याद्यविवेको बुद्ध्याद्यविवेके जाते कार्यावि-

b. The state of the case is this: as, when the soul has been discriminated from the *body*, it is impossible but that it should be discriminated from the *colour* and other [properties], the effects of the body, [which is the substantial cause of its own properties]; so, by parity of reasoning, from the departure of the cause, when soul, in its character of *unalterableness*, &c., has been discriminated from *Nature*, it is impossible that there should remain a conceit of [the soul's being any of] the *products* thereof [i. e., of Nature], such as the 'understanding,' and the like, which have the character of being *modifications*[1] [of primal Nature, while the soul, on the other hand, is a thing unalterable].

c. But then [some one may say], 'What proof is there that there is a conceit [entertained by people in general,] of a *Nature* [or primal principle] different from the conceit of an 'understanding,' &c., [which, you tell us, are products of this supposed first principle]? For all the various conceits [that the soul falls into], such as, 'I am ignorant,' and so on, can be accounted for on the ground simply of an 'understanding,' &c., [without postulating a primal Nature which is to assume the shape of an 'understanding,' &c.]:'

वेकस्य कार्यतयानादिकारणाविवेकमूलकत्वात्तस्य प्रधानाविवेकहाने सत्यवश्यं हानमित्यर्थः ॥

[1] यथा शरीरादात्मनि विविक्ते शरीरकार्येषु रूपादिष्वविवेको न संभवति तथा कूटस्थत्वादिधर्मैः प्रधानात्पुरुषे विविक्ते तत्कार्येषु परिणामादिधर्मकेषु बुद्ध्यादिष्वभिमानो न स्यातुमुत्सहते तुल्यन्यायात्कारणनाशाच्चेति भावः ॥

well, if any one says this, I reply, 'no;' because, unless there were such a thing as Nature, we could not account for such conceits as the following, viz., 'Having died, having died, again, when there is a creation, let me be a denizen of Paradise, and not of hell;' because no *products*, such as the 'understanding,' when they have perished, can be created anew,[1] [any more than [a gold-bracelet, melted down, can be reproduced, though another like it may be produced from the materials].

The soul's confounding itself with Nature is logically antecedent to its confounding itself with anything else.

d. Moreover, it is inadmissible to say that men's conceit of [the identity of themselves with their] 'understanding,' &c., is [the *primary* cause of the soul's bondage, and is] not preceded by anything; because 'understanding' and the rest [as you will not deny] are *effects*. Now, while it is to be expected that there should be some predetermining agency to establish a conceit of [ownership in, or of one's identity with,] any *effects*, it is clear that it is a conceit of [ownership, &c.,] in respect of the *cause*, and nothing else, that must be the predetermining agency: for we see this in ordinary life; and our theories are bound to conform [deferentially] to experience. For [to explain,] we see, in ordinary life, that the conceit of [the ownership of] the grain, &c., pro-

---

[1] ननु बुद्ध्याद्यभिमानातिरिक्ते प्रधानाभिमाने किं प्रमाणमहमज्ञ इत्याद्यखिलाभिमानानां बुद्ध्यादिविषयत्वेनैवोपपत्तेरिति चेन्न मृत्वा मृत्वा पुनः सृष्टौ स्वर्गी स्यां मा च नारकीत्याद्यभिमानानां प्रधानविषयत्वं विनानुपपत्तेरतीतानां बुद्ध्याद्यखिलकार्याणां पुनः सृष्ट्यभावात् ॥

duced by a field, results from the conceit of [the ownership of] the field; and, from the conceit of [the ownership of] gold, the conceit of [the ownership of] the bracelets, or other things, formed of that gold; and, by the removal of these [i.e., the removal of the logically antecedent conceits, that the field, or the gold, is one's property], there is the removal of those,[1] [i.e., the removal of the conceits that the grain, &c., and that the bracelets, &c., the corresponding products or effects of the field and of the gold, are one's property: and so the soul will cease to confound itself with the 'understanding,' when it ceases to confound itself with Nature, of which the 'understanding' is held to be a product].

e. [And, if it be supposed that we thus lay ourselves open to the charge of a *regressus in infinitum,* seeing that, whatever we may assign as the *first* cause, we may, on our own principles, be asked what was the 'predetermining agency' in regard to *it;* or if it be supposed that we are chargeable with reasoning in a circle, when we hold that the soul's confounding itself with Nature is the cause of

---

[1] किं च बुद्ध्यादिषु पुरुषाणामभिमानोऽनादिर्वक्तुं न शक्यते बुद्ध्यादीनां कार्यत्वात्। कार्येष्वभिमानव्यवस्थार्थं नियामकाकाङ्क्षायां कारणाभिमान एव नियामकतया सिद्ध्यति लोके दृष्टत्वात्कल्पनायाश्च दृष्टानुसारित्वात्। दृष्टो हि लोके क्षेत्राभिमानात्क्षेत्रजन्यधान्यादिष्वभिमानः सुवर्णाभिमानात्तज्जन्यकटकादिष्वभिमानस्तयोर्निवृत्त्या च तयोर्निवृत्तिरिति॥

its *continuing* so to confound itself, and its continuing so to confound itself is, reciprocally, the cause why it confounds itself; we reply, that] there is no occasion to look for any other 'predetermining agency,' in the case of the conceit of [the identity of the soul with] Nature, or in the case of the self-continuance[1] thereof, [i. e., of that error of confounding one's self with Nature]; because [these two are alike] without antecedent, like seed and sprout,[2] [of which it is needless to ask which is the first; the old puzzle, 'which was first, the acorn, or the oak?' being a frivolous question].

f. But then [some one may say], if we admit the soul's bondage [at one time], and its freedom [at another], and its discrimination [at one time], and its non-discrimination [at another], then this is in contradiction to the assertion [in § 19], that it is 'ever essentially a pure and free intelligence;' and it is in contradiction to such texts as this, viz., 'The absolute truth is this, that neither is there destruction [of the soul], nor production [of it]; nor is it bound, nor is it an effecter [of any work], nor is it desirous of liberation, nor is it, indeed, *liberated*; [seeing that that cannot desire or obtain liberation, which was never *bound*].'[3] This [charge of inconsistency] he repels:[4]

---

[1] To render *vásána*, on which see 2, at p. 29, *supra*. *Ed.*

[2] प्रधानाभिमानतद्वासनयोश्च बीजाङ्कुरवदनादित्वान्न तदभिमाने नियामकान्तरापेक्षेति ॥

[3] *Amṛitabindu Upanishad*, v. 10. See Dr. Albrecht Weber's *Indische Studien*, vol. ii., p. 61, note 2. *Ed.*

[4] ननु पुरुषस्य चेद्बन्धमोक्षौ विवेकाविवेकौ च स्वीकृतौ तर्हि नित्यशुद्धबुद्धमुक्तत्वोक्तिविरोधस्तथा

वाङ्मात्रं न तु[1] तत्त्वं चित्तस्थितेः ॥ ५८ ॥

The bondage of the soul is merely verbal.

Aph. 58. It is merely verbal, and not a reality [this so-called bondage of the soul]; since it [the bondage] *resides* in the *mind*, [and not in the soul].

a. That is to say: since bondage, &c., all reside only in the *mind* [and not in the soul], all this, as regards the soul, is merely verbal, i.e., it is *vox et praeterea nihil;* because is is merely a *reflexion,* like the redness of [pellucid] crystal [when a China-rose is near it], but not a reality, with no false imputation, like the redness of the China-rose itself. Hence there is *no* contradiction to what had been said before, [as the objector (under § 57. *f.*) would insinuate]: such is the state of the case.[2]

च न निरोधो न चोत्पत्तिर्न बद्धो न च साधकः। न मुमुक्षुर्न वै मुक्त इत्येषा परमार्थतेत्यादिश्रुतिविरोधश्चेति तां परिहरति ॥

[1] Aniruddha has, instead of न तु, तु न. Hence: 'But it is merely verbal, not a reality,' &c. *Ed.*

[2] बन्धादीनां सर्वेषां चित्त एवावस्थानात्तत्सर्वं पुरुषे वाङ्मात्रं शब्दमात्रं स्फटिकलौहित्यवत्प्रतिबिम्बमात्रत्वान्न तु तत्त्वमनारोपितं जवालौहित्यवदित्यर्थः। अतो नोक्तविरोध इति भावः ॥

F

Whether Testimony, or Inference, without Perception, might not avail to dissipate the soul's bondage.

b. But then, if bondage, &c., as regards the soul, be merely verbal, let them be set aside by *hearing* [that they are merely verbal], or by argument [establishing that they are so]. Why, in the Scripture and the Law, is there enjoined, as the cause of liberation, a discriminative knowledge [of Soul, as distinguished from Non-soul], going the length of *immediate cognition?* To this he replies:[1]

युक्तितोऽपि न बाध्यते दिङ्मूढवदपरोक्षादृते ॥ ५९ ॥

The truth must be directly discerned, and not merely accepted on the ground of Testimony, or of Inference.

Aph. 59. Moreover, it [the non-discrimination of Soul from Nature,] is not to be removed by argument; as that of the person perplexed about the points of the compass [is not to be removed] without immediate cognition.

a. By 'argument' we mean thinking. The word 'moreover' is intended to aggregate [or take in, along with 'argument'] 'testimony,'[2] [or verbal authority, which, no more than 'argument,' or inference, can remove the evil, which can be removed by nothing short of direct intuitive *perception* of the real state of the case].

---

[1] ननु बन्धादिकं चेत्पुरुषे वाङ्मात्रं तर्हि श्रवणेन युक्त्या वा तस्य बाधो भवतु। किमर्थं श्रुतिस्मृत्योः साक्षात्कारपर्यन्तं विवेकज्ञानमुपदिश्यते मोक्षहेतुतयेति। तत्राह॥

[2] युक्तिर्मननम्। अपिशब्दः श्रवणसमुच्चयार्थः।

b. That is to say: the bondage, &c., of the soul though [granted to be] merely verbal, are not to be removed by merely hearing, or inferring, without immediate cognition, without directly perceiving; just as the contrariety in regard to the [proper] direction, though merely verbal [as resulting from misdirection], in the case of [1] a person who is mistaken as to the points of the compass [and hence as to his own bearings], is not removed by testimony, or by inference, without immediate cognition, i. e., without [his] directly perceiving[2] [how the points of the compass really lie, to which immediate perception 'testimony,' or 'inference,' may conduce, but the necessity of which these *media*, or instruments of knowledge, cannot supersede].

c. Or it [Aph. 59] may be explained as follows, viz.: But then, [seeing that] it is declared, by the assertion [in Aph. 56], viz., that 'The removal of it is to be effected by the necessary means,' that knowledge, in the shape of discrimination [between Soul and Nature], is the remover of *non*-discrimination [in regard to the matter in question], tell us, is that knowledge of a like nature with the hearing

---

[1] Here I have had to make several insertions and other alterations. Dr. Ballantyne had: 'That is to say, the bondage, &c., [of the soul] is not to be removed by merely hearing, or inferring, without *perceiving;* just as the contrariety in regard to the proper direction, in the case,' &c. *Ed.*

[2] वाङ्मात्रमपि पुरुषस्य बन्धादिकं श्रवणमननमात्रेण न बाध्यतेऽपरोक्षादृते साक्षात्कारं विना यथा दिङ्मूढजनस्य वाङ्मात्रमपि दिग्वैपरीत्यं श्रवणयुक्तिभ्यां न बाध्यते साक्षात्कारं विनेत्यर्थः ॥

[of Testimony], &c.? Or is it something peculiar? A reply to this being looked for, he enounces the aphorism [§ 59]: 'Moreover, it is not to be removed by argument,' &c. That is to say: non-discrimination is not excluded, is not cut off, by argument, or by testimony, unless there be discrimination as an immediate perception; just as is the case with one who is bewildered in regard to [his] direction; because the only thing to remove an *immediate* error is an immediate individual perception[1] [of the truth. For example, a man with the jaundice perceives *white* objects as if they were *yellow*. He may *infer* that the piece of chalk which he looks at is really white; or he may believe the *testimony* of a friend, that it *is* white; but still nothing will remove his erroneous *perception* of yellowness in the chalk, except a direct perception of its whiteness].

d. Having thus, then, set forth the fact that Liberation results from the immediate discrimination [of Soul from

---

[1] अथवेत्थं व्याख्येयं ननु नियतकारणात्तदुच्छित्तिरित्यनेन विवेकज्ञानमविवेकोच्छेदकमुक्तं तज्ज्ञानं किं श्रवणादिसाधारणमुतास्ति कश्चिद्विशेष इत्याकाङ्क्षायामाह युक्तितोऽपीत्यादिसूत्रम्। अविवेको युक्तितः श्रवणतश्च न बाध्यते नोच्छिद्यते विवेकापरोक्षं विना दिङ्मोहवदित्यर्थः साक्षात्कारभ्रमे साक्षात्कारविशेषदर्शनस्यैव विरोधित्वादिति॥

Nature], the next thing to be set forth is the 'discrimination'[1] [here referred to].

e. This being the topic, in the first place, since only if Soul and Nature exist, liberation can result from the discrimination of the one from the other, therefore that 'instrument of right knowledge' (*pramáṇa*) which establishes the existence of these [two *imperceptible* realities] is [first] to be set forth :[2]

अचाक्षुषाणामनुमानेन बोधो धूमादिभिरिव वह्नेः ॥ ६० ॥

The evidence for things imperceptible.

Aph. 60. The knowledge of things imperceptible is by means of Inference; as that of fire [when not directly perceptible,] is by means of smoke, &c.

a. That is to say: 'of things imperceptible,' i.e., of things not cognizable by the senses, e.g., Nature and the Soul, 'the knowledge,' i.e., the fruit lodged in the soul, is brought about by means of that instrument of right knowledge [which may be called] 'Inference' (*anumána*), [but which (see Nyáya Aphorisms, I., § 5) is, more correctly, 'the recognition of a Sign']; as [the knowledge that there is] fire [in such and such a locality, where we cannot directly

---

[1] तदेवं विवेकसाक्षात्कारान्मोक्षं प्रतिपाद्यातः परं विवेकः प्रतिपादनीयः ॥

[2] तत्रादौ प्रकृतिपुरुषसिद्धौ हि तद्विवेकान्मोक्षः स्यादतस्तत्सिद्धौ प्रमाणमुपन्यस्यते ॥

perceive it,] is brought about by the 'recognition of a Sign,' occasioned by smoke, &c.[1]

b. Moreover, it is to be understood that that which is [true, but yet is] not established by 'Inference,' is established by Revelation. But, since 'Inference' is the chief [among the instruments of knowledge], in this [the Sánkhya] System, 'Inference' only is laid down [in the aphorism,] as the *chief* thing; but Revelation is not disregarded[2] [in the Sánkhya system; as will be seen from Aph. 88 of this Book].

c. He [next] exhibits the order of creation of those things among which Nature is the first, and the relation of cause and effect [among these, severally], preparatorily to the argument that will be [afterwards] stated:[3]

---

[1] अचाक्षुषाणामप्रत्यक्षाणां प्रकृतिपुरुषादीनामनुमानेन प्रमाणेन बोधः पुरुषनिष्ठं फलं सिद्धं भवति यथा धूमादिभिर्जनितेनानुमानेन वह्नेः सिद्धिरित्यर्थः ॥

[2] अनुमानासिद्धमप्यागमात्सिध्यतीत्यपि बोध्यम्। अस्य शास्त्रस्यानुमानप्राधान्यात्तु केवलानुमानस्य मुख्यतयैवोपन्यासो न त्वागमस्यानपेक्षेति ॥

[3] प्रकृत्यादीनां सृष्टिक्रमं वक्ष्यमाणानुमानोपयोगिकार्यकारणभावं च दर्शयति ॥

सत्त्वरजस्तमसां साम्यावस्था प्रकृतिः प्रकृतेर्महान्महतोऽहंकारोऽहंकारात्पञ्च तन्मात्राण्युभयमिन्द्रियं तन्मात्रेभ्यः[1] स्थूलभूतानि पुरुष इति पञ्चविंशतिर्गणः ॥ ६१ ॥

The twenty-five Realities enumerated.

Aph. 61. Nature (*prakṛiti*) is the state of equipoise of Goodness (*sattwa*), Passion (*rajas*), and Darkness (*tamas*): from Nature [proceeds] Mind (*mahat*); from Mind, Self-consciousness (*ahankára*); from Self-consciousness, the five Subtile Elements (*tan-mátra*), and both sets [external and internal,] of Organs (*indriya*); and, from the Subtile Elements, the Gross Elements (*sthúla-bhúta*). [Then there is] Soul (*purusha*). Such is the class of twenty-five.

a. 'The state of equipoise' of the [three] things called 'Goodness,' &c., is their being neither less nor more [one than another]; that is to say, the state of *not* being [developed into] an *effect* [in which one or other of them predominates]. And thus 'Nature' is the triad of 'Qualities' (*guṇa*), distinct from the products [to which this triad gives rise]: such is the complete meaning.[2] [3]

b. These things, viz., 'Goodness,' &c., [though spoken of as the three *Qualities*], are not 'Qualities' (*guṇa*) in the *Vaiśeshika* sense of the word; because [the 'Qualities' of

---

[1] My MSS. of Aniruddha omit तन्मात्रेभ्यः. *Ed.*

[2] सत्त्वादिद्रव्याणां या साम्यावस्थान्यूनानतिरिक्तावस्थाकार्यावस्थेत्यर्थः । एवं च कार्यभिन्नं गुणत्रयं प्रकृतिरिति पर्यवसितोऽर्थः ॥

[3] For a translation of a slightly different text, see the *Rational Refutation*, &c., p. 43. *Ed.*

the *Vaiśeshika* system have, themselves, *no* qualities (see Kaṇáda's 16th Aph.); while] *these* have the qualities of Conjunction, Disjunction, Lightness, Force,[1] Weight, &c.[2] In this [Sánkhya] system, and in Scripture, &c., the word 'Quality' (*guṇa*) is employed [as the name of the three things in question],[3] because they are subservient to Soul [and, therefore, hold a secondary rank in the scale of being], and because they form the *cords* [which the word *guṇa* also signifies], viz., 'Mind,' &c., which consist of the three [so-called] 'Qualities,' and which *bind*, as a [cow, or other] brute-beast, the Soul.[4] [5]

c. Of this [Nature] the principle called 'the great one' (*mahat*), viz., the principle of 'Understanding' (*buddhi*), is the product. 'Self-consciousness' is a conceit [of separate personality]. Of this there are two products, (1) the

---

[1] *Balavattwa;* for which I find the variant *chalatwa*, 'mobility.' *Ed.*

[2] Read: 'Goodness and the rest are substances, not specific qualities; for they [themselves] possess [qualities, viz., those of] contact and separation, and also have the properties of levity, mobility, gravity, &c.' *Vaiśeshiká guṇaḥ* is equivalent to the *viśesha-guṇáḥ* in the original of Book V., 25. *a.* For the 'specific qualities,' see the *Bháshá-parichchheda*, st. 90. *Ed.*

[3] For 'is employed,' &c., read, 'is applied to these (*teshu*), [namely, goodness, passion, and darkness].' *Ed.*

[4] सत्त्वादीनि द्रव्याणि न वैशेषिका गुणाः संयोगविभागवत्त्वाल्लघुत्वबलवत्त्वगुरुत्वादिधर्मकत्वाच्च। तेष्वत्र शास्त्रे श्रुत्यादौ च गुणशब्दः पुरुषोपकरणत्वात्पुरुषपशुबन्धकत्रिगुणात्मकमहदादिरज्जुनिर्मातृत्वाच्च प्रयुज्यते ॥

[5] For a different translation, see the *Rational Refutation*, &c., pp. 43, 44. *Ed.*

'Subtile Elements' and (2) the two sets of 'Organs.' The 'Subtile Elements' are [those of] Sound, Touch, Colour, Taste, and Smell. The two sets of 'Organs,' through their division into the external and the internal, are of eleven kinds. The products of the 'Subtile Elements' are the five 'Gross Elements.' But 'Soul' is something distinct from either product or cause. Such is the class of twenty-five, the aggregate of things. That is to say, besides these there is nothing.[1]

d. He [next], in [several] aphorisms, declares the order of the inferring[2] [of the existence of these principles, the one from the other:

स्थूलात्पञ्चतन्मात्रस्य ॥ ६२ ॥

The existence of the 'Subtile Elements' is inferred from that of the 'Gross.'

Aph. 62. [The knowledge of the existence] of the five 'Subtile Elements' is [by inference,] from the 'Gross Elements.'

---

[1] तस्याः कार्यं महत्तत्त्वं बुद्धितत्त्वम्। अहंकारोऽभिमानः। तस्य कार्यद्वयं तन्मात्राण्युभयमिन्द्रियं च। तन्मात्राणि शब्दस्पर्शरूपरसगन्धाः। उभयमिन्द्रियं बाह्याभ्यन्तरभेदेनैकादशविधम्। तन्मात्राणां कार्याणि पञ्च स्थूलभूतानि। पुरुषस्तु कार्यकारणविलक्षण इति। इत्येवं पञ्चविंशतिर्गणः पदार्थव्यूहः। एतदतिरिक्तः पदार्थो नास्तीत्यर्थः॥

[2] अनुमानक्रममाह सूत्रैः॥

a. 'The knowledge, by inference,' so much is supplied,'[1] [to complete the aphorism, from Aph. 60].

b. Earth, &c., the 'Gross Elements,' are proved to exist, by Perception; [and] thereby [i. e., from that Perception; for Perception must precede Inference, as stated in Gotama's 5th Aphorism,] are the 'Subtile Elements' inferred, [the *στοιχεῖα στοιχείων* of Empedocles]. And so the application [of the process of inference to the case] is as follows:

(1) The Gross Elements, or those which have not reached the absolute limit [of simplification, or of the atomic], consist of things [Subtile Elements, or Atoms,] which have distinct qualities; [the earthy element having the distinctive quality of Odour; and so of the others]:

(2) Because they are gross;

(3) [And everything that is gross is formed of something less gross, or, in other words, more subtile,] as jars, webs, &c.;[2] [the gross web being formed of the less gross threads; and so of the others].

बाह्याभ्यन्तराभ्यां तैश्चाहंकारस्य[3] ॥ ६३ ॥

And thence that of Self-consciousness.

Aph. 63. [The knowledge of the existence] of Self-consciousness is [by inference,] from the external and inter-

---

[1] अनुमानेन बोध इत्यनुवर्तते ॥

[2] स्थूलं पृथिव्यादि प्रत्यक्षसिद्धं तेन तन्मात्राणामनुमानम् । तथा चापकर्षकाष्ठापन्नानि स्थूलभूतानि सविशेषगुणवद्द्रव्योपादानकानि स्थूलत्वाद्घटपटादिवदिति प्रयोगः ॥

[3] In my MSS. of Aniruddha there is no च after तैः. *Ed.*

nal [organs], and from these ['Subtile Elements,' mentioned in Aph. 62].

a. By inference from [the existence of] the external and internal organs, and from [that of] these 'Subtile Elements,' there is the knowledge of [the existence of such a principle as] Self-consciousness.[1]

b. The application [of the process of inference to the case] is in the following [somewhat circular] manner:

(1) The Subtile Elements and the Organs are made up of things consisting of Self-consciousness:

(2) Because they are products of Self-consciousness:

(3) Whatever is not so [i. e., whatever is *not* made out of Self-consciousness] is not thus [i. e., is not a *product* of Self-consciousness]; as the Soul, [which, not being made up thereof, is not a product of it].[2]

c. But then, if it be thus [i. e., if it be, as the Sánkhyas declare, that all objects, such as jars, are made up of Self-consciousness, while Self-consciousness depends on 'Understanding,' or 'Intellect,' or 'Mind,' the *first* product of 'Nature' (see Aph. 61)], then [some may object, that], since it would be the case that the Self-consciousness of the potter is the material of the jar, the jar made by him would disappear, on the beàtification of the potter, whose internal organ [or 'Understanding'] then surceases.

---

[1] बाह्याभ्यन्तराभ्यामिन्द्रियाभ्यां तैस्तन्मात्रैश्चाहंकारस्यानुमानेन बोधः ॥

[2] तन्मात्रेन्द्रियाण्यभिमानवद्द्रव्योपादानकान्यभिमानकार्यद्रव्यत्वात् । यन्नैवं तन्नैवं यथा पुरुष इति प्रयोगः ॥

And this [the objector may go on to say,] is not the case; because *another* man [*after* the beatification of the potter,] recognizes that 'This is that same jar[1] [which, you may remember, was fabricated by our deceased acquaintance].'

d. [In reply to this we say,] it is *not* thus; because, on one's beatification, there is an end of only those modifications of his internal organ [or 'Intellect'] which could be causes [as the *jar* no longer can be,] of the emancipated soul's *experiencing* [either good or ill], but not an end of the modifications of intellect in general, nor [an end] of intellect altogether:[2] [so that we might spare ourselves the trouble of further argument, so far as concerns the objection grounded on the assumption that the intellect of the potter *surceases*, on his beatification: but we may go further, and admit, for the sake of argument, the surcease of the 'intellect' of the beatified potter, without conceding any necessity for the surcease of his pottery. This alternative theory of the case may be stated as follows]:

e. Or [as Berkeley suggests, in his Principles of Human knowledge, Ch. vi.], let the Self-consciousness of the *Deity* be the cause why jars and the like [continue to exist], and

---

[1] नन्वेवं कुलालाहंकारस्यापि घटोपादानत्वापत्त्या कुलालमुक्तौ तदन्तःकरणनाशे तन्निर्मितघटनाशः स्यात्। न चैतद्युक्तं पुरुषान्तरेण स एवायं घट इति प्रत्यभिज्ञायमानत्वादिति॥

[2] मैवं मुक्तपुरुषभोगहेतुपरिणामस्यैव तदन्तःकरणे मोक्षोत्तरमुच्छेदान्न तु परिणामसामान्यस्यान्तःकरणस्वरूपस्य वोच्छेदः॥

not the Self-consciousness of the potter, &c.,[1] [who may lose their Self-consciousness, whereas the Deity, the sum of all life, *Hiraṇyagarbha* (see *Vedánta-śara*, § 62), never loses *his* Self-consciousness, while aught living continues].

तेनान्तःकरणस्य ॥ ६४ ॥

And thence that of Intellect.

Aph. 64. [The knowledge of the existence] of Intellect is [by inference,] from that [Self-consciousness, § 63].

a. That is to say: by inference from [the existence of] 'that,' viz., Self-consciousness, which is a product, there comes the knowledge of 'Intellect' (*buddhi*), the *great* 'inner organ' (*antaḥkaraṇa*), [hence] called 'the great one' (*mahat*), [the existence of which is recognized] under the character of the *cause* of this[2] [product, viz., Self-consciousness].

b. And so the application [again rather circular, of the process of inference to the case,] is as follows:

(1) The thing called Self-consciousness is made out of the things that consist of the moods of judgment [or mind];

(2) Because it is a thing which is a product of judgment [proceeding in the Cartesian order of *cogito, ergo sum;* and]

---

[1] अथवा घटादिष्वपि हिरण्यगर्भाहंकार एव कारणमस्तु न कुलालाद्यहंकारः ॥

[2] तेनाहंकारेण कार्येण तत्कारणतया मुख्यस्यान्तःकरणस्य महदाख्यस्य बुद्धेरनुमानेन बोध इत्यर्थः ॥

(3) Whatever is not so [i. e., whatever is *not* made out of judgment, or mental assurance], is not thus [i. e., is not a product of mental assurance]; as the Soul, [which is not made out of this or of anything antecedent], &c.[1]

c. Here the following reasoning is to be understood: Every one, having first determined anything under a concept [i. e., under such a form of thought as is expressed by a general term; for example, that this which presents itself is a jar, or a human body, or a possible action of one kind or other], after that makes the judgment, 'This is I,' or 'This ought to be done by me,' and so forth: so much is quite settled; [and there is no dispute that the fact is as here stated]. Now, having, in the present instance, to look for some *cause* of the thing called 'Self-consciousness' [which manifests itself in the various judgments just referred to], since the relation of cause and effect subsists between the two functions [the occasional conception, and the subsequent occasional judgment, which is a function of Self-consciousness], it is assumed, for simplicity, merely that the relation of cause and effect exists between the two substrata to which the [two sets of] functions belong; [and this is sufficient,] because it follows, as a matter of course, that the occurrence of a *function* of the effect must result from the occurrence of a *function* of the cause;[2] [nothing, according to the Sánkhya, being in any

---

[1] तथा चायं प्रयोगः । अहंकारद्रव्यं निश्चयवृत्तिमद्द्रव्योपादानकं निश्चयकार्यद्रव्यत्वात् । यन्नैवं तन्नैवं यथा पुरुषादिरिति ॥

[2] अत्रायं तर्को बोध्यः । सर्वोऽपि लोकः पदार्थमादौ स्वरूपतो निश्चित्य पश्चादभिमन्यतेऽयमहं

product, except so far, and in such wise, as it preexisted in the cause of that product].

ततः प्रकृतेः ॥ ६५ ॥

And thence that of Nature.

Aph. 65. [The knowledge of the existence] of Nature is [by inference,] from that ['Intellect,' § 64].

a. By inference from [the existence of] 'that,' viz., the principle [of Intellect, termed], 'the Great one,' which is a *product*, there comes the knowledge of [the existence of] Nature, as [its] cause.[1]

b. The application [of the process of inference to the case] is as follows:

(1) Intellect, the affections whereof are Pleasure, Pain, and Dulness, is produced from something which has these affections, [those of] Pleasure, Pain, and Dulness:

(2) Because, whilst it is a *product* [and must, therefore, have arisen from something consisting of that which itself now consists of], it consists of Pleasure, Pain, and Dulness; [and]

मयेदं कर्तव्यमित्यादिरूपेणेति तावत्सिद्धमेव। तत्राहंकारद्रव्यकारणाकाङ्क्षायां वृत्त्योः कार्यकारणभावेन तदाश्रययोरेव कार्यकारणभावो लाघवात्कल्प्यते कारणस्य वृत्तिलाभेन कार्यवृत्तिलाभस्यौत्सर्गिकत्वादिति ॥

[1] ततो महत्त्वात्कार्यात्कारणतया प्रकृतेरनुमानेन बोधः ॥

(3) [Every *product* that has the affections of, or that occasions, Pleasure, Pain, or Dulness, takes its rise in something which consists of these]; as lovely women, &c.[1]

c. For an agreeable woman gives pleasure to her husband, and, therefore, [is known to be mainly made up of, or] partakes of the quality of 'Goodness;' the indiscreet one gives pain to him, and, therefore, partakes of the quality of 'Foulness;' and she who is separated [and perhaps forgotten,] occasions indifference, and so partakes of the quality of 'Darkness.'[2]

d. And the appropriate refutation [of any objection], in this case, is [the principle], that it is fitting that the qualities of the effect should be [in every case,] in conformity with the qualities of the cause.[3]

e Now he states how, in a different way, we have [the evidence of] inference for [the existence of] Soul, which is void of the relation of cause and effect that has been men-

---

[1] अयं प्रयोगः। सुखदुःखमोहधर्मिणी बुद्धिः सुखदुःखमोहधर्मकद्रव्यजन्या कार्यत्वे सति सुखदुःखमोहात्मकत्वात्कान्तादिवदिति॥

[2] कान्ता हि भर्तुः सुखदेति सात्त्विकी। अविनया दुःखदेति राजसी। विरहिणी मोहदेति तामसी भवति॥

[3] कारणानुसारेणैव कार्यगुणौचित्यं चाचानुकूलस्तर्कः॥

tioned,[1] [in the four preceding aphorisms, as existing between Nature and its various products]:

संहतपरार्थत्वात्पुरुषस्य ॥ ६६ ॥

The argument for the existence of Soul.

Aph. 66. [The existence] of Soul [is inferred] from the fact that the combination [of the principles of Nature into their various effects] is for the sake of another [than unintelligent Nature, or any of its similarly unintelligent products].

a. 'Combination,' i.e., conjunction, which is the cause [of all products; these resulting from the conjunction of their constituent parts]. Since whatever has this quality, as Nature,[2] Mind, and so on [unlike Soul, which is *not* made up of parts], is for the sake of some other; for this reason it is understood that Soul exists: such is the remainder,[3] [required to complete the aphorism].

b. But the application [of the argument, in this particular case, is as follows]:

(1) The thing in question, viz., Nature the 'Great one,' with the rest [of the aggregate of the unintelligent], has, as its fruit [or end], the [mundane] experiences and the [eventual] Liberation of some other than itself:

---

[1] अथ यथोक्तकार्यकारणभावशून्यस्य पुरुषस्य प्रकारान्तरेणानुमानमाह ॥

[2] Here indicated by the adjective *avyakta*, 'the indiscrete.' See Aph. 136 of this Book. *Ed.*

[3] संहतः कारणीभूतसंयोगः । तद्वतोऽव्यक्तमहदादेः परार्थत्वाद्धेतोः पुरुषस्य बोध इति शेषः ॥

(2) Because it is a combination [or *compages*];

(3) [And every combination,] as a couch, or a seat, or the like, [is for another's use, not for its own; and its several component parts render no mutual service].[1]

c. Now, in order to establish that it is the cause of all [products], he establishes the *eternity* of Nature (*prakṛiti*):[2]

मूले मूलाभावादमूलं मूलम्[3] ॥ ६७ ॥

Argument for the eternity of Nature.

Aph. 67. Since the root has no root, the root [of all] is rootless.

a. Since 'the root' *(múla)*, i.e., the cause of the twenty-three principles, [which, with Soul and the root itself, make up the twenty-five realities recognized in the Sánkhya,] 'has no root,' i.e., has no cause, the 'root,' viz., Nature *(pradhána)*, is 'rootless,' i.e., void of root. That is to say, there is no other cause of Nature; because there would be

---

[1] प्रयोगस्तु विवादास्पदं प्रकृतिमहदादिकं स्वेतरस्य भोगापवर्गफलकं संहतत्वाच्छय्यासनादिवदिति ॥

[2] इदानीं सर्वकारणत्वोपपत्तये प्रकृतेर्नित्यत्वमुपपादयति ॥

[3] This seems to mean: 'There being no root to a root, the root [or radical principle, in the Sánkhya,] is rootless.'

In several MSS. which I consulted in India I found the strange reading: मूलं मूलाभावादमूलं मूलानाम् । 'The root of roots, since it has no root, is rootless.' This is very like saying that A=A. *Ed.*

a *regressus in infinitum*,[1] [if we were to suppose another cause, which, by parity of reasoning, would require another cause; and so on without end].

b. He states the argument [just mentioned] in regard to this, [as follows]:[2]

पारम्पर्येऽप्येकत्र परिनिष्ठेति संज्ञामात्रम् ॥ ६८ ॥

---

[1] मूले त्रयोविंशतितत्त्वानां कारणे मूलाभावात्कारणाभावान्मूलं प्रधानममूलं मूलशून्यम्। अनवस्थापत्त्या प्रधानस्य न कारणान्तरमस्तीत्यर्थः ॥

The source of the preceding exposition I have not ascertained. Vijnána has: त्रयोविंशतितत्त्वानां मूलमुपादानं प्रधानं मूलशून्यमनवस्थापत्त्या तत्र मूलान्तरासंभवादित्यर्थः। Nágeśa: मूलं सर्वेषामुपादानं प्रधानं मूलशून्यमनवस्थापत्त्या मूलभूते तत्र मूलान्तरासंभवादित्यर्थः। Aniruddha: मूलप्रकृतेर्मूलाभावात्कारणाभावादमूलं यत्कारणं तन्मूलम्। सा प्रकृतिः। Vedánti Mahádeva: त्रयोविंशतितत्त्वानां मूले प्रधानेऽनवस्थापत्त्या कारणाभावादकारणं प्रधानमित्यर्थः। *Ed.*

[2] अत्र युक्तिमाह ॥

The employment of the term Primal Agency, or Nature, is merely to debar the regressus in infinitum.

Aph. 68. Even if there be a succession, there is a halt at some *one* point; and so it is merely a name [that we give to the point in question, when we speak of the *root* of things, under the the name of 'Nature'].

a. Since there would be the fault of *regressus in infinitum,* if there were a succession of causes,—another cause of Nature, and another [cause] of that one, again,—there must be, at last, a halt, or conclusion, at some one point, somewhere or other, at some one, uncaused, eternal thing. Therefore, that at which we stop is the *Primal Agency (pra-kriti)*; for this [word *prakriti,* usually and conveniently rendered by the term *Nature,*] is nothing more than a sign to denote the cause which is the *root:* such is the meaning.[1]

b. But then [some Vedántí may object, according to this view of matters], the position that there are just twenty-five realities is not made out; for, in addition to[2] the 'Indiscrete' [or primal Nature], which [according to you,] is the cause of Mind,[3] *another* unintelligent principle, named 'Ignorance' [see *Vedánta-sára,* § 21], presents

---

[1] प्रकृतेरन्यत्कारणं तस्याप्यन्यदिति कारणपारम्पर्येऽप्यनवस्थादोषादन्ततोऽकारण एकस्मिन्यत्रकुत्रचिन्नित्ये परिनिष्ठा पर्यवसानं भविष्यतीति । अतो यत्र पर्यवसानं सैव प्रकृतिरिति हि मूलकारणस्य संज्ञामात्रमित्यर्थः ॥

[2] Read 'in connexion with.' *Ed.*

[3] Literally, instead of 'Mind,' 'the principle [termed] the Great one.' *Ed.*

itself. Having pondered this doubt, he declares [as follows]:[1]

समानः प्रकृतेर्द्वयोः ॥ ६९ ॥

Nature and Soul alike uncreated.

Aph. 69. Alike, in respect of Nature, and of both [Soul and Nature, is the argument for the uncreated existence].[2]

a. In the discussion of the Primal Agent [Nature], the cause which is the root [of all products], the same side is taken by us both, the asserter [of the Sánkhya doctrine] and the opponent [Vedántí]. This may be thus stated: As there is mention, in Scripture, of the *production* of Nature, so, too, is there of that of *Ignorance*, in such texts as this, viz.: 'This Ignorance, which has five divisions, was produced from the great Spirit.' Hence it must needs be that a figurative production is intended to be asserted, in respect of *one* of these [and not the *literal* production of both; else we should have no root at all]; and, of the two, it is with *Nature* only that a figurative production, in the shape of a manifestation through conjunction with Soul, &c., is congruous. A production [such as that metaphorical one here spoken of,] the characteristic of which is conjunction *is* mentioned; for there is mention

---

[1] ननु पञ्चविंशतितत्त्वानीति नोपपद्यते महत्तत्त्वकारणाव्यक्तापेक्षयाविद्याख्यजडतत्त्वान्तरापत्तेरित्याशङ्क्याह ॥

[2] This is Dr. Ballantyne's revised translation, suggested by a remark of Vijnána, quoted and translated below, in *b*. The rendering now replaced runs: 'Alike [is the opinion] of both [of us], in respect of Nature.' The side-note was formerly correspondent to *a*., viz.: 'He meets a Vedántic objection.' *Ed.*

of [such] a figurative origination of Soul and Nature, in a passage of the *Kaurma* [*Puráṇa*], beginning, 'Of action [or the Primal Agency], and knowledge [or Soul],' and so on. And, as there is no mention, in Scripture, of the origin of *Ignorance*, as figurative, *it* is *not* from eternity. And Ignorance, which consists of false knowledge, has been declared, in an aphorism of the *Yoga*, to be [not a separate entity, but] 'an affection of the mind.' Hence there is no increase to the [list of the twenty-five] Realities,[1] [in the shape of a twenty-sixth principle, to be styled Ignorance].

b. Or [according to another, and more probable, inter-

---

[1] प्रकृतेर्मूलकारणविचारे द्वयोर्वादिप्रतिवादिनोरावयोः समानः पक्षः। एतदुक्तं भवति यथा प्रकृतेरुत्पत्तिः श्रूयत एवमविद्याया अपि। अविद्या पञ्चपर्वैषा प्रादुर्भूता महात्मन इत्यादिवाक्यैः। अत एकस्या अवश्यं गौण्युत्पत्तिर्वक्तव्या तच्च च प्रकृतेरेव पुरुषसंयोगादिभिरभिव्यक्तिरूपा गौण्युत्पत्तिर्युक्ता। संयोगलक्षणोत्पत्तिः कथ्यते कर्मज्ञानयोरिति कौर्मवाक्ये प्रकृतिपुरुषयोर्गौणोत्पत्तिस्मरणात्। अविद्यायाश्च क्वापि गौणोत्पत्त्यश्रवणात्तस्या अनादिता। अविद्या च मिथ्याज्ञानरूपा बुद्धिधर्म इति योगे सूचितम्। अतो न तत्त्वाधिक्यम्॥

pretation of the aphorism,] the meaning is this, that the argument is the same in support of both, i.e., of both Soul and Nature: such is the meaning.[1]

c. But then, there being [as has been shown,] a mode of arriving, by inference, at [a knowledge of the saving truth in regard to] Nature, Soul, &c., whence is it that reflexion, in the shape of discrimination [between Soul and Nature], does not take place in the case of *all* [men]? In regard to this point, he states [as follows]:[2]

अधिकारित्रैविध्यान्न नियमः ॥ ७० ॥

All do not profit by the saving truth; because it is only the best kind of people that are fully amenable to reason.

Aph. 70. There is no rule [or necessity, that *all* should arrive at the truth]; because those who are privileged [to engage in the inquiry] are of three descriptions.

a. For those privileged [to engage in the inquiry] are of three descriptions, through their distinction into those who, in reflecting, are dull, mediocre, and best. Of these, by the dull the [Sánkhya] arguments are frustrated [and altogether set aside], by means of the sophisms that have been uttered by the *Bauddhas*, &c. By the mediocre they [are brought into doubt, or, in other words,] are made to appear as if there were equally strong arguments on the other side, by means of arguments which really prove the reverse [of what these people employ them to prove], or by

---

[1] अथ वा द्वयोः प्रकृतिपुरुषयोः समान एव न्याय इत्यर्थः ॥

[2] ननु प्रकृतिपुरुषाद्यनुमानप्रकारसत्त्वे सर्वेषां विवेकमननं कुतो न जायते । तत्राह ॥

arguments which are not true: [see the section on Fallacies in the *Tarka-sangraha*]. But it is only the *best* of those privileged, that reflect in the manner that has been set forth [in our exposition of the process of reflexion which leads to the discriminating of Soul from Nature]: such is the import. But there is no rule that *all* must needs reflect in the manner so set forth: such is the literal meaning.[1]

b. He now, through two aphorisms, defines 'the Great one' and 'Self-consciousness';[2] [the reader being presumed to remember that Nature consists of the three 'Qualities' in equipoise, and to be familiar with the other principles, such as the 'Subtile elements' (see § 61)]:

महदाख्यमाद्यं कार्यं तन्मनः ॥ ७१ ॥

By 'the Great one' is meant Mind.

Aph. 71. The first product [of the Primal Agent, Nature], which is called 'the Great one,' is Mind.

a. 'Mind' (*manas*). 'Mind' [is so called], because its function is 'thinking' (*manana*). By 'thinking' is here meant 'judging' (*niśchaya*). That of which this is the func-

---

[1] मनने हि मन्दमध्यमोत्तमभेदेन त्रिविधा ऽधिकारिणः। तत्र मन्दैर्बौद्धाद्युक्तकुतर्कैरनुमानानि बाध्यन्ते। मध्यमैर्विरुद्धासल्लिङ्गैः सत्प्रतिपक्षितानि क्रियन्ते। उत्तमाधिकारिणामेव तूक्तरीत्या मननमिति भावः। सर्वेषामेव तूक्तरीत्या मनननियमो नेत्यक्षरार्थः॥

[2] महदहंकारयोः स्वरूपमाह सूत्राभ्याम्॥

tion is 'intellect' (*buddhi*); and *that* is the first product, that called 'the Great one' (*mahat*): such is the meaning.[1]

चरमोऽहंकारः ॥ ७२ ॥

The relation of Self-consciousness to Mind.

Aph. 72. 'Self-consciousness' is that which is subsequent [to Mind.]

a. 'Self-consciousness,' the function of which is a conceit [that '*I* exist,' '*I* do this, that, and the other thing'], is that which is subsequent: that is to say, 'Self-consciousness' is the next after 'the Great one'[2] [§ 71].

b. Since 'Self-consciousness' is that whose function is a conceit [which brings out the *Ego*, in every case of cognition, the matter of which cognition would, else, have lain dormant in the bosom of Nature, the formless Objective], it therefore follows that the others [among the phenomena of mundane existence,] are effects of this [Self-consciousness]; and so he declares [as follows]:[3]

---

[1] मन इति। मननवृत्तिकं मनः। मननमत्र निश्चयः। तद्वृत्तिका बुद्धिः। तन्महदाख्यमाद्यं कार्यमित्यर्थः ॥

[2] अहंकारोऽभिमानवृत्तिकः पदार्थश्चरमो महतोऽनन्तरोऽहंकार इत्यर्थः।

[3] यतोऽभिमानवृत्तिकोऽहंकारोऽतस्तत्कार्यत्वमुत्तरेषामुपपन्नमित्याह ॥

तत्कार्यत्वमुत्तरेषाम्[1] ॥ ७३ ॥

All products, save Mind, result from Self-consciousness.

Aph. 73. To the others it belongs to be products thereof, [i.e., of Self-consciousness].

a. 'To be products thereof,' i.e., to be products of Self-consciousness: that is to say, the fact of being products thereof belongs to the others,[2] the eleven 'Organs' (*indriya*), the five 'Subtile elements,' and, mediately, to the [gross] Elements, also, the products of the Subtile elements.[3]

b. But then, if it be thus [some one may say], you relinquish your dogma, that *Nature* is the cause of the whole world. Therefore he declares [as follows]:[4]

आद्यहेतुता तद्द्वारा पारम्पर्येऽप्यणुवत् ॥ ७४ ॥

---

[1] Instead of उत्तरेषां, which seems to be peculiar to Vijnána, Aniruddha and others have the preferable lection अन्येषां. *Ed.*

[2] To render अन्येषां. Paragraph *a* is taken, with slight alterations at the beginning and at the end, from Aniruddha. *Ed.*

[3] तत्कार्यत्वमहंकारकार्यत्वमन्येषामेकादशेन्द्रियाणां पञ्च तन्मात्राणां पारम्पर्येण तन्मात्रकार्याणामपि भूतानां तत्कार्यत्वमित्यर्थः ॥

[4] ननु यद्येवं तर्हि प्रधानं सर्वजगत्कारणमिति सिद्धान्तहानिरत आह ॥

Nature, immediately the cause of Mind, is, mediately, the cause of all other products.

Aph. 74. Moreover, mediately, through that [i.e., the 'Great one' (§71)], the first [cause, viz., Nature,] is the cause [of all products]; as is the case with the Atoms, [the causes, though not the immediate causes, of jars, &c.].

a. 'Moreover, mediately,' i.e., moreover, not in the character of the immediate cause, 'the first,' i.e., Nature, *is* the cause of 'Self-consciousness' and the rest, [mediately,] through 'the Great one' and the rest; as, in the theory of the *Vaiśeshikas*, the Atoms are the cause of a jar, or the like, only [mediately,] through combinations of two atoms, and so on: such is the meaning.[1]

b. But then, since, also, both Nature and Soul are eternal, which of them is [really] the cause of the creation's commencing? In regard to this, he declares [as follows]:[2]

पूर्वभावित्वे द्वयोरेकतरस्य हानेऽन्यतरयोगः[3] ॥ ७५ ॥

---

[1] पारम्पर्येऽपि साक्षादहेतुत्वेऽप्याद्यायाः प्रकृतेर्हेतुताहंकारादिषु महदादिद्वारास्ति यथा वैशेषिकमतेऽणूनां घटादिहेतुता द्व्यणुकादिद्वारैवेत्यर्थः ॥

[2] ननु प्रकृतिपुरुषयोर्द्वयोरपि नित्यत्वात्सृष्ट्यादौ कस्य कारणत्वमित्यत आह ॥

[3] Slightly better, perhaps, than this reading is that of Aniruddha: पूर्वभावित्वे द्वयोरेकतरहानेनान्यतरयोगः। Aniruddha's explanation here follows: न पूर्वभावित्वमात्रेण कारणत्वं किं त्वन्वयव्यतिरेकाभ्यां द्वयोर्मध्य एकस्य

Why Nature is the sole cause.

Aph. 75. While both [Soul and Nature] are antecedent [to all products], since the one [viz., Soul,] is devoid [of this character of being a cause], it is applicable [only] to the other of the two, [viz., Nature].

a. That is to say: 'while both,' viz., Soul and Nature, are preexistent to every product, still, 'since the one,' viz., Soul, from the fact of its not being modified [into anything else, as clay is modified into a jar], must be 'devoid,' or lack the nature of a cause, 'it is applicable,' i.e., the nature of a cause must belong, to the other of the two.[1]

b. But then [some one may say], let *Atoms* alone be causes; since there is no dispute [that *these* are causal]. In reply to this, he says:[2]

परिच्छिन्नं न[3] सर्वोपादानम् ॥ ७६ ॥

पुरुषस्य कारणत्वयोग्यताहानिरविकारित्वश्रुतेः । अतोऽन्यतरस्य प्रधानस्य कारणत्वयोगः । *Ed.*

[1] द्वयोरेव पुंप्रकृत्योरखिलकार्यपूर्वभावित्वेऽप्येकतरस्य पुरुषस्यापरिणामित्वेन हाने कारणताहान्यामन्यतरस्य योगः कारणतासंभव इत्यर्थः ॥

[2] नन्वविवादात्परमाणूनामेव कारणत्वमस्त्वित्यत आह ॥

[3] Aniruddha has, according to both my MSS., परिच्छिन्नत्वान्न. *Ed.*

Why the theory of a plastic Nature is preferable to that of Atoms.

Aph. 76. What is limited cannot be the substance of all [things].

a. That which is limited cannot be the substance of all [things]; as yarn cannot be the [material] cause of a jar. Therefore it would [on the theory suggested,] be necessary to mention separate causes of [all] things severally; and it is simpler to assume a single cause. Therefore Nature alone is the cause. Such is the meaning.[1]

b. He alleges Scripture in support of this:[2]

तदुत्पत्तिश्रुतेश्च ॥ ७७ ॥

Scripture declares in favour of the theory.

Aph. 77. And [the proposition that Nature is the cause of all is proved] from the text of Scripture, that the origin [of the world] is therefrom, [i.e., from Nature].

a. An argument, in the first instance, has been set forth [in § 76; for, till argument fails him, no one falls back upon authority]. Scripture, moreover, declares that Nature is the cause of the world, in such terms as, 'From Nature the world arises,' &c.[3]

---

[1] यत्परिच्छिन्नं न तत्सर्वोपादानं यथा न तन्तुर्घटस्य कारणम् । तस्मात्पदार्थानां पृथक्पृथक्कारणं वक्तव्यमेककारणत्वे च लाघवम् । तस्मात्प्रधानस्यैव कारणत्वमित्यर्थः ॥

[2] अत्र श्रुतिं दर्शयति ॥

[3] युक्तिस्तावत्प्रोक्ता । श्रुतिरपि प्रधानस्य जगत्कारणतामाह प्रधानाज्जगज्जायत इति ॥

b. But then [some one may say], a jar which antecedently did not exist is seen to come into existence. Let, then, *antecedent non-existence* be the cause [of each product]; since this is an invariable antecedent, [and, hence, a cause; 'the invariable antecedent being denominated a cause,' if Dr. Brown, in his 6th lecture, is to be trusted]. To this he replies:[1]

नावस्तुनो वस्तुसिद्धिः ॥ ७८ ॥

Ex nihilo nihil fit. *Aph.* 78. A thing is not made out of nothing.

a. That is to say: it is not possible that out of nothing, i.e., out of a nonentity, a thing should be made, i.e., an entity should arise. If an entity were to arise out of a nonentity, then, since the character of a cause is visible in its product, the *world*, also, would be unreal: such is the meaning.[2]

b. Let the world, too, *be* unreal: what harm is that to *us?* [If any ask this,] he, therefore, declares [as follows]:[3]

अबाधाददुष्टकारणजन्यत्वाच्च नावस्तुत्वम् ॥ ७९ ॥

---

[1] ननु प्रागसतो घटस्य भवनं दृश्यते। नियतपूर्वभावित्वात्प्रागभावः कारणमस्त्वित्यत आह ॥

[2] अवस्तुनोऽभावाद्वस्तुसिद्धिर्भावोत्पत्तिर्न संभवतीत्यर्थः। यद्यभावाद्भावोत्पत्तिस्तर्हि कारणरूपं कार्ये दृश्यत इति जगतोऽप्यवस्तुत्वं स्यादित्यर्थः ॥

[3] भवतु जगदप्यवस्तु का नो हानिरित्यत आह ॥

Reasons why the world is not to be supposed unreal.

Aph. 79. It [the world] is not unreal; because there is no fact contradictory [to its reality], and because it is not the [false] result of depraved causes, [leading to a belief in what ought not to be believed].

a. When there is the notion, in regard to a shell [of a pearl-oyster, which sometimes glitters like silver], that it is silver, its being silver is contradicted by the [subsequent and more correct] cognition, that this is *not* silver. But, in the case in question [that of the world regarded as a reality], no one ever has the cognition, 'This world is *not* in the shape of an entity,' by which [cognition, if any one ever really had such,] its being an entity might be opposed.[1]

b. And it is held that that is false which is the result of a *depraved* cause; e.g., some one's cognition of a [white] conch-shell as *yellow*, through such a fault as the jaundice, [which depraves his eye-sight]. But, in the case in question, [that of the world regarded as a reality], there is no such [temporary or occasional] depravation [of the senses]; because all, at all times, cognize the world as a reality. Therefore the world is *not* an unreality.[2]

---

[1] शुक्तौ रजतमिति ज्ञाने नेदं रजतमिति ज्ञानाद्रजतबाधः । न चात्र नेदं भावरूपं जगदिति कस्यापि ज्ञानं येन भावरूपबाधः स्यात् ॥

[2] दुष्टकारणजन्यत्वाच्च मिथ्येत्यवगम्यते यथा कामलादिदोषात्पीतशङ्खज्ञानं कस्यचित् । अत्र च जगज्ज्ञानस्य सर्वेषां सर्वदा सत्त्वान्न दोषोऽस्ति । तस्मान्नावस्तु जगदिति ॥

c. But then [some one may suggest], *let* a nonentity be the [substantial] cause of the world; still the world will not [necessarily, therefore,] be unreal. In regard to this, he declares [as follows]:[1]

भावे तद्योगेन तत्सिद्धिरभावे तदभावात्कुतस्तरां तत्सिद्धिः ॥ ८० ॥

The product of something is something; and that of nothing, nothing.

Aph. 80. If it [the substantial cause,] be an entity, then this would be the case, [that the product would be an entity], from its union [or identity] therewith; [but] if [the cause be] a nonentity, then how could it possibly be the case [that the product would be real], since *it* is a nonentity, [like the cause with which it is united, in the relation of identity]?

a. If an *entity* were the substantial cause [of the world], then, since [it is a maxim that] the qualities of the cause present themselves in the product, 'this would be the case,' i.e., it would be the case that the product was real, 'because of union therewith,' i.e., because of the union [of the product] with the reality [which is its substratum]. [But,] since, [by parity of reasoning], if a *nonentity* [were the substantial cause], the world would be a nonentity, then, by reason of its being a nonentity, i.e., by reason of the world's being [on that supposition,] necessarily a nonentity, [like its supposed cause], how could this be the case,[2] [that it would be *real*]?

---

[1] नन्वभावः कारणमस्तु तथाप्यभावत्वं न जगतो भविष्यतीति । तत्राह ॥

[2] भाव उपादानकारणे कारणगुणाः कार्ये इति

b. But then [a follower of the *Mímáṅsá* may say], since [it would appear that] nonentity can take no shape but that of nonentity, let *works* alone be the cause of the world. What need have we of the hypothesis of 'Nature'? To this he replies :[1]

न कर्मण उपादानायोगात्[2] ॥ ८१ ॥

Action cannot serve as a substratum.

Aph. 81. No; for *works* are not adapted to be the *substantial* cause [of any product].

a. Granting that 'the unseen' [merit or demerit arising from actions] may be an *instrumental* cause, [in bringing about the mundane condition of the agent], yet we never see merit or demerit in the character of the *substantial* cause [of any product] : and our theories ought to show deference to our experience. 'Nature' is to be accepted; because Liberation arises [see § 56,[3] and § 83,] from discerning the distinction between Nature and the Soul.[4]

तद्योगेन भावयोगेन तत्सिद्धिः कार्यस्य वस्तुत्वसिद्धिः। अभावे जगतोऽभावत्वे तदभावाज्जगदभावस्यावश्यंभावात्कुतस्तत्सिद्धिरिति ॥

[1] नन्वभावस्याभावरूपत्वात्कर्मैव जगत्कारणमस्तु। किं प्रधानकल्पनयेत्यत आह ॥

[2] उपादानत्वायोगात् is the lection accepted by Vijnána, and by him only. *Ed.*

[3] It is the bracketed Aph. 56, at p. 58, *supra*, that is here referred to. *Ed.*

[4] निमित्तं कारणमदृष्टमस्तु धर्माधर्मयोस्तूपा-

b. But then [some one may say], since Liberation can be attained by undertaking the things directed by the Veda, what occasion is there for [our troubling ourselves about] *Nature?* To this he replies :[1]

नानुश्रविकादपि तत्सिद्धिः साध्यत्वेनावृत्तियोगा-
दपुरुषार्थत्वम् ॥ ८२ ॥

Salvation is not to be obtained by ritual observances.

Aph. 82. The accomplishment thereof [i.e., of Liberation,] is not, moreover, through Scriptural rites: the chief end of man does not consist in this [which is gained through such means]; because, since this consists of what is accomplished through *acts*, [and is, therefore, a *product*, and not *eternal*], there is [still left impending over the ritualist,] the liability to repetition of births.

a. 'Scriptural means,' such as sacrifices, [are so called], because they are heard from [the mouth of the instructor in] Scripture. Not thereby, moreover, is 'the accomplishment thereof,' i.e., the accomplishment of Liberation; 'because one is liable to repetition of births, by reason of the fact that it [the supposed Liberation,] was accomplished by *means*,' i.e., because the [thus far] liberated

---

दानकारणत्वं न क्वचिद्दृष्टं कल्पना हि दृष्टानुसारेणैव भवति। प्रकृतिपुरुषविवेकदर्शनान्मुक्तिरिति प्रकृतिस्वीकारः ॥

[1] ननु वेदोक्तार्थानुष्ठानादेव मुक्तिसंभवात्किं प्रकृत्येत्यत आह ॥

[soul] is still liable to repetition of births,[1] inasmuch as this [its supposed Liberation,] is not *eternal*, [just] because it is [the result of] *acts*. For *this* reason, the chief end of man does not consist in this,[2] [which is gained through ritual observances].

b. He shows what *does* constitute the chief end of man:[3]

तत्र प्राप्तविवेकस्यानावृत्तिश्रुतिः ॥ ८३ ॥

In regard to the attainment of the chief end of man, the Scripture concurs with the Sánkhya.

Aph. 83. There is Scripture for it, that he who has attained to discrimination, in regard to these [i.e., Nature and Soul], has no repetition of births.

a. 'In regard to these,' i.e., in regard to Nature and Soul, of him who has attained to discrimination, there is a text declaring, that, in consequence of his knowledge of the distinction, there will be no repetition of births; the text, viz., '*He* does not return again,'[4] &c.[5]

---

[1] Literally, 'liable to return to mundane existence.' *Ed.*

[2] वेदादनुश्रूयत इत्यानुश्रविको यज्ञादिः। तस्मादपि न तत्सिद्धिर्मोक्षसिद्धिः साध्यत्वेनावृत्तियोगात्कर्मत्वेनानित्यत्वान्मुक्तस्य पुनः संसारावृत्तियोगः। तस्मादपुरुषार्थत्वम् ॥

[3] पुरुषार्थत्वं दर्शयति ॥

[4] Compare the *Chhándogya Upanishad*, viii., xv. *Ed.*

[5] तत्र प्रकृतिपुरुषयोः प्राप्तविवेकस्य विवेकज्ञानादनावृत्तिश्रुतिः। न स पुनरावर्तेत इति श्रुतिः ॥

b. He states an objection to the opposite view:[1]

दुःखाद्दुःखं जलाभिषेकवन्न जाड्यविमोकः ॥ ८४ ॥

Pain can lead only to pain, not to liberation from it.

Aph. 84. From pain [occasioned, e.g., to victims in sacrifice,] must come pain [to the sacrificer, and not *liberation* from pain]; as there is not relief from chilliness, by affusion of water.

a. If Liberation were to be effected by *acts,* [such as sacrifices], then, since the acts involve a variety of pains, Liberation itself [on the principle that every effect includes the qualities of its cause,] would include a variety of pains; and it would be a grief, from the fact that it must eventually end: for, to one who is distressed by chilliness the affusion of water does not bring liberation from his chilliness, but, rather, [additional] chilliness.[2]

b. But then [some one may say], the fact that the act is productive of pain is not the *motive* [to the performance of sacrifice]; but the [real] reason is this, that the act is productive of *things desirable.* And, in accordance with this, there is the text, 'By means of acts [of sacrifice] they may partake of immortality,' &c. To this he replies:[3]

---

[1] विपक्षे दोषमाह ॥

[2] यदि कर्मसाध्यो मोक्षो भवेत्कर्मणो दुःखबहुलत्वान्मोक्षोऽपि दुःखबहुलः स्यादन्ततः क्षयित्वेनापि दुःखं स्यान्नहि जाड्यार्त्तस्य जाड्यविमोको जलाभिषेकात्प्रत्युत जाड्यमेवेति ॥

[3] ननु दुःखस्य कर्मसाध्यत्वमप्रयोजकं किं तु का-

काम्येऽकाम्येऽपि[1] साध्यत्वाविशेषात् ॥ ८५ ॥

The character of the end contemplated makes no difference in regard to the transitoriness of what is effected by works.

Aph. 85. [Liberation cannot arise from acts]; because, whether the end be something desirable, or undesirable, [and we admit that the *motive* of the sacrifice is not the giving pain to the victim], this makes no difference in regard to its being the result of *acts*, [and, therefore, not eternal, but transitory].

a. Grant that pain is not what is [intended] to be accomplished by works done without desire, [on the part of the virtuous sacrificer], still, though there *is* a difference [as you contend,] between [an act done to secure] something enjoyable and an act done without reference to enjoyment, this makes no difference with respect to the fact of the Liberation's being produced by *acts*, [which, I repeat, *permanent* Liberation cannot be]: there must still again be pain; for it [the Liberation supposed to have been attained through works,] must be perishable, because it is a *production*. The text which declares that works done without desire are instruments of Liberation has reference to *knowledge*, [which, I grant, may be gained by such means]; and Liberation comes through knowledge; so that these [works] are instruments of Liberation

---

म्यकर्मसाध्यत्वं हेतुः। तथा च श्रुतिः कर्मभ्यो ऽमृतत्वमानशुरिति। तत्राह ॥

[1] The reading of Aniruddha, according to my MSS., is काम्याकामेऽपि. *Ed.*

mediately:[1] [but you will recollect that the present inquiry regards the *immediate* cause].

b. [But then, some one may say], supposing that Liberation may take place [as you Sánkhyas contend,] through the knowledge of the distinction between Nature and Soul, still, since, from the perishableness [of the Liberation effected by *this* means, as well as any other means], mundane life may return, we are both on an equality, [*we*, whose Liberation you Sánkhyas look upon as transitory, and you Sánkhyas, whose Liberation we, again, look upon as being, by parity of reasoning, in much the same predicament]. To this he replies:[2]

निजमुक्तस्य बन्धध्वंसमात्रे[3] परं न समानत्वम् ॥ ८६ ॥

---

[1] मा भून्निष्कामकर्मसाध्यं दुःखं तथापि काम्यान्निष्कामकर्मविशेषेऽपि मोक्षस्य कर्मसाध्यत्वमविशिष्टं साध्यत्वात्क्षयित्वेन पुनरपि दुःखं स्यात् । निष्कामकर्मणो मोक्षसाधनत्वश्रुतिः ज्ञानार्थं ज्ञानाच्च मोक्ष इति पारम्पर्येण मोक्षसाधनत्वम् ॥

[2] यदि प्रकृतिपुरुषविवेकज्ञानान्मोक्षो भवेत्तथापि क्षयित्वात्पुनरपि संसार इत्यावयोस्तुल्यत्वमित्यत आह ॥

[3] Dr. Ballantyne, on republishing the Sánkhya Aphorisms in the *Bibliotheca Indica*, adopted the genuine reading, बन्धध्वंसमात्रं, instead of that given above, which I find, indeed, in the Serampore edition of the *Sánkhya-pravachana-bháshya*, but in no MS. He ought, however, at the same time, to have altered his translation,

The right means effect Liberation once for all.

Aph. 86. Of him who is essentially liberated, his bonds having absolutely perished, it [i.e., the fruit of his saving knowledge,] is absolute: there is no parity [between his case and that of him who relies on works, and who may thereby secure a temporary sojourn in Paradise, only to return again to earth].

a. Of him 'who is essentially liberated,' who, in his very essence, is free, there is the destruction of bondage. The bond [see § 56,[1]] is Non-discrimination [between Nature and Soul]. By the removal thereof there is the destruction, the annihilation, of Non-discrimination: and how is it possible that there should again be a return of the mundane state, when the destruction of Non-discrimination is *absolute?* Thus there is no [such] similarity,[2] [between the two cases, as is imagined, by the objector, under § 85.*b.*].

b. It has been asserted [in § 61,] that there is a class of twenty-five [things which are realities]; and, since these cannot be ascertained [or made out to be *true*], except by

---

which, in conformity with the unadulterated text, might have run somewhat as follows: 'Of him who is, in himself, liberated all extinction of bondage is final,' &c. Such is the interpretation which, on comparison of the various commentaries, seems to be the most eligible. *Ed.*

[1] This is the Aphorism bracketed at p. 58, *supra. Ed.*

[2] निजमुक्तस्य स्वभावमुक्तस्य बन्धध्वंसः। बन्धो ऽविवेकः। तद्विरोधेनाविवेकध्वंसो नाशः। अविवेकनाशस्य च प्रध्वंसत्वात्कुतः संसारस्य पुनरावर्तनमिति न समत्वम् ॥

proof, therefore he displays this;[1] [i.e., he shows what he *means* by proof]:

द्वयोरेकतरस्य[2] वाप्यसंनिकृष्टार्थपरिच्छित्तिः प्रमा। तत्साधकतमं[3] यत्तत् ॥ ८७ ॥

What is meant by evidence.

Aph. 87. The determination of something not [previously] lodged in both [the Soul and the Intellect], nor in one or other of them, is 'right notion' (*pramá*). What is, in the highest degree, productive thereof [i. e., of any given 'right notion'], is that; [i. e., is what we mean by proof, or evidence, (*pramáṇa*)].

a. 'Not lodged,' i. e., not deposited in 'one rightly cognizing' (*pramátṛi*); in short, not previously known. The 'determination,' i.e., the ascertainment [or right apprehension] of such a thing, or reality, is 'right notion'; and, whether this be an affection 'of *both*,' i.e., of Intellect, and also of Soul [as some hold that it is], or of only one or other of the two, [as others hold,] *either* way, 'what is, in the highest degree, productive' of this 'right notion' is [what we term proof, or] evidence, (*pramáṇa*): such is the definition of evidence in general; [the definition of its several species falling to be considered hereafter]: such is the meaning.[4]

---

[1] पञ्चविंशतिर्गण इत्युक्तं तत्सिद्धिश्च न प्रमाणेन विनेति तद्दर्शयति ॥

[2] Nágeśa has वासं°. *Ed.*

[3] Some MSS. have the inferior reading -साधकं. *Ed.*

[4] असंनिकृष्टः प्रमातर्यनारूढोऽनधिगत इति

b. It is with a view to the exclusion of Memory, Error, and Doubt, in their order, that we employ [when speaking of the result of evidence,] the expressions 'not previously known' [which excludes things remembered], and 'reality' [which excludes mistakes and fancies], and 'discrimination,'[1] [which excludes doubt].

c. In regard to this [topic of knowledge and the sources of knowledge], if 'right notion,' is spoken of as located in the *Soul* [see § 87. *a.*], then the [proof, or] evidence is an affection of the *Intellect.* If [on the other hand, the 'right notion' is spoken of as] located in the Intellect, in the shape of an affection [of that the affections of which are mirrored by the Soul], then it [the proof, or evidence, or whatever we may choose to call that from which 'right notion' results,] is just the conjunction of an organ [with its appropriate object; such conjunction giving rise to sense-perception], &c. But, if *both* the Soul's cognition and the affections of the Intellect are spoken of as [cases of] 'right notion,' then *both* of these aforesaid [the affection of the Intellect, in the first case, and the conjunction of an organ with its appropriate object, &c., in the other

---

यावत् । एवंभूतस्यार्थस्य वस्तुनः परिच्छित्तिरवधारणं प्रमा सा च द्वयोर्बुद्धिपुरुषयोरेव धर्मो भवतु किं वैकतरमात्रस्योभयथैव तस्याः प्रमाया यत्साधकतमं तत्प्रमाणमिति प्रमाणसामान्यलक्षणमित्यर्थः ॥

[1] स्मृतिभ्रमसंशयव्युदासाय क्रमेणानधिगत इति वस्तुन इत्यवधारणमिति ॥

case,] are [to receive the name of] proof (*pramáṇa*). You are to understand, that, when the organ of vision, &c., are spoken of as 'evidence,' it is only as being *mediately*[1] [the sources of right knowledge].

d. How many [kinds of] proofs [then,] are there? To this he replies :[2]

त्रिविधं प्रमाणं[3] तत्सिद्धौ सर्वसिद्धेर्नाधिक्यसिद्धिः ॥ ८८ ॥

There are three kinds of evidence.

Aph. 88. Proof is of three kinds: there is no establishment of more; because, if these be established, then all [that is true] can be established [by one or other of these three proofs].

a. 'Proof is of three kinds;' that is to say, 'perception'

---

[1] अत्र यदि प्रमारूपं फलं पुरुषनिष्ठमुच्यते तदा बुद्धिवृत्तिरेव प्रमाणम्। यदि बुद्धिनिष्ठं वृत्तिरूपं तदा तदेन्द्रियसंनिकर्षादिरेव। यदि तु पौरुषेयबोधो बुद्धिवृत्तिश्चोभयमपि प्रमेत्युच्यते तदोक्तमुभयमेव प्रमाणं भवति। चक्षुरादिषु प्रमाणव्यवहारः परंपरयैवेति बोध्यम् ॥

[2] कति प्रमाणानीत्यत आह ॥

[3] So reads Aniruddha; but Vijnána, Nágeśa, and Vedánti Mahádeva end the eighty-seventh Aphorism with these two words. Hence: 'That which is, in the highest degree, productive thereof is proof, of three kinds.' *Ed.*

(*pratyaksha*), 'the recognition of signs' (*anumána*), and 'testimony' (*śabda*), are the [three kinds of] proofs.[1]

b. But then [some one may incline to say], let 'comparison' [which is reckoned, in the Nyáya, a specifically distinct source of knowledge], and the others [such as 'Conjecture,' &c., which are reckoned, in like manner, in the Mímáṅsá], also be instruments of right knowledge, [as well as these three], in [the matter of] the discriminating of Nature and Soul: he therefore says, 'because, if these [three] be established,' &c. And, since, if there be the three kinds of proof established,' everything [that is really true] can be established [by means of them], there is no establishment of more;' no addition to the proofs can be fairly made out; because of the cumbrousness [that sins against the philosophical maxim, that we are not to assume more than is necessary to account for the case]: such is the meaning.[2]

c. For the same reason, Manu, also, has laid down only a triad of proofs, where he says [see the Institutes, Ch. xii., v. 105]: 'By that man who seeks a distinct knowledge of his duty, [these] three [sources of right knowledge] must be well understood, viz., Perception, Inference, and Scriptural authority in its various shapes [of legal institute,

---

[1] त्रिविधं प्रमाणमिति प्रत्यक्षानुमानशब्दाः प्रमाणानीत्यर्थः ॥

[2] ननूपमानाद्यपि प्रकृतिपुरुषविवेकप्रमाणमस्त्विति। अत आह तत्सिद्धाविति। त्रिविधप्रमाणसिद्धौ च सर्वस्यार्थस्य सिद्धेर्नाधिक्यसिद्धिर्न प्रमाणाधिक्यं सिद्ध्यति गौरवादित्यर्थः ॥

&c.].' And 'Comparison,' and 'Tradition' *(aitihya)*, and the like, are included under Inference and Testimony; and 'Non-perception' *(anupalabdhi)* and the like are included under Perception;[1] [for the non-perception of an absent jar on a particular spot of ground is nothing else than the perception of that spot of ground *without* a jar on it].

d. He [next] states the definitions of the varieties[2] [of proof, having already (§ 87) given the general definition]:

[3]यत्संबद्धं[4] सत्तदाकारोल्लेखि विज्ञानं तत्प्रत्यक्षम् ॥ ८९ ॥

Perception defined.

Aph. 89. Perception *(pratyaksha)* is that discernment which, being in conjunction [with the thing perceived], portrays the form thereof.

a. 'Being in conjunction,' [literally,] 'existing in con-

---

[1] अत एव मनुनापि प्रमाणत्रयमेवोपन्यस्तम्। प्रत्यक्षमनुमानं च शास्त्रं च विविधागमम्। त्रयं सुविदितं कार्यं धर्मशुद्धिमभीप्सतेति। उपमानैतिह्यादीनां चानुमानशब्दयोः प्रवेशोऽनुपलब्ध्यादीनां च प्रत्यक्षे प्रवेश इति ॥

[2] विशेषलक्षणमाह ॥

[3] Aniruddha has यत्संबन्धसिद्धं तदा°, yielding 'determined by,' &c., instead of 'being in,' &c. *Ed.*

[4] Vedánti Mahádeva has यत्संबन्धं (?). *Ed.*

junction;' 'portrays the form thereof,' i.e., assumes the form of the thing with which it is in conjunction [as water assumes the form of the vessel into which it is poured]; what 'discernment,' or affection of the Intellect, [does *this*], that [affection of the Intellect (see Yoga Aphorisms, I., § 5 and § 8. *b*.)] is the evidence [called] Perception: such is the meaning.[1]

b. But then, [some one may say,] this [definition of Perception (§ 89)] does not extend [as we conceive it ought, and presume it is intended, to do,] to the perception, by adepts in the *Yoga*, of things past, future, or concealed [by stone walls, or such intervening things as interrupt ordinary perception]; because there is, here, no 'form of the thing, in *conjunction*' [with the mind of him who perceives it, while absent]: having pondered this doubt, he corrects it by [stating, as follows,] the fact, that this [supernatural sort of perception] is not what he intends to define:[2]

योगिनामबाह्यप्रत्यक्षत्वान्न दोषः ॥ ९० ॥

---

[1] संबद्धं सत्संबद्धं भवत्तदाकारोल्लेखि संबद्धवस्त्वाकारधारि भवति यद्विज्ञानं बुद्धिवृत्तिस्तत्प्रत्यक्षं प्रमाणमित्यर्थः ॥

[2] ननु योगिनामतीतानागतव्यवहितवस्तुप्रत्यक्षेऽव्याप्तिः संबद्धवस्त्वाकाराभावादित्याशङ्क्य तस्यालक्ष्यत्वेन समाधत्ते ॥

The definition not to be blamed, though it should not apply to the perceptions of the mystic.

Aph. 90. It is not a fault [in the definition, that it does not apply to the perceptions of adepts in the *Yoga*]; because that of the adepts in the *Yoga* is not an *external* perception.

a. That is to say: it is only *sense*-perception that is to be here defined; and the adepts of the Yoga do not perceive through the *external* [organs of sense]. Therefore there is no fault [in our definition]; i.e., there is no *failure* to include the perceptions of these;[1] [because there is no *intention* to include them].

b. [But, although this reply is as much as the objector has any right to expect,] he states the real justification[2] [of the definition in question]:

लीनवस्तुलब्धातिशयसंबन्धाद्वादोषः[3] ॥ ९१ ॥

But the definition does apply to the perceptions of the mystic.

Aph. 91. Or, there is no fault [in the definition], because of the conjunction, with *causal* things, of that [mystical mind] which has attained exaltation.[4]

---

[1] ऐन्द्रियकप्रत्यक्षमेवात्र लक्ष्यं योगिनश्चाबाह्यप्रत्यक्षकाः। अतो न दोषो न तत्प्रत्यक्षेऽव्याप्तिरित्यर्थः ॥

[2] वास्तवं समाधानमाह ॥

[3] Thus Vijnána and Vedánti Mahádeva. Aniruddha has -संबन्धान्न दोषः. The reading of Nágeśa is -संबन्धाद्वा न दोषः. *Ed.*

[4] For the term *atiśaya*, again rendered, in the next page, by 'exaltation,' *vide infra*, p. 115, note 4. *Ed.*

a. Or, be it so that the perception of the *Yogí*, also, shall be the thing to be defined; still there is no fault [in our definition, § 89]; it does not fail to extend [to this, also]; since the mind of the *Yogí*, in the exaltation gained from the habitude produced by concentration, *does* come into conjunction with things [as existent] in their causes,[1] [whether or not with the things as developed into products perceptible by the external senses].

b. Here the word rendered 'causal' *(lína)* denotes the things, *not* in conjunction [with the senses], alluded to by the objector [in § 89. *b.*]; for *we,* who assert that effects *exist* [from eternity, in their causes, before taking the shape of effects, and, likewise, in these same causes, when again resolved into their causes], hold that even what is past, &c., still essentially exists, and that, hence, its conjunction [with the mind of the mystic, or the clairvoyant,] is possible.[2]

Objection, that the definition does not apply to the perceptions of the 'Lord.'

c. But then, [some one may say,] still this [definition] does not extend to the Lord's perceptions; because, since these are from everlasting, they can-

---

[1] अथ वास्तु योगिप्रत्यक्षमपि लक्ष्यं तथापि न दोषो नाव्याप्तिर्यतो लीनवस्तुषु लब्धयोगजधर्मजन्यातिशयस्य योगिचित्तस्य संबन्धो घटते ॥

[2] अत्र लीनशब्दः पराभिप्रेतासंनिकृष्टवाची सत्कार्यवादिनां ह्यतीतादिकमपि स्वरूपतोऽस्तीति तत्संबन्धः संभवेदिति ॥

not *result* from [emergent] conjunction. To this he replies:[1]

ईश्वरासिद्धेः ॥ ९२ ॥

That any 'Lord' exists is not proved.

Aph. 92. [This objection to the definition of Perception has no force]; because it is not proved that there *is* a Lord (*íśwara*).

a. That there is no fault [in the definition of Perception], because there is no proof that there *is* a Lord, is supplied[2] [from § 90].

b. And this demurring to there being any 'Lord' is merely in accordance with[3] the arrogant dictum of [certain] partisans [who hold an opinion not recognized by the majority]. Therefore, it is to be understood, the expression employed is, 'because it is *not proved* that there is a Lord,' but not the expression, 'because there *is no* Lord.'[4]

---

[1] ननु तथापीश्वरप्रत्यक्षेऽव्याप्तिस्तस्य नित्यत्वेनासंनिकर्षजन्यत्वात् । तत्राह ॥

[2] ईश्वरे प्रमाणाभावाददोष इत्यनुवर्तते ॥

[3] Rather, 'And this [mere] taking exception to a Lord is expressly owing to,' &c. The aphorist would not be confounded with those who denied what he waited to see evidenced. The attitude which he assumed is that of suspense of judgment on the point of theism, as against the positiveness of the professed atheist. Vijnána, here followed, then goes on to say: अन्यथा हीश्वराभावादित्येवोच्येत । 'For, otherwise [i.e., if the aphorist had been atheistic], it would have been explicitly declared, Because of the non-existence of a Lord.' *Ed.*

[4] अयं चेश्वरप्रतिषेध एकदेशिनां प्रौढवादेनैवे-

c. But, on the implication[1] that there *is* a 'Lord,' what we mean to speak of [in our definition of Perception, (§89),] is merely the being of the [same] kind with what is produced by conjunction[2] [of a sense-organ with its object; and the perceptions of the 'Lord' may be of the same *kind* with such perceptions, though they were not to come from the same *source*].

d. Having pondered the doubt, '*How* should the Lord not be proved [to exist] by the Scripture and the Law, [which declare his existence]?' he states a dilemma which excludes [this]:[3]

मुक्तबद्धयोरन्यतराभावान्न तत्सिद्धिः ॥ ९३ ॥

A dilemma, to exclude proof that there is any 'Lord.'

Aph. 93. [And, further,] it is not proved that he [the 'Lord,'] exists; because [whoever exists must be either free or bound; and], of free and bound, he can be neither the one nor the other.

a. The 'Lord' whom you imagine, tell us, is he free from troubles, &c.? Or is he in bondage through these?

ति । अत एवेश्वरासिद्धेरित्युक्तं न त्वीश्वराभावादिति बोध्यम् ॥

1 Rather, 'the view being accepted' (*abhyupagame*).

2 ईश्वराभ्युपगमे तु संनिकर्षजन्यजातीयत्वमेव विवक्षितम् ॥

3 श्रुतिस्मृतिभ्यां कथमीशो न सिध्येदित्याशङ्क्य तर्कविरोधं बाधकमाह ॥

Since he is not, cannot be, either the one or the other, it is not proved that there is a 'Lord:' such is the meaning.[1]

b. He explains this very point:[2]

उभयथाप्यसत्करत्वम्[3] ॥ ९४ ॥

The force of the dilemma.

Aph. 94. [Because,] either way, he would be inefficient.

a. Since, if he were free, he would have no desires, &c., which [as compulsory motives,] would instigate him to create; and, if he were bound, he would be under delusion; he must be [on either alternative,] unequal to the creation, &c.[4] [of this world].

b. But then, [it may be asked,] if such be the case, what becomes of the Scripture-texts which declare the 'Lord?' To this he replies:[5]

---

[1] ईश्वरोऽभिमतः किं क्लेशादिभिर्मुक्तो वा तैर्बद्धो वा । अन्यतरस्याप्यभावादसंभवान्नेश्वरसिद्धिरित्यर्थः ॥

[2] तदेवाह ॥

[3] The reading, in a later handwriting, of one of my MSS. of Aniruddha is -सत्कर्तृत्वम्. *Ed.*

[4] मुक्तत्वे सृष्टिप्रयोजकरागाद्यभावाद्बद्धत्वे च मूढत्वान्न सृष्ट्यादिक्षमत्वमित्यर्थः ॥

[5] नन्वेवमीश्वरप्रतिपादकश्रुतीनां का गतिः । तत्राह ॥

मुक्तात्मनः प्रशंसा[1] उपासा सिद्धस्य[2] वा ॥ ९५ ॥

The import of the texts which speak of the 'Lord.'

Aph. 95. [The Scriptural texts which make mention of the 'Lord' are] either glorifications of the liberated Soul, or homages to the recognized[3] [deities of the Hindu pantheon].[4]

a. That is to say: accordingly as the case may be, *some* text [among those in which the term 'Lord' occurs,] is intended, in the shape of a glorification [of Soul], as the 'Lord,' [as Soul is held to be], merely in virtue of junction [with Nature], to incite [to still deeper contemplation], to exhibit, as what is to be known, the liberated Soul, i. e., absolute Soul in general; and some other text, declaratory, for example, of creatorship, &c., preceded by resolution [to create, is intended] to extol [and to purify the mind of the contemplator, by enabling him to take a part in extolling] the eternity, &c., of the familiarly known[3] Brahmá,

---

[1] Another reading, that of Nágeśa and of Vedánti Mahádeva, प्रशंसोपा°, makes this word of the singular number. *Ed.*

[2] उपासासिद्धस्य, a compound, is the reading of Aniruddha, followed by Vedánti Mahádeva. See 4, below. *Ed.*

[3] In both places, *siddha,* 'possessor of supernatural powers.' *Ed.*

[4] Aniruddha's exposition of this Aphorism is as follows: रागाद्यभावान्मुक्तात्मन इव मुक्तात्मनो न तु मुक्तस्य तस्य संकल्पकर्तृत्वाद्यभावात्। तत्प्रशंसा विधिवाक्योत्तम्भनाय। उपासासिद्धस्य। उपासनया लब्धातिशयस्य योगिनोऽणिमादिसिद्धस्य प्रशंसा-

Vishṇu, Śiva, or other *non*-eternal 'Lord;' since these, though possessed of the conceit [of individuality], &c., [and, in so far, liable to perish], have immortality, &c., in a secondary sense;[1] [seeing that the Soul, in *every* combination, is immortal, though the combination itself is not so].

b. But then, [some one may say], even if it were thus [as alleged under § 95], what is heard in Scripture, [viz.], the fact that it [viz., Soul] is the *governor* of Nature, &c., would not be the case; for, in the world, we speak of government in reference only to modifications [preceded and determined] by resolutions [that so and so shall take place], &c. To this he replies:[2]

भ्यासोत्तम्भनायेति । According to this, the term *íśwara*, 'mighty one,' 'lord,' is applied, by way of eulogy, either to a soul as it were liberated, or to a person who, through devotion, has acquired transcendent faculties, that is to say, the *Yogí*. Resolution, agentship, and the like, are impredicable of one absolutely liberated; and such a one, being inert and impassive, cannot be intended by *íśwara*, 'a power.' Hence the expression, 'as it were liberated.' Also see, for *atiśaya*,—translated, above, 'transcendent faculties,'—Book IV., Aph. 24. *Ed.*

1 यथायोगं काचिच्छ्रुतिर्मुक्तात्मनः केवलात्मसामान्यस्य ज्ञेयताविधानाय संनिधिमात्रैश्वर्येण स्तुतिरूपा प्ररोचनार्था काचिच्च संकल्पपूर्वकस्रष्टृत्वादिप्रतिपादिका श्रुतिः सिद्धस्य ब्रह्मविष्णुहरादेरेवानित्येश्वरस्याभिमानादिमतोऽपि गौणनित्यत्वादिमत्त्वान्नित्यत्वाद्युपासापरेत्यर्थः ॥

2 ननु तथापि प्रकृत्याद्यधिष्ठातृत्वं श्रूयमाणं नो-

तत्संनिधानादधिष्ठातृत्वं मणिवत् ॥ ९६ ॥

Soul, like the lodestone, acts not by resolve, but through proximity.

Aph. 96. The governorship [thereof, i.e., of Soul over Nature] is from [its] proximity thereto, [not from its resolving to act thereon]; as is the case with the gem, [the lodestone, in regard to iron].

a. If it were alleged that [its, Soul's,] creativeness, or [its] governorship, was through a *resolve* [to create, or to govern], then this objection [brought forward under § 95. *b.*] would apply. But [it is not so; for,] by *us* [Sánkhyas,] it is held that the Soul's governorship, in the shape of creatorship, or the like, is merely from [its] *proximity* [to Nature]; 'as is the case with the [lodestone] gem.'[1]

b. As the gem, the lodestone, is attracted by iron merely by proximity, without resolving [either to act or to be acted on], &c., so, by the mere conjunction of the primal Soul, Nature is changed into the principle [called] the 'Great one,' [or Mind, (see § 61. *c.*)]. And in this alone consists [what we speak of as] its acting as *creator* towards that which is superadded to it: such is the meaning.[2]

पपद्यते लोके संकल्पादिना परिणमनस्यैवाधिष्ठानव्यवहारादिति । तत्राह ॥

[1] यदि संकल्पेन स्रष्टृत्वमधिष्ठातृत्वमुच्यते तदायं दोषः स्यात् । अस्माभिस्तु पुरुषस्य संनिधानादेवाधिष्ठातृत्वं स्रष्टृत्वादिरूपमिष्यते मणिवत् ॥

[2] यथायस्कान्तमणेः सान्निध्यमात्रेण लोहाकर्षकत्वं संकल्पादिना विना तथैवादिपुरुषस्य संयो-

c. And thus it is declared, [in some one of the Puráṇas[1]]: 'As the iron acts, whilst the gem [the lodestone,] stands void of volition, just so this world is created by a deity who is mere Existence. Thus it is, that there are, in the Soul, both agency [seemingly,] and non-agency, [really]. It is *not* an agent, inasmuch as it is void of volition; [and it *is*] an agent, merely through approximation [to Nature].'[2]

d. In respect of worldly products, also, animal souls overrule, merely through their approximation [to Nature]: so he declares [as follows]:[3]

विशेषकार्येष्वपि[4] जीवानाम् ॥ ९७ ॥

गमात्रेण प्रकृतेर्महत्तत्त्वरूपेण परिणमनम् । इद-
मेव च स्वोपाधिस्रष्टृत्वमित्यर्थः ॥

[1] The Translator's authority for this attribution has not been discovered. *Ed.*

[2] तथा चोक्तम् । निरिच्छे संस्थिते रत्ने यथा लोहः प्रवर्तते । सत्तामात्रेण देवेन तथैवेयं जगज्जनिः । अत आत्मनि कर्तृत्वमकर्तृत्वं च संस्थितम् । निरिच्छत्वादकर्तासौ कर्ता सन्निधिमात्रत इति ॥

[3] लौकिककार्येष्वपि जोवानां संनिधिमात्रेणै-वाधिष्ठातृत्वमित्याह ॥

[4] Aniruddha has विशेषकार्येऽपि. *Ed.*

In like manner, embodied souls do not energize.

Aph. 97. In the case of individual products, also, [the apparent agency] of animal souls [is solely through proximity].

a. 'The agency is solely through proximity:' so much is supplied[1] [from § 96].

b. The meaning is this, that, in the case, also, of particular productions,—the creation, &c., of things individual [as contradistinguished from that of all things in the lump, (see *Vedánta-sára*, § 67)],—animal souls, i. e., souls in which the intellects [of individuals] reflect themselves [see § 99. *a.*], overrule, merely through proximity, but not through any effort; seeing that these [animal souls] are none other than the motionless Thought.[2]

c. But then, [some one may say], if there were no eternal and omniscient 'Lord,' through the doubt of a blind tradition, [in the absence of an intelligently effective guardianship], the *Vedas* would cease to be an authority; [a possibility which, of course, cannot be entertained for an instant]. To this he replies:[3]

---

1 अधिष्ठातृत्वं संनिधानादेवेत्यनुषज्यते ॥

2 विशेषकार्येषु व्यष्टिसृष्ट्यादिष्वपि जीवानामन्तःकरणप्रतिबिम्बितचेतनानां संनिधानादेवाधिष्ठातृत्वं न तु केनापि व्यवहारेण कूटस्थचिन्मात्रत्वादित्यर्थः ॥

3 ननु नित्यसर्वज्ञेश्वराभावेऽन्धपरंपराशङ्कया वेदाप्रामाण्यं स्यात् । अत आह ॥

सिद्धरूपबोद्धृत्वाद्वाक्यार्थोपदेशः ॥ ९८ ॥

How the Vedas need not the 'Lord' to authenticate them.

Aph. 98. The declaration of the texts or sense [of the Veda, by Brahmá, for example], since *he* knows the truth, [*is* authorative evidence].

a. To complete [the aphorism, we must say], 'since *Hiranyagarbha* [i.e., *Brahmá,*] and others [viz., *Vishnu* and *Śiva*], are knowers of what is certain, i.e., of what is true, the declaration of the texts or sense of the Vedas, where *these* are the speakers, *is* evidence[1] [altogether indisputable].

b. But then, if Soul, by its simple proximity [to Nature (§ 96)], is an overruler in a *secondary* sense [only of the term,—as the magnet may be said, in a secondary sense, to draw the iron, while the conviction is entertained, that, actually and literally, the iron draws the magnet],—who is the *primary* [or actual,] overruler? In reference to this, he says:[2]

---

[1] हिरण्यगर्भादीनां सिद्धरूपस्य यथार्थस्य बोद्धृत्वात्तद्वक्तृको वेदवाक्यार्थोपदेशः प्रमाणमिति शेषः ॥

[2] ननु पुरुषस्य चेत्संनिधिमात्रेण गौणमधिष्ठातृत्वं तर्हि मुख्यमधिष्ठातृत्वं कस्येत्याकाङ्क्षायामाह ॥

अन्तःकरणस्य[1] तदुज्ज्वलितत्वाल्लोहवदधिष्ठातृत्वम् ॥ ९९ ॥

It is in the shape of the internal organ, that Nature affects Soul.

Aph. 99. The internal organ, through its being enlightened thereby [i.e., by Soul], is the overruler; as is the iron, [in respect of the magnet].

a. The internal organ, i.e., the understanding, is the overruler, through its fancying itself to be Soul, [as it does fancy,] by reason of its being enlightened by the Soul, through its happening to reflect itself in [and contemplate itself in,] Soul; 'just as the iron,' that is to say, as the attracting iron, though inactive, draws [the magnet], in consequence of [its] mere proximity,[2] [and so acquires magnetism by magnetic induction].

b. He [now, having discussed the evidence that consists in direct perception,] states the definition of inference[3] (*anumána*):

---

[1] Aniruddha has महतोऽन्तःकरणस्य; prefixing to 'the internal organ' the synonymous 'the Great One.' *Ed.*

[2] अन्तःकरणस्य बुद्धेः पुरुषच्छायापत्त्या तेन चैतन्येनोज्ज्वलितत्वाच्चेतनत्वाभिमानादधिष्ठातृत्वं लोहवदिति यथाकर्षको लोहो निष्क्रियोऽपि संनिधिमात्रेण कर्षतीति ॥

[3] अनुमानलक्षणमाह ॥

प्रतिबन्धदृशः[1] प्रतिबद्धज्ञानमनुमानम् ॥ १०० ॥

Inference defined. *Aph.* 100. The knowledge of the connected [e.g., fire], through perception of the connexion [e.g., of fire with smoke], is inference.

a. That is to say: inference [or conviction of a general truth,] is [a kind of] evidence consisting in a [mental] modification, [which is none other than] the knowledge of the connected, i.e., of the constant accompanier, through the knowledge of the constant accompaniment: by 'connexion' (*pratibandha*) here being meant 'constant attendedness' (*vyápti*); and through the perception thereof[2] [it being that the mind has possession of any general principle].

b. But a conclusion (*anumiti*) is knowledge of the soul;[3] [whilst an Inference, so far forth as it is an instrument in the establishment of knowledge deducible from it, is an affection of the internal organ, or understanding (see §87. *c.*)]

c. He [next] defines testimony[4] (*śabda*):

---

[1] प्रतिबद्धदृशः is the reading of Nágeśa and of Vedánti Mahádeva. *Ed.*

[2] प्रतिबन्धो व्याप्तिस्तद्दृशो व्याप्तिज्ञानात्प्रतिबद्धस्य व्यापकस्य ज्ञानं वृत्तिरूपमनुमानं प्रमाणमित्यर्थः ॥

[3] अनुमितिस्तु पौरुषेयो बोध इति ॥

[4] शब्दं लक्षयति ॥

आप्तोपदेशः शब्दः ॥ १०१ ॥

Valid testimony defined.

Aph. 101. Testimony [such as is entitled to the name of evidence,] is a declaration by one worthy [to be believed].

a. Here 'fitness' means 'suitableness;' and so the evidence which is called 'Testimony' is the knowledge arising from a suitable declaration: such is the meaning. And [while this belongs to the understanding, or internal organ (see § 100. *b.*)] the result is that [knowledge] in the Soul, [which is called] 'knowledge by hearing'[1] (*śabda-bodha*).

b. He [next] volunteers to tell us what is the use of his setting forth [the various divisions of] evidence:[2]

उभयसिद्धिः प्रमाणात्तदुपदेशः ॥ १०२ ॥

Why the kinds of Evidence have been here set forth.

Aph. 102. Since the establishment of [the existence of] both [soul and non-soul] is by means of evidence, the declaration thereof [i.e., of the kinds of evidence, has been here made].

a. It is only by means of evidence that both Soul and non-soul are established as being distinct, [the one from the

---

[1] आप्तिरत्र योग्यता तथा च योग्यः शब्दस्तज्जन्यं ज्ञानं शब्दाख्यं प्रमाणमित्यर्थः। फलं च पौरुषेयः शाब्दबोध इति ॥

[2] प्रमाणप्रतिपादनस्य स्वयमेव फलमाह ॥

other]: therefore has this, viz., evidence, been here declared: such is the meaning.[1]

b. Among these [several kinds of proof], he [now] describes that one by which, especially, viz., by a proof which is one kind of inference, Nature and Soul are here to be established discriminatively:[2]

सामान्यतो दृष्टादुभयसिद्धिः[3] ॥ १०३ ॥

The existence of Soul and Nature argued from analogy.

Aph. 103. The establishment of both [Nature and Soul] is by analogy.

a. [Analogy (*sámányato dṛishṭa*) is that kind of evidence which is employed in the case] where, by the force [as an argument,] which the residence of any property in the subject derives from a knowledge of its being constantly accompanied [by something which it may therefore betoken], when we have had recourse to [as the means of determining this constant accompaniment,] what is, for instance, generically of a perceptible kind, [where, under such circumstances, we repeat,] anything of a *different* kind, i.e., *not* cognizable by the senses, is established; as when,

---

[1] उभयोरात्मानात्मनोर्विवेकेन सिद्धिः प्रमाणादेव भवति। अतस्तस्य प्रमाणस्योपदेशः कृत इत्यर्थः ॥

[2] तत्र येनानुमानविशेषेण प्रमाणेन मुख्यतोऽत्र प्रकृतिपुरुषौ विविच्य साधनीयौ तद्दर्शयति ॥

[3] My MS. of Nágeśa has दृष्टात्सिद्धिः. *Ed.*

for example, having apprehended a constant accompaniment, [e.g., that an act implies an instrument], by taking into consideration such instruments as axes, &c., which are of earthy and other kinds, a quite heterogeneous, imperceptible, instrument of *knowledge*, viz., [the instrument named] Sense, is established [or inferred to exist]; such is what we mean by Analogy; and it is by *this* [species of inference], that both, [viz.,] Nature and Soul, are proved [to exist]: such is the meaning.[1]

b. Of these [viz., Nature and Soul,] the argument from analogy for [the existence of] Nature is as follows: the Great Principle [viz., Understanding (see § 61. *c.*)] is formed out of the things [called] Pleasure, Pain, and Delusion, [to the aggregate of which three in equipoise (see § 61) the name of Nature is given]; because, whilst it is [undeniably,] a production, it has the characters of Pleasure, Pain, and Delusion; just as a bracelet, or the like, formed of gold, or the like,[2] [has the characteristic pro-

---

[1] यच्च सामान्यतः प्रत्यक्षादिजातीयमादाय व्याप्तिग्रहात्पक्षधर्मताबलेन तद्विजातीयोऽप्रत्यक्षार्थः सिध्यति यथा पृथिवीत्वादिजातोयं कुठारादिकरणमादाय व्याप्तिं गृहीत्वा तद्विजातीयमतीन्द्रियं ज्ञानकरणमिन्द्रियं साध्यत इति तत्सामान्यतो दृष्टं तस्मादुभयोः प्रकृतिपुरुषयोः सिद्धिरित्यर्थः ॥

[2] तत्र प्रकृतेः सामान्यतो दृष्टमनुमानं यथा महत्तत्त्वं सुखदुःखमोहद्रव्योपादानकं कार्यत्वे सति सुखदुःखमोहधर्मकत्वात्सुवर्णादिजकुण्डलादिवदिति ॥

perties of the gold, or the like, and is thereby known to have been formed out of gold, or the like].

c. But, [as regards the argument from analogy, in proof of the existence] of Soul, [it is, as stated before, under § 66, to the following effect]: Nature is for the sake of *another;* because it is something that acts as a combination; as a house, for instance, [which is a combination of various parts combined for the benefit of the tenant]. In this instance, having gathered, in regard to houses, &c., the fact established on sense-perception, that they exist for the sake of [organized] bodies, for example, something of a different kind therefrom, [i.e., from Nature, viz.], Soul, is inferred [by analogy,] as something other than Nature, &c., [which, as being a compound thing, is not designed for itself]: such is the meaning.[1]

d. But then [some one may say], since Nature is eternal, and exertion is habitual to her, [and the result of her action is the bondage of the Soul], there should constantly be experience [whether of pleasure or of pain], and, hence, no such thing as thorough emancipation. To this he replies:[2]

चिदवसानो भोगः ॥ १०४ ॥

---

[1] पुरुषस्य तु प्रधानं परार्थं संहत्यकारित्वाद्गृहादिवदिति। अत्र प्रत्यक्षसिद्धं देहाद्यर्थकत्वं गृहादिषु गृहीत्वा तद्विजातीयः पुरुषः प्रधानादिपरत्वेनानुमीयत इति ॥

[2] ननु प्रकृतेर्नित्यत्वात्प्रवृत्तिशीलत्वाच्च सर्वदा भोग इत्यनिर्मोक्षः स्यादित्यत आह ॥

When it is that experience ceases.

Aph. 104. Experience [whether of pain or pleasure,] ends with [the discernment of] Thought, [or Soul, as contradistinguished from Nature].

a. By 'Thought' [we mean] Soul. Experience [whether of pain or pleasure,] ceases, on the discerning thereof. As 'antecedent non-existence,' though devoid of a beginning, [see *Tarka-sangraha*, § 92], surceases [when the thing antecedently non-existent begins to be], so, eternal Nature [eternal, as regards the absence of any beginning,] continues [no further than] till the discernment of the difference [between Nature and Soul]; so that experience whether of pain or pleasure,] does *not* at all times occur: such is the state of the case.[1]

b. [But some one say], if Nature be agent, and Soul experiencer, then it must follow [which seems unreasonable,] that another is the experiencer of [the results of] the acts done by one different. To this he replies:[2]

अकर्तुरपि फलोपभोगोऽन्नाद्यवत् ॥ १०५ ॥

The fruit of the action is not always the agent's.

Aph. 105. The experience of the fruit *may* belong even to another than the agent; as in the case of food, &c.

---

[1] चिदात्मा। तद्विवेकावसानो भोगः। यथानादिरपि प्रागभावो नश्यति तथा नित्यायाः प्रकृतेर्विवेकज्ञानपर्यन्तः प्रसर इति न सर्वदा भोगापत्तिरिति भावः॥

[2] यदि कर्तृ प्रधानं भोक्ता पुरुषस्तर्ह्यन्यकृतस्य कर्मणोऽन्यो भोक्तेति स्यादित्याह॥

a. As it belongs to the cook to prepare the food, &c., and to one who was not the agent, viz., the master, to enjoy the fruit [thereof, i. e., the fruit of the cook's actions], so is the case here, also.[1]

b. Having stated an exoteric principle [which may serve, in practice, to silence, by the *argumentum ad hominem*, him on whose principles it may be valid], he [next] declares his own doctrine,[2] [in regard to the doubt started under § 104. *b.*]:

अविवेकाद्वा तत्सिद्धेः कर्तुः फलावगमः ॥ १०६ ॥

To suppose that Soul acts and experiences is an error.

Aph. 106. Or, [to give a better account of the matter than that given in § 105], since it is from non-discrimination that it is derived, the notion that the *agent* [soul being mistaken for an agent,] has the fruit [of the act is a wrong notion].

a. The soul is neither an agent nor a patient; but, from the fact that the Great Principle [the actual agent (see § 97. *b.*)] is reflected in it, there arises the *conceit* of its being an agent. 'Or, since it is from non-discrimination;' that is to say, because it is from the failure to discriminate between Nature and Soul, that this takes place, i.e., that conceit takes place, that it is the *agent* that experiences the fruit;[3] [whereas the actual agent is Nature, which, being unintelligent, can experience neither pain nor pleasure].

---

[1] यथा सूपकारस्यान्नादिकर्तृत्वमकर्तुरीश्वरस्य फलोपभोक्तृत्वे तथाचापीति ॥

[2] व्यवहारसिद्धान्तमुक्त्वा स्वसिद्धान्तमाह ॥

[3] न पुरुषः कर्ता न वा भोक्ता किं तु महत्तत्त्वप्र-

b. The opposite of this [wrong view, referred to in § 106,] he states [as follows]:[1]

नोभयं च तत्त्वाख्याने ॥ १०७ ॥

Soul is really neither agent nor experiencer.

Aph. 107. And, when the truth is told, there is [seen to be] neither [agency, in Soul, nor experience].

a. 'When the truth is told' [and discerned], i.e., when, by means of evidence, Nature and Soul are *perceived* [in their entire distinctness, one from the other], 'there is neither,' i.e., neither the condition [as regards soul,] of an agent nor that of a patient.[2]

b. Having discussed [the topic of] evidence, he [now] states the distribution of the subject-matter of evidence:[3]

विषयोऽविषयोऽप्यतिदूरादेर्हानोपादानाभ्या-
मिन्द्रियस्य ॥ १०८ ॥

तिविम्बितत्वात्कर्तृत्वाभिमानः। अविवेकाद्वेति प्रकृतिपुरुषयोर्विवेकाग्रहात्तत्सिद्धेः कर्तुः फलोपभोगाभिमानसिद्धेरिति ॥

[1] एतद्व्यतिरेकमाह ॥

[2] तत्त्वाख्याने प्रमाणेन प्रकृतिपुरुषयोः साक्षात्कारे नोभयं न कर्तृत्वं न भोक्तृत्वमिति ॥

[3] प्रमाणमुक्त्वा प्रमेयव्यवस्थामाह ॥

What is perceptible, under certain circumstances, may be imperceptible, under others.

Aph. 108. [A thing may be] an object [perceptible], and also [at another time,] not an object, through there being, in consequence of great distance, &c., a want of [conjunction of the sense with the thing], or [on the other hand,] an appliance of the sense [to the thing].

a. An object [is a perceived object], through the proximity, or conjunction, of the sense [with the object]. [A thing may be] not an object [perceived], through the want of the sense, i.e., through the want of conjunction [between the sense and what would otherwise be its object]. And [this] want of conjunction [may result] from the junction's being prevented by great distance, &c.[1]

What may prevent perception.

b. [To explain the '&c.,' and to exemplify the causes that may prevent the conjunction, required in order to perception, between the thing and the sense, we may remark, that] it is in consequence of great distance, that a bird [flying very high up] in the sky is not perceived; [then again,] in consequence of extreme proximity, the collyrium located in the eye [is not perceived by the eye itself]; a thing placed in [the inside of, or on the opposite side of,] a wall [is not perceived], in consequence of the obstruction; from distraction of mind, the unhappy, or other [agitated person], does not perceive the thing that is at his side [or under his very nose]; through its subtilty,

---

[1] इन्द्रियस्योपादानात्संबन्धाद्विषयः । इन्द्रियस्य हानात्संबन्धाभावादविषयः । असंबन्धश्चातिदूरादेरयोग्यत्वात् ॥

an atom [is not perceived]; nor is a very small sound, when overpowered by the sound of a drum; and so on.[1]

c. How [or, for which of the possible reasons just enumerated,] comes the imperceptibleness of *Nature?* In regard to this, he declares:[2]

सौक्ष्म्यात्तदनुपलब्धिः[3] ॥ १०९ ॥

The subtilty of Nature. *Aph.* 109. Her imperceptibleness arises from [her] subtilty.

a. 'Her,' i.e., *Nature's*, imperceptibleness is from subtilty. By subtilty is meant the fact of being difficult to investigate; not [as a Naiyáyika might, perhaps, here prefer understanding the term,] the consisting of atoms; for Nature is [not atomic, in the opinion of the Sánkhyas, but] all-pervasive.[4]

---

[1] अतिदूराद्वियति पक्षी नोपलभ्यते। अतिसामीप्याल्लोचनस्थाञ्जनम्। व्यवधानात्कुड्यस्थं वस्तु। मनोऽनवस्थानाच्छोकादिग्रस्तस्य पार्श्वस्थवस्त्वग्रहणम्। सौक्ष्म्यादणोः। अभिभवान्मर्दलध्वनिना स्वल्पध्वनेरित्यादि॥

[2] प्रकृतेः कथमनुपलब्धिरित्यत आह॥

[3] Aniruddha, according to the MSS. seen by me, has सौक्ष्म्यादनुपलब्धिः. *Ed.*

[4] तस्याः प्रकृतेरनुपलब्धिः सौक्ष्म्यात्। दुरूहत्वं सौक्ष्म्यं नत्वणुत्वं प्रकृतेर्विभुत्वादिति॥

b. How, then, [it may be asked,] is [the existence of] Nature determined? To this he replies:[1]

कार्यदर्शनात्तदुपलब्धेः ॥ ११० ॥

Nature inferred from the existence of productions.

Aph. 110. [Nature exists;] because her existence is gathered from the beholding of productions.

a. As the knowledge of [there being such things as] atoms comes from the beholding of jars, &c., [which are agglomerations], so the knowledge of Nature comes from the beholding of products which have the three Qualities;[2] [(see § 62. *a*.) and the existence of which implies a cause, to which the name of Nature is given, in which these constituents exist from eternity].

b. Some [the Vedántís,] say that the world has *Brahma* as its cause; others [the Naiyáyikas], that it has atoms as its cause; but our seniors [the transmitters of the Sánkhya doctrine], that it has *Nature* as its cause. So he sets forth a doubt [which might naturally found itself] thereon:[3]

वादिविप्रतिपत्तेस्तदसिद्धिरिति चेत् ॥ १११ ॥

---

[1] कथं तर्हि प्रकृतिव्यवस्थेत्यत आह ॥

[2] यथा घटादिदर्शनात्परमाणुज्ञानं तथा त्रिगुणकार्यदर्शनात्प्रकृतिज्ञानमिति ॥

[3] ब्रह्मकारणं जगदिति केचित्परमाणुकारणमित्यन्ये प्रधानकारणकमिति वृद्धा इति। तत्र संशयमाह ॥

A doubt thrown on the existence of Nature, by the contradiction of dissentients.

Aph. 111. If [you throw out the doubt that] it [viz., the existence of Nature,] is not established, because of the contradiction of asserters [of other views, then you will find an answer in the next aphorism].

a. 'Because of the contradiction of asserters [of the Vedánta or Nyáya], *it* is not established,' i. e., Nature [as asserted by the Sánkhyas,] is not established.'[1]

b. But then, [to set forth the objection of these counter-asserters], if a product existed antecedently to its production [as that product], *then* an eternal Nature [such as you Sánkhyas contend for,] would be proved to exist as the [necessary] substratum thereof; since you will declare that a cause is inferred only as the [invariable] accompanier of an effect; but it is denied, by us asserters [of the Vedánta, &c.], that the effect *does* exist [antecedently to its production; well,] *if* [this doubt be thrown out]: such is the meaning[2] [of the aphorism].

c. He states [his] doctrine [on this point]:[3]

तथाप्येकतरदृष्ट्यैकतरसिद्धेर्नापलापः ॥ ११२ ॥

---

[1] वादिनां विप्रतिपत्तेस्तदसिद्धिः प्रधानासिद्धिः ॥

[2] ननु कार्यं चेदुत्पत्तेः प्राक्सिद्धं स्यात्तदा तदाधारतया नित्या प्रकृतिः कार्यसाहित्येनैव कारणानुमानवक्ष्यमाणत्वाद्वादिविप्रतिपत्तेस्तत्कार्यस्यैवासिद्धिरिति यदीत्यर्थः ॥

[3] सिद्धान्तमाह ॥

Mutual denials settle nothing.

Aph. 112. Still, since[1] each [doctrine] is established in the opinion of each, a [mere unsupported] denial is not [decisive].

a. If one side were disproved merely by the dissent of the opponent, then [look you,] there is dissent against the other side, too: so how could *it* be established? If the one side is established by there being inevitably attendant the recognition of the constant accompanier, on the recognition of that which is constantly accompanied [by it], it is the same with *my* [side], also: therefore [my] inference from effect [to cause] is not to be denied[2] [in this peremptory fashion].

b. Well, then, [the opponent may say], let [the inference of] cause from effect be granted; how is it that this [cause] is *Nature*, and nothing else, [such as Atoms, for instance]? To this he replies:[3]

---

[1] I have corrected the translator's 'But, since thus,' which rendered the unwarranted reading तथा तु, now replaced by तथापि, the correlative of चेत् at the end of the preceding Aphorism. *Ed.*

[2] यदि वादिविप्रतिपत्तिमात्रेण पक्षासिद्धत्वं विपक्षेऽपि विप्रतिपत्तिरस्तीति कथं तत्सिद्धिः। यदि व्याप्यज्ञानाद्व्यापकज्ञानस्याविनाभावित्वात्पक्षसिद्धिस्तर्हि ममाप्येवमिति न कार्यादनुमानापलापः॥

[3] ननु कार्यात्कारणमस्तु तच्च प्रकृतिरेवेति कथमित्यत आह॥

त्रिविधविरोधापत्तेः[1] ॥ ११३ ॥

Nature the only hypothesis consistent with what appears.

Aph. 113. Because [if we were to infer any other cause than Nature,] we should have a contradiction to the threefold [aspect which things really exhibit].

a. Quality is threefold [see § 61. *a.*], viz., Goodness, Passion, and Darkness: there would be a contradiction to *these*: such is the meaning.[2]

b. The drift here is as follows: If the character of cause [of all things around us] belonged to Atoms, or the like, then there would be a contradiction to the fact of being an aggregate of pleasure, pain, and delusion, which is recognizable in the world;[3] [because nothing, we hold, can exist in the effect, which did not exist in the cause and pleasure, pain, &c., are no properties of Atoms].

c. He now repels the doubt as to whether the production of an effect is that of what existed [antecedently], or of what did not exist:[4]

---

[1] Vedánti Mahádeva ends this Aphorism with the word च; and so does Vijnána, according to some MSS. *Ed.*

[2] त्रिविधो गुणः सत्त्वरजस्तमांसि तद्विरोध इत्यर्थः ॥

[3] इदमत्राकूतं यदि परमाण्वादीनां कारणत्वं तदा जगत्युपलभ्यमानस्य सुखदुःखमोहात्मकत्वस्य विरोधः स्यादिति ॥

[4] इदानीं कार्यस्य सत उत्पत्तिरसतो वेति संशयं निरस्यति ॥

नासदुत्पादो नृशृङ्गवत् ॥ ११४ ॥

What never existed will never exist.

Aph. 114. The production of what is no entity, as a man's horn, does not take place.

a. Of that which, like the horn of a man, is not an entity, even the production is impossible: such is the meaning. And so the import is, that that effect alone which [antecedently] exists is [at any time] produced.[1]

b. He states an argument why an effect must be some [previously existent] entity:[2]

उपादाननियमात् ॥ ११५ ॥

A product cannot be of nothing.

Aph. 115. Because of the rule, that there must be some material [of which the product may consist].

a. And only when both are extant is there, from the presence of the cause, the presence of the effect. Otherwise, everywhere and always, every [effect] might be produced; [the presence of the cause being, on the supposition, superfluous]. This he insists upon [as follows]:[3]

---

[1] नरशृङ्गतुल्यस्यासत उत्पादोऽपि न संभवतीत्यर्थः। तथा च सदेव कार्यमुत्पद्यत इत्याशयः॥

[2] सत्कार्ये न्यायमाह॥

[3] कारणसंबन्धात्कार्यसंबन्धश्च विद्यमानयोरेव। अन्यथा सर्वत्र सर्वदा सर्वोत्पत्तिः स्यात्। एतदेवाह।

सर्वत्र सर्वदा सर्वासंभवात् ॥ ११६ ॥

Else, anything might occur at any time, anywhere.

Aph. 116. Because everything is not possible everywhere and always, [which might be the case, if materials could be dispensed with].

a. That is to say: because, in the world, we see that everything is *not* possible, i. e., that everything is *not* produced; 'everywhere,' i. e., in every place; 'always,' i. e., at all times.[1]

b. For the following reason, also, he declares, there is no production of what existed not[2] [antecedently]:

शक्तस्य शक्यकरणात् ॥ ११७ ॥

Effects preexist, potentially, in their causes.

Aph. 117. Because it is that which is competent [to the making of anything] that makes what is possible, [as a product of it].

a. Because the being the material [of any future product] is nothing else than the fact of [being it, *potentially*, i. e., of] having the competency to be the product; and [this] competency is nothing else than the product's condition as that of what has not yet come to pass: therefore, since 'that which is competent,' viz., the cause, makes the product which is 'possible' [to be made out of it], it is not of any *nonentity* that the production takes

---

[1] सर्वत्र सर्वस्मिन्देशे सर्वदा सर्वस्मिन्काले सर्वासंभवात्सर्वानुत्पत्तेर्लोकदर्शनादित्याशयः ॥

[2] इतश्च नासदुत्पाद इत्याह ॥

place, [but of an entity, whose *esse*, antecedently, was *possibility*] : such is the meaning.[1]

b. He states another argument:[2]

कारणभावाच्च ॥ ११८ ॥

The product is nothing else than the cause.

Aph. 118. And because it [the product,] is [nothing else than] the cause, [in the shape of the product].

a. It is declared, in Scripture, that, previously to production, moreover, there is no difference between the cause and its effect; and, since it is thereby settled that a product is an entity, production is not of what [previously] existed not: such is the meaning.[3]

b. He ponders a doubt:[4]

न भावे भावयोगश्चेत् ॥ ११९ ॥

A doubt whether that which is can be said to become.

Aph. 119. If [it be alleged that] there is no possibility of that's *becoming* which already *is*, [then the answer will be found in the next aphorism].

---

[1] कार्यशक्तिमत्त्वमेव ह्युपादानत्वं शक्तिश्च कार्यस्यानागतावस्थैवेति शक्तस्य कारणस्य शक्यकार्यकरणादपि नासत उत्पाद इत्यर्थः ॥

[2] अपरं न्यायमाह ॥

[3] उत्पत्तेः प्रागपि कार्यस्य कारणाभेदः श्रूयते तस्माच्च सत्कार्यसिद्ध्या नासदुत्पाद इत्यर्थः ॥

[4] शङ्कते ॥

a. That is to say: but then, if it be thus [that every effect exists antecedently to its production], since the effect [*every* effect,] must be eternal [without beginning], there is no possibility of [or room for] the adjunction of *becoming*, the adjunction of *arising*, in the case of a product which is [already, by hypothesis,] in the shape of an entity; because the employment of [the term] '*arising*' [or the fact of being produced] has reference solely to what did *not* exist [previously]; if this be urged: such is the meaning.[1]

b. He declares the doctrine [in regard to this point]:[2]

नाभिव्यक्तिनिबन्धनौ व्यवहाराव्यवहारौ ॥ १२० ॥

Production is only manifestation; and so of the opposite.

Aph. 120. No; [do not argue that what *is* cannot become; for] the employment and the non-employment [of the term 'production'] are occasioned by the *manifestation* [and the non-manifestation of what is spoken of as produced, or not].

a. 'No;' the view stated [in § 119] is not the right one: such is the meaning.[3]

b. As the whiteness of white cloth [which has become] dirty is brought manifestly out by means of washing, &c.,

---

[1] नन्वेवं सति कार्यस्य नित्यत्वे सति भावरूपे कार्ये भावयोग उत्पत्तियोगो न संभवत्यसत एवोत्पत्तिव्यवहारादिति चेदित्यर्थः ॥

[2] सिद्धान्तमाह ॥

[3] न नोक्तपक्षो युक्त इत्यर्थः ॥

so, by the operation of the potter, is the pot brought into manifestness; [whereas], on the blow of a mallet, it becomes hidden,[1] [and no longer appears as a *pot*].

c. And manifestation [is no fiction of ours; for it] is seen; for example, that of oil, from sesamum-seeds, by pressure; of milk, from the cow, by milking; of the statue, which resided in the midst of the stone, by the operation of the sculptor; of husked rice, from rice in the husk, by threshing; &c.[2]

d. Therefore, the employment and the non-employment of the [term] 'the *production* of an effect' are dependent on *manifestation*, dependent on the manifestation of the *effect:* that is to say, the employment of [the term] 'production' is in consequence of the manifestation [of what is spoken of as produced]; and the non-employment of [the term] 'production' is in consequence of there being no manifestation [of that which is, therefore, not spoken of as produced]; but [the employment of the term 'production' is] not in consequence of that's becoming an entity which was not an entity.[3]

---

[1] यथा शुक्लपटस्य मलिनस्य क्षालनादिना शुक्लत्वमभिव्यज्यते तथा कुलालस्य व्यापाराद्घटोऽभिव्यज्यते मुद्गराभिघातात्तिरोभूयते ॥

[2] दृष्टा चाभिव्यक्तिः पीडनेन तिलेषु तैलस्य दोहनेन गवि पयसः शिलामध्यस्थप्रतिमाया लैङ्गिकव्यापारेणावघातेन धान्ये तण्डुलस्येत्यादि ॥

[3] तस्मात्कार्योत्पत्तेर्व्यवहाराव्यवहारा अभिव्यक्तिनिबन्धनौ कार्याभिव्यक्तिनिमित्तकौ। अभिव्य-

e. But if [the employment of the term] 'production' is occasioned by [the fact of] *manifestation,* by what is occasioned [the employment of the term] *destruction?*[1] To this he replies:[2]

नाशः कारणलयः ॥ १२१ ॥

What is meant by destruction.

Aph. 121. Destruction [of anything] is the resolution [of the thing spoken of as destroyed,] into the cause [from which it was produced].

a. The resolution, by the blow of a mallet, of a jar into its cause [i.e., into the particles of clay which constituted the jar], to *this* are due both [the employment of] the term 'destruction,' and the kind of action [or behaviour] belonging to anything[3] [which is termed its destruction].[4]

क्ति उत्पत्तिव्यवहारोऽभिव्यक्त्यभावाच्चोत्पत्तिव्यवहाराभावो नत्वसतः सत्तयेत्यर्थः ॥

1 'If production is occasioned by manifestation, by what is destruction occasioned?' Aniruddha, here quoted, has, in my MSS.: अभिव्यक्तिनिबन्धनोत्पत्तिः. *Ed.*

2 अभिव्यक्तिनिबन्धनात्तूत्पत्तिः किंनिबन्धनो विनाश इत्यत आह ॥

3 मुद्गराभिघाताद्घटस्य कारणे यो लयः तन्निबन्धनो नाश इति शब्दार्थक्रियाभेदौ ॥

4 'From the blow of a mallet [results] the resolution of a jar into its material cause: by this the destruction [of it] is occasioned. Such is the meaning of the word [*náśa*], and [such is] the particular action [which]

b. [But some one may say], if there were [only] a resolution [of a product into that from which it arose], a resurrection [or παλιγγενεσία] of it might be seen; and this is *not* seen: well [we reply], it is not seen by blockheads; but it *is* seen by those who can discriminate. For example, when thread is destroyed, it is changed into the shape of earth [as when burned to ashes]; and the earth is changed into the shape of a cotton-tree; and this [successively] changes into the shape of flower, fruit, and thread [spun again from the fruit of the cotton-plant]. So is it with all entities.[1]

c. Pray [some one may ask], is [this] *manifestation* [that you speak of under § 120] something real, or something not real? If it be something real [and which, therefore, never anywhere ceases to be], then [all] effects [during this constant manifestation] ought constantly to be *perceived;* and, if it be *not* real, then there would be the absence of [all] products, [in the absence of all manifestation. Manifestation, therefore, must be something *real;* and] there must be [in order to give rise to it,] another manifestation of it, and of this another; [seeing that a *manifestation* can be the result of nothing else than a manifes-

---

it expresses.' This is from Aniruddha, who, in the MSS. to which I have access, has no यो before लयः. *Ed.*

[1] यदि लयः पुनरुद्भवो दृश्येत न च दृश्यत इति मूढैर्न दृश्यते विवेचकैर्दृश्यत एव। तथा हि तन्तौ नष्टे मृद्रूपेण परिणामो मृदश्च कार्पासवृक्षरूपेण परिणामस्तस्य पुष्पफलतन्तुरूपेण परिणामः। एवं सर्वे भावा इति॥

tation, on the principle that an effect consists of neither more nor less than its cause]; and thus we have a *regressus in infinitum.* To this he replies:[1]

पारम्पर्यतोऽन्वेषणाद्बीजाङ्कुरवत्[2] ॥ १२२ ॥

How manifestation may occur without being an entity.

Aph. 122. Because they seek each other reciprocally,[3] as is the case with seed and plant, [manifestation may generate manifestation, from eternity to eternity].

a. Be it so, that there are thousands of manifestations; still there is no fault; for there *is* no starting-point; as is the case with seed and plant,[4] [which people may suppose to have served, from eternity, as sources, one to another, reciprocally].

---

[1] किमभिव्यक्तिः सत्यसती वा। सती चेन्नित्यकार्योपलब्धिः स्यात्। असती चेत्सत्कार्यहानिस्तस्या अप्यभिव्यक्तिरन्या तस्या अप्यन्येत्यनवस्थेत्यत आह ॥

[2] अन्वेषणात्, the reading here given, is that of Aniruddha and Vedánti Mahádeva. Vijnána has अन्वेषणा. *Ed.*

[3] Translating the Sánkhya Aphorisms in the *Bibliotheca Indica*, Dr. Ballantyne, adopting the lection *anveshaṇá*, inconsiderately rendered: 'You are to understand, that, successively,' instead of 'There is a continual following of one after the other.' Vijnána explains *anveshaṇá* by *anudhávana;* and Vedánti Mahádeva has, in definition of it, the synonymous *anusaraṇa.* *Ed.*

[4] भवत्वभिव्यक्तिसहस्रं तथापि न दोषोऽनादित्वाद्बीजाङ्कुरवदिति ॥

b. He states another argument:[1]

उत्पत्तिवद्वादोषः ॥ १२३ ॥

The objections to the theory of manifestation retorted.

Aph. 123. Or, [at all events, our theory of 'manifestation' is as] blameless as [your theory of] 'production.'

a. Pray [let us ask], is *production* produced, or is it not? If it is produced, then of this [production of production] there must be production; so that there is a *regressus in infinitum*, [such as you allege against *our* theory, under § 121. *c*.]. If it be *not* produced, then, pray, is this because it is *unreal*, or because it is eternal? If because it is unreal, then production never is at all; so that it would never be perceived, [as you allege that it is]. Again, if [production is not something produced,] because it is *eternal*, then there would be at, all times, the production of [all possible] effects, [which you will scarcely pretend is the case]. Again, if you say, since 'production' itself *consists* of production, what need of supposing an ulterior production [of production]? then, in like manner, [*I* ask,] since 'manifestation' itself *consists* of manifestation, what need of supposing an ulterior manifestation [of manifestation]? The view which you hold on this point is *ours*, also;[2] [and

---

[1] युक्त्यन्तरमाह ॥

[2] किमुत्पत्तिरुत्पद्यते न वा। उत्पद्यते चेदस्या उत्पत्तिरित्यनवस्था। नोत्पद्यते चेत्किमसत्त्वान्नित्यत्वाद्वा। यद्यसत्त्वात्कदाचिदप्युत्पत्तिर्नास्तीति सर्वदानुपलम्भः स्यात्। अथ नित्यत्वात्सर्वदा का-

thus every objection stated or hinted under § 121. *c.*, is capable of being retorted].

b. He [now] states the community of properties [that exists] among the products of Nature, mutually :[1]

हेतुमदनित्यमव्यापि[2] सक्रियमनेकमाश्रितं लिङ्गम् ॥ १२४ ॥

The characters common to all products.

Aph. 124. [A product of Nature is] caused, uneternal, not all-pervading, mutable, multitudinous, dependent, mergent.

a. 'Caused,' i.e., having a cause. 'Uneternal,' i.e., destructible. 'Not all-pervading,' i.e., not present everywhere. 'Mutable,' i.e., distinguished by the acts of leaving [one form], and assuming [another form], &c. It [the soul,] leaves the body it has assumed, [and, probably, takes another]; and bodies, &c., move [and are mutable, as is notorious]. 'Multitudinous,' i.e., in consequence of the distinction of souls; [every man, e.g., having a separate body]. 'Dependent,' [i.e.,] on its cause. 'Mergent,' that is to say, it [i.e., every product, in due time,] is resolved into that from which it originated.[3]

र्योत्पत्तिः स्यात् । अथोत्पत्तेः स्वयमेवोत्पत्तिरूपत्वात्किमुत्पत्त्यन्तरकल्पनयेति तर्ह्यभिव्यक्तेरप्यभिव्यक्तिरूपत्वात्किमभिव्यक्त्यन्तरकल्पनयेति तुल्यम् । तच्च यस्तव सिद्धान्तः सोऽस्माकमपि ॥

[1] प्रकृतिकार्याणामन्योन्यं साधर्म्यमाह ॥

[2] Aniruddha omits अव्यापि. *Ed.*

[3] हेतुमत्कारणवत् । अनित्यं विनाशि । अव्या-

b. [But, some one may say], if realities be the twenty-five [which the Sánkhyas enumerate (see § 61), and no more], pray, are such common operations as knowing, enjoying, &c., absolutely *nothing*; you accordingly giving up what you *see*, [in order to save an hypothesis with which what you see is irreconcilable]? To this he replies:[1]

आञ्जस्यादभेदतो वा गुणसामान्यादेस्तत्सिद्धिः
प्रधानव्यपदेशाद्वा ॥ १२५ ॥

The qualities of the Nyáya are implied in the term Nature.

Aph. 125. There is the establishment of these [twenty-four 'Qualities' of the *Nyáya*, which you fancy that we do not recognize, because we do not explicitly enumerate them], either by reason that these ordinary qualities [as contradistinguished from the *three* Qualities of the Sánkhya], &c., are, in reality, nothing different; or [to put it in another point of view,] because they are hinted by [the term] Nature, [in which, like our own three Qualities, they are implied].

प्यसर्वगम् । सक्रियं त्यागोपादानादिक्रियाविशिष्टम् । उपात्तदेहं त्यजति शरीरादयश्च स्पन्दन्ते । अनेकं पुरुषभेदात् । आश्रितं स्वकारणे । लिङ्गं स्वकारणे लयं गच्छतीति ॥

[1] यदि पञ्चविंशतितत्त्वं किं ज्ञानसुखादीनां सामान्यकर्मणामभाव एव तथा च दृष्टपरित्याग इत्यत आह ॥

a. Either from their being nothing different from the twenty-four principles, 'in reality,' truly, quite evidently,—since the character of these [twenty-four] fits the ordinary qualities, &c., [which you fancy are neglected in our enumeration of things,]—'there is the establishment of these,' i.e., there is their establishment [as realities,] through their being implied just in those[1] [twenty-four principles which are explicitly specified in the Sánkhya].

b. The word 'or' shows that there is another alternative [reply, in the aphorism, to the objection in question]. 'Or because they are hinted by [the term] Nature;' that is to say, the qualities, &c. [such as Knowledge], are established [as realities], just because they are hinted by [the term] Nature, by reason that [these] qualities are, mediately, products of Nature; for there is no difference between product and cause. But the omission to mention them [explicitly] is not by reason of their not being at all.[2]

c. He [next] mentions the points in which Nature and [her] products agree:[3]

---

[1] आञ्जस्यात्स्वरूपतः प्रत्यक्षत एव वा चतुर्विंशतितत्त्वादभेदतस्तल्लक्षणयोगाद्गुणसामान्यादीनां तत्सिद्धिस्तेष्वेवान्तर्भावात्सिद्धिः ॥

[2] वाशब्दः पक्षान्तरं सूचयति। प्रधानव्यपदेशाद्वा गुणानां पारम्पर्येण प्रधानकार्यत्वेन कार्यकारणयोरभेदात्प्रधानव्यपदेशादेव गुणादिसिद्धिः। नत्वभावादननुकीर्तनमिति ॥

[3] प्रकृतिकार्ययोः साधर्म्यमाह ॥

त्रिगुणाचेतनत्वादि द्वयोः ॥ १२६ ॥

The characters common to Nature and her products.

Aph. 126. Of both [Nature and her products] the fact that they consist of the three Qualities [§ 61. *a.*], and that they are irrational, &c., [is the common property].

a. Consisting of the three qualities, and being irrational, [such in the meaning of the compound term with which the aphorism commences]. By the expression '&c.' is meant [their] being intended for *another*, [see § 66]. 'Of both,' i.e., of the cause [viz., Nature], and of the effects [viz., all natural products]. Such is the meaning.[1]

b. He [next] states the mutual differences of character among the three Qualities which [see § 61] are the [constituent] parts of Nature :[2]

प्रीत्यप्रीतिविषादाद्यैर्गुणानामन्योन्यं वैधर्म्यम् ॥ १२७ ॥

In what the three Qualities differ.

Aph. 127. The Qualities [§ 62] differ in character, mutually, by pleasantness, unpleasantness, lassitude, &c., [in which forms, severally, the Qualities present themselves].

a. 'Pleasantness,' i. e., Pleasure. By the expression

---

[1] त्रिगुणत्वमचेतनत्वम् । आदिशब्दात्परार्थत्वम् । द्वयोरिति कार्यकारणयोरित्यर्थः ॥

[2] प्रकृतिविभागस्य त्रिगुणस्यान्योन्यवैधर्म्यमाह ॥

'&c.' ismeant Goodness (*sattwa*), which is light [i. e., not heavy,] and illuminating. 'Unpleasantness,' i. e., Pain. By the expression '&c.' [in reference to this,] is meant Passion (*rajas*), which is urgent and restless. 'Lassitude,' i. e., stupefaction. By the expression '&c.' is meant Darkness (*tamas*), which is heavy and enveloping. It is by these habits that the Qualities, viz., Goodness, Passion, and Darkness, differ: such is the remainder,[1] [required to complete the aphorism].

b. At the time of telling their differences, he tells in what respects they agree:[2]

लघ्वादिधर्मैरन्योन्यं साधर्म्यं वैधर्म्यं गुणानाम्[3] ॥ १२८ ॥

In what respects the Qualities agree, as well as differ.

Aph. 128. Through Lightness and other habits the Qualities mutually agree and differ.

a. The meaning is as follows: the enunciation [in the

---

[1] प्रीतिः सुखम्। आदिशब्दाल्लघु प्रकाशकं सत्त्वम्। अप्रीतिर्दुःखम्। आदिशब्दादुपष्टम्भकं चलं च रजः। विषादो मोहः। आदिशब्द्राद्गुरुवरणकं तमः। एतैर्धर्मैर्गुणानां सत्त्वरजस्तमसां वैधर्म्यं भवतीति शेषः॥

[2] तेषां वैधर्म्यकथनावसरे साधर्म्यमाह॥

[3] So reads Aniruddha only. Vijnána, Nágeśa, and Vedánti Mahádeva have: लघ्वादिधर्मैः साधर्म्यं वैधर्म्यं च गुणानाम्। *Ed.*

shape of the term *laghu*, 'light,' is not one intended to call attention to the concrete, viz., what things are light, but] is one where the abstract [the nature of light things, viz., 'lightness' (*laghutwa*)] is the prominent thing. 'Through Lightness and other habits,' i. e., through the characters of Lightness, Restlessness, and Heaviness, the Qualities differ. Their *agreement* is through what is hinted by the expression 'and other.' And this consists in their mutually predominating [one over another, from time to time], producing one another, consorting together, and being reciprocally present, [one in another], for the sake of Soul.[1]

b. By [the expressions, in § 124,] 'caused,' &c., it is declared that the 'Great one' [or Mind], &c., are *products*. He states the proof of this:[2].

उभयान्यत्वात्कार्यत्वं महदादेर्घटादिवत् ॥ १२९ ॥

Proof that Mind &c. are products.

Aph. 129. Since they are other than both [Soul and Nature, the only two uncaused entities], Mind and the rest are products; as is the case with a jar, or the like.

a. That is to say: like a jar, or the like, Mind and the

---

[1] अयमर्थः। भावप्रधानो निर्देशः। लघ्वादिधर्मैर्लघुचलनगुरुत्वैर्गुणानां वैधर्म्यम्। आदिपदसूचितेन साधर्म्यम्। तच्च पुरुषार्थमन्योन्याभिभवजननमिथुनवृत्तित्वम् ॥

[2] हेतुमदित्यादिना महदादीनां कार्यत्वमुक्तम्। तत्र प्रमाणमाह ॥

rest are products; because they are something other than the two which [alone] are eternal, viz., Nature and Soul.[1]

b. He states another reason:[2]

परिमाणात् ॥ १३० ॥

A second proof. *Aph.* 130. Because of [their] measure, [which is a limited one].

a. That is to say: [Mind and the rest are products]; because they are limited in measure;[3] [whereas the only two that are uncaused, viz., Nature and Soul, are unlimited].

b. He states another argument:[4]

समन्वयात् ॥ १३१ ॥

A third proof *Aph.* 131. Because they conform [to Nature].

a. [Mind and the rest are products]; because they well [follow and] correspond with Nature; i. e., because the Qualities of Nature [§ 61] are seen in all things:[5] [and it

---

[1] नित्याभ्यां प्रकृतिपुरुषाभ्यामन्यत्वाद्घटादेरिव महदादेः कार्यत्वमित्यर्थः ॥

[2] हेत्वन्तरमाह ॥

[3] परिमितत्वादित्यर्थः ॥

[4] अपरां युक्तिमाह ॥

[5] प्रधानेन सह सम्यगन्वयात्प्रधानगुणानां सर्वपदार्थेषु दर्शनात् ॥

is a maxim, that what is in the effect was derived from the cause and implies the cause.

b. He states the same thing,[1] [in the next aphorism]:

शक्तितश्चेति ॥ १३२ ॥

A fourth proof. *Aph.* 132. And, finally, because it is through the power [of the cause alone, that the product can do aught].

a. It is by the power of its cause, that a product energizes, [as a chain restrains an elephant, only by the force of the iron which it is made of]; so that Mind and the rest, being [except through the strength of Nature,] powerless, produce *their* products in subservience to Nature. Otherwise, since it is their habit to energize, they would at all times produce their products,[2] [which it will not be alleged that they do].

b. And the word *iti*, in this place, is intended to notify the completion of the set of [positive] reasons[3] [why Mind and the others should be regarded as *products*].

c. He [next] states [in support of the same assertion,] the argument from negatives,[4] [i.e., the argument drawn

---

[1] एतदेवाह ॥

[2] कारणशक्त्या कार्यं प्रवर्तत इति महदादयः क्षीणाः सन्तः प्रकृत्यनुसारेण कार्यं जनयन्ति। अन्यथा प्रवृत्तिशीलत्वात्सर्वदा कार्यं जनयेयुः ॥

[3] इतिशब्दश्चात्र हेतुवर्गसमाप्तिसूचनार्थः ॥

[4] व्यतिरेकमाह ॥

from the consideration as to what becomes of Mind and the others, when they are *not* products]:

तद्धाने प्रकृतिः पुरुषो वा ॥ १३३ ॥

Converse proof of the same.

Aph. 133. On the quitting thereof [quitting the condition of product], there is Nature, or Soul, [into one or other of which the product must needs have resolved itself].

a. Product and non-product; such is the pair of alternatives. 'On the quitting thereof;' i. e., when Mind and the rest quit the condition of product, Mind and the rest [of necessity] enter into Nature, or Soul;[1] [these two alone being non-products].

b. [But perhaps some one may say, that] Mind and the rest may exist quite independently of the pair of alternatives [just mentioned]. In regard to this, he declares [as follows]:[2]

तयोरन्यत्वे तुच्छत्वम्[3] ॥ १३४ ॥

---

[1] कार्यमकार्यं चेति कोटिद्वयम् । तद्धाने महदादेः कार्यताहाने प्रकृतौ पुरुषे वा महदादीनां प्रवेश इति ॥

[2] उभयकोटिविनिर्मुक्ता एव महदादयो भविष्यन्तीत्याह ।

[3] Nágeśa has तुच्छता. *Ed.*

Mind and the rest would not be at all, if neither product nor non-product.

Aph. 134. If they were other than these two, they would be void; [seeing that there is nothing self-existent, besides Soul and Nature].

a. If Mind and the rest were 'other than these two,' i. e., than product or non-product [§ 133], they would be in the shape of what is 'void,' i. e., in the shape of nonentity.[1]

b. Well now, [some one may say,] why should it be under the character of a *product*, that Mind and the rest are a sign of [there being such a principle as] Nature? They may be [more properly said to be] a sign, merely in virtue of their not *occurring apart* from it. To this he replies:[2]

कार्यात्कारणानुमानं तत्साहित्यात् ॥ १३५ ॥

What kind of causes can be inferred from their effects.

Aph. 135. The cause is inferred from the effect, [in the case of Nature and her products]; because it accompanies it.

a. That [other relation, other than that of material and product, which you would make out to exist between Nature and Mind,] exists, indeed, where the nature [or

---

[1] तयोः कार्याकार्ययोरन्यत्वे महदादीनां तुच्छरूपत्वमभावरूपत्वम् ॥

[2] अथ किमर्थं महदादयः कार्यत्वेन प्रकृतेर्लिङ्गम् । अविनाभावादेव लिङ्गं भविष्यन्तीत्यत्राह ॥

essence] of the cause is not seen in the effect; as [is the case with] the inference, from the rising of the moon, that the sea is swollen [into full tide; rising, with maternal affection, towards her son who was produced from her bosom on the occasion of the celebrated Churning of the Ocean. Though the swelling of the tide does not occur apart from the rising of the moon, yet here the cause, moon-rise, is not seen in the effect, tide; and, consequently, though we infer the effect from the cause, the cause could not have been inferred from the effect]. But, in the present case, since we see, in Mind and the rest, the characters of Nature, the cause *is* inferred from the effect. 'Because it accompanies it,' i. e., because, in Mind and the rest, we see the properties of Nature,[1] [i. e., Nature herself actually present; as we see the clay which is the cause of a jar, actually present in the jar].

b. [But it may still be objected,] if it be thus, then let that principle itself, the 'Great one' [or Mind], be the cause of the world: what need of *Nature?* To this he replies:[2]

अव्यक्तं त्रिगुणाल्लिङ्गात् ॥ १३६ ॥

---

[1] भवत्येवं यत्र कारणरूपं कार्ये न दृश्यते यथा चन्द्रोदयात्समुद्रवृद्ध्यनुमानम्। अत्र तु प्रधानरूपस्य महदादौ दर्शनात्कार्यात्कारणानुमानमेव। तत्साहित्यात्प्रकृतिरूपस्य महदादौ दर्शनात् ॥

[2] एवं चेन्महत्तत्त्वमेव जगत्कारणमस्तु किं प्रधानेनेत्यत आह ॥

How Mind must have an antecedent.

Aph. 136. The indiscrete, [Nature, must be inferred] from its [discrete and resolvable] effect, [Mind], in which are the three Qualities, [which constitute Nature].

a. 'It is resolved;' such is the import of [the term] *linga*, [here rendered] 'effect.' From that [resolvable effect], viz., the 'Great principle' [or Mind], in which are the three Qualities, Nature must be inferred. And that the 'Great principle,' in the shape of ascertainment [or distinct intellection], is discrete [or limited] and perishable, is established by direct observation. Therefore [i. e., since Mind, being perishable, must be resolvable into something else,] we infer that into which it is resolvable,[1] [in other words, its 'cause,' here analogously termed *lingin*, since 'effect' has been termed *linga*].

b. But then, [some one may say], still something quite different may be the cause [of all things]: what need of [this] *Nature* [of yours]? In regard to this, he remarks [as follows]:[2]

तत्कार्यतस्तत्सिद्धेर्नापलापः ॥ १३७ ॥

---

[1] लयं गच्छतीति लिङ्गं कार्यम् । तस्मात्त्रिगुणान्महत्तत्त्वात्प्रधानमनुमातव्यम् । महत्तत्त्वं चाध्यवसायरूपं व्यक्तं विनाशि प्रत्यक्षसिद्धम् । तेन लिङ्ग्यनुमानम् ॥

[2] ननु तथाप्यन्यदेव कारणं भविष्यति किं प्रकृत्येत्यत्राह ॥

Why Nature, and nothing else, must be the root of all.

Aph. 137. There is no denying that it [Nature,] *is;* because of its effects, [which will be in vain attributed to any other source].

a. Is the cause of this [world] a product, or not a product? If it were a product, then, the same being [with equal propriety to be assumed to be] the case with *its* cause, there would be a *regressus in infinitum.* If effects be from any *root* [to which there is nothing antecedent], then *this* is that [to which we give the name of *Nature*]. 'Because of its effects,' that is to say, because of the effects of Nature. There is no denying 'that it *is*,' i. e., that *Nature* is.[1]

b. Be it so, [let us grant,] that Nature *is;* yet [the opponent may contend,] *Soul* positively cannot be; for [if the existence of causes is to be inferred from their products, Soul cannot be thus demonstrated to exist, seeing that] it has *no* products. In regard to this, he remarks [as follows]:[2]

सामान्येन विवादाभावाद्धर्मवन्न साधनम् ॥ १३८ ॥

---

[1] तत्कारणं कार्यमकार्यं वा । कार्यत्वे तत्कारणस्यापि तथात्वे सत्यनवस्था । मूलकार्यत्वे तदेव सेति । तत्कार्यत इति प्रकृतिकार्यत इत्यर्थः । तत्सिद्धेः प्रकृतिसिद्धेर्नापलापः ॥

[2] भवतु प्रकृतिसिद्धिः पुरुषस्य सिद्धिस्तु न स्यादेव नहि तस्य कार्यमस्तीत्यत्राह ॥

It is not from any effect that Soul is inferred.

Aph. 138. [The relation of cause and effect is] not [alleged as] the means of establishing [the existence of Soul]; because, as is the case with [the disputed term] 'merit,' there is no dispute about there being such a kind of thing; [though *what* kind of thing *is* matter of dispute].

a. There is no dispute about 'there being such a kind of thing,' i.e., as to there being Soul, simply; [since everybody who does not talk stark nonsense must admit a Soul, or *self*, of *some* kind]; for the dispute is [not as to its *being*, but] as to its peculiarity [of being], as [whether it be] multitudinous, or sole, all-pervading, or *not* all-pervading, and so forth; just as, in every [philosophical system, or] theory, there is no dispute as to [there being something to which may be applied the term] 'merit' (*dharma*); for the difference of opinion has regard to the particular kind of [thing,—such as sacrifices, according to the Mímáńsá creed, or good works, according to the Nyáya,—which shall be held to involve] 'merit.'[1]

b. 'Not the means of establishing' that [viz., the existence of soul]; i. e., the relation of cause and effect is not the means of establishing it. This intends, 'I will mention *another* means of establishing it.'[2]

---

[1] सामान्येन तावदात्मनि विवादो नास्ति विशेषे हि विवादोऽनेक एको व्यापकोऽव्यापक इत्यादि यथा सर्वस्मिन्दर्शने धर्म इत्यविवादो धर्मविशेषे हि विप्रतिपत्तिः ॥

[2] न तत्साधनं न तत्र कार्यकारणभावः साधनम् । अन्यत्साधनं वक्ष्यामीत्यभिसन्धिः ॥

b. [But some one may say,] Souls are nothing else than the body, and its organs, &c.: what need of imagining anything else? To this he replies:[1]

शरीरादिव्यतिरिक्तः पुमान् ॥ १३९ ॥

Materialism scouted.

Aph. 139. Soul is something else than the body, &c.

a. [The meaning of the aphorism is] plain.[2]

b. He propounds an argument in support of this:[3]

संहतपरार्थत्वात् ॥ १४० ॥

The discerptible is subservient to the indiscerptible.

Aph. 140. Because that which is combined [and is, therefore, discerptible,] is for the sake of some other, [*not* discerptible].

a. That which is discerptible is intended for something else that is indiscerptible. If it were intended for something else that is discerptible, there would be a *regressus in infinitum*.[4]

b. And combinedness [involving (see § 67) discerptible-

---

[1] देहेन्द्रियादय एवात्मानः किमन्यकल्पनयेत्यत आह ॥

[2] व्यक्तम् ॥

[3] अत्र न्यायमाह ॥

[4] यत्संहतं तदसंहतपरार्थम् । संहतपरार्थत्वे ऽनवस्था स्यात् ॥

ness,] consists in the Qualities' making some product by their state of mutual commixture; or [to express it otherwise,] combinedness is the state of the soft and the hard, [which distinguishes matter from spirit]. And this exists occultly in Nature, as well as the rest; because, otherwise, discerptibleness would not prove discoverable in the products thereof, viz., the 'Great one,' &c.[1]

c. He elucidates this same point:[2]

त्रिगुणादिविपर्ययात् ॥ १४१ ॥

Soul presents no indication of being material.

Aph. 141. [And Soul is something else than the body, &c.]; because there is [in Soul,] the reverse of the three Qualities, &c.

a. Because there is, in Soul, 'the reverse of the three Qualities,' &c., i. e., because they are not seen [in it]. By the expression '&c.' is meant, because the *other* characters of Nature, also, are not seen[3] [in Soul].

b. He states another argument:[4]

---

[1] संहतत्वं च गुणानामन्योन्यमिथुनभावेन कार्यकरणम् । अथ वा द्रवकठिनता संहतत्वम् । तच्च प्रकृत्यादौ तिरोभूतमस्ति । अन्यथा तत्कार्येषु महदादिषु संहततादर्शनप्रसङ्गात् ॥

[2] तदेव स्पष्टयति ॥

[3] पुरुषे त्रिगुणादिविपर्ययात्तददर्शनात् । आदिशब्दादन्येषां प्रकृतिधर्माणामप्यदर्शनादिति ॥

[4] न्यायान्तरमाह ॥

अधिष्ठानाच्चेति ॥ १४२ ॥

Another proof that Soul is not material.

Aph. 142. And [Soul is not material;] because of [its] superintendence [over Nature].

a. For a superintendent is an intelligent being; and Nature is unintelligent: such is the meaning.[1]

b. He states another argument:[2]

भोक्तृभावात् ॥ १४३ ॥

Another proof.

Aph. 143. [And Soul is not material;] because of [its] being the experiencer.

a. It is Nature that is experienced; the experiencer is Soul. Although Soul, from its being unchangeably the same, is not [really] an experiencer, still the assertion [in the aphorism,] is made, because of the fact that the reflexion of the Intellect befalls it,[3] [and thus makes it *seem* as if it experienced (see § 58. *a.*)].

b. Efforts are engaged in for the sake of Liberation. Pray, is this [for the benefit] of the Soul, or of Nature;

---

[1] चेतनो ह्यधिष्ठाता भवति प्रकृतिश्च जडेत्यर्थः ॥

[2] युक्त्यन्तरमाह ॥

[3] भोग्या प्रकृतिर्भोक्ता पुरुषः । यद्यपि कूटस्थत्वादात्मनो भोक्तृत्वं नास्ति तथापि बुद्धिच्छायापत्त्येत्युक्तम् ॥

[since Nature, in the shape of Mind, is, it seems, the experiencer]? To this he replies:[1]

कैवल्यार्थं प्रवृत्तेः[2] ॥ १४४ ॥

For Soul, not Nature, is Liberation wanted.

Aph. 144. [It is for Soul, and not for Nature;] because the exertions are with a view to isolation [from all qualities; a condition to which Soul is competent, but Nature is not].

a. The very essence of Nature cannot depart from it [so as to leave it in the state of absolute, solitary isolation contemplated]; because the three Qualities are its very essence, [the departure of which from it would leave nothing behind], and because it would thus prove to be *not* eternal, [whereas, in reality, it *is* eternal]. The isolation (*kaivalya*) of that alone is possible of which the qualities are reflexional, [and not constitutive (see § 58. *a.*)]; and that is Soul.[3]

b. Of what nature is this [Soul]? To this he replies:[4]

---

[1] मोक्षार्थं प्रवृत्तिः । सा किमात्मनः प्रकृतेर्वेत्यत आह ॥

[2] This lection is that of Aniruddha alone. Vijnána, Nágeśa, and Vedánti Mahádeva end the Aphorism with च, necessitating 'and because,' &c. *Ed.*

[3] त्रिगुणस्वभावत्वात्प्रकृतेर्न स्वभावप्रच्यवोऽनित्यत्वप्रसङ्गाच्च । यस्यौपाधिकगुणास्तस्य कैवल्यं संभवति स चात्मेति ॥

[4] स किंरूप इत्यत आह ॥

जडप्रकाशायोगात्प्रकाशः ॥ १४५ ॥

The nature of the Soul.

Aph. 145. Since light does not pertain to the unintelligent, light, [which must pertain to something or other, is the essence of the Soul, which, self-manifesting, manifests whatever else is manifest].

a. It is a settled point, that the unintelligent is not light; [it is not self-manifesting]. If Soul, also, were unintelligent [as the Naiyáyikas hold it to be, in *substance;* knowledge being, by them, regarded not as its essence or substratum, but as one of its *qualities*], then there would need to be another light for *it;* and, as the simple theory, let Soul itself consist, essentially, of light.[1]

b. And there is Scripture [in support of this view; for example, the two following texts from the *Bṛihadáraṇyaka Upanishad*[2]]: 'Wherewith shall one distinguish that wherewith one distinguishes all this [world]?' 'Wherewith shall one take cognizance of the cognizer?'[3]

c. [But the Naiyáyika may urge,] *let* Soul be unintelligent [in its substance], but have Intelligence as its

---

[1] जडो न प्रकाशत इति सिद्धम् । यद्यात्मापि जडः स्यात्तस्याप्यन्येन प्रकाशेन भवितव्यं लाघवाच्चात्मैव प्रकाशरूपोऽस्तु ॥

[2] II., 4, 14; or *Śatapatha-bráhmaṇa*, xiv., 5, 4, 16. The two sentences quoted are continuous. *Ed.*

[3] श्रुतिश्च येनेदं सर्वं विजानाति तं केन विजानीयात् । विज्ञातारमरे केन विजानीयादिति ॥

attribute. *Thereby* it manifests all things; but it is not, essentially, Intelligence. To this he replies:[1]

निर्गुणत्वान्न चिद्धर्मा ॥ १४६ ॥

Soul has no quality.

Aph. 146. It [Soul,] has not Intelligence as its attribute; because it is without quality.

a. If soul were associated with attributes, it would be [as we hold everything to be, that is associated with attributes,] liable to alteration; and, therefore, there would be no Liberation;[2] [its attributes, or susceptibilities, always keeping it liable to be affected by something or other; or, the absolutely simple being the only unalterable].

b. He declares that there is a contradiction to Scripture in this,[3] [i. e., in the view which he is contending against]:

श्रुत्या सिद्धस्य नापलापस्तत्प्रत्यक्षबाधात् ॥ १४७ ॥

Scripture is higher evidence than supposed intuition.

Aph. 147. There is no denial [to be allowed] of what is established by Scripture; because the [supposed] evidence of intuition for this [i. e., for the existence of qualities in the Soul,] is confuted [by the Scriptural declaration of the contrary].

---

[1] जडोऽप्यात्मास्तु चिद्धर्मा। तेन जगत्प्रकाशयति नतु चिद्रूप इत्यत आह ॥

[2] यद्यात्मनो धर्मयोगः स्यात्परिणामित्वं स्यात्तश्चानिर्मोक्ष इति ॥

[3] अत्र श्रुतिविरोधमाह ॥

a. The text, 'For this Soul is uncompanioned,'[1] &c., would be confuted, if there were any annexation of qualities[2] [to Soul: and the notion of confuting Scripture is not to be entertained for a moment].

b. But the literal meaning [of the aphorism] is this, that the fact, established by Scripture, of its [i. e., soul's,] being devoid of qualities, &c., cannot be denied; because the Scripture itself confutes the [supposed] intuitive perception thereof, i. e., the [supposed] intuitive perception of qualities, &c.,[3] [in the soul].

सुषुप्त्याद्यसाक्षित्वम्[4] ॥ १४८ ॥

Argument against the soul's being unintelligent.

Aph. 148. [If soul were unintelligent,] it would not be witness [of its own comfort,] in profound [and dreamless] sleep, &c.

a. If soul were unintelligent, then, in deep sleep, &c., it would not be a witness, a knower. But that this is not

---

1 *Bṛihadáraṇyaka Upanishad*, iv., 3, 16; or *Śatapatha-bráhmaṇa*, xiv., 7, 1, 17. *Ed.*

2 असङ्गो ह्ययं पुरुष इत्यादिश्रुतिर्गुणयोगे सा बाधिता स्यात् ॥

3 अक्षरार्थस्तु श्रुत्या सिद्धस्य निर्गुणत्वादेर्नापलापः संभवति तत्प्रत्यक्षस्य गुणादिप्रत्यक्षस्य श्रुत्यैव बाधात् ॥

4 सुषुप्त्याद्यवस्थासाक्षित्वम् । Nágeśa. सुषुप्त्याद्यस्य साक्षित्वम् । Vedánti Mahádeva. *Ed.*

the case [may be inferred] from the phenomenon, that 'I slept *pleasantly*.' By the expression '&c.' [in the aphorism,] dreaming is included.[1]

b. The Vedántís say that 'soul is *one* only'; and so, again, 'For Soul is eternal, omnipresent, changeless, void of blemish:' 'Being one [only], it is divided [into a seeming multitude] by Nature (*śakti*), i.e., Illusion (*máyá*), but not through its own essence, [to which there does not belong multiplicity].' In regard to this, he says [as follows]:[2]

जन्मादिव्यवस्थातः पुरुषबहुत्वम्[3] ॥ १४९ ॥

There is a multiplicity of souls.

Aph. 149. From the several allotment of birth, &c., a multiplicity of souls [is to be inferred].

a. 'Birth, &c.' By the '&c.,' growth, death, &c., are included. 'From the several allotment' of these, i.e., from their being appointed; [birth to one, death to another, and so on]. 'A multiplicity of souls;' that is to say, souls

---

[1] यद्यात्मा जडः स्यात्सुषुप्त्यादावसाक्षित्वमज्ञातृत्वं स्यात्। न चैवं सुखमहमस्वाप्समिति प्रतिभासनात्। आदिशब्दात्स्वप्नग्रहणम् ॥

[2] एक एवात्मेति वेदान्तिनः। तथा च। नित्यः सर्वगतो ह्यात्मा कूटस्थो दोषवर्जितः। एकः स भिद्यते शक्त्या मायया न स्वभावतः। अत्राह ॥

[3] Vedánti Mahádeva has, agreeably to some copies of his work, पुरुषस्य बहुत्वम्. *Ed.*

are many. If soul were one only, then, when *one* is born, *all* must be born, &c.[1]

b. He ponders, as a doubt, the opinion of the others,[2] [viz., of the Vedántís]:

उपाधिभेदेऽप्येकस्य नानायोग आकाशस्येव घटादिभिः ॥ १५० ॥

The view of the Vedánta on this point.

Aph. 150. [The Vedántís say, that,] there being a difference in its investments, moreover, multiplicity attaches [seemingly,] to the one [Soul]; as is the case with Space, by reason of jars, &c., [which mark out the spaces that they occupy].

a. As Space is one,—[and yet], in consequence of the difference of adjuncts, [as] jars, &c., when a jar is destroyed, it is [familiarly] said, 'the jar's space is destroyed' [for then there no longer exists a *space marked out by the jar*];[3] —so, also, on the hypothesis of there being but one Soul, since there is a difference of corporeal limitation, on the destruction thereof, [i. e., of the limitation occasioned by any particular human body], it is merely a way of talking [to say], 'The soul has perished.' [This, indeed, is so far true, that there is really no perishing of Soul; but

---

[1] जन्मादीति। आदिनोपचयमरणादि गृह्यते। तद्व्यवस्थातस्तन्नियमात्। पुरुषबहुत्वं बहव आत्मान इत्यर्थः। यद्येक एवात्मैकस्मिञ्जायमाने सर्वे जायेरन्निति ॥

[2] परमतमाशङ्कते ॥

[3] *Vide supra*, p. 53, Aph. 51, &c. *Ed.*

then it is true,] also on the hypothesis that there are *many* souls. [And it must be true:] otherwise, since Soul is eternal, [without beginning or end, as both parties agree], how could there be the appointment of birth and death?[1]

b. He states [what may serve for] the removal of doubt[2] [as to the point in question]:

उपाधिर्भिद्यते नतु तद्वान् ॥ १५१ ॥

Refutation of the Vedánta on this point.

Aph. 151. The investment is different, [according to the Vedántís], but not that to which this belongs; [and the absurd consequences of such an opinion will be seen].

a. 'The investment is different,' [there are diverse bodies of John, Thomas, &c.]; 'that to which this belongs,' i. e. that [Soul] to which this investment [of body, in all its multiplicity,] belongs, is *not* different, [but is one only]: such is the meaning. And, [now consider], in consequence of the destruction of one thing, we are not to speak as if there were the destruction of something else; because this [if it were evidence of a thing's being destroyed,] would present itself where it ought not;[3] [the destruction of De-

---

[1] यथैकमाकाशं घटाद्युपाधिभेदाद्धटे नष्टे घटाकाशं नष्टमिति व्यपदिश्यते तथैकात्मपक्षेऽपि देहावच्छेदभेदात्तन्नाश आत्मा नष्ट इति व्यपदेशमात्रम्। नानात्मपक्षेऽपि। अन्यथात्मनो नित्यत्वात्कथं जन्ममरणव्यवस्थेति ॥

[2] समाधानमाह ॥

[3] *Vide supra*, p. 16, note 3. *Ed.*

vadatta, e. g., presenting itself, as a fact, when we are considering the case of Yajnadatta, who is not, for *that* reason, to be assumed to be dead]: and, on the hypothesis that Soul is one, the [fact that the Vedánta makes an] imputation of inconsistent conditions is quite evident; since Bondage and Liberation do not [and cannot,] belong [simultaneously] to *one.* But the conjunction and [simultaneous] non-conjunction of the sky [or space] with smoke, &c., [of which the Vedántí may seek to avail himself, as an illustration,] are *not* contradictory; for Conjunction is not pervasion;[1] [whereas, on the other hand, it would be nonsense to speak of Bondage as affecting one portion of a monad, and Liberation as affecting another portion; as a monkey may be in conjunction with a branch of a tree, without being in conjunction with the stem].

b. What may be [proved] by this? To this he replies:[2]

एवमेकत्वेन परिवर्तमानस्य न विरुद्धधर्माध्यासः ॥ १५२ ॥

The Sánkhya is free from the charge of absurdity to which the Vedánta is open.

Aph. 152. Thus, [i. e., by taking the Sánkhya view,] there is no imputation of contradictory conditions to [a Soul

---

[1] उपाधिर्भिद्यते तद्वाननुपाधिमान्न भिद्यत इत्यर्थः। न चान्यनाशादन्यच नाशव्यवहारोऽतिप्रसङ्गादेकात्मपक्षे च व्यक्त एव विरुद्धधर्माध्यास एकस्य बन्धमोक्षाभावात्। आकाशस्य तु धूमादियोगायोगावविरुद्धौ संयोगस्याव्याप्यवृत्तित्वात् ॥

[2] एतेन किं स्यादिति। अत आह ॥

supposed to be] everywhere present as *one* [infinitely extended monad].

a. 'Thus,' i. e., [if you regard the matter rightly,] according to the manner here set forth, there is no 'imputation,' or attribution, 'of incompatible conditions,' Bondage, Liberation, &c., to a soul 'existing everywhere,' throughout all, as one,[1] [i. e., as a monad].

b. [But, the Vedántí may contend,] we *see* the condition of another attributed even to one quite different; as, e.g., Nature's character as an agent [is attributed] to Soul, which is another [than Nature]. To this he replies:[2]

अन्यधर्मत्वेऽपि नारोपात्तत्सिद्धिरेकत्वात् ॥ १५३ ॥

Imputation' is not proof.

Aph. 153. Even though there be [imputed to Soul] the possession of the condition of another, this [i.e., that it really possesses such,] is not established by the imputation; because it [Soul,] is *one* [absolutely simple, unqualified entity].

a. [The notion] that Soul is an agent is a mistake; because, that Soul is *not* an agent is true, and the imputation [of agency to Soul] is *not* true, and the combination of the true and the untrue is not real. Neither birth nor

---

[1] एवमुक्तरीत्यैकत्वेन परितः सर्वतो वर्तमानस्यात्मनो बन्धमोक्षादिविरुद्धधर्माणामध्यास आरोपो न भवतीत्यर्थः ॥

[2] अन्यधर्मस्याप्यन्यत्रारोपो दृष्टो यथा प्रकृतेः कर्तृत्वं पुरुषेऽन्यत्रेति । अत्राह ॥

death or the like is compatible with Soul; because it is uncompanioned,[1] [i.e., unattended either by qualities or by actions].

b. [But the Vedántí may say:] and thus there will be an opposition to the Scripture. For, according to that, 'Brahma is one without a second:'[2] 'There is nothing here diverse; death after death does he [deluded man,] obtain, who here sees, as it were, a multiplicity.'[3] To this he replies:[4]

नाद्वैतश्रुतिविरोधो जातिपरत्वात् ॥ १५४ ॥

Scripture, speaking of Soul as one, is speaking of it generically.

Aph. 154. There is no opposition to the Scriptures [declaratory] of the non-duality [of Soul]; because the reference [in such texts,] is to the *genus*, [or to Soul in general].

a. But there is no opposition [in our Sánkhya view of the matter,] to the Scriptures [which speak] of the oneness of Soul; because those [Scriptural texts] refer to the *genus*.

---

[1] पुरुषकर्तृत्वं भ्रान्तं पुरुषाकर्तृत्वस्य सत्त्वादारोपस्यासत्यत्वान्न च सत्यासत्ययोः संबन्धस्तात्त्विको भवति । असङ्गित्वादात्मनो न जन्ममरणादि संभवति ॥

[2] *Chhándogya Upanishad*, vi., 1. But the word ब्रह्म does not occur there. *Ed.*

[3] *Kaṭha Upanishad*, iv., 11. Instead of आप्नोति, however, the correct reading is गच्छति. *Ed.*

[4] एवं च श्रुतिविरोधः स्यात् । तथा चैकमेवा-

By *genus* we mean sameness, the fact of being of the same nature: and it is to this alone that the texts about the non-duality [of Soul] have reference. It is not the indivisibleness [of Soul,—meaning, by its indivisibleness, the impossibility that there should be more souls than one,—that is meant in such texts]; because there is no motive [for viewing Soul as *thus* indivisible]: such is the meaning.[1]

b. But then, [the Vedántí may rejoin,] Bondage and Liberation are just as incompatible in any single soul, on the theory of him who asserts that souls are many, [and that each is at once bound and free]. To this he replies:[2]

विदितबन्धकारणस्य दृष्ट्या तद्रूपम्[3] ॥ १५५ ॥

द्वितीयं ब्रह्म नेह नानास्ति किं चन मृत्योः स मृत्युमाप्नोति य इह नानेव पश्यति । अत्राह ॥

[1] आत्मैक्यश्रुतीनां विरोधस्तु नास्ति तासां जातिपरत्वात् । जातिः सामान्यमेकरूपत्वं तत्रैवाद्वैतश्रुतीनां तात्पर्यात् । नाखण्डत्वं प्रयोजनाभावादित्यर्थः ॥

[2] नन्वनेकात्मवादिनोऽप्येकस्यात्मनो बन्धमोक्षौ विरुद्धाविति । अत्राह ॥

[3] All the commentators but Aniruddha read दृष्ट्यातद्रूपम्; and they differ widely from him, as they often do, in their elucidations of the Aphorism. Nágeśa's explanation of it is as follows: विदितं प्रसिद्धं बन्धकारणमविवेको यत्र तादृशभ्रान्तपुरु-

The compatibility of Bondage and Freedom.

Aph. 155. Of him [i. e., of that soul,] by whom the cause of Bondage is known, there is that condition [of isolation, or entire liberation], by the perception [of the fact, that Nature and soul are distinct, and that he, really, was *not* bound, even when he seemed to be so].

a. By whom is known 'the cause of bondage,' viz., the non-perception that Nature and soul are distinct, of him, 'by the perception' [of it], i. e., by cognizing the distinction, there is 'that condition,' viz., the condition of isolation, [the condition (see § 144) after which the soul aspires. The soul in Bondage which is no real bondage may be typified by Don Quixote, hanging, in the dark, from the ledge of a supposed enormous precipice, and holding on for life, as he thought, from not knowing that his toes were within six inches of the ground].[1]

षदृष्ट्यैव पुरुषेष्वतद्रूपत्वं नानारूपत्वं तन्नार्थकारीति भावः। The substance of this is, that, only in the eyes of the mistaken man who is influenced by the notorious cause of bondage, or in other words, who is unable to discriminate, is the essential condition of souls multeity, a condition the reverse of the one before referred to, unity; and that is inconclusive. The Aphorism, thus understood, must be assumed to proceed from a Vedántic disputant against the Sánkhya. Whether as read by Aniruddha, or as read by others, it is susceptible, with reference to the previous context, of a variety of renderings. *Ed.*

[1] विदितं बन्धकारणं प्रकृतिपुरुषविवेकादर्शनं यस्य तस्य दृष्ट्या विवेकज्ञानेन तद्रूपं कैवल्यरूपम् ॥

b. [Well, rejoins the Vedántí,] Bondage [as you justly observe,] is dependent on non-perception [of the truth], and is not real. It is a maxim, that non-perception is removed by perception; and, on this showing, we recognize as correct the theory that Soul is one, but not that of Soul's being multitudinous. To this he replies:[1]

नान्धादृष्ट्या चक्षुष्मतामनुपलम्भः ॥ १५६ ॥

He jeers the Vedánti. *Aph.* 156. No: because the blind do not see, can those who have their eyesight not perceive?

a. What! because a blind man does not see, does also one who has his eyesight not perceive? There are *many* arguments [in support of the view] of those who assert that souls are many, [though *you* do not see them]: such is the meaning.[2]

b. He declares, for the following reason, also, that Souls are many:[3]

---

[1] विवेकादर्शननिमित्तो बन्धो न तात्त्विकः। दर्शनाददर्शनं निवर्तत इति युक्तिः। एवं चैकात्मपक्ष एव न्याय्यं पश्यामो न नानात्मक इति। अत्राह ॥

[2] अन्धो न पश्यतीति चक्षुष्मानपि किं नोपलभते। नानात्मवादिनामनेके न्यायाः सन्तीत्यर्थः ॥

[3] इतोऽपि नानात्मान इत्याह ॥

वामदेवादिर्मुक्तो नाद्वैतम्[1] ॥ १५७ ॥

Scripture proof that Souls are many.

Aph. 157. Vámadeva, as well as others, has been liberated, [if we are to believe the Scriptures; therefore] non-duality is not [asserted, in the same Scriptures, in the Vedántic sense].

a. In the Puráṇas, &c., we hear, 'Vámadeva has been liberated,' 'Śuka has been liberated,' and so on. If Soul were *one*, since the liberation of all would take place, on the liberation of one, the Scriptural mention of a diversity [of separate and successive liberations] would be self-contradictory.[2]

b. [But the Vedántí may rejoin :] on the theory that Souls are many, since the world has been from eternity, and from time to time some one or other is liberated, so, by degrees, *all* having been liberated, there would be a universal void. But, on the theory that Soul is *one*, Liberation is merely the departure of an adjunct, [which, the Vedántí flatters himself, does not involve the inconsistency which he objects to the Sánkhya]. To this he replies :[3]

---

1 Aniruddha perhaps has वामदेवादिमुक्तेर्नाद्वैतम् । *Ed.*

2 पुराणादौ श्रुतं वामदेवो मुक्तः शुको मुक्त इत्यादि । यद्येक एवात्मैकमुक्तौ सर्वमुक्तेर्भेदश्रुतिबाधः स्यात् ॥

3 नानात्मपक्षेऽनादौ संसारे कदापि कोऽपि मुच्यत इति क्रमेण सर्वमुक्तौ सर्वशून्यता स्यात् ।

अनादावद्य यावदभावाद्भविष्यदप्येवम् ॥ १५८ ॥

As it has been, so will it be.

Aph. 158. Though it [the world,] has been from eternity, since, up to this day, there has not been [an entire emptying of the world], the future, also, [may be inferentially expected to be] thus [as it has been heretofore].

a. Though the world *has been* from eternity, since, up to this day, we have not seen it become a void, there is no proof [in support] of the view that there will be Liberation[1] [of *all* Souls, so as to leave a void].

b. He states another solution [of the difficulty]:[2]

इदानीमिव सर्वत्र नात्यन्तोच्छेदः ॥ १५९ ॥

The stream of mundane things will flow on for ever.

Aph. 159. As now [things are, so], everywhere [will they continue to go on: hence there will be] no absolute cutting short [of the course of mundane things].

a. Since souls are [in number,] without end, though Liberation successively take place, there will not be [as a necessary consequence,] a cutting short of the world. As now, so everywhere,—i.e., in time to come, also,—there

---

एकात्मपक्षे तूपाधिविगम एव मोक्ष इति। अत्राह ॥

[1] अनादौ संसारेऽद्य यावच्छून्यताया अदर्शनाद्भविष्यति मुक्तिरिति पक्षे नास्ति प्रमाणम् ॥

[2] समाधानान्तरमाह ॥

will be Liberation, but not, therefore, an absolute cutting short [of the world]; since of this the on-flowing is eternal.[1]

b. On the theory, also, that Liberation is the departure of an adjunct [§ 157. *b.*], we should find a universal void; so that the doubt[2] is alike, [in its application to either view]. Just as there might be an end of all things, on the successive liberation of many souls, so, since all adjuncts would cease, when [the fruit of] works [this fruit being in the shape of Soul's association with body, as its adjunct,] came to an end, the world would become void,[3] [on the Vedánta theory, as well as on the Sáṅkhya].

c. Now, [if the Vedántí says,] there will not be a void, because adjuncts are [in number,] endless, then it is the same, on the theory that Souls are many. And thus [it has been declared]:[4] 'For this very reason, indeed, though those who are knowing [in regard to the fact that Nature

---

[1] अनन्तत्वादात्मनां क्रमेण मुक्तिरपि स्यात्संसारोच्छेदोऽपि न स्यात्। इदानीमिव सर्वत्र भविष्यत्कालेऽपि मुक्तिर्भविष्यतीति नात्यन्तोच्छेदोऽस्य प्रवाहनित्यत्वात्॥

[2] *Anuyoga,* here rendered 'doubt,' rather signifies 'difficulty raised,' 'question.' *Ed.*

[3] उपाधिविगमो मोक्ष इति पक्षेऽपि सर्वशून्यताप्रसङ्ग इति तुल्योऽनुयोगः। यथा नानात्मनां क्रमेण मुक्तौ सर्वोच्छेदस्तथा कर्मोच्छेदे सर्वोपाधिनाशाज्जगच्छून्यं स्यात्॥

[4] The source of the stanza here translated I have not ascertained. *Ed.*

and Soul are different], are continually being liberated, there will not be a void, inasmuch as there is no end of multitudes of souls in the universe.'[1]

d. Pray, [some one may ask,] is Soul [*essentially*] bound? Or free? If [essentially] bound, then, since its essence cannot depart, there is no Liberation; for, if it [the essence,] departed, then it [Soul,] would [cease, with the cessation of its essence, and] not be eternal. If [on the other hand, you reply that it is essentially] free, then meditation and the like [which you prescribe for the attainment of liberation,] are unmeaning. To this he replies:[2]

व्यावृत्तो भूयरूपः[3] ॥ १६० ॥

---

[1] अथोपाधीनामनन्तत्वान्न शून्यता नानात्मपक्षे तुल्यत्वम् । तथा च । अत एव हि विद्वत्सु मुच्यमानेषु संततम् । ब्रह्माण्डजीवलोकानामनन्तत्वादशून्यता ॥

[2] किमात्मा बद्धो मुक्तो वा । बद्धत्वे स्वरूपस्याप्रच्यवादनिर्मोक्षः प्रच्यवेऽनित्यत्वम् । मुक्तत्वे व्यर्थो ध्यानादिरिति । अत आह ॥

[3] This reading I find nowhere, but, instead of it, व्यावृत्तोभयरूपः, 'Clear of both conditions [*i.e.*, that of being bound and that of being freed, is Soul, which is eternally free].'

Messrs. Böhtlingk and Roth call Dr. Ballantyne's भूयरूपः 'Fehlerhaft für भूयोरूपः.' Their substitute is, so far as I know, conjectural.

According to most interpreters, however, the preceding Aphorism has reference to the question whether it be only after Soul is

Soul is ever free, though it may seem bound in all sorts of ways.

Aph. 160. It [Soul,] is altogether free, [but seemingly] multiform, [or different, in appearance, from a free thing, through a delusive semblance of being bound].

a. It is not bound; nor is it liberated; but it is ever free, [see § 19]. But the destruction of ignorance [as to its actual freedom,] is effected by meditation, &c.,[1] [which are, therefore, not unmeaning, as alleged in § 159. *d.*].

b. It has been declared that Soul is a witness.[2] Since it is a witness [some one may object], even when it has attained to discriminating [between Nature and Soul], there

---

liberated, or, on the other hand, at all times, that simplicity, or unchanging fixedness, of essential condition (*ekarúpatwa*) is predicable of it.

Introductions to the Aphorism, with expositions of it, here follow. Vedánti Mahádeva: पुरुषस्य यदेकरूपत्वं तत्किं मोक्षकाल उत सर्वदेत्याकाङ्क्षायामाह । Nágeśa: पुरुषाणां चैकरूपत्वं मोक्षकाल इव सर्वदेत्याह । Vedánti Mahádeva: श्रुतिस्मृतिन्यायेभ्यो व्यावृत्ते नित्यनिवृत्ते उभयरूपे उभे रूपे रूपभेद इति यावद्यस्मात्तथा । Nágeśa: पुरुषो व्यावृत्तो नित्यव्यावृत्त उभयरूपभेदो यस्मात्तथेत्यर्थः । Also see the commentaries on the *Sánkhya-káriká*, st. 19; and § 144. *a.*, at p. 162, *supra.* *Ed.*

[1] न बद्धो नायं मुच्यते किं तु नित्यमुक्तः । अज्ञाननाशस्तु ध्यानादिना क्रियत इति ॥

[2] *Vide supra*, p. 56, § 54. *a.*, and p. 165, § 148. *Ed.*

is no Liberation; [Soul, on this showing, being not an absolutely simple entity, but something *combined* with the character of a spectator or witness]. To this he replies:[1]

[2]अक्षसंबन्धात्साक्षित्वम् ॥ १६१ ॥

How Soul is a spectator.

Aph. 161. It [Soul,] is a witness, through its connexion with sense-organs, [which quit it, on liberation].

a. A sense-organ is an organ of sense. Through its connexion therewith, it [Soul,] is a witness. And where is [its] connexion with sense-organs, [these products of Nature (see § 61)], when discrimination [between Nature and Soul] has taken place?[3]

b. [Well, some one may ask], at all times of *what* nature is Soul? To this he replies:[4]

नित्यमुक्तत्वम्[5] ॥ १६२ ॥

---

[1] आत्मनः साक्षित्वमुक्तम् । प्राप्तविवेकस्यापि साक्षित्वेऽनिर्मोक्ष इति । अचाह ॥

[2] Only Aniruddha recognizes this reading. Vijnána, Nágeśa, and Vedánti Mahádeva have साक्षात्सं°. *Ed.*

[3] अक्षमिन्द्रियम् । तत्संबन्धात्साक्षित्वम् । विवेके च क्वेन्द्रियसंबन्ध इति ॥

[4] सर्वदा किंरूप आत्मेति । अत आह ॥

[5] Vijnána says that this Aphorism and that next following specify notes of Soul which establish that its essential condition is neither

The real condition of Soul.

Aph. 162. [The nature of Soul is] constant freedom.

a. 'Constant freedom:' that is to say; Soul is, positively, always devoid of the Bondage called Pain [see §§ 1 and 19]; because Pain and the rest are modifications of Understanding,[1] [which (see § 61) is a modification of Nature, from which Soul is really distinct].

औदासीन्यं चेति ॥ १६३ ॥

Soul's indifference.

Aph. 163. And, finally, [the nature of Soul is] indifference [to Pain and Pleasure, alike].

a. By 'indifference' is meant non-agency. The word *iti* [rendered 'finally,'] implies that the exposition of the Nature of Soul is completed.[2]

b. [Some one may say, the fact of] Soul's being an agent is declared in Scripture. How is this, [if, as you say, it be *not* an agent]? To this he replies:[3]

---

of those alluded to in Aph. 160: उभयरूपत्वाभावसिद्ध्यर्थं पुरुषस्यापरौ विशेषावाह सूत्राभ्याम् । *Ed.*

[1] नित्यमुक्तत्वं सदैव पुरुषस्य दुःखाख्यबन्धशून्यत्वं दुःखादेर्बुद्धिपरिणामत्वादित्यर्थः ॥

[2] औदासीन्यमकर्तृत्वम् । इतिशब्दः पुरुषधर्मप्रतिपादनसमाप्तौ ॥

[3] आत्मनः कर्तृत्वं श्रूयते । तत्कथमिति । अत आह ॥

उपरागात्कर्तृत्वं चित्सान्निध्याच्चित्सान्निध्यात्
॥ १६४ ॥

How Soul, which is not an agent, is yet spoken of as such.

Aph. 164. [Soul's *fancy* of] being an agent is, through the influence [of Nature],[1] from the proximity of Intellect, from the proximity of Intellect.

a. [Its] 'being an agent,' i. e., Soul's *fancy* of being an agent, is 'from the proximity of Intellect,' 'through the influence' of Nature,[2] [(see § 19,) of which Intellect (see § 61) is a modification].

b. The repetition of the expression 'from the proximity of Intellect' is meant to show that we have reached the conclusion: for thus do we see [practised] in the Scriptures,[3] [e. g., where it is said, in the Veda: 'Soul is to be known; it is to be discriminated from Nature: thus it does not come again, it does not come again'[4]].

---

[1] The translator inadvertently omitted the words 'through,' &c. *Ed.*

[2] चित्सान्निध्येन प्रकृत्युपरागादात्मनः कर्तृत्वं कर्तृत्वाभिमानः ॥

[3] चित्सान्निध्यादिति वीप्सा परिसमाप्तौ श्रुतौ तथा दृष्टत्वादिति ॥

[4] These words are taken from Colebrooke: see his *Miscellaneous Essays* (Prof. Cowell's edition), vol. i., p. 249. The original is found, as a quotation, &c., in Váchaspati Miśra's *Tattwa-kaumudí*, near the beginning of the comment on st. 2 of the *Sánkhya-káriká*: आत्मा वा अरे ज्ञातव्यः। प्रकृतितो विवेक्तव्यः।

c. So much, in this Commentary[1] on the illustrious Kapila's Aphorisms declaratory of the Sánkhya, for the First Book, that on the [topics or] subject-matter[2] [of the Sánkhya system].

न स पुनरावर्तते न स पुनरावर्तते । Of ज्ञातव्यः there is a variant, द्रष्टव्यः, in one of my MSS. The words प्र॰ वि॰ are obviously a gloss; and I have punctuated accordingly. They are preceded, I take it, by one text, and are followed by another. The source of the first has not been discovered. For what is very similar to the second, see the conclusion of the *Chhándoyya Upanishad.* Colebrooke's 'thus' is unrepresented in the Sanskrit as I find it. *Ed.*

1 Aniruddha's is intended, though many passages in the preceding pages are from other commentaries. *Ed.*

2 इति श्रीकापिलसाङ्ख्यप्रवचनसूत्रवृत्तौ विषयाध्यायः प्रथमः ॥

END OF BOOK I.

BOOK II.

a. The subject-matter [of the Institute] has been set forth [in Book I.]. Now, in order to prove that it is not the *Soul* that undergoes the alterations [observable in the course of things], he will tell, very diffusely, in the Second Book, how the creation is formed out of the Primal Principle. There, too, the nature of the products of Nature is to be declared fully, with a view to the very clear discrimination of Soul from these. Therefore, according to [the verses],[1]

b. 'Whoso rightly knows its changes, and the Primal Agent [Nature], and Soul, the eternal, he, thirsting no more, is emancipated,'

c. we remark, that, with reference to the character, &c., of Emancipation, all the three [things mentioned in these verses] require to be known. And here, in the first place, with advertence to the consideration, that, if Nature, which is unintelligent, were to create without a motive, we should find even the emancipated one bound, he states the *motive* for the creation of the world:[2]

---

[1] Here add, 'in the *Moksha-dharma*, &c.'; and read, instead of 'we remark .... Emancipation,' 'there is the declaration that.'

The verses quoted are from the *Mahábhárata*, xii., 7879, and occur in Chap. ccxvi., in the Section entitled *Moksha-dharma*. *Ed.*

[2] शास्त्रस्य विषयो निरूपितः। साम्प्रतं पुरुषस्यापरिणामित्वोपपादनाय प्रकृतितः सृष्टिप्रक्रियामतिविस्तरेण द्वितीयाध्याये वक्ष्यति। तत्रैव

विमुक्तमोक्षार्थं स्वार्थं वा प्रधानस्य ॥ १ ॥

The motive for creation.

Aph. 1. Of Nature [the agency, or the being a maker, is] for the emancipation of what is [really, though not apparently,] emancipated, or else for [the removal of] itself.

a. The expression 'the being a maker' is borrowed from the last aphorism of the preceding Book. Nature makes the world for the sake of removing the pain, which is [really] a shadow [Book I., § 58], belonging to the Soul, which is, in its very nature, free from the bonds of pain; or [to explain it otherwise,] for the sake of removing pain [connected] by means of but a shadowy link; or [on the other hand,] it is 'for the sake of itself,' that is to say, for the sake of removing the actually real pain [which consists] of itself.[1]

प्रधानकार्याणां स्वरूपं विस्तरतो वक्तव्यं तेभ्योऽपि पुरुषस्यातिस्फुटविवेकाय। अत एव।

विकारं प्रकृतिं चैव पुरुषं च सनातनम्।
यो यथावद्विजानाति स वितृष्णो विमुच्यते॥

इति मोक्षधर्मादिषु त्रयाणामेव ज्ञेयत्ववचनम्। तत्र चादावचेतनायाः प्रकृतेर्निष्प्रयोजनसृष्टृत्वे मुक्तस्यापि बन्धप्रसङ्ग इत्याशयेन जगत्सर्जने प्रयोजनमाह॥

[1] कर्तृत्वमिति पूर्वाध्यायशेषसूत्रादनुषज्यते। स्वभावतो दुःखबन्धाद्विमुक्तस्य पुरुषस्य प्रतिबिम्ब-

b. Although experience [of good and ill], also, as well as Emancipation, is a motive for creation, yet Emancipation alone is mentioned, inasmuch as it is the principal one.[1]

c. But then, if creation were for the sake of Emancipation, then, since Emancipation might take place through creation once for all, there would not be creation again and again; to which he replies:[2] [3]

विरक्तस्य तत्सिद्धेः ॥ २ ॥

Successive creation why.

Aph. 2. Because this [Emancipation] is [only] of him that is void of passion.

a. Emancipation does not take place through creation once for all; but it is [the lot only] of him that has been extremely tormented many times by the various pain of birth, death, sickness, &c.; and, therefore, [successive creation goes on] because Emancipation actually occurs in the case only of him in whom complete dispassion has

---

रूपदुःखमोक्षार्थं प्रतिबिम्बसंबन्धेन दुःखमोक्षार्थं वा प्रधानस्य जगत्कर्तृत्वमथ वा स्वार्थं स्वस्य पारमार्थिकदुःखमोक्षार्थमित्यर्थः ॥

[1] यद्यपि मोक्षवद्भोगोऽपि सृष्टेः प्रयोजनं तथापि मुख्यत्वान्मोक्ष एवोक्तः ॥

[2] ननु मोक्षार्थं चेत्सृष्टिस्तर्हि सकृत्सृष्ट्यैव मोक्षसंभवे पुनः पुनः सृष्टिर्न स्यादिति तत्राह ॥

[3] For another rendering of the original of *a.*, *b.*, and *c.*, see my translation of the *Rational Refutation*, &c., p. 62. *Ed.*

arisen through the knowledge of the distinctness of Nature and Soul: such is the meaning.[1]

b. He tells the reason why dispassion does not take place through creation once for all:[2]

न श्रवणमात्रात्तत्सिद्धिरनादिवासनाया बलवत्त्वात्[3] ॥ ३ ॥

Force of the foregoing reason.

Aph. 3. It is not effected by the mere hearing; because of the forcibleness of the impressions[4] from eternity.

a. Even the hearing [of Scripture, in which the distinctness of Nature from Soul is enounced,] comes [not to all alike, but only] through the merit of acts done in many births, [or successive lives]. Even then dispassion is not established through the mere hearing, but through direct cognition; and direct cognition does not take place suddenly, because of the forcibleness of false impressions that

---

[1] नैकदा सृष्टेर्मोक्षः किं तु बहुशो जन्ममरणव्याध्यादिविविधदुःखेन भृशं तप्तस्य ततश्च प्रकृतिपुरुषयोर्विवेकख्यात्योत्पन्नपरवैराग्यस्यैव मोक्षोत्पत्तिसिद्धेरित्यर्थः ॥

[2] सकृत्सृष्ट्या वैराग्यासिद्धौ हेतुमाह ॥

[3] This reading is peculiar to Vijnána, but seems to have some countenance from Nágeśa. Aniruddha and Vedánti Mahádeva have -वासनापटुत्वात्. *Ed.*

[4] *Vásaná.* *Vide supra*, p. 29, note 2. *Ed.*

have existed from eternity, but [the required direct cognition takes place] through the completion of Concentration; and there is an abundance of obstacles to Concentration [see Yoga Aphorisms, Book II]: therefore, only after many births do dispassion and Emancipation take place at any time of any one at all: such is the meaning.[1]

b. He states another reason for the continuous flow of creation:[2]

बहुभृत्यवद्वा प्रत्येकम् ॥ ४ ॥

Another reason for continuous creation.

Aph. 4. Or as people have, severally, many dependants.

a. As householders have, severally, many who are dependent upon them, according to the distinctions of wife, children, &c., so, also, the Qualities, viz., Goodness, &c., [Book I., § 61. *b.*] have to emancipate innumerable Souls, severally. Therefore, however many Souls may have been emancipated, the onflow of creation takes place for the emancipation of other Souls; for Souls are [in number,] without end: such is the meaning. And so the Yoga aphorism [Book II., § 22] says: 'Though it have ceased

---

[1] श्रवणमपि बहुजन्मकृतपुण्येन भवति । तत्रापि श्रवणमात्रान्न वैराग्यसिद्धिः किं तु साक्षात्कारात्साक्षात्कारश्च झटिति न भवत्यनादिमिथ्यावासनाया बलवत्त्वात्किं तु योगनिष्ठया योगे च प्रतिबन्धबाहुल्यमिति । अतो बहुजन्मभिरेव वैराग्यं मोक्षश्च कदाचित्कस्यचिदेव सिध्यतीत्यर्थः ॥

[2] सृष्टिप्रवाहे हेत्वन्तरमाह ॥

to be, in respect of him that has done the work, it has not [absolutely] ceased to be; because it is common to others besides him.'[1]

b. But then why is it asserted that Nature alone creates, when, by the text, 'From that or this Soul proceeded the Ether,'[2] &c., it is proved that *Soul*, also, creates? To this he replies:[3]

प्रकृतिवास्तवे च पुरुषस्याध्याससिद्धिः ॥ ५ ॥

Nature, not Soul, creates.

Aph. 5. And, since it [the character of creator,] belongs, really, to Nature, it follows that it is fictitiously attributed to Soul.

---

[1] यथा गृहस्थानां प्रत्येकं बहवो भर्तव्या भवन्ति स्त्रीपुत्रादिभेदेनैवं सत्त्वादिगुणानामपि प्रत्येकमसंख्यपुरुषा विमोचनीया भवन्ति। अतः कियत्पुरुषमोक्षेऽपि पुरुषान्तरमोचनार्थं सृष्टिप्रवाहो घटते पुरुषाणामानन्त्यादित्यर्थः। तथा च योगसूत्रं कृतार्थं प्रति नष्टमप्यनष्टं तदन्यसाधारणत्वादिति ॥

[2] *Taittiriya Upanishad*, ii., 1. But read: 'From this, from this same self,' &c. *Ed.*

[3] ननु प्रकृतेरेव स्रष्टृत्वं कथमुच्यते तस्माद्वा एतस्मादात्मन आकाशः संभूत इति श्रुत्या पुरुषस्यापि स्रष्टृत्वसिद्धेरिति तत्राह ॥

a. And, since Nature's character of creator is decided to be real, there is, really, in the Scriptures, only a fictitious [or figurative] attribution of creativeness to Soul.[1]

b. But then, if it be thus, how is it laid down that Nature's creativeness, moreover, is *real;* since we are told [in Scripture,] that creation, moreover, is on a level with a dream? To this he replies:[2]

कार्यतस्तत्सिद्धेः[3] ॥ ६ ॥

The reality of Nature's creativeness.

Aph. 6. Since it is proved from the products.

a. That is to say: because the real creative character of Nature is established just 'from the products,' viz., by that evidence [see Book I., § 110,] which acquaints us with the subject [in which the creative character inheres]; for *products* are real, inasmuch as they produce impressions and exhibit acts.[4] [The reality of eternal things is established here, just as it is by Locke, who says: 'I think

---

[1] प्रकृतौ स्रष्टृत्वस्य वस्तुत्वे च सिद्धे पुरुषस्य स्रष्टृत्वाध्यास एव श्रुतिषु सिध्यति ॥

[2] नन्वेवं प्रकृतावपि स्रष्टृत्वं वास्तवमिति कुतोऽवधृतं सृष्टेः स्वप्नादितुल्यतायाऽपि श्रवणादिति तत्राह ॥

[3] Aniruddha alone has कार्यतस्तत्सिद्धिः, which reading Dr. Ballantyne at first accepted. *Ed.*

[4] कार्याणामर्थक्रियाकारितया वास्तवत्वेन का-

God has given me assurance enough as to the existence of things without me; since, by their different application, I can produce, in myself, both *pleasure and pain (artha)*, which is one great concernment of my present state.' These existing products being admitted, the Sánkhya argues that they must have a cause; and, as this cause means neither more nor less than something creative, whatever proves the existence of the cause proves, at the same time, its creative character.]

b. But then [it may be said], on the alternative [see § 1] that Nature works for *herself*, she must energize with reference to the *emancipated* Soul, also. To this he replies:[1]

चेतनोद्देशान्नियमः कण्टकमोक्षवत् ॥ ७ ॥

Who escape nature. *Aph.* 7. The rule is with reference to one knowing; just as escape from a thorn.

a. The word *chetana* here means 'one knowing;' because the derivation is from *chit*, 'to be conscious'. As one and the same thorn is not a cause of pain to him who, being 'one knowing,' i.e., aware of it, escapes from that same, but actually is so in respect of *others;* so Nature, also, is escaped by 'one knowing,' one aware, one who has accomplished the matter: to *him* it does not consist of pain; but to others, who are *not* knowing, it actually is a cause of pain: such is

---

यैत एव धर्मिग्राहकप्रमाणेन प्रकृतेर्वास्तवस्रष्टृत्वसिद्धेरित्यर्थः ॥

[1] ननु प्रकृतेः स्वार्थत्वपक्षे मुक्तपुरुषं प्रत्यपि सा प्रवर्तेत । तत्राह ॥

the 'rule,' meaning, the distribution. Hence, also, of Nature, which is, by its own nature, bound [inasmuch as it *consists* of bonds], the self-emancipation is possible; so that it does not energize with reference to the emancipated Soul[1] [§ 6. *b*.].

b. But then [suggests some one], what was said [at § 5], that, in respect of Soul, the creative character is only fictitiously attributed, this is not proper; because it is fitting, that, by the conjunction of Nature, *Soul*, also, should be modified into Mind, &c.; for a modification of wood, &c., resembling earth, &c., through the conjunction of earth, &c., is seen: to which he replies:[2]

---

[1] चिती संज्ञान इति व्युत्पत्त्या चेतनोऽत्राभिज्ञः। यथैकमेव कण्टकं यश्चेतनोऽभिज्ञस्तस्मादेव मुच्यते तं प्रत्येव दुःखात्मकं न भवत्यन्यान्प्रति तु भवत्येव तथा प्रकृतिरपि चेतनादभिज्ञात्कृतार्थादेव मुच्यते तं प्रत्येव दुःखात्मिका न भवत्यन्याननभिज्ञान्प्रति तु दुःखात्मिका भवत्येवेति नियमो व्यवस्थेत्यर्थः। एतेन स्वभावतो बद्धाया अपि प्रकृतेः स्वमोक्षो घटत इति। अतो न मुक्तपुरुषं प्रति प्रवर्तत इति॥

[2] ननु पुरुषे स्रष्टृत्वमध्यस्तमात्रमिति यदुक्तं तन्न युक्तं प्रकृतिसंयोगेन पुरुषस्यापि महदादिपरिणामौचित्याद्दृष्टो हि पृथिव्यादियोगेन काष्ठादेः पृथिव्यादिसदृशः परिणाम इति। तत्राह॥

अन्ययोगेऽपि तत्सिद्धिर्नाञ्जस्येनायोदाहवत् ॥ ८ ॥

Soul not creative, though associated with what is so.

Aph. 8. Even though there be conjunction [of Soul] with the other [viz., Nature], this [power of giving rise to products] does not exist in it immediately; just like the burning action of iron.

a. Even though there be conjunction with Nature, there belongs to Soul no creativeness, 'immediately,' i.e., directly. An illustration of this is, 'like the burning action of iron:' as iron does not possess, directly, a burning power; but this is only fictitiously attributed to it, being through the fire conjoined with it: such is the meaning. But, in the example just mentioned, it is admitted that there is an alteration of both; for this is proved by sense-evidence: but, in the instance under doubt, since the case is accounted for by the modification of one only, there is cumbrousness in postulating the modification of both; because, otherwise, by the conjunction of the China-rose, it might be held that the colour of the crystal was changed.[1]

---

[1] प्रकृतियोगेऽपि पुरुषस्य न स्रष्टृत्वसिद्धिराञ्जस्येन साक्षात्। तत्र दृष्टान्तोऽयोदाहवत्। यथायसो न दग्धृत्वं साक्षादस्ति किं तु स्वसंयुक्ताग्निद्वारकमध्यस्तमेवेत्यर्थः। उक्तदृष्टान्ते तूभयोः परिणामः प्रत्यक्षसिद्धत्वादिष्यते संदिग्धस्थले त्वेकस्यैव परिणामेनोपपत्तावुभयोः परिणामकल्पने गौरवम्। अन्यथा जपासंयोगात्स्फटिकस्य रागपरिणामापत्तेरिति ॥

b. It has already been stated [§ 1] that the fruit of creation is emancipation. Now he states the principal occasional cause of creation :[1]

रागविरागयोर्योगः सृष्टिः ॥ ९ ॥

Creation when.

Aph. 9. When there is passion, or dispassion, there is concentration, [in the latter case, and] creation, [in the former].

a. When there is passion, there is creation ; and, when there is dispassion, there is 'concentration,' i. e., the abiding [of Soul] in its own nature [see Yoga Aphorisms, Book I., § 3[2]] ; in short, emancipation, or the hindering of the modifications of the thinking principle [Yoga Aphorisms, Book I., § 2[2]] : such is the meaning. And so the import is, that Passion is the cause of creation ; because of their being[3] simultaneously present or absent.[4]

b. After this he begins to state the manner of creation :[5]

---

[1] सृष्टेः फलं मोक्ष इति प्रागुक्तम् । इदानीं सृष्टेर्मुख्यं निमित्तकारणमाह ॥

[2] *Vide infra*, p. 211, note 6. *Ed.*

[3] 'Simultaneously,' &c., is to render *anwayavyatirekau*, on which *vide supra*, p. 43, note 2. *Ed.*

[4] रागे सृष्टिर्वैराग्ये च योगः स्वरूपेऽवस्थानं मुक्तिरिति यावदथ वा चित्तवृत्तिनिरोध इत्यर्थः । तथा चान्वयव्यतिरेकाभ्यां रागः सृष्टिकारणमित्याशयः ॥

[5] इतः परं सृष्टिप्रक्रियां वक्तुमारभते ॥

महदादिक्रमेण [1]पञ्चभूतानाम् ॥ १० ॥

Order of creation.

Aph. 10. In the order [see § 12. *b.*] of Mind, &c., [is the creation] of the five elements, [or of the material world].

a. 'Creation' is supplied from the preceding aphorism.[2]

b. He mentions a distinction[3] [between these successively creative energies and the primal one]:

आत्मार्थत्वात्सृष्टेर्नैषामात्मार्थ आरम्भः ॥ ११ ॥

Nature's products not for themselves.

Aph. 11. Since creation is for the sake of Soul, the origination of these [products of Nature] is not for their own sake.

a. 'Of these,' i.e., of Mind, &c., since the creativeness is 'for the sake of Soul,' i.e., for the sake of the emancipation of Soul, the 'origination,' i.e., the creativeness, is not for the sake of themselves; since, inasmuch as they are perishable, they [unlike Nature, (see § 1)] are not susceptible of emancipation: such is the meaning.[4]

b. He declares the creation of limited space and time:[5]

---

[1] Nágeśa has, instead of पञ्च°, च. *Ed.*

[2] सृष्टिरिति पूर्वसूत्रादनुवर्तते ॥

[3] विशेषमाह ॥

[4] एषां महदादीनां स्रष्टृत्वस्यात्मार्थत्वात्पुरुषमोक्षार्थत्वान्न स्वार्थ आरम्भः स्रष्टृत्वं विनाशित्वेन मोक्षायोगादित्यर्थः ॥

[5] खण्डदिक्कालयोः सृष्टिमाह ॥

दिक्कालावाकाशादिभ्यः ॥ १२ ॥

Relative time and space whence.

Aph. 12. [Relative] Space and Time [arise] from the Ether, &c.

a. The Space and Time which are *eternal* [and absolute], being the *source* of the Ether, are, really, sorts of qualities of Nature: therefore it is consistent that Space and Time should be all-pervading. But the Space and Time which are limited arise from the Ether, through the conjunction of this or that limiting object: such is the meaning. By the expression '&c.,' [in the aphorism,] is meant 'from the apprehending of this or that limiting object.'[1]

b. Now he exhibits, in their order, through their nature and their habits, the things mentioned [in § 10] as 'in the order of Mind, &c.':[2]

अध्यवसायो बुद्धिः ॥ १३ ॥

Aph. 13. Intellect is judgment.

Mind or Intellect defined.

a. 'Intellect' is a synonym of 'the Great Principle' [or Mind (see Book I., § 71)]; and 'judgment,' called [also] ascertainment, is its

---

[1] नित्यौ यौ दिक्कालौ तावाकाशप्रकृतिभूतौ प्रकृतेर्गुणविशेषावेव। अतो दिक्कालयोर्विभुत्वोपपत्तिः। यौ तु खण्डदिक्कालौ तौ तत्तदुपाधिसंयोगादाकाशादुत्पद्येते इत्यर्थः। आदिशब्देनोपाधिग्रहणादिति ॥

[2] इदानीं महदादिक्रमेणेत्युक्तान्स्वरूपतो धर्मतश्च क्रमेण दर्शयति ॥

peculiar modification: such is the meaning. But they are set forth as identical, because a property and that of which it is the property are indivisible.[1] And it is to be understood, that this Intellect is 'Great,' because it pervades all effects other than itself, and because it is of great power.[2]

b. He mentions other properties, also, of the Great Principle:[3]

तत्कार्यं धर्मादिः[4] ॥ १४ ॥

Products of intellect.

Aph. 14. Merit, &c., are products of it.

a. The meaning is, that Merit, Knowledge, Dispassion, and Supernatural Power, moreover, are formed out of *intellect*, not formed of *self-consciousness* (*ahankára*), &c.; because intellect alone [and not self-consciousness,] is a product of superlative Purity,[5] [without admixture of Passion and Darkness].

---

[1] See, for a different rendering, the *Rational Refutation*, &c., p. 45. *Ed.*

[2] महत्तत्त्वस्य पर्यायो बुद्धिरिति । अध्यवसायश्च निश्चयाख्यस्तस्यासाधारणी वृत्तिरित्यर्थः । अभेद-निर्देशस्तु धर्मधर्म्यभेदात् । अस्याश्च बुद्धेर्महत्त्वं स्वेतरसकलकार्यव्यापकत्वान्महैश्वर्याच्च मन्तव्यम् ॥

[3] महत्तत्त्वस्यापरानपि धर्मानाह ॥

[4] From copying a typographical error, Dr. Ballantyne had, in both his editions, धर्मादि. *Ed.*

[5] धर्मज्ञानवैराग्यैश्वर्याण्यपि बुद्ध्युपादानकानि

b. But then, if it be thus, how can the prevalence of demerit, in the portions of intellect lodged in men, cattle, &c., be accounted for? To this he replies:[1]

महदुपरागाद्विपरीतम् ॥ १५ ॥

Opposite products of intellect.

Aph. 15. The Great one [intellect,] becomes reversed through tincture.[2]

a. That same 'Great one,' i.e., the Great Principle [or intellect], through being tinged with Passion and Darkness, also becomes 'reversed' [see § 14. *a*.], i.e., vile, with the properties of Demerit, Ignorance, Non-dispassion, and want of Supernatural Power: such is the meaning.[3]

b. Having characterized the Great Principle, he defines its product, Self-consciousness:[4]

नाहंकाराद्युपादानकानि बुद्धेरेव निरतिशयसत्त्वकार्यत्वादित्यर्थः ॥

[1] नन्वेवं कथं नरपश्वादिगतानां बुद्ध्यंशानामधर्मप्राबल्यमुपपद्यताम् । तत्राह ॥

[2] I.e., 'influence.' *Ed.*

[3] तदेव महन्महत्तत्त्वं रजस्तमोभ्यामुपरागाद्विपरीतं क्षुद्रमधर्माज्ञानावैराग्यानैश्वर्यधर्मकमपि भवतीत्यर्थः ॥

[4] महत्तत्त्वं लक्षयित्वा तत्कार्यमहंकारं लक्षयति ॥

अभिमानोऽहंकारः ॥ १६ ॥

Self-consciousness. *Aph.* 16. Self-consciousness is a conceit.

a. 'Self-consciousness' is what makes the Ego, as a potter [makes a pot]; the thing [called] the internal instrument (*antaḫ-karaṉa*): and this, inasmuch as a property and that of which it is the property are indivisible, is spoken of as 'a conceit,'[1] [viz., of personality], in order to acquaint us that this is its peculiar modification. Only when a thing has been determined by intellect [i.e., by an act of judgment (see § 13. *a.*)], do the making of an Ego and the making of a Meum take place.[2]

b. He mentions the product of Self-consciousness, which has arrived in order:[3]

एकादशपञ्चतन्मात्रं तत्कार्यम् ॥ १७ ॥

Product of Self-consciousness. *Aph.* 17. The product of it [viz., of Self-consciousness,] is the eleven [organs], and the five Subtile Elements.

a. The meaning is, that the eleven organs, with the

---

[1] For another version, see the *Rational Refutation*, &c., p. 45. *Ed.*

[2] अहं करोतीत्यहंकारः कुम्भकारवदन्तःकरणद्रव्यं स च धर्मधर्म्यभेदादभिमान इत्युक्तोऽसाधारणवृत्तितासूचनाय। बुद्ध्या निश्चित एवार्थेऽहंकारममकारौ जायेते ॥

[3] क्रमागतमहंकारस्य कार्यमाह ॥

five Subtile Elements, viz., Sound, &c., are the product of Self-consciousness.[1]

b. Among these, moreover, he mentions a distinction :[2]

सात्त्विकमेकादशकं प्रवर्तते वैकृतादहंकारात् ॥१८॥

The Mind whence.

Aph. 18. The eleventh, consisting of [the principle of] Purity, proceeds from modified Self-consciousness.

a. The 'eleventh,' i.e., the completer of the eleven, viz., Mind, [or the 'internal organ,'—which is not to be confounded with 'the Great one,' called also Intellect and Mind,—alone,] among the set consisting of sixteen [§ 17], consists of Purity; therefore it is produced from Self-consciousness 'modified,' i.e., pure: such is the meaning. And hence, too, it is to be reckoned that the ten organs are from the Passionate Self-consciousness; and the Subtile Elements, from the Dark Self-consciousness.[3]

b. He exhibits the eleven organs :[4]

---

[1] एकादशेन्द्रियाणि शब्दादिपञ्चतन्मात्रं चाहंकारस्य कार्यमित्यर्थः ॥

[2] अत्रापि विशेषमाह ॥

[3] एकादशानां पूरणमेकादशकं मनः षोडशात्मगणमध्ये सात्त्विकमतस्तद्वैकृतात्सात्त्विकाहंकाराज्जायत इत्यर्थः । अतश्च राजसाहंकाराद्दशेन्द्रियाणि तामसाहंकाराच्च तन्मात्राणीत्यवगन्तव्यम् ॥

[4] एकादशेन्द्रियाणि दर्शयति ॥

कर्मेन्द्रियबुद्धीन्द्रियैरान्तरमेकादशकम् ॥ १९ ॥

Of the Organs.

Aph. 19. Along with the organs of action and the organs of understanding another is the eleventh.

a. The organs of action are five, viz., the vocal organ, the hands, the feet, the anus, and the generative organ; and, the organs of understanding are five, those called the organs of sight, hearing, touch, taste, and smell. Along with these ten, 'another,' viz., Mind, is 'the eleventh,' i.e., is the eleventh organ: such is the meaning.[1]

b. He refutes the opinion that the Organs are formed of the Elements:[2]

आहङ्कारिकत्वश्रुतेर्न भौतिकानि ॥ २० ॥

The Nyâya view rejected.

Aph. 20. They [the organs,] are not formed of the Elements; because there is Scripture for [their] being formed of Self-consciousness.

a. Supply 'the organs.'[3]

b. Pondering a doubt, he says:[4]

---

[1] कर्मेन्द्रियाणि वाक्पाणिपादपायूपस्थानि पञ्च ज्ञानेन्द्रियाणि च चक्षुःश्रोत्रत्वग्रसनघ्राणाख्यानि पञ्च। एतैर्दशभिः सहान्तरं मन एकादशकमेकादशेन्द्रियमित्यर्थः ॥

[2] इन्द्रियाणां भौतिकत्वमतं निराकरोति ॥

[3] इन्द्रियाणीति शेषः ॥

[4] आशङ्क्याह ॥

देवतालयश्रुतिर्नारम्भकस्य[1] ॥ २१ ॥

A text explained. *Aph.* 21. The Scripture regarding absorption into deities is not [declaratory] of an originator.

a. That Scripture which there is about absorption into deities is not 'of an originator,' that is to say, it does not refer to an originator; because [although a thing, e.g., a jar, when it ceases to be a jar, is usually spoken of as being resolved into its originator, viz., into earth, yet] we see the absorption of a drop of water into what, nevertheless, is *not* its originator, viz., the ground; [and such is the absorption into a deity from whom the Mind absorbed did not originally emanate].[2]

b. Some say that the Mind, included among the organs, is eternal. He repels this:[3]

---

[1] Aniruddha has, instead of -श्रुतिः, -श्रुतेः. His comment is as follows: कारणे कार्यलय इति स्थितम्। आदित्यं वै चक्षुर्गच्छतीति देवे लयः श्रूयते। तस्मान्नारम्भकस्य नारम्भकाभिमतस्य भूतस्य कारणत्वमिति। *Ed.*

[2] देवतासु या लयश्रुतिः सा नारम्भकस्य नारम्भकविषयिणीत्यर्थोऽनारम्भकेऽपि भूतले जलबिन्दोर्लयदर्शनात् ॥

[3] इन्द्रियान्तर्गतं मनो नित्यमिति केचित्। तत्परिहरति ॥

तदुत्पत्तिश्रुतेर्विनाशदर्शनाच्च[1] ॥ २२ ॥

No organ eternal.

Aph. 22. [None of the organs is eternal, as some hold the Mind to be ;] because we have Scripture for their beginning to be, and because we see their destruction.

a. All these organs, without exception, have a beginning; for the Scripture says, 'From this are produced the vital air, the mind, and all the organs;'[2] &c., and because we are certified of their destruction by the fact that, in the conditions of being aged, &c., the mind, also, like the sight and the rest, decays, &c.: such is the meaning.[3]

b. He rebuts the atheistical opinion that the sense [for example,] is merely the set of eye-balls, [&c.]:[4]

अतीन्द्रियमिन्द्रियं भ्रान्तानामधिष्ठाने[5] ॥ २३ ॥

---

[1] Aniruddha's reading is तदुत्पत्तिः श्रूयते विनाश°. *Ed.*

[2] *Muṇḍaka Upanishad*, ii., i., 3. *Ed.*

[3] तेषां सर्वेषामेवेन्द्रियाणामुत्पत्तिरस्त्येतस्माज्जायते प्राणो मनः सर्वेन्द्रियाणि चेत्यादिश्रुतेर्वृद्धाद्यवस्थासु चक्षुरादीनामिव मनसोऽप्यपचयादिना विनाशनिर्णयाच्चेत्यर्थः ॥

[4] गोलकजातमेवेन्द्रियमिति नास्तिकमतमपाकरोति ॥

[5] This is taken from my edition, where, however, it is corrected in the corrigenda. See the next two notes. *Ed.*

The Sense not to be confounded with its site.

Aph. 23. The Sense is supersensuous; [it being the notion] of mistaken persons [that the Sense exists] in [identity with] its site.

a. Every Sense is supersensuous, and not perceptible; but only in the opinion of mistaken persons does the Sense exist 'in its site,' e.g., [Sight,] in the eye-ball, in the condition of identity [with the eye-ball]: such is the meaning. The correct reading is: ['The sense is something supersensuous; to confound it with] the site,[1] [is a mistake].'[2]

b. He rebuts the opinion that one single Sense, through diversity of powers, performs various offices:[3]

शक्तिभेदेऽपि भेदसिद्धौ नैकत्वम् ॥ २४ ॥

All the organs are not one organ.

Aph. 24. Moreover, a difference being established if a difference of *powers* be [conceded], there is not a oneness [of the organs].

---

[1] इन्द्रियं सर्वमतीन्द्रियं नतु प्रत्यक्षं भ्रान्तानामेव त्वधिष्ठानं गोलकं तादात्म्येनेन्द्रियमित्यर्थः। अधिष्ठानमित्येव पाठः ॥

[2] The original of this shows that Vijnána emphasizes अधिष्ठानं as the true reading. He seems to point to अधिष्ठाने, which Aniruddha has, and, after him, Vedánti Mahádeva. *Ed.*

[3] एकमेवेन्द्रियं शक्तिभेदाद्विलक्षणकार्यकारीति मतमपाकरोति ॥

a. Even by the admission that a diversity of *powers* belongs to one single organ, the diversity of organs is established; because the *powers* are, assuredly, organs; therefore, there is not a singleness of organ: such is the meaning.[1]

b. But then [it may be said], there is something unphilosophical in supposing various kinds of organs to arise from one single Self-consciousness. To this he replies:[2]

न कल्पनाविरोधः प्रमाणदृष्टस्य[3] ॥ २५ ॥

Theoretical considerations cannot upset facts.

Aph. 25. A theoretical discordance is not [of any weight,] in the case of what is matter of ocular evidence.

a. This is simple.[4]

b. He tells us that, of the single leading organ, the Mind, the other ten are kinds of powers:[5]

---

[1] एकस्यैवेन्द्रियस्य शक्तिभेदस्वीकारेऽपीन्द्रियभेदः सिध्यति शक्तीनामपीन्द्रियत्वादतो नैकत्वमिन्द्रियस्येत्यर्थः ॥

[2] नन्वेकस्मादहंकारान्नानाविधेन्द्रियोत्पत्तिकल्पनायां न्यायविरोधः । तत्राह ॥

[3] Nágeśa is peculiar in having प्रमाणदृष्टत्वात्. *Ed.*

[4] सुगमम् ॥

[5] एकस्यैव मुख्येन्द्रियस्य मनसोऽन्ये दश शक्तिभेदा इत्याह ॥

उभयात्मकं[1] मनः ॥ २६ ॥

Diversified operation of Mind.

Aph. 26. The Mind identifies itself with both.

a. That is to say: the Mind identifies itself with the organs of intellection and of action.[2]

b. Of his own accord, he explains the meaning of the expression 'identifies itself with both:'[3]

गुणपरिणामभेदान्नानात्वमवस्थावत् ॥ २७ ॥

How this happens.

Aph. 27. By reason of the varieties of transformation of [which] the Qualities [are susceptible], there is a diversity [of their product, the Mind,] according to circumstances.

a. As one single man supports a variety of characters, through the force of association,—being, through association with his beloved, a lover; through association with one indifferent, indifferent; and, through association with some other, something other,—so the Mind, also, through association with the organ of vision, or any other, becomes various, from its becoming one with the organ of vision, or any other; by its being [thereby] distinguished by the modification of seeing, or the like. The argument in support of this is, 'of the Qualities,' &c.; the meaning being, because of the adaptability of the Qualities, Goodness, &c., to varieties of transformation.[4]

---

[1] All the commentators but Vijnána here insert च. *Ed.*

[2] ज्ञानकर्मेन्द्रियात्मकं मन इत्यर्थः ॥

[3] उभयात्मकमित्यस्यार्थं स्वयं विवृणोति ॥

[4] यथैक एव नरः सङ्गवशान्नानात्वं भजते का-

b. He mentions the object of the organs of intellection and of action:[1]

रूपादिरसमलान्त[2] उभयोः ॥ २८ ॥

What the organs deal with.

Aph. 28. Of both [sets of organs the object is that list of things], beginning with Colour, and ending with the dirt of Taste.

a. The 'dirt' of the tastes of food, &c., means ordure, &c.,[3] [into which the food, consisting of the *quality* Taste, &c., is partly transformed].

b. Of what Soul (*indra*), through what service, these are termed Organs (*indriya*), both these things he tells us:[4]

द्रष्टृत्वादिरात्मनः करणत्वमिन्द्रियाणाम् ॥ २९ ॥

मिनीसङ्गात्कामुको विरक्तसङ्गाद्विरक्तोऽन्यसङ्गाच्चान्य एवं मनोऽपि चक्षुरादिसङ्गाच्चक्षुराद्येकीभावेन दर्शनादिवृत्तिविशिष्टतया नाना भवति। तत्र हेतुर्गुणेत्यादि गुणानां सत्त्वादीनां परिणामभेदेषु सामर्थ्यादित्यर्थः ॥

[1] ज्ञानकर्मेन्द्रिययोर्विषयमाह ॥

[2] Aniruddha reads, in lieu of -मल°, -वर्ग°. *Ed.*

[3] अन्नरसानां मलः पुरीषादिः ॥

[4] यस्येन्द्रस्य येनोपकारेणैतानीन्द्रियाणीत्युच्यते तदुभयमाह ॥

The Organs and their possessors.

Aph. 29. The being the seer, &c., belongs to the Soul; the instrumentality belongs to the Organs.

a. For, as a king, even without himself energizing, becomes a warrior through his instrument, his army, by directing this by orders simply, so the Soul, though quiescent, through all the organs, of vision, &c., becomes a seer, a speaker, and a judger, and the like, merely through the proximity called 'Conjunction;' because it moves these, as the lodestone[1] [does the iron, without exerting any effort].

b. Now he mentions the special modifications of the triad of internal organs:[2]

त्रयाणां स्वालक्षण्यम् ॥ ३० ॥

Differences in the internal organs.

Aph. 30. Of the three [internal organs] there is a diversity among themselves.

---

[1] यथा हि महाराजः स्वयमव्याप्रियमाणोऽपि सैन्येन करणेन योद्धा भवत्याज्ञामात्रेण प्रेरकत्वात्तथा कूटस्थोऽपि पुरुषश्चक्षुराद्यखिलकरणैर्द्रष्टा वक्ता संकल्पयिता चेत्येवमादिर्भवति संयोगाख्यसान्निध्यमात्रेणैव तेषां प्रेरकत्वादयस्कान्तमणिवदिति ॥

[2] इदानीमन्तःकरणत्रयस्यासाधारणवृत्तीराह ॥

a. The aspect of Intellect is attention[1]; of Self-consciousness, conceit [of personality]; of the Mind, decision and doubt.[2]

b. He mentions, also, a common aspect of the three:[3]

सामान्यकरणवृत्तिः प्राणाद्या वायवः पञ्च ॥ ३१ ॥

A character common to the three.

Aph. 31. The five airs, viz., Breath, &c., are the modification, in common, of the [three internal] instruments.

a. That is to say: the five, in the shape of Breath, &c., which are familiarly known as 'airs', because of their circulating as the air does, these [animal spirits] are the joint or common 'modification,' or kinds of altered form, 'of the instruments,' i.e., of the triad of internal instruments.[4]

b. The opinion is not ours, as it is that of the Vaiśeshi-

---

[1] *Adhyavasáya*, rendered 'ascertainment' and 'judgment' at pp. 156 and 196, *supra*. Also see the *Rational Refutation*, &c., p. 46. *Ed.*

[2] बुद्धेर्वृत्तिरध्यवसायोऽभिमानोऽहंकारस्य संकल्पविकल्पौ मनस इति ॥

[3] त्रयाणां साधारणीं वृत्तिमप्याह ॥

[4] प्राणादिरूपाः पञ्च वायुवत्संचाराद्वायवो ये प्रसिद्धास्ते सामान्या साधारणी करणस्यान्तःकरणत्रयस्य वृत्तिः परिणामभेदा इत्यर्थः ॥

kas, that the modifications of the organs take place successively only, and not simultaneously. So he says:[1]

क्रमशोऽक्रमशश्चेन्द्रियवृत्तिः ॥ ३२ ॥

Sense-impressions, &c., not exclusively successive.

Aph. 32. The modifications of the organs take place both successively and simultaneously.

a. This is simple.[2]

b. Lumping the modifications of the understanding, with a view to showing how they are the cause of the world, he, in the first place, exhibits [them]:[3]

वृत्तयः पञ्चतय्यः क्लिष्टाक्लिष्टाः[4] ॥ ३३ ॥

The ideas which constitute the world.

Aph. 33. The modifications [of the understanding, which are to be shown to be the cause of the world, and] which are of five kinds, are [some of them,] painful and [others,] not painful.

---

[1] वैशेषिकाणामिवास्माकं नायं नियमो यदिन्द्रियवृत्तिः क्रमेणैव भवति नैकदेत्याह ॥

[2] सुगमम् ॥

[3] पिण्डीकृत्य बुद्धिवृत्तीः संसारनिदानताप्रतिपादनार्थमादौ दर्शयति ॥

[4] Literally the same words are found in the Yoga Aphorisms, Book I., § 5. *Ed.*

a. That the modifications are of five sorts is declared by Patanjali's aphorism,[1] [see Yoga Aphorisms, Book I., § 6 [2]].

b. He acquaints [us] with the nature of Soul:[3]

तन्निवृत्तावुपशान्तोपरागः स्वस्थः ॥ ३४ ॥

Soul's relation thereto.

Aph. 34. On the cessation thereof [viz., of mundane influences], its tincture[4] ceasing, it [Soul,] abides in itself.

a. That is to say: during the state of repose of these modifications, it [the Soul], the reflexion of these having ceased, is abiding in itself; being, at *other* times, also, as it were, in isolation, [though seemingly not so]. And to this effect there is a triad of Aphorisms of the Yoga,[5] [viz., Book I., §§ 2, 3, and 4[6]].

---

[1] वृत्तीनां पञ्चप्रकारत्वं पातञ्जलसूत्रेणोक्तम् ॥

[2] Namely: प्रमाणविपर्ययविकल्पनिद्रास्मृतयः । 'Evidence, misprision, chimera, unconsciousness, memory.' *Ed.*

[3] पुरुषस्य स्वरूपं परिचाययति ॥

[4] I. e., 'influence', as in Aph. 15, at p. 198, *supra*. *Ed.*

[5] तासां वृत्तीनां विरामदशायां शान्ततत्प्रतिबिम्बकः स्वस्थो भवति कैवल्य इवान्यदापीत्यर्थः । तथा च योगसूत्रत्रयम् ॥

[6] योगश्चित्तवृत्तिनिरोधः । 'Concentration (*yoga*) is the hindering of the modifications of the thinking principle.' तदा द्रष्टुः स्वरूपेऽवस्थानम् । 'Then [i. e., at the time of Con-

b. He explains this by an illustration:[1]

कुसुमवच्च मणिः ॥ ३५ ॥

This illustrated. *Aph.* 35. And as [by] a flower, the gem.

a. The 'and' implies that this is the *reason* [of what was asserted in the preceding aphorism]; the meaning being, as the gem [is tinged, apparently,] by a flower. As the gem called rock-crystal, by reason of a flower of the Hibiscus, becomes red, not abiding in its own state, and, on the removal thereof, becomes colourless, abiding in its own state, in like manner[2] [is the Soul apparently tinged by the adjunction of the Qualities].

b. But then [it may be asked], by whose *effort* does the aggregate of the organs come into operation; since Soul is motionless, and since it is denied[3] that there is any Lord [or Demiurgus]? To this he replies:[4]

---

centration,] it [the Soul,] abides in the form of the spectator [without a spectacle].' वृत्तिसारूप्यमितरत्र । 'At other times [than that of Concentration] it [the Soul,] is in the same form as the modifications [of the internal organ].' Dr. Ballantyne's translation is here quoted. *Ed.*

[1] एतदेव दृष्टान्तेन विवृणोति ॥

[2] चकारो हेतौ कुसुमेनेव मणिरित्यर्थः । यथा जपाकुसुमेन स्फटिकमणी रक्तोऽस्वस्थो भवति तन्निवृत्तौ च रागशून्यः स्वस्थो भवति तद्वदिति ॥

[3] 'Demurred to' is preferable. *Vide supra*, p. 112. *Ed.*

[4] ननु कस्य प्रयत्नेन करणजातं प्रवर्ततां पुरु-

पुरुषार्थं करणोद्भवोऽप्यदृष्टोल्लासात् ॥ ३६ ॥

What moves the Organs to operate.

Aph. 36. The Organs also arise, for the sake of Soul, from the development of *desert*.

a. The meaning is, that, just as Nature energizes 'for the sake of Soul,' so 'the Organs also arise;' i. e., the energizing of the Organs is just in consequence of the development of the deserts of the Soul: [see Yoga Aphorisms, Book II., § 13. *b.*]. And the desert belongs entirely to the investment;[1] [the Soul not really possessing either merit or demerit].

b. He mentions an instance of a thing's spontaneously energizing for the sake of another:[2]

धेनुवद्वत्साय ॥ ३७ ॥

An illustration.

Aph. 37. As the cow for the calf.

a. As the cow, for the sake of the calf, quite spontaneously secretes milk, and awaits no other effort, just so, for the sake of the master, Soul, the Organs energize quite spontaneously: such is the meaning. And it is *seen*, that,

---

षस्य कूटस्थत्वादीश्वरस्य च प्रतिषिद्धत्वादिति। तत्राह ॥

[1] प्रधानप्रवृत्तिवत्पुरुषार्थं करणोद्भवः करणानां प्रवृत्तिरपि पुरुषस्यादृष्टाभिव्यक्तेरेव भवतीत्यर्थः। अदृष्टं चोपाधेरेव ॥

[2] परार्थं स्वतः प्रवृत्तौ दृष्टान्तमाह ॥

out of profound sleep, the understanding of its own accord wakes up.[1]

b. With reference to the question, how many Organs there are, external and internal combined, he says:[2]

करणं [3]त्रयोदशविधमवान्तरभेदात् ॥ ३८ ॥

The number of the Organs.

Aph. 38. Organ is of thirteen sorts, through division of the subordinates.

a. The triad of internal organs, and the ten external organs, combined, are thirteen. He says 'sorts,' in order to declare that, of these, moreover, there is an infinity, through [their] distinction into individuals. He says 'through division of the subordinates,' with a reference to the fact, that it is *understanding* which is the *principal* organ; the meaning being, because the organs [or functions,] of the single organ, called understanding, are more than one.[4]

---

[1] यथा वत्सार्थं धेनुः स्वयमेव क्षीरं स्रवति नान्यं यत्नमपेक्षते तथैव स्वामिनः पुरुषस्य कृते स्वयमेव करणानि प्रवर्तन्त इत्यर्थः। दृश्यते च सुषुप्तात्स्वयमेव बुद्धेरुत्थानमिति ॥

[2] बाह्याभ्यन्तरैर्मिलित्वा कियन्ति करणानीत्याकाङ्क्षायामाह ॥

[3] The reading of Vedánti Mahádeva, and of him alone, is त्रयोदशविधं बाह्यान्तरभेदात्. *Ed.*

[4] अन्तःकरणत्रयं दश बाह्यकरणानि मिलित्वा

b. But then, since understanding [it seems,] alone is the principal instrument in furnishing its object [of emancipation] to Soul, and the instrumentality of the others is secondary, in this case what is [meant by] *secondariness?*[1] [Why are they said to be instrumental *at all?*] In regard to this he says:[2]

इन्द्रियेषु साधकतमत्वगुणयोगात्कुठारवत् ॥ ३९ ॥

Efficiency of the Organs whence.

Aph. 39. Because the quality of being most efficient is conjoined with the organs; as in the case of an axe.

a. The quality of the [principal] organ, the understanding, in the shape of being most efficient on behalf of soul, exists, derivatively, in the [other derivative] organs. Therefore it is made out that an organ is of thirteen kinds: such is the connexion with the preceding aphorism.[3]

त्रयोदश। तेष्वपि व्यक्तिभेदेनानन्त्यं प्रतिपादयितुं विधमित्युक्तम्। बुद्धिरेव मुख्यं करणमित्याशयेनोक्तमवान्तरभेदादित्येकस्यैव बुद्ध्याख्यकरणस्य करणानामनेकत्वादित्यर्थः॥

[1] Instead of 'in this case,' &c., read, 'what is the character of these [i. e., organs]?' *Ed.*

[2] ननु बुद्धिरेव पुरुषेऽर्थसमर्पकत्वान्मुख्यं करणमन्येषां च करणत्वं गौणं तत्र को गुण इत्याकाङ्क्षायामाह॥

[3] इन्द्रियेषु पुरुषार्थसाधकतमत्वरूपः करणस्य

b. 'As in the case of an axe.' As, although the blow itself, since it is this that puts an end to our non-possession of the result, is the principal efficient in the cutting, yet the axe, also, is an efficient, because of its close proximity to the quality of being the principal efficient, so [here, also]: such is the meaning. He does not here say that Self-consciousness is secondarily efficient, meaning to imply that it is one with the internal organ.[1]

c. Specifying the precise state of the case in regard to the condition of secondary and principal, he says:[2]

द्वयोः प्रधानं मनो लोकवद्भृत्यवर्गेषु ॥ ४० ॥

Preeminent efficiency of Mind illustrated.

Aph. 40. Among the two [the external and the internal organs], the principal is Mind; just as, in the world, among troops of dependants.

a. 'Among the two,' viz., the external and the internal, 'Mind,' i. e., understanding, simply, is 'the principal,' i. e.,

---

बुद्धेर्गुणः परंपरयास्ति । अतस्त्रयोदशविधं करणमुपपद्यत इति पूर्वसूत्रेणान्वयः ॥

[1] कुठारवदिति । यथा फलायोगव्यवच्छिन्नतया प्रहारस्यैव छिदायां मुख्यकरणत्वेऽपि प्रकृष्टसाधनत्वगुणयोगात्कुठारस्यापि करणत्वं तथेत्यर्थः । अन्तःकरणस्यैकत्वमभिप्रेत्याहंकारस्य गौणकरणत्वमत्र नोक्तम् ॥

[2] गौणमुख्यभावे व्यवस्थां विशिष्याह ॥

chief; in short, is the immediate cause; because it is that which furnishes Soul with its end; just as, among troops of dependants, some one single person is the prime minister of the king; and the others, governors of towns, &c., are his subordinates: such is the meaning.[1]

b. Here the word 'Mind' does not mean the third internal organ,[2] [(§ 30. *a.*) but Intellect, or 'the Great One.']

c. He tells, in three aphorisms, the reasons why Intellect [or understanding] is the principal:[3]

अव्यभिचारात् ॥ ४१ ॥

A reason why Understanding is the principal.

Aph. 41. [And Intellect is the principal, or immediate and direct, efficient in Soul's emancipation;] because there is no wandering away.

a. That is to say: because it [understanding,] per-

---

[1] द्वयोर्बाह्यान्तरयोर्मध्ये मनो बुद्धिरेव प्रधानं मुख्यं साक्षात्करणमिति यावत्पुरुषेऽर्थसमर्पकत्वाद्यथा भृत्यवर्गेषु मध्ये कश्चिदेव लोको राज्ञः प्रधानो भवत्यन्ये च तदुपसर्जनीभूता ग्रामाध्यक्षादयस्तद्वदित्यर्थः ॥

[2] अत्र मनःशब्दो न तृतीयान्तःकरणवाची ॥

[3] बुद्धेः प्रधानत्वे हेतूनाह त्रिभिः सूत्रैः ॥

vades all the organs; or because there is no result apart from it.[1]

तथाशेषसंस्काराधारत्वात् ॥ ४२ ॥

Another reason. *Aph.* 42. So, too, because it [the understanding,] is the depository of all self-continuant impressions.

a. Understanding alone is the depository of all self-continuant impressions, and not the Sight, &c., or Self-consciousness, or the Mind; else it could not happen that things formerly seen, and heard, &c., would be remembered by the blind, and deaf, &c.[2]

स्मृत्यानुमानाच्च ॥ ४३ ॥

Another reason. *Aph.* 43. And because we infer this [its preeminence] by reason of its meditating.

a. That is to say: and because we infer its preeminence, 'by reason of its meditating,' i.e., its modification in the shape of meditation. For the modification of thought called 'meditation' is the noblest of all the modifications [incident to Soul, or pure Thought, whose blessedness, or state of emancipation, it is to have no *modification* at all]; and the Understanding itself, which, as being the depository thereof, is, further, named Thought [*chitta,* from the

---

[1] सर्वकरणव्यापकत्वात्फलाव्यभिचाराद्वेत्यर्थः ॥

[2] बुद्धेरेवाखिलसंस्काराधारता नतु चक्षुरादेरहंकारमनसोर्वा पूर्वदृष्टश्रुताद्यर्थानामन्धबधिरादिभिः स्मरणानुपपत्तेः ॥

same root as *chintá*[1]], is nobler than the organs whose modifications are other than this: such is the meaning.[2]

b. But then, suppose that the modification 'meditation' belongs only to the *Soul*, [suggests some one]. To this he replies:[3]

संभवेन्न स्वतः ॥ ४४ ॥

Meditation not essential to Soul.

Aph. 44. It cannot be of its own nature.

a. That is to say: meditation cannot belong to Soul essentially; because of the immobility[4] [of Soul; whereas 'meditation' is an effort].

b. But then, if thus the preeminence belongs to understanding alone, how was it said before [at § 26,] that it is the *Mind* that takes the nature of both [sets of organs, in

---

[1] The two words are, respectively, from *chit* and *chint*, which are cognate. *Ed.*

[2] स्मृत्या चिन्तनरूपया वृत्त्या प्राधान्यानुमानाच्चेत्यर्थः । चिन्तावृत्तिर्हि ध्यानाख्या सर्ववृत्तिभ्यः श्रेष्ठा तदाश्रयतया च चित्तापरनाम्नी बुद्धिरेव श्रेष्ठान्यवृत्तिककरणेभ्य इत्यर्थः ॥

[3] ननु चिन्तावृत्तिः पुरुषस्यैवास्तु । तत्राह ॥

[4] स्वतः पुरुषस्य स्मृतिर्न संभवेत्कूटस्थत्वादित्यर्थः ॥

apparent contradiction to the view propounded at § 39]? To this he replies:[1]

आपेक्षिको गुणप्रधानभावः क्रियाविशेषात् ॥ ४५ ॥

An organ may be, relatively, principal, or secondary.

Aph. 45. The condition [as regards Soul's instruments,] of secondary and principal is relative; because of the difference of function.

a. In respect to the difference of function, the condition, as secondary, or principal, of the instruments [of Soul] is relative. In the operations of the Sight, &c., the Mind is principal; and, in the operation of the Mind, Self-consciousness, and, in the operation of Self-consciousness, Intellect, is principal[2] [or precedent].

b. But then, what is the cause of this arrangement; viz., that, of this [or that] Soul, this [or that] Intellect, alone, and not another Intellect, is the instrument? With reference to this, he says:[3]

---

[1] नन्वेवं बुद्धेरेव प्राधान्ये कथं मनस उभयात्मकत्वं प्रागुक्तम् । तत्राह ॥

[2] क्रियाविशेषं प्रति करणानामापेक्षिको गुणप्रधानभावः । चक्षुरादिव्यापारेषु मनः प्रधानं मनोव्यापारे चाहंकारोऽहंकारव्यापारे च बुद्धिः प्रधानम् ॥

[3] नन्वस्य पुरुषस्येयं बुद्धिरेव करणं न बुद्ध्यन्तरमित्येवं व्यवस्था किंनिमित्तिकेत्याकाङ्क्षायामाह ॥

तत्कर्मार्जितत्वात्तदर्थमभिचेष्टा[1] लोकवत् ॥ ४६ ॥

Every one reaps as he has sowed.

Aph. 46. The energizing [of this or that Intellect] is for the sake of this [or that Soul]; because of [its] having been purchased by the works [or deserts] of this [or that Soul]; just as in the world.

a. The meaning is, that, 'the energizing,' i.e., all operation, of the instrument is for the sake of this [or that] Soul; because of [its] having been purchased by this [or that] Soul's works [or deserts]; just as in the world. As, in the world [or in ordinary affairs], whatever axe, or the like, has been purchased by the act, e.g., of buying, by whatever man, the operation of that [axe, or the like], such as cleaving, is only for the sake of that man [who purchased it]: such is the meaning. The import is, that *therefrom* is the distributive allotment of instruments[2] [inquired about under § 45. *b.*]

b. Although there is *no* act in Soul, because it is im-

---

[1] Nágeśa differs from all the other commentators in reading -र्थमपि चेष्टा. *Ed.*

[2] तत्पुरुषीयकर्मजन्यात्करणस्य तत्पुरुषार्थमभिचेष्टा सर्वव्यापारो भवति लोकवदित्यर्थः । यथा लोके येन पुरुषेण क्रयादिकर्मणार्जितो यः कुठारादिस्तत्पुरुषार्थमेव तस्य छिदादिव्यापार इत्यर्थः । अतः करणव्यवस्थेति भावः ॥

movable, still, since it is the means of Soul's experience, it is *called* the act of Soul; just like the victories, &c., of a king [which are, really, the acts of his servants]; because of Soul's being the owner[1] [of the results of acts; as the king is of the results of the actions of his troops].

c. In order to make clear the chiefship of Intellect, he sums up,[2] [as follows]:

समानकर्मयोगे बुद्धेः प्राधान्यं लोकवल्लोकवत् ॥ ४७ ॥

Summing up.

Aph. 47. Admitting that they [the various instruments of Soul, all] equally act, the preeminence belongs to Intellect; just as in the world, just as in the world.

a. Although the action of all the instruments is the same, in being for the sake of Soul, still the preeminence belongs to Intellect alone: just as in the world. The meaning is, because it is just as the preeminence, in the world, belongs to the prime minister, among the rulers of towns, and the rest, even although there be no difference so far as regards their being [all alike workers] for the sake of the king. Therefore, in all the Institutes, Intellect alone is celebrated as 'the Great One.' The repetition

---

[1] यद्यपि कूटस्थतया पुरुषे कर्म नास्ति तथापि पुरुषभोगसाधनतया पुरुषस्वामिकत्वेन राज्ञो जयादिवदेव पुरुषस्य कर्मोच्यते ॥

[2] बुद्धेः प्राधान्यं प्रकटीकर्तुमुपसंहरति ॥

[viz., 'just as in the world, just as in the world,'] implies the completion of the Book.[1]

b. So much for [this abstract of] the Second Book, on the Products of Nature, in the commentary, on Kapila's Declaration of the Sánkhya, composed by the venerable Vijnána Áchárya.[2]

---

[1] यद्यपि पुरुषार्थत्वेन समान एव सर्वेषां करणानां व्यापारस्तथापि बुद्धेरेव प्राधान्यं लोकवत्। लोके हि राजार्थकत्वाविशेषेऽपि ग्रामाध्यक्षादिषु मध्ये मन्त्रिणः प्राधान्यं तद्वदित्यर्थः। अत एव बुद्धिरेव महानिति सर्वशास्त्रेषु गीयत इति। वीप्साध्यायसमाप्तौ॥

[2] इति श्रीविज्ञानाचार्यनिर्मिते कापिलसाङ्ख्यप्रवचनस्य भाष्ये प्रधानकार्याध्यायो द्वितीयः॥

END OF BOOK II.

BOOK III.

a. In the next place, the gross product of Nature, viz., the great elements and the dyad of bodies, is to be described; and, after that, the going into various wombs, and the like; [this description being given] with a view to that less perfect degree of dispassionateness which is the cause of one's engaging upon the means of knowledge; and, after that, with a view to perfect freedom from passion, all the means of knowledge are to be told: so the Third [Book] commences:[1]

अविशेषाद्विशेषारम्भः ॥ १ ॥

The elements whence.

Aph. 1. The origination of the diversified [world of sense] is from that which has no difference.

a. '[Which] has no difference,' i.e., that in which there exists not a distinction, in the shape of calmness, fierceness, dulness, &c., viz., the Subtile Elements, called 'the five somethings, simply;' from this [set of five] is the origina-

---

[1] इतः परं प्रधानस्य स्थूलकार्यं महाभूतानि शरीरद्वयं च वक्तव्यं ततश्च विविधयोनिगत्यादयो ज्ञानसाधनानुष्ठानहेत्वपरवैराग्यार्थं ततश्च परवैराग्याय ज्ञानसाधनान्यखिलानि वक्तव्यानीति तृतीयारम्भः ॥

tion of 'the diversified,' [so called] from their possessing a difference, in the shape of the calm, &c., viz., the gross, the great Elements: such is the meaning. For, the fact of consisting of pleasure, or the like, in the shape of the calm, and the rest, is manifested, in the degrees of greater, and less, &c., in the gross Elements only, not in the Subtile; because *these*, since they have but the one form of the calm, are manifest to the concentrated,[1] [practitioners of meditation, but to no others].

b. So then, having stated, by composing the preceding Book, the origin of the twenty-three Principles, he states the origination, therefrom, of the dyad of bodies:[2]

तस्माच्छरीरस्य ॥ २ ॥

The Body whence. *Aph.* 2. Therefrom, of the Body.

a. 'Therefrom,' i.e., from the twenty-three Principles,

---

[1] नास्ति विशेषः शान्तघोरमूढत्वादिरूपो यच्चेत्यविशेषो भूतसूक्ष्मं पञ्चतन्मात्राख्यं तस्माच्छान्तादिरूपविशेषवत्त्वेन विशेषाणां स्थूलानां महाभूतानामारम्भ इत्यर्थः। सुखाद्यात्मकता हि शान्तादिरूपा स्थूलभूतेष्वेव तारतम्यादिभिरभिव्यज्यते न सूक्ष्मेषु तेषां शान्तैकरूपतयैव योगिष्वभिव्यक्तेरिति॥

[2] तदेवं पूर्वाध्यायमारभ्य त्रयोविंशतितत्त्वानामुत्पत्तिमुक्त्वा तस्माच्छरीरद्वयोत्पत्तिमाह॥

there is the origination of the pair of Bodies, the Gross [Body] and the Subtile: such is the meaning.[1]

b. Now he proves that mundane existence could not be accounted for otherwise than on the ground of the twenty-three Principles:[2]

तद्बीजात्संसृतिः ॥ ३ ॥

Mundane existence whence.

Aph. 3. From the seed thereof is mundane existence.

a. 'Thereof,' i.e., of the Body; 'from the seed,' i.e., from the Subtile one, as its cause, in the shape of the twenty-three Principles, is 'mundane existence,' i.e., do the going and coming of Soul take place; for it is impossible that, of itself, there should be a going, &c., of that which, in virtue of [its] all-pervadingness, is immovable: such is the meaning. For Soul, being conditioned by the twenty-three Principles, only by means of that investment migrates from Body to Body, with a view to experiencing the fruits of previous works.[3]

---

[1] तस्मात्त्रयोविंशतितत्त्वात्स्थूलसूक्ष्मशरीरद्वयस्यारम्भ इत्यर्थः ॥

[2] संप्रति त्रयोविंशतितत्त्वं संसारान्यथानुपपत्तिं प्रमाणयति ॥

[3] तस्य शरीरस्य बीजात्त्रयोविंशतितत्त्वरूपात्सूक्ष्माद्धेतोः पुरुषस्य संसृतिर्गतागते भवतः कूटस्थस्य विभतया स्वतो गत्याद्यसंभवादित्यर्थः ।

b. He states, also, the limit of mundane existence:[1]

आविवेकाच्च प्रवर्तनमविशेषाणाम् ॥ ४ ॥

Mundane existence till when.

Aph. 4. And, till there is discrimination, there is the energizing of these, which have no differences.

a. The meaning is, that, of all Souls whatever, void of the differences of being Lord, or not Lord, &c., [though, seemingly, possessed of such differences,] 'energizing,' i.e., mundane existence, is inevitable, even till there is discrimination [of Soul from its seeming investments]; and it does not continue after that.[2]

b. He states the reason of this:[3]

उपभोगादितरस्य ॥ ५ ॥

The reason of this.

Aph. 5. Because of [the necessity of] the other's experiencing.

a. The meaning is: because of the necessity that the

त्रयोविंशतितत्त्वेऽवस्थितो हि पुरुषस्तेनैवोपाधिना पुर्वकृतकर्मभोगार्थं देहाद्देहं संसरति ॥

[1] संसृतेरवधिमप्याह ॥

[2] ईश्वरानीश्वरत्वादिविशेषरहितानां सर्वेषामेव पुंसां विवेकपर्यन्तमेव प्रवर्तनं संसृतिरावश्यकी विवेकोत्तरं च न सेत्यर्थः ॥

[3] तत्र हेतुमाह ॥

other, i.e., that that very [Soul], which does not discriminate, should experience the fruit of its own [reputed] acts.[1]

b. He states, that, even while there is a Body, during the time of mundane existence, fruition [really] is not:[2]

संप्रति परिमुक्तो[3] द्वाभ्याम् ॥ ६ ॥

Soul's bondage only seeming.

Aph. 6. It [Soul,] is now quite free from both.

a. 'Now,' i.e., during the time of mundane existence, Soul is quite free 'from both,' i.e., from the pairs, viz., cold and heat, pleasure and pain, &c.: such is the meaning.[4]

b. He next proceeds to describe, separately, the dyad of Bodies:[5]

मातापितृजं स्थूलं प्रायश इतरन्न तथा ॥ ७ ॥

The Gross and the Subtile Bodies distinguished.

Aph. 7. The Gross [Body] usually arises from father and mother; the other one is not so.

---

[1] इतरस्याविवेकिन एव स्वीयकर्मफलभोगाव-श्यंभावादित्यर्थः ॥

[2] देहसत्त्वेऽपि संसृतिकाले भोगो नास्तीत्याह ॥

[3] Aniruddha has परिष्वक्तो, and comments accordingly. *Ed.*

[4] संप्रति संसृतिकाले पुरुषो द्वाभ्यां शीतोष्ण-सुखदुःखादिद्वन्द्वैः परिमुक्तो भवतीत्यर्थः ॥

[5] अतः परं शरीरद्वयं विशिष्य वक्तुमुपक्रमते ॥

a. The Gross one arises from father and mother, 'usually,' i.e., for the most part; for there is mention also of a Gross Body *not* born of a womb: and 'the other,' i.e., the Subtile Body, is 'not so,' i.e., does not arise from a father and mother; because *it* arises from creation, &c.: such is the meaning.[1]

b. He decides [the question], through disguise by which one of the Bodies, Gross and Subtile, the conjunction of the pairs [pleasure and pain, &c.,] with Soul takes place.[2]

पूर्वोत्पत्तेस्तत्कार्यत्वं भोगादेकस्य नेतरस्य ॥ ८ ॥

Which of the bodies is the cause of Soul's bondage.

Aph. 8. To that which arose antecedently it belongs to be that whose result is this; because it is to the one that there belongs fruition, not to the other.

a. 'To be that whose result is this,' i.e., to have pleasure and pain as its effect [reflected in Soul], belongs to that Subtile Body alone whose origin was 'antecedent,' i.e., at the commencement of the creation [or annus magnus]. Why? Because the fruition of what is called pleasure and pain belongs only to 'the one,' i.e., the Subtile Body, but not to 'the other,' i.e., the Gross Body; because all are

---

[1] स्थूलं मातापितृजं प्रायशो बाहुल्येनायोनिजस्यापि स्थूलशरीरस्य स्मरणादितरच्च सूक्ष्मशरीरं न तथा न मातापितृजं सर्गाद्युत्पन्नत्वादित्यर्थः ॥

[2] स्थूलसूक्ष्मशरीरयोर्मध्ये किमुपाधिकः पुरुषस्य द्वन्द्वयोगस्तदवधारयति ॥

agreed that there is neither pleasure nor pain, &c., in a body of *earth*: such is the meaning.[1]

b. He tells the nature of the Subtile Body just mentioned:[2]

सप्तदशैकं लिङ्गम् ॥ ९ ॥

The Subtile Body how constituted.

Aph. 9. The seventeen, as one, are the Subtile Body.

a. The Subtile Body, further, through its being container and contained, is twofold. Here the seventeen, [presently mentioned,] mingled, are the Subtile Body; and that, at the beginning of a creation, is but one, in the shape of an aggregate; [as the forest, the aggregate of many trees, is but one]: such is the meaning. The seventeen are the eleven organs, the five Subtile Elements, and Understanding. Self-consciousness is included under Understanding.[3]

---

[1] पूर्वं सर्गादावुत्पत्तिर्यस्य लिङ्गशरीरस्य तस्यैव तत्कार्यत्वं सुखदुःखकार्यकत्वम्। कुतः। एकस्य लिङ्गदेहस्यैव सुखदुःखाद्युपभोगान्वितरस्य स्थूलशरीरस्य मृतशरीरे सुखदुःखाद्यभावस्य सर्वसंमतत्वादित्यर्थः ॥

[2] उक्तस्य सूक्ष्मशरीरस्य स्वरूपमाह ॥

[3] सूक्ष्मशरीरमप्याधाराधेयभावेन द्विविधं भवति। तत्र सप्तदश मिलित्वा लिङ्गशरीरं तच्च सर्गादौ समष्टिरूपमेकमेव भवतीत्यर्थः। एकादशेन्द्रियाणि पञ्च तन्मात्राणि बुद्धिश्चेति सप्तदश। अहंकारस्य बुद्धावेवान्तर्भावः ॥

b. But [one may ask,] if the Subtile Body be *one*, how can there be diverse experiences accordingly as Souls are [numerically] distinct, [one from another]? To this he replies:[1]

व्यक्तिभेदः कर्मविशेषात् ॥ १० ॥

How there come to be individuals.

Aph. 10. There is distinction of individuals, through diversity of desert.

a. Although, at the beginning of the creation [or annus magnus], there was but one Subtile Body, in the shape of that investment [of Soul (see *Vedánta-sára*, § 62,) named] *Hiranyagarbha*, still, subsequently, moreover, there becomes a division of it into individuals,—a plurality, partitively, in the shape of individuals;—as, at present, there is, of the one Subtile Body of a father, a plurality, partitively, in the shape of the Subtile Body of son, daughter, &c. He tells the cause of this, saying, 'through diversity of desert;' meaning, through actions, &c., which are causes of the experiences of other animal souls.[2 3]

---

[1] ननु लिङ्गं चेदेकं तर्हि कथं पुरुषभेदेन विलक्षणा भोगाः स्युः । तत्राह ॥

[2] यद्यपि सर्गादौ हिरण्यगर्भोपाधिरूपमेकमेव लिङ्गं तथापि तस्य पश्चाद्व्यक्तिभेदो व्यक्तिरूपेणांशतो नानात्वमपि भवति यथेदानीमेकस्य पितृलिङ्गदेहस्य नानात्वमंशतो भवति पुत्रकन्यादिलिङ्गदेहरूपेण । तत्र कारणमाह कर्मविशेषादिति जीवान्तराणां भोगहेतुकर्मादेरित्यर्थः ॥

[3] See, for another rendering, the *Rational Refutation*, &c., p. 36. *Ed.*

b. But then, on this showing, since the Subtile one alone, from its being the site of fruition, is [what ought to be denoted by the term] *Body*, how is the term Body applied to the Gross one? To this he replies:[1]

तदधिष्ठानाश्रये देहे तद्वादात्तद्वादः ॥ ११ ॥

Why the Gross Body is called a Body.

Aph. 11. From its being applied to *it*, [viz., to the Subtile one], it is applied to the Body, which is the tabernacle of the abiding thereof.

a. But then, what proof is there of another body,—other than the one consisting of the six sheaths,—serving as a tabernacle for the Subtile Body? With reference to this, he says:[2]

न स्वातन्त्र्यात्तदृते छायावच्चित्रवच्च ॥ १२ ॥

The Subtile Body dependent on the Gross Body.

Aph. 12. Not independently [can the Subtile Body exist], without that [Gross Body]; just like a shadow and a picture.

a. That is to say: the Subtile Body does not stand independently, 'without that,' i. e., without a support; as a shadow, or as a picture, does not stand without a support. And so, having abandoned a Gross Body, in order to go

---

[1] नन्वेवं भोगायतनतया लिङ्गस्यैव शरीरत्वे स्थूले कथं शरीरव्यवहारः । तत्राह ॥

[2] ननु षाट्कौशिकातिरिक्ते लिङ्गशरीराधिष्ठानभूते शरीरान्तरे किं प्रमाणमित्याकाङ्क्षायामाह ॥

to another world, it is settled that the Subtile Body takes another body, to serve as its tabernacle: such is the import.[1]

b. But then [it may be said], of the Subtile Body, since it is limited substance, as the Air, or the like, let the *Ether* [or *Space*], without [its] being attached [to anything], be the site: it is purposeless to suppose [its] attachment to anything else. To this he replies:[2]

मूर्त्तत्वेपि न सङ्घातयोगात्तरणिवत् ॥ १३ ॥

For it must have a material support.

Aph. 13. No, even though it be limited; because of [its] association with masses; just like the sun.

a. Though it be limited, it does not abide independently, without association; for, since, just like the sun, it consists of *light*, it is inferred to be associated with a mass: such is the meaning. All lights, the sun and the rest, are seen only under the circumstances of association [of the luminiferous imponderable] with earthy substances; and the Subtile Body

---

[1] तल्लिङ्गशरीरं तदृतेऽधिष्ठानं विना स्वातन्त्र्यान्न तिष्ठति यथा छाया निराधारा न तिष्ठति यथा वा चित्रमित्यर्थः । तथा च स्थूलदेहं त्यक्त्वा लोकान्तरगमनाय लिङ्गदेहस्याधारभूतं शरीरान्तरं सिध्यतीति भावः ॥

[2] ननु मूर्तद्रव्यतया वाय्वादेरिव लिङ्गस्याकाशमेवासङ्गेनाधारोऽस्तु व्यर्थमन्यत्र सङ्गकल्पनमिति । तत्राह ॥

consists of 'Purity,' which is Light: therefore it must be associated with the Elements.[1]

b. He determines the magnitude of the Subtile Body:[2]

अणुपरिमाणं तत्कृतिश्रुतेः[3] ॥ १४ ॥

Size of the Subtile Body. *Aph.* 14. It is of atomic magnitude; for there is a Scripture for its acting.

a. 'It,' the Subtile Body, is 'of atomic magnitude,' i. e., limited, but not absolutely an *atom;* because it is declared to have parts. Wherefore? 'For there is Scripture for its acting;' i. e., because there is Scripture about its acting. When a thing is all-prevading, it cannot act; [action being motion]. But the proper reading is, 'because there is Scripture for its *moving*.'[4]

---

[1] मूर्तत्वेऽपि न स्वातन्त्र्यादसङ्गतयावस्थानं प्रकाशरूपत्वेन सूर्यस्येव सङ्घातसङ्गानुमानादित्यर्थः। सूर्यादीनि सर्वाणि तेजांसि पार्थिवद्रव्यसङ्गेनैवावस्थितानि दृश्यन्ते लिङ्गं च सत्त्वप्रकाशमयम्। अतो भूतसङ्गतमिति ॥

[2] लिङ्गस्य परिमाणमवधारयति ॥

[3] The reading तद्गतिश्रुतेः, on which Vijnána remarks, is accepted by Nágeśa.

Aniruddha is singular in here inserting, as an Aphorism: न्यायश्चान्यत्र प्रपञ्चित इति। *Ed.*

[4] तल्लिङ्गमणुपरिमाणं परिच्छिन्नं नत्वत्यन्तमे-

b. He states another argument for its being limited:[1]

[2]तदन्नमयत्वश्रुतेश्च[3] ॥ १५ ॥

Another proof of this. *Aph.* 15. And because there is Scripture for its being formed of food.

a. That is to say: it, viz., the Subtile Body, cannot be all-pervading; because there is a Scripture for its being partially formed of food; for, if it were all-prevading, it would be eternal. Although Mind, &c., are not formed of the Elements, still it is to be understood that they are spoken of as formed of food, &c.; because they are filled with homogeneous particles, through contact with food;[4] [as the light of a lamp is supplied by contact with the oil].

b. For what purpose is the mundane existence, the migrating from one body to another [Gross] body, of Sub-

---

वाणु सावयवत्वस्योक्तत्वात् । कुतः । कृतिश्रुतेः क्रियाश्रुतेः । विभुत्वे सति क्रिया न संभवति । तद्गतिश्रुतेरिति पाठस्तु समीचीनः ॥

[1] परिच्छिन्नत्वे युक्त्यन्तरमाह ॥

[2] Nágeśa has the reading अन्न° . *Ed.*

[3] Aniruddha and Nágeśa omit the word च . *Ed.*

[4] तस्य लिङ्गस्यैकदेशतोऽन्नमयत्वश्रुतेर्न विभुत्वं संभवतीति विभुत्वे सति नित्यतापत्तेरित्यर्थः । यद्यपि मनआदीनि न भौतिकानि तथाप्यन्नसंसृष्टसजातीयांशपूरणादन्नमयत्वादिव्यवहारो बोध्यः ॥

tile Bodies, which are *unintelligent?* With reference to this, he says:[1]

पुरुषार्थं संसृतिर्लिङ्गानां सूपकारवद्राज्ञः ॥ १६ ॥

Why the Subtile Body migrates.

Aph. 16. The mundane existence of Subtile Bodies is for the sake of Soul; just like a king's cooks.

a. That is to say: as the cooks of a king frequent the kitchens for the sake of the king, so the Subtile Bodies transmigrate for the sake of Soul.[2]

b. The Subtile Body has been discussed in respect of all its peculiarities. He now likewise discusses the Gross Body, also:[3]

पाञ्चभौतिको देहः ॥ १७ ॥

The Gross Body whence.

Aph. 17. The Body consists of the five elements.

---

[1] अचेतनानां लिङ्गानां किमर्थं संसृतिर्देहाद्देहान्तरसंचार इत्याशङ्कायामाह ॥

[2] यथा राज्ञः सूपकाराणां पाकशालासु संचारो राजार्थं तथा लिङ्गशरीराणां संसृतिः पुरुषार्थमित्यर्थः ॥

[3] लिङ्गशरीरमशेषविशेषतो विचारितम् । इदानीं स्थूलशरीरमपि तथा विचारयति ॥

a. That is to say: the Body is a modification of the five elements mingled.[1]

b. He mentions another opinion:[2]

चातुर्भौतिकमित्येके ॥ १८ ॥

Another opinion. *Aph.* 18. Some say it consists of *four* elements.

a. This [is alleged] with the import that the *Ether* does not originate[3] [anything].

ऐकभौतिकमित्यपरे[4] ॥ १९ ॥

Another opinion. *Aph.* 19. Others say that it consists of *one* element.

a. The import is, that the body is of Earth only, and the other elements are merely supporters. Or 'of one element' means, of one or other element:[5] [see the Rosicrucian doctrine in the *Tarka-sangraha*, § 13., &c].

---

[1] पञ्चानां भूतानां मिलितानां परिणामो देह इत्यर्थः ॥

[2] मतान्तरमाह ॥

[3] आकाशस्यानारम्भकत्वमभिप्रेत्येदम् ॥

[4] One of my MSS. of Aniruddha omits the word इति. *Ed.*

[5] पार्थिवमेव शरीरमन्यानि च भूतान्युपष्टम्भकमात्राणीति भावः । अथ वैकभौतिकमेकैकभौतिकमित्यर्थः ॥

b. He tells us what is proved by the fact that the Body consists of the Elements:[1]

न सांसिद्धिकं चैतन्यं प्रत्येकादृष्टेः ॥ २० ॥

Intellect not the result of organization.

Aph. 20. Intellect is not natural [a natural result of organization]; because it is not found in them severally.

a. That is to say: since we do not find intellect in the separated Elements, intellect is not natural to the Body,—which consists of the Elements,—but is adventitious.[2]

b. He states another refutation[3] [of the notion that Intellect is a property of the Body]:

प्रपञ्चमरणाद्यभावश्च ॥ २१ ॥

A further argument.

Aph. 21. And [if the Body had intellect natural to it,] there would not be the death, &c., of anything.

a. That is to say: and, if the Body had intellect natural to it, there would not be the death, the profound sleep, &c., 'of anything,' of all things. For death, profound sleep, &c., imply the body's being non-intelligent; and this, if it were, by its own nature, intelligent, would not take

---

[1] देहस्य भौतिकत्वेन यत्सिध्यति तदाह ॥

[2] भूतेषु पृथक्कृतेषु चैतन्यादर्शनाद्भौतिकस्य देहस्य न स्वाभाविकं चैतन्यं किं त्वौपाधिकमित्यर्थः ॥

[3] बाधकान्तरमाह ॥

place; because the essential nature of a thing remains as long as the thing remains.[1]

b. Pondering a doubt, as to the assertion [in § 20], viz., 'because it is not found in them severally,' he repels it:[2]

मदशक्तिवच्चेत्प्रत्येकपरिदृष्टे सांहत्ये[3] तदुद्भवः ॥ २२ ॥

An illustrative objection disposed of.

Aph. 22. If [you say that Intellect results from organization, and that] it is like the power of something intoxicating, [the ingredients of which, separately, have no intoxicating power, we reply, that] this might arise, on conjunction, if we had seen, in each [element, something conducive to the result].

a. But then, as an intoxicating power, though not residing in the substances severally, resides in the mixed substance, so may Intellect, also, be; if any one say this, it is not so. If it *had been* seen in each [constituent], its appearance in the compound might have had place; but, in the case in question, it is not the case that it is seen in each.

---

[1] प्रपञ्चस्य सर्वस्यैव मरणसुषुप्त्याद्यभावश्च देहस्य स्वाभाविकचैतन्ये सति स्यादित्यर्थः । मरणसुषुप्त्यादिकं हि देहस्याचेतनता सा च स्वाभाविकचैतन्ये सति नोपपद्यते स्वभावस्य यावद्द्रव्यभावित्वादिति ॥

[2] प्रत्येकादृष्टेरिति यदुक्तं तच्चाशङ्क्य परिहरति ॥

[3] Aniruddha and Vedánti Mahádeva read सौक्ष्म्यात्सांहत्ये. *Ed.*

Therefore, in the illustration [of something intoxicating resulting from mixture], it being established, by the Institutes, &c., that there is, in each ingredient, a *subtile* tendency to intoxicate, it is settled only that, at the time when these combine, there will be a *manifestation* of the [latent] power of intoxicating; but, in the thing illustrated, it is not established, by any proof whatsoever, that there is intelligence, in a subtile [or undeveloped] state, in the elements separately: such is the meaning.[1]

b. It was stated [§ 16,] that the Subtile Bodies transmigrate for the sake of Soul. In regard to this, he tells, in two aphorisms, by what operation, dependent on the birth of the Subtile Bodies, which means their transmigrations into Gross Bodies, what aims of Soul are accomplished:[2]

---

[1] ननु यथा मादकता शक्तिः प्रत्येकद्रव्यावृत्तिरपि मिलितद्रव्ये वर्तत एवं चैतन्यमपि स्यादिति चेन्न। प्रत्येकपरिदृष्टे सति सांहत्ये तदुद्भवः संभवेत्प्रकृते तु प्रत्येकपरिदृष्टत्वं नास्ति। अतो दृष्टान्ते प्रत्येकं शास्त्रादिभिः सूक्ष्मतया मादकत्वे सिद्धे संहतभावकाले मादकत्वाविर्भावमात्रं सिध्यति दार्ष्टान्तिके तु प्रत्येकभूतेषु सूक्ष्मतया न केनापि प्रमाणेन चैतन्यं सिद्धमित्यर्थः॥

[2] पुरुषार्थं संसृतिर्लिङ्गानामित्युक्तम्। तत्र लिङ्गानां स्थूलदेहसंचाराख्यजन्मना यो यः पुरुषार्थो येन येन व्यापारेण सिध्यति तदाह सूत्राभ्याम्॥

ज्ञानान्मुक्तिः ॥ २३ ॥

Purpose of the Subtile Body's taking a gross one.

Aph. 23. From knowledge [acquired during mundane existence, comes] salvation, [Soul's *chief* end].

a. That is to say: by the transmigration of the Subtile Body, through birth, there takes place the direct operation of discrimination [between Soul and Non-Soul]; [and] thence, in the shape of emancipation, Soul's [chief] End.[1]

बन्धो विपर्ययात् ॥ २४ ॥

Bondage whence.

Aph. 24. Bondage [which may be viewed as one of the ends which Soul could arrive at only through the Subtile Body,] is from Misconception.

a. Through the transmigration of the subtile body, from misconception, there is that [less worthy] end of soul, in the shape of bondage, consisting of pleasure and pain: such is the meaning.[2]

b. Liberation and Bondage, [resulting] from knowledge and misconception [respectively], have been mentioned. Of these, in the first place, he explains Liberation [arising] from knowledge:[3]

---

[1] लिङ्गसंसृतितो जन्मद्वारा विवेकसाक्षात्कारस्तस्मान्मुक्तिरूपः पुरुषार्थो भवतीत्यर्थः ॥

[2] विपर्ययात्सुखदुःखात्मको बन्धरूपः पुरुषार्थो लिङ्गसंसृतितो भवतीत्यर्थः ॥

[3] ज्ञानविपर्ययाभ्यां मुक्तिबन्धावुक्तौ । तत्रादौ ज्ञानान्मुक्तिं विचारयति ॥

नियतकारणत्वान्न समुच्चयविकल्पौ ॥ २५ ॥

Knowledge has neither cooperator nor substitute, in liberating Soul.

Aph. 25. Since this [viz., knowledge,] is the precise cause [of liberation], there is neither association [of anything else with it, e. g., good works,] nor alternativeness, [e. g., of good works, in its stead].

a. In respect of there being neither association nor alternativeness, he states an illustration :[1]

स्वप्नजागराभ्यामिव मायिकामायिकाभ्यां नोभयोर्मुक्तिः पुरुषस्य ॥ २६ ॥

This illustrated.

Aph. 26. The emancipation of Soul does not depend on both [knowledge and works, or the like]; as [any end that one aims at is not obtained] from dreams and from the waking state, [together, or alternatively, which are, severally,] illusory and not illusory.

a. But, even if it be so, [some one may say,] there may be association, or alternativeness, of knowledge of the truth with that knowledge which is termed Worship of [the One, all-constitutive, divine] Soul; since there is no *illusoriness* in *this* object of Worship. To this he replies :[2]

---

[1] समुच्चयविकल्पयोरभावे दृष्टान्तमाह ॥

[2] नन्वेवमप्यात्मोपासनाख्यज्ञानेन सह तत्त्वज्ञानस्य समुच्चयविकल्पौ स्यातामुपास्यस्यामायिकत्वादिति तत्राह ॥

इतरस्यापि नात्यन्तिकम् ॥ २७ ॥

Man's conception of the All is faulty.

Aph. 27. Even of that other it is not complete.

a. Even of 'that other,' i.e., of the [just-mentioned] object of worship, the non-illusoriness is not complete; because imaginary things, also, enter into [our conception of, and overlie, and disguise,] the object of worship, the [One, all-constitutive] Soul: such is the meaning.[1]

b. He states in what *part* [of it] is the illusoriness of the [object of] Worship,[2] [just referred to]:

संकल्पितेऽप्येवम् ॥ २८ ॥

Where the fault applies.

Aph. 28. Moreover, it is in what is *fancied* that it is thus [illusory].

a. That is to say: 'moreover, it is thus,' i.e., moreover, there is illusoriness, in that portion of the thing meditated which [portion of it] is fancied by the Mind, [while it does not exist in reality]; for, the object of worship having been declared in such texts as, 'All this, indeed, is Brahma,'[3] the illusoriness belongs entirely to that portion [of the impure conception of 'the All' which presents itself, to the undiscriminating, under the aspect] of the world.[4]

---

[1] इतरस्याप्युपास्यस्य नात्यन्तिकममायिकत्वमुपास्यात्मन्यध्यस्तपदार्थानामपि प्रवेशादित्यर्थः ॥

[2] उपासनस्य मायिकत्वं यस्मिन्नंशे तदाह ॥

[3] *Chhándogya Upanishad*, iii., xiv., 1. *Ed.*

[4] मनःसंकल्पिते ध्येयांश एवमपि मायिकत्व-

b. Then what profit is there in Worship? With reference to this, he declares [as follows]:[1]

भावनोपचयाच्छुद्धस्य सर्वं प्रकृतिवत् ॥ २९ ॥

The fruit of Worship. *Aph.* 29. From the achievement of [the worship termed] meditation there is, to the pure [Soul], all [power]; like Nature.

a. Through the effecting of the worship which is termed meditation, there becomes, to the 'pure,' i. e., the sinless, Soul, all power; as belongs to Nature: such is the meaning. That is to say: as Nature creates, sustains, and destroys, so also the Purity of the understanding of the worshipper, by instigating Nature, creates, &c.[2] [But this is not Liberation, or Soul's chief end.]

b. It has been settled that Knowledge alone is the means of Liberation. Now he mentions the *means* of Knowledge:[3]

मपीत्यर्थः। सर्वं खल्विदं ब्रह्मेत्यादिश्रुत्युक्ते ह्युपास्ये प्रपञ्चांशस्य मायिकत्वमेवेति ॥

[1] तर्ह्युपासनस्य किं फलमित्याकाङ्क्षायामाह ॥

[2] भावनाख्योपासनानिष्पत्त्या शुद्धस्य निष्पापस्य पुरुषस्य प्रकृतेरिव सर्वमैश्वर्यं भवतीत्यर्थः। प्रकृतिर्यथा सृष्टिस्थितिसंहारं करोत्येवमुपासकस्य बुद्धिसत्त्वमपि प्रकृतिप्रेरणेन सृष्ट्यादिकर्तृ भवतीति ॥

[3] ज्ञानमेव मोक्षसाधनमिति स्थापितम्। इदानीं ज्ञानसाधनान्याह ॥

रागोपहतिर्ध्यानम् ॥ ३० ॥

Removal of obstacles to knowledge.

Aph. 30. Meditation is [the cause of] the removal of Desire.

a. That is to say: Meditation is the cause of the removal of that affection of the mind by objects, which is a hinderer of knowledge.[1]

b. With advertence to the fact that knowledge arises from the effectuation of Meditation, and not from merely commencing upon it, he characterizes the effectuation of Meditation:[2]

वृत्तिनिरोधात्तत्सिद्धिः ॥ ३१ ॥

Meditation at what point perfected.

Aph. 31. It [Meditation,] is perfected by the repelling of the modifications [of the Mind, which ought to be abstracted from all thoughts of anything].

a. He mentions also the means of Meditation:[3]

धारणासनस्वकर्मणा तत्सिद्धिः ॥ ३२ ॥

Practices conducive to meditation.

Aph. 32. This [Meditation,] is perfected by Restraint, Postures, and one's Duties.

---

[1] ज्ञानप्रतिबन्धको यो विषयोपरागश्चित्तस्य तदुपघातहेतुर्ध्यानमित्यर्थः ॥

[2] ध्याननिष्पत्त्यैव ज्ञानोत्पत्तिर्नारम्भमात्रेणेत्याशयेन ध्याननिष्पत्तेर्लक्षणमाह ॥

[3] ध्यानस्यापि साधनान्याह ॥

a. That is to say: Meditation results from the triad, which shall be mentioned, viz., Restraint, &c.[1]

b. By means of a triad of aphorisms he characterizes, in order, Restraint, &c.:[2]

निरोधश्छर्दिविधारणाभ्याम् ॥ ३३ ॥[3]

Restraint of the breath. *Aph.* 33. Restraint [of the breath] is by means of expulsion and retention.

a. That it is 'of the breath' is gathered from the notoriousness[4] [of its being so].

b. He characterizes Postures, which come next in order:[5]

स्थिरसुखमासनम् ॥ ३४ ॥

Postures. *Aph.* 34. Steady and [promoting] ease is a [suitable] Posture.

a. That is to say: that is a Posture which, being steady, is a cause of pleasure; such as the crossing of the arms.[6]

---

[1] वक्ष्यमाणेन धारणादित्रयेण ध्यानं भवतीत्यर्थः ॥

[2] धारणादित्रयं क्रमात्सूत्रत्रयेण लक्षयति ॥

[3] Aniruddha and Vedánti Mahádeva transpose Aphorisms 33 and 34. *Ed.*

[4] प्राणस्येति प्रसिद्ध्या लभ्यते ॥

[5] क्रमप्राप्तमासनं लक्षयति ॥

[6] यत्स्थिरं सत्सुखसाधनं भवति स्वस्तिकादि तदासनमित्यर्थः ॥

b. He characterizes one's Duty:[1]

स्वकर्म स्वाश्रमविहितकर्मानुष्ठानम् ॥ ३५ ॥

One's duty. *Aph.* 35. One's Duty is the performance of the actions prescribed for one's religious order.

a. Simple.[2]

वैराग्यादभ्यासाच्च ॥ ३६ ॥

Knowledge by Concentration how attained. *Aph.* 36. Through Dispassion and Practice.

a. Simply through mere Practice, in the shape of Meditation, accompanied by Dispassion, Knowledge, with its instrument, Concentration, takes place in the case of those who are most competent [to engage in the matter]: such is the meaning. Thus has liberation through knowledge been expounded.[3]

b. After this, the cause of Bondage, viz., Misconception, declared in [the assertion,] 'Bondage is from Misconception,' [§ 24], is to be expounded. Here he first states the nature of Misconception:[4]

---

[1] स्वकर्म लक्षयति ॥

[2] सुगमम् ॥

[3] केवलाभ्यासाद्ध्यानरूपादेव वैराग्यसहिताज्ज्ञानं तत्साधनयोगश्च भवत्युत्तमाधिकारिणामित्यर्थः । तदेवं ज्ञानान्मोक्षो व्याख्यातः ॥

[4] अतः परं बन्धो विपर्ययादित्युक्तो बन्धकारणं

विपर्ययभेदाः पञ्च ॥ ३७ ॥

Misconception divided. *Aph.* 37. The kinds of Misconception are five.

a. That is to say: the subdivisions of Misconception, which is the cause of Bondage, are Ignorance, Egoism, Desire, Aversion, and Fear of Dissolution; the five mentioned in the *Yoga*,[1] [see *Yoga Aphorisms*, Book II., § 3[2]].

b. Having stated the nature of Misconception, he states also the nature of its cause, viz., Disability:[3]

अशक्तिरष्टाविंशतिधा तु[4] ॥ ३८ ॥

The varieties of Disability. *Aph.* 38. But Disability is of twenty-eight sorts.[5]

a. Simple;[6] [as explained in the *Yoga*].

विपर्ययो व्याख्यास्यते। तत्रादौ विपर्ययस्य स्वरूपमाह ॥

[1] अविद्यास्मितारागद्वेषाभिनिवेशाः पञ्च योगोक्ता बन्धहेतुविपर्ययस्यावान्तरभेदा इत्यर्थः ॥

[2] The five are there called 'afflictions' (*kleśa*). *Ed.*

[3] विपर्ययस्य स्वरूपमुक्त्वा तत्कारणस्याशक्तेरपि स्वरूपमाह ॥

[4] This word is omitted by Aniruddha and by Vedánti Mahádeva. *Ed.*

[5] See, for these, Dr. Ballantyne's edition of the *Tattwa-samása*, § 63. *Ed.*

[6] सुगमम् ॥

b. In a couple of aphorisms he mentions [those] two, Acquiescence and Perfection, on the prevention of which come two sorts of Disability of the Understanding:[1]

तुष्टिर्नवधा ॥ ३९ ॥

Acquiescence. *Aph.* 39. Acquiescence is of nine sorts.

a. He will, himself, explain how it is of nine sorts.[2]

सिद्धिरष्टधा ॥ ४० ॥

Perfections. *Aph.* 40. Perfection is of eight sorts.

a. This, also, he will, himself, explain.[3]

b. Of the aforesaid, viz., Misconception, Disability, Acquiescence, and Perfection, since there may be a desire to know the particulars, there is, in order, a quaternion of aphorisms:[4]

अवान्तरभेदाः पूर्ववत् ॥ ४१ ॥

---

[1] ययोर्विघाते बुद्धेरशक्ती ते तुष्टिसिद्धी सूत्रद्वयेनाह ॥

[2] स्वयमेव नवधात्वं वक्ष्यति ॥

[3] एतदपि स्वयं वक्ष्यति ॥

[4] उक्तानां विपर्ययाशक्तितुष्टिसिद्धीनां विशेषजिज्ञासायां क्रमेण सूत्रचतुष्टयं प्रवर्तते ॥

Their subdivisions.

Aph. 41. The subdivisions [of Misconception] are as [declared] aforetime.

a. The subdivisions of Misconception, which, in a general way, have been stated as five, are to be understood to be particularized 'as aforetime,' i. e., just as they have been declared by preceding teachers: they are not explained here, for fear of prolixity: such is the meaning.[1]

एवमितरस्याः ॥ ४२ ॥

Of this further.

Aph. 42. So of the other [viz., Disability].

a. That is to say: 'so,' i. e., just as aforetime [§ 41], the divisions 'of the other,' viz., of Disability, also, which are twenty-eight, are to be understood, as regards their particularities.[2]

आध्यात्मिकादिभेदान्नवधा तुष्टिः ॥ ४३ ॥

Acquiescence divided.

Aph. 43. Acquiescence is ninefold, through the distinctions of 'the internal and the rest.'

---

[1] विपर्ययस्यावान्तरभेदा ये सामान्यतः पञ्चोक्तास्ते पूर्ववत्पूर्वाचार्यैर्यथोक्तास्तथैव विशिष्यावधार्या विस्तरभयान्नेहोच्यन्त इत्यर्थः ॥

[2] एवं पूर्ववदेवेतरस्या अशक्तेरप्यवान्तरभेदा अष्टाविंशतिर्विशेषतोऽवगन्तव्या इत्यर्थः ॥

a. This aphorism is explained by a memorial verse,[1] [No. 50[2]].

ऊहादिभिः सिद्धिः ॥ ४४ ॥

Perfection divided. *Aph.* 44. Through Reasoning, &c., [which are its subdivisions,] Perfection [is eightfold].

a. That is to say: Perfection is of eight kinds, through its divisions, viz., Reasoning, &c. This aphorism, also, has been explained in a memorial verse,[3] [No 51[4]].

---

[1] इदं सूत्रं कारिकया व्याख्यातम् ॥

[2] Quoted below, from the *Sánkhya-káriká,* with Mr. John Davies's translation:

आध्यात्मिकाश्चतस्रः प्रकृत्युपादानकाल-
भाग्याख्याः ।
बाह्या विषयोपरमात्पञ्च नव तुष्टयोऽभि-
मताः ॥

'Nine varieties of acquiescence are set forth; four internal, named from Nature, means, time, and fortune; five external, relating to abstinence from objects of sense.' *Ed.*

[3] ऊहादिभेदैः सिद्धिरष्टधा भवतीत्यर्थः । इद-मपि सूत्रं कारिकया व्याख्यातम् ॥

[4] Here appended, with Mr. Davies's translation:

ऊहः शब्दोऽध्ययनं दुःखविघातास्त्रयः सुहृत्प्राप्तिः ।
दानं च सिद्धयोऽष्टौ सिद्धेः पूर्वोऽङ्कुशस्त्रिविधः ॥

'The eight perfections (or means of acquiring perfection) are reasoning (*úha*), word or oral instruction (*śabda*), study or reading (*adhya-*

b. But then, how is it said that Perfection consists only of 'Reasoning, &c.,' seeing that it is determined, in all the Institutes, that the eight Perfections, viz., [the capacity of assuming] atomic bulk, &c., result from recitations, austerity, meditation, &c.? To this he replies:[1]

नेतरादितरहानेन विना ॥ ४५ ॥

The enumeration defended.

Aph. 45. Not from any other [than what we have just stated does real Perfection arise; because what does arise therefrom, e.g., from austerities, is] without abandonment of something else, [viz., Misconception].

a. 'From any other,' i.e., from anything different from the pentad, 'Reasoning, &c.,' e.g., from Austerity, &c., there is no real Perfection. Why? 'Without abandonment of something else;' i.e., because *that* Perfection [which you choose to call such] takes place positively without abandonment of something else, i.e., of Misconception: therefore [*that* Perception], since it is no antagonist to mundane existence, is only a *semblance* of a Perfection, and not a real Perfection: such is the meaning.[2]

---

yana), the suppression of the three kinds of pain, acquisition of friends, and liberality (*dána*). The three fore-mentioned (conditions) are checks to perfection.' *Ed.*

[1] ननूहादिभिरेव कथं सिद्धिरुच्यते मन्त्रतपःसमाध्यादिभिरप्यणिमाद्यष्टसिद्धेः सर्वशास्त्रसिद्धत्वादिति तत्राह ॥

[2] इतरादूहनादिपञ्चकभिन्नात्तपआदेस्तात्त्विकी न सिद्धिः। कुतः। इतरहानेन विना यतः सा

b. Now the individuated creation, which was mentioned concisely in the assertion, 'There is distinction of individuals through diversity of desert,' [§ 10], is set forth diffusely :[1]

दैवादिप्रभेदा ॥ ४६ ॥

The creation viewed in its parts.

Aph. 46. [The creation is that] of which the subdivisions are the demons, &c.

a. Supply, such is that creation, of which 'the subdivisions,' the included divisions, are the demons, &c. This is explained in a memorial verse,[2] [No. 53[3]].

सिद्धिरितरस्य विपर्ययस्य हानं विनैव भवत्यतः संसारापरिपन्थित्वात्सा सिद्ध्याभास एव नतु तात्त्विकी सिद्धिरित्यर्थः ॥

[1] साम्प्रतं व्यक्तिभेदः कर्मविशेषादिति संक्षेपादुक्ता व्यष्टिसृष्टिर्विस्तरतः प्रतिपाद्यते ॥

[2] दैवादिः प्रभेदोऽवान्तरभेदो यस्याः सा तथा सृष्टिरिति शेषः । तदेतत्कारिकया व्याख्यातम् ॥

[3] It here follows, with the translation of Mr. Davies :

अष्टविकल्पो दैवस्तैर्यग्योनश्च पञ्चधा भवति ।
मानुष्यश्चैकविधः समासतो भौतिकः सर्गः ॥

'The divine class has eight varieties; the animal, five. Mankind is single in its class. This is, in summary, the world (*sarga*, emanation,) of living things.' *Ed.*

b. He states that the aforesaid subdivided creation, also, is for the sake of Soul :[1]

आब्रह्मस्तम्बपर्यन्तं तत्कृते सृष्टिराविवेकात् ॥ ४७ ॥

This creation, also, for Soul's sake. *Aph.* 47. From Brahmá down to a post, for its [Soul's,] sake is creation, till there be discrimination [between Soul and Nature].

a. He mentions, further, the division of the subdivided creation, in three aphorisms :[2]

ऊर्ध्वं सत्त्वविशाला ॥ ४८ ॥

The celestial world. *Aph.* 48. Aloft, it [the creation,] abounds in [the quality of] Purity.

a. That is to say: 'aloft,' above the world of mortals, the creation has chiefly [the Quality of] Purity.[3]

तमोविशाला मूलतः ॥ ४९ ॥

The infernal world. *Aph.* 49. Beneath, it [the creation,] abounds in Darkness.

a. 'Beneath,' that is to say, under the world of mortals.[4]

---

[1] अवान्तरसृष्टेरप्युक्तायाः पुरुषार्थत्वमाह ॥

[2] व्यष्टिसृष्टावपि विभागमाह सूत्रत्रयेण ॥

[3] ऊर्ध्वं भूर्लोकादुपरि सृष्टिः सत्त्वाधिका भवतीत्यर्थः ॥

[4] मूलतो भूर्लोकादध इत्यर्थः ॥

मध्ये रजोविशाला ॥ ५० ॥

The world of mortals.

Aph. 50. In the midst, it [the creation,] abounds in Passion.

a. 'In the midst,' that is to say, in the world of mortals.[1]

b. But then, for what reason are there, from one single Nature, creations diverse in having, affluently, purity and the rest? With reference to this, he says:[2]

कर्मवैचित्र्यात्प्रधानचेष्टा गर्भदासवत् ॥ ५१ ॥

Why Nature operates diversely.

Aph. 51. By reason of diversity of desert is Nature's [diverse] behaviour; like a born-slave.

a. Just by reason of diverse desert is the behaviour of Nature, as asserted, in the shape of diversity of operation. An illustration of the diversity is [offered in the example], 'like a born-slave.' That is to say: as, of him who is a slave from the embryo-state upwards, there are, through the aptitude arising from the habit[3] of being a dependant, various sorts of behaviour, i. e., of service, for the sake of his master, so[4] [does Nature serve Soul in various ways].

---

[1] मध्ये भूर्लोक इत्यर्थः ॥

[2] नन्वेकस्या एव प्रकृतेः केन निमित्तेन सत्त्वादिविशालतया विचित्राः सृष्टय इत्याकाङ्क्षायामाह ॥

[3] *Vásaná.* *Vide supra*, p. 29, note 2. *Ed.*

[4] विचित्रकर्मनिमित्तादेव यथोक्ता प्रधानस्य

b. But then, if the creation aloft is abundant in Purity [the element of joy], since Soul's object is really thereby effected, what need is there of *Liberation?* To this he replies:[1]

आवृत्तिस्तत्राप्युत्तरोत्तरयोनियोगाद्धेयः ॥ ५२ ॥

Why Heaven is to be shunned.

Aph. 52. Even there there is return [to miserable states of existence]: it is to be shunned, by reason of the successive subjections to birth, [from which the inhabitants of Heaven enjoy no immunity].

a. Moreover:[2]

समानं[3] जरामरणादिजं दुःखम्[4] ॥ ५३ ॥

Transitoriness of heavenly bliss.

Aph. 53. Alike [belongs to all] the sorrow produced by decay and death.

चेष्टा कार्यवैचित्र्यरूपा भवति। वैचित्र्ये दृष्टान्तो गर्भदासवदिति। यथा गर्भावस्थामारभ्य यो दासस्तस्य भृत्यवासनापाटवेन नानाप्रकारा चेष्टा परिचर्या स्वाम्यर्थं भवति तद्वदित्यर्थः ॥

1 ननु चेदूर्ध्वं सत्त्वविशाला सृष्टिरस्ति तर्हि तत एव कृतार्थत्वात्पुरुषस्य किं मोक्षेणेति। तत्राह ॥

2 किं च ॥

3 Vedánti Mahádeva has, instead of समानं, सर्वत्र. *Ed.*

4 Nágeśa, according to my sole MS., has जरामरणादिदुःखम्. *Ed.*

a. Common to all alike, those that are aloft and those beneath, beginning with Brahmá and ending with a stock, is the 'sorrow produced by decay and death'; therefore, moreover, it [heaven,] is to be shunned: such is the meaning.[1]

b. What need of more? The end is not effected by absorption into the cause, either; as he tells us:[2]

न कारणलयात्कृतकृत्यता मग्नवदुत्थानात् ॥ ५४ ॥

Absorption into Nature ineffectual.

Aph. 54. Not by absorption into the cause is there accomplishment of the end; because, as in the case of one who has dived, there is a rising again.

a. In the absence of knowledge of the distinction [between Soul and Nature], when indifference towards Mind, &c., has resulted from worship of Nature, then absorption into Nature takes place; for it is declared: 'Through Dispassion there is absorption into Nature.' Even through this, i.e., the absorption into the cause, the end is not gained; 'because there is a rising again; as in the case of one who has dived.' As a man who has dived under water rises again, exactly so do Souls which have been absorbed into Nature reappear, [at the commencement of a new annus magnus], in the condition of Lords; because it is

---

[1] ऊर्ध्वाधोगतानां ब्रह्मादिस्थावरान्तानां सर्वेषामेव जरामरणादिजं दुःखं साधारणमतोऽपि हेय इत्यर्थः ॥

[2] किं बहुना । कारणे लयादपि न कृतकृत्यतेत्याह ॥

impossible that one's Faults should be consumed, without a familiarity with the distinction [between Soul and Nature], in consequence of the reappearance of Passion, by reason of the non-destruction of habits,[1] &c.: such is the meaning.[2]

b. But then, the cause is not by any one caused to act. Being independent, then, why does she [Nature,] make that grief-occasioning resurrection of her own worshipper? To this he replies:[3]

अकार्यत्वेऽपि तद्योगः पारवश्यात् ॥ ५५ ॥

Nature free to act, yet guided by an end.

Aph. 55. Though she be not constrained to act, yet this is fitting; because of her being devoted to another.

---

1 To render *sanskāra*. *Ed.*

2 विवेकज्ञानाभावे यदा महदादिषु वैराग्यं प्रकृत्युपासनया भवति तदा प्रकृतौ लयो भवति वैराग्यात्प्रकृतिलय इति वचनात्। तस्मात्कारणलयादपि न कृतकृत्यतास्ति मग्नवदुत्थानात्। यथा जले मग्नः पुरुषः पुनरुत्तिष्ठत्येवमेव प्रकृतिलीनाः पुरुषा ईश्वरभावेन पुनराविर्भवन्ति संस्कारादेरक्षयेण पुना रागाभिव्यक्तेर्विवेकख्यातिं विना दोषदाहानुपपत्तेरित्यर्थः ॥

3 ननु कारणं केनापि न कार्यते। अतः सा स्वतन्त्रा कथं स्वोपासकस्य दुःखनिदानमुत्थानं पुनः करोति। तत्राह ॥

a. Though Nature is 'not constrained to act,' not instigated, not subject to the will of another, yet 'this is fitting;' it is proper that he who is absorbed in her should rise again. Why? 'Because of her being devoted to another;' i. e., because she seeks Soul's end. The meaning is, that he who is absorbed in her is again raised up, by Nature, for the sake of Soul's end, which consists in knowledge of the distinction [between Nature and Soul]. And Soul's end, and the like, are not *constrainers* of Nature, but occasions for the energizing of her whose very being is to energize; so that there is nothing detracted from her independence.[1]

b. He mentions, further, a proof that Soul rises from absorption into Nature:[2]

स हि सर्ववित्सर्वकर्ता ॥ ५६ ॥

The gain of absorption into Nature.

Aph. 56. [He who is absorbed into Nature must rise again;] for he becomes omniscient and omnipotent [in a subsequent creation].

---

[1] प्रकृतेरकार्यत्वेऽप्यप्रेर्यत्वेऽप्यन्येच्छानधीनत्वेऽपि तद्योगः पुनरुत्थानौचित्यं तल्लीनस्य । कुतः । पारवश्यात्पुरुषार्थतन्त्रत्वात् । विवेकख्यातिरूपपुरुषार्थवशेन प्रकृत्या पुनरुत्थाप्यते स्वलीन इत्यर्थः । पुरुषार्थादयश्च प्रकृतेर्न प्रेरकाः किं तु प्रवृत्तिस्वभावायाः प्रवृत्तौ निमित्तानीति न स्वातन्त्र्यक्षतिः ॥

[2] प्रकृतिलयात्पुरुषस्योत्थाने प्रमाणमप्याह ॥

a. For 'he,' viz., he who, in a previous creation, was absorbed into the Cause, in a subsequent creation becomes 'omniscient and omnipotent;' the Lord, the First Spirit.[1]

b. But then, if that be so, it is impossible to deny[2] a *Lord*, [which, nevertheless, the *Sánkhyas* seem to do]. To this he replies:[3]

ईदृशेश्वरसिद्धिः सिद्धा ॥ ५७ ॥

In what sense there is a Lord.

Aph. 57. The existence of *such* a Lord is a settled point.

a. It is quite agreed, by all, that there is an emergent Lord, he who had been absorbed into Nature; for the ground of dispute [between *Sánkhyas* and the rest,] is altogether about an *eternal* Lord: such is the meaning.[4]

b. He expounds diffusely the motive for Nature's creating, which was mentioned only indicatorily in the first aphorism of the Second Book:[5]

---

[1] स हि पूर्वसर्गे कारणलीनः सर्गान्तरे सर्ववित्सर्वकर्तेश्वर आदिपुरुषो भवति ॥

[2] *Pratishedha*, on which *vide supra*, p. 112, note 3. *Ed.*

[3] नन्वेवमीश्वरप्रतिषेधानुपपत्तिः । तत्राह ॥

[4] प्रकृतिलीनस्य जन्येश्वरस्य सिद्धिः सर्वसंमतैव नित्येश्वरस्यैव विवादास्पदत्वादित्यर्थः ॥

[5] प्रधानसृष्टेः प्रयोजनं द्वितीयाध्यायस्यादिसूत्रे दिङ्मात्रेणोक्तं विस्तरतः प्रतिपादयति ॥

प्रधानसृष्टिः परार्थं स्वतोऽप्यभोक्तृत्वादुष्ट्रकुङ्कुमवहनवत् ॥ ५८ ॥

Nature's disinterestedness.

Aph. 58. Nature's creating is for the sake of another, though it be spontaneous;—for she is not the experiencer;—like a cart's carrying saffron [for the sake of its master].

a. But then, it is quite impossible that Nature, being unintelligent, should be, spontaneously, a creator; for we see that a cart, or the like, operates only by reason of the efforts of another. To this he replies:[1]

अचेतनत्वेऽपि क्षीरवच्चेष्टितं प्रधानस्य ॥ ५९ ॥

Nature's spontaneous action illustrated.

Aph. 59. Though she be unintelligent, yet Nature acts; as is the case with milk.

a. That is to say: as milk, without reference to men's efforts, quite of itself changes into the form of curd, so Nature, although she be unintelligent, changes into the form of Mind, &c., even without the efforts of any other.[2]

---

[1] ननु प्रधानस्याचेतनस्य स्वतः स्रष्टृत्वमेव नोपपद्यते रथादेः परप्रयत्नेनैव प्रवृत्तिदर्शनादिति। तत्राह ॥

[2] यथा क्षीरं पुरुषप्रयत्ननैरपेक्ष्येण स्वयमेव दधिरूपेण परिणमत एवमचेतनत्वेऽपि परप्रयत्नं

b. This is not rendered tautological by this aphorism, 'As the cow for the calf,' [Book II., § 37]; because there the question was only of the operation of *instruments*, and because cows *are* intelligent.[1]

c. By means of the exhibition of another illustration, he mentions the cause of the thing asserted as aforesaid:[2]

कर्मवद्दृष्टेर्वा कालादेः[3] ॥ ६० ॥

Another illustration.

Aph. 60. Or as is the case with the acts [or on-goings]—for we see them—of Time, &c.

a. Or as is the case with the acts [or on-goings,] of Time, &c., the spontaneous action of Nature is proved from what is seen. The action of Time, for example, takes place quite spontaneously, in the shape of one season's now departing and another's coming on: let the behaviour of Nature, also, be thus; for the supposition conforms to observed facts: such is the meaning.[4]

विनापि महदादिरूपपरिणामः प्रधानस्य भवतीत्यर्थः ॥

[1] धेनुवद्वत्सायेत्यनेन सूत्रेणास्य न पौनरुक्त्यं तत्र करणप्रवृत्तेरेव विचारितत्वाद्धेनूनां चेतनत्वाच्चेति ॥

[2] दृष्टान्तान्तरप्रदर्शनपूर्वकमुक्तार्थहेतुमाह ॥

[3] One of my MSS. of Aniruddha has कालादेव. *Ed.*

[4] कालादेः कर्मवद्वा स्वतः प्रधानस्य चेष्टितं

b. But, still, a senseless Nature would never energize, or would energize the wrong way; because of there being [in her case,] no such communing as, 'This is my means of producing experience, &c.' To this he replies: [1]

स्वभावाच्चेष्टितमनभिसंधानाद्भृत्यवत् ॥ ६१ ॥

Nature acts from habit.

Aph. 61. From her own nature she acts, not from thought; like a servant.

a. That is to say: as, in the case of an excellent servant, naturally, just from habit,[2] the appointed and necessary service of the master is engaged in, and not with a view to his own enjoyment, just so does Nature energize from habit alone.[3]

सिध्यति दृष्टत्वात् । अथैको गच्छत्यृतुरितरश्च प्रवर्तत इत्यादिरूपं कालादिकर्म स्वत एव भवत्येवं प्रधानस्यापि चेष्टा स्यात्कल्पनाया दृष्टानुसारित्वादित्यर्थः ॥

[1] ननु तथापि ममेदं भोगादिसाधनमिति प्रतिसंधानाभावान्मूढायाः प्रकृतेः कदाचित्प्रवृत्तिरपि न स्याद्विपरीता च प्रवृत्तिः स्यात् । तत्राह ॥

[2] As here, so again just below, this word renders *sanskára*. *Ed.*

[3] यथा प्रकृष्टभृत्यस्य स्वभावात्संस्कारादेव प्रतिनियतावश्यकी च स्वामिसेवा प्रवर्तते नतु स्वभोगाभिप्रायेण तथैव प्रकृतेश्चेष्टितं संस्कारादेवेत्यर्थः ॥

कर्माकृष्टेर्वानादितः[1] ॥ ६२ ॥

Or through the influence of Desert.

Aph. 62. Or from attraction by Deserts, which have been from eternity.

a. Here the word 'or' is for connecting [this aphorism with the preceding one]. Since Desert has been from eternity, therefore, moreover, through attraction by Deserts, the energizing of Nature is necessary and rightly distributed:[2] such is the meaning.[3]

b. It being thus settled, then, that Nature is creative for the sake of another, he tells us, in the following section,[4] that, on the completion of that other's purpose, Liberation takes place through Nature's quite spontaneously ceasing to act:[5]

विविक्तबोधात्सृष्टिनिवृत्तिः प्रधानस्य सूदवत्पाके ॥ ६३ ॥

---

[1] Aniruddha inserts अपि after वा. *Ed.*

[2] वाशब्दोऽत्र समुच्चये। यतः कर्मानाद्यतः कर्मभिराकर्षणादपि प्रधानस्यावश्यकी व्यवस्थिता च प्रवृत्तिरित्यर्थः ॥

[3] See the *Rational Refutation*, &c., p. 36. *Ed.*

[4] Read, instead of 'in the following section,' 'by an enunciation.' *Ed.*

[5] तदेवं प्रधानस्य परार्थतः स्रष्टृत्वे सिद्धे परप्रयोजनसमाप्तौ स्वत एव प्रधाननिवृत्त्या मोक्षः सिध्यतीत्याह प्रघट्टकेन ॥

Nature desists when the end is gained.

Aph. 63. From discriminative knowledge there is a cessation of Nature's creating; as is the case with a cook, when the cooking has been performed.

a. When Soul's aim has been accomplished, by means of indifference to all else, through discriminative knowledge of Soul, Nature's creating ceases; as, when the cooking is completed, the labour of the cook ceases: such is the meaning.[1]

b. But, at that rate, since Nature's creating ceases through the production of discriminative knowledge in the case of a single Soul, we should find *all* liberated. To this he replies:[2]

इतर इतरवत्तद्दोषात्[3] ॥ ६४ ॥

Liberation of one involves not that of all.

Aph. 64. Another remains like another, through her fault.

a. But 'another,' i. e., one *devoid* of discriminative knowledge, remains 'like another,' i. e., just like one bound by

---

[1] विविक्तपुरुषज्ञानात्परवैराग्येण पुरुषार्थसमाप्तौ प्रधानस्य सृष्टिर्निवर्तते यथा पाके निष्पन्ने पाचकस्य व्यापारो निवर्तत इत्यर्थः ॥

[2] नन्वेवमेकपुरुषस्योपाधौ विवेकज्ञानोत्पत्त्या प्रकृतेः सृष्टिनिवृत्तौ सर्वमुक्तिप्रसङ्ग इति। तत्राह ॥

[3] Aniruddha's lection of this Aphorism is: इतर इतरत्तद्दोषात्। *Ed.*

Nature. Why? 'Through her fault,' i.e., through the fault which may be described as her not accomplishing that soul's aim: such is the meaning.[1]

b. He mentions the fruit of Nature's ceasing to act:[2]

द्वयोरेकतरस्य वौदासीन्यमपवर्गः ॥ ६५ ॥

Liberation consists of what.

Aph. 65. [The fruit of Nature's ceasing to act], the solitariness of both [Nature and Soul], or [which comes to the same thing,] of either, is liberation.

a. 'Of both,' i.e., of Nature and Soul, the 'solitariness,' i.e., the being alone, the mutual disjunction, in short, this is liberation.[3]

b. But then, how would Nature, having attained indifference, through the mood in the shape of discrimination, on the liberation of a single Soul, again engage in creation, for the sake of another Soul? And you are not to say that this is no objection, because Nature consists of different portions, [it is not *another* Nature, but the same]; because we see, that, even out of the [mortal] constituents of the

---

[1] इतरस्तु विविक्तबोधरहित इतरवद्बद्धवदेव प्रकृत्या तिष्ठति । कुतः । तद्दोषात्तस्य प्रधानस्यैव तत्पुरुषार्थासमापनाख्यदोषादित्यर्थः ॥

[2] सृष्टिनिवृत्तेः फलमाह ॥

[3] द्वयोः प्रधानपुरुषयोरेवौदासीन्यमेकाकिता परस्परवियोग इति यावत्सोऽपवर्गः ॥

liberated person, viz., his dust, &c., things are created for the experience of another. To this he replies:[1]

अन्यसृष्ट्युपरागेऽपि न[2] विरज्यते[3] प्रबुद्धरज्जुतत्त्व-[4]स्यैवोरगः[5] ॥ ६६ ॥

---

[1] नन्वेकपुरुषमुक्तावेव विवेकाकारवृत्त्या विरक्ता प्रकृतिः कथमन्यपुरुषार्थं पुनः सृष्टौ प्रवर्तताम्। न च प्रकृतेरंशभेदान्नैष दोष इति वाच्यं मुक्तपुरुषोपकरणैरपि पृथिव्यादिभिरन्यस्य भोग्यसृष्टिदर्शनादिति। तत्राह ॥

[2] Nágeśa has अन्यसृष्ट्युपरागान्न. *Ed.*

[3] Vijnána's genuine reading seems to be विरतोऽ. His comment, however, recognizes also विरज्यतेऽ, the reading of Aniruddha. One MS. of his work which has been consulted has, like Vedánti Mahádeva, विरमतेऽ. Nágeśa has निवर्ततेऽ. *Ed.*

[4] -स्यै°, instead of -स्ये°, appears to have very little good warrant; and Dr. Ballantyne, indeed, translates इव, not एव. *Ed.*

[5] Of this Aphorism, and of the comment on it, MSS. of Vijnána's treatise afford a much better text than that here reprinted. In one of its more approved forms, that which Vijnána seems to elect, the original enunciation runs thus: अन्यसृष्ट्युपरागेऽपि न विरतोऽप्रबुद्धरज्जुतत्त्वस्येवोरगः। 'Furthermore, she [Nature,] does not give over effecting creation, with reference to another, [i.e., another soul than that of the spiritual sage, though she creates for such a sage no longer; and she acts, in so doing,] analogously to a snake, with reference to him who is unenlightened as to the real

How Nature affects one, and not another.

Aph. 66. Moreover, [when Nature has left off distressing the emancipated,] she does not desist, in regard to her creative influence on another; as is the case with the snake, [which ceases to be a terror,] in respect of him who is aware of the truth in regard to the rope [which another mistakes for a snake].

a. Nature, though, in respect of one Soul, she have desisted, in consequence of discriminative knowledge, does not desist as regards her creative influence on another Soul, but *does* create in respect of *that* one; as the snake [so to speak,] does not produce fear, &c., in the case of him who is aware of the truth in regard to the rope, but *does* produce it, in respect of him who is ignorant [that what

---

character of the rope' [which is mistaken for it; this illusory snake keeping him constantly in a state of alarm, though it ceases to affect him who has discovered that it is nothing more formidable than a yard or two of twisted hemp]. More closely, so far as regards the construction of the original: 'Furthermore, in like manner as a snake goes on influencing him who . . . . . [Nature persists] in effecting creation,' &c.

That *upardga*, as embodied in the expression *sṛishṭyupardga*, signifies 'causing,' 'effecting,' is the view of both Aniruddha and Vedánti Mahádeva, who define it by *karaṇa*.

The Aphorism in question, mainly as just exhibited, together with preferable deviations from the comment as given by Dr. Ballantyne, will be found at p. 13 of the variants appended to my edition of the *Sánkhya-pravachana-bhdshya*. Nágeśa, following Vijnána very closely, explains the Aphorism as follows: यथा प्रबुद्धरज्जुतत्त्वं प्रति निवृत्तोऽप्यहिरप्रबुद्धरज्जुतत्त्वस्य भयादिसृष्ट्युपरागान्न निवर्तते तथा ज्ञानिनं प्रति निवृत्तापि प्रकृतिरन्यं प्रति सृष्टौ प्रवर्तत इत्यर्थः। *Ed.*

he looks upon is a rope, and not a snake]: such is the meaning. And Nature is likened to a snake, because of her disguising Soul, which is likened to a rope. Certain unintelligent persons, calling themselves *Vedántís*, having quite failed to understand that such is the drift of such examples as those of the rope, the snake, &c., suppose that Nature is an absolute nothing, or something merely imaginary. The matters of Scripture and of the legal institutes are to be *elucidated* by means of this [or that] example offered by the *Sánkhyas*, who assert the reality of Nature: it is not the case that the matter is simply *established* to be as is the example;[1] [the analogy of which is not to be overstrained, as if the cases were parallel throughout].

कर्मनिमित्तयोगाच्च ॥ ६७ ॥

---

[1] एकस्मिन्पुरुषे विविक्तबोधाद्विरक्तमपि प्रधानं नान्यस्मिन्पुरुषे सृष्ट्युपरागाय विरक्तं भवति किं तु तं प्रति सृजत्येव यथा प्रबुद्धरज्जुतत्त्वस्यैवोरगो भयादिकं न जनयति मूढं प्रति तु जनयत्येवेत्यर्थः। उरगतुल्यत्वं च प्रधानस्य रज्जुतुल्ये पुरुषे समारोपणादिति। एवंविधं रज्जुसर्पादिदृष्टान्तानामाशयमबुद्ध्वैवाबुधाः केचिद्वेदान्तिब्रुवाः प्रकृतेरत्यन्ततुच्छत्वं मनोमात्रत्वं वा तुलयन्ति। एतेन प्रकृतिसत्यतावादिसाङ्ख्योक्तदृष्टान्तेन श्रुतिस्मृत्यर्था बोधनीया न केवलं दृष्टान्तवत्त्वेनायमर्थः सिध्यति ॥

Another consideration why Nature should act.

Aph. 67. And from connexion with Desert, which is the cause.

a. 'Desert,' which is the cause of creation, in consequence of the conjunction of this, also, she creates, for the sake of another Soul [than the emancipated one]: such is the meaning.[1]

b. But then, since all Souls are alike indifferent, inasmuch as they do not desire [Nature's interference], what is it that here determines Nature to act only in regard to this one, and to desist in regard to that one? And *Desert* is not the determiner; because here, too, there is nothing to determine of which Soul what is the Desert; [Desert being inferrible only from, and, therefore, not cognizable antecendently to, its *fruits*]. To this he replies:[2]

नैरपेक्ष्येऽपि प्रकृत्युपकारेऽविवेको निमित्तम् ॥ ६८ ॥

Nature's selection how determined.

Aph. 68. Though there is [on Soul's part, this] indifference, yet want of discrimination is the cause of Nature's service.

---

[1] सृष्टौ निमित्तं यत्कर्म तस्य संबन्धादप्यन्यपुरुषार्थं सृजतीत्यर्थः ॥

[2] ननु सर्वेषां पुरुषाणामप्रार्थकतया नैरपेक्ष्याविशेषेऽपि कंचित्प्रत्येव प्रधानं प्रवर्तते कंचित्प्रति च निवर्तेत इत्यत्र किं नियामकम् । न च कर्म नियामकं कस्य पुरुषस्य किं कर्मेत्यत्रापि नियामकाभावादिति । तत्राह ॥

a. That is to say: although Souls *are* indifferent, yet Nature, just through [her own] non-discrimination, saying, 'This is my master,' 'This is I myself,' serves Souls, [towards their eventual emancipation], by creation, &c. And so, to what Soul, not having discriminated herself [therefrom], she has the habit[1] of showing herself, in respect just of that one does Nature energize; and this it is that determines her: such is the import.[2]

b. Since it is her *nature* to energize, how can she desist, even when discrimination has taken place? To this he replies:[3]

नर्तकीवत्प्रवृत्तस्यापि निवृत्तिश्चारितार्थ्यात् ॥ ६९ ॥

Nature energizes only till the end is attained.

Aph. 69. Like a dancer does she, though she had been energizing, desist; because of the end's having been attained.

a. Nature's disposition to energize is only for the sake of Soul, and not universally. Therefore is it fitting that

---

1 *Vásaná. Vide supra*, p. 29, note 2. *Ed.*

2 पुरुषाणां नैरपेक्ष्येऽप्ययं मे स्वाम्ययमेवाहमित्यविवेकादेव प्रकृतिः सृष्ट्यादिभिः पुरुषानुपकरोतीत्यर्थः। तथा च यस्मै पुरुषायात्मानमविविच्य दर्शयितुं वासना वर्तते तं प्रत्येव प्रधानं प्रवर्तत इत्येव नियामकमिति भावः॥

3 प्रवृत्तिस्वभावत्वात्कथं विवेकेऽपि निवृत्तिरुपपद्यताम्। तत्राह॥

Nature should desist, though she has been energizing, when the end has been attained, in the shape of the effectuation of Soul's aim; as a dancer, who has been performing, with the view of exhibiting a dance to the spectators, desists, on the accomplishment of this: such is the meaning.[1]

b. He states another reason for the cessation:[2]

दोषबोधेऽपि नोपसर्पणं प्रधानस्य कुलवधू-
वत् ॥ ७० ॥

This illustrated.

Aph. 70. Moreover, when her fault is known, Nature does not approach [Soul]; like a woman of good family.

a. That is to say: Nature, moreover, ashamed at Soul's having seen her fault,—in her transformations, and her taking the shape of pain, &c.,—does not again approach Soul; 'like a woman of good family,' i.e.; as a [frail] woman of good family, ashamed at ascertaining that her fault

---

[1] पुरुषार्थमेव प्रधानस्य प्रवृत्तिस्वभावो नतु सामान्येन। अतः प्रवृत्तस्यापि प्रधानस्य पुरुषार्थसमाप्तिरूपे चरितार्थत्वे सति निवृत्तिर्युक्ता यथा परिषद्भ्यो नृत्यदर्शनार्थं प्रवृत्ताया नर्तक्यास्तत्सिद्धौ निवृत्तिरित्यर्थः ॥

[2] निवृत्तौ हेत्वन्तरमाह ॥

has been seen by her husband, does not approach her husband.[1] [2]

b. But then, if Nature's energizing be for the sake of Soul, Soul must be *altered* by Bondage and Liberation, [and not remain the unalterable entity which you allege it to be]. To this he replies:[3]

नैकान्ततो बन्धमोक्षौ पुरुषस्याविवेकादृते ॥ ७१ ॥

Soul's relation to Bondage.

Aph. 71. Bondage and Liberation do not actually belong to Soul, [and would not even appear to do so,] but for non-discrimination.

a. Bondage and Liberation, consisting in the conjunction of Pain, and its disjunction, do not 'actually,' i. e., really, belong to Soul; but, in the way mentioned in the fourth aphorism, they result only from non-discrimination: such is the meaning.[4]

---

[1] पुरुषेण परिणामित्वदुःखात्मकत्वादिदोषदर्शनादपि लज्जितायाः प्रकृतेः पुनर्न पुरुषं प्रत्युपसर्पणं कुलवधूवद्यथा स्वामिना मे दोषो दृष्ट इत्यवधारणेन लज्जिता कुलवधूर्न स्वामिनमुपसर्पति तद्वदित्यर्थः ॥

[2] See the *Rational Refutation*, &c., p. 61.

[3] ननु पुरुषार्थं चेत्प्रधानप्रवृत्तिस्तर्हि बन्धमोक्षाभ्यां पुरुषस्य परिणामापत्तिरिति । तत्राह ॥

[4] दुःखयोगवियोगरूपौ बन्धमोक्षौ पुरुषस्य नै-

b. But, in reality, Bondage and Liberation, as declared, belong to Nature alone: so he asserts:[1]

प्रकृतेराञ्जस्यात्ससङ्गत्वात्पशुवत् ॥ ७२ ॥

Bondage is really Nature's.

Aph. 72. They really belong to Nature, through consociation; like a beast.

a. Bondage and Liberation, through Pain, really belong to Nature,[2] 'through consociation,' i. e., through her being hampered by the habits, &c., which are the causes of Pain; as a beast, through its being hampered by a rope, experiences Bondage and Liberation: such is the meaning.[3]

b. Here, by what causes is there Bondage? Or by what is there Liberation? To this he replies:[4]

कान्ततस्तत्त्वतः किं तु चतुर्थसूत्रवक्ष्यमाणप्रकारेणाविवेकादेवेत्यर्थः ॥

[1] परमार्थतस्तु यथोक्तौ बन्धमोक्षौ प्रकृतेरेवेत्याह ॥

[2] Read: 'Bondage and Liberation belong to Nature alone; because to it, in truth, belongs misery.' *Ed.*

[3] प्रकृतेरेव तत्त्वतो दुःखेन बन्धमोक्षौ ससङ्गत्वाद्दुःखसाधनैर्धर्मादिभिर्लिप्तत्वाद्यथा पशू रज्ज्वा लिप्ततया बन्धमोक्षभागी तद्वदित्यर्थः ॥

[4] तत्र कैः साधनैर्बन्धः कैर्वा मोक्ष इत्याकाङ्क्षायामाह ॥

रूपैः सप्तभिरात्मानं बध्नाति प्रधानं [1]कोशकारवद्विमोचयत्येकरूपेण[2] ॥ ७३ ॥

How Nature binds and liberates herself.

Aph. 73. In seven ways does Nature bind herself; like the silk-worm: in one way does she liberate herself.

a. By Merit, Dispassion, Supernatural Power, Demerit, Ignorance, Non-dispassion, and Want of Power, viz., by habits, causes of Pain, in the shape of these seven, 'does Nature bind herself' with Pain; 'like the silk-worm;' i. e., as the worm that makes the cocoon binds itself by means of the dwelling which itself constructs. And that same Nature liberates herself from Pain 'in one way,' i. e., by Knowledge alone: such is the meaning.[3]

b. But then, that which you assert, viz., that Bondage and Liberation result from Non-discrimination alone, is improper; because Non-discrimination can neither be

---

[1] Nágeśa has कोशकारवन्मो°. *Ed.*

[2] Aniruddha and Vedánti Mahádeva have -मोचयत्येकेन रूपेण. *Ed.*

[3] धर्मवैराग्यैश्वर्याधर्माज्ञानावैराग्यानैश्वर्यैः सप्तभी रूपैर्धर्मैर्दुःखहेतुभिः प्रकृतिरात्मानं दुःखेन बध्नाति कोशकारवत्कोशकारकृमिर्यथा स्वनिर्मितेनावासेनात्मानं बध्नाति तद्वत् । सैव च प्रकृतिरेकरूपेण ज्ञानेनैवात्मानं दुःखान्मोचयतीत्यर्थः ॥

quitted nor assumed, and because, in the world, Pain, and its negative, Pleasure, &c., can, themselves, be neither quitted nor assumed: otherwise, [if you still insist on retaining the opinion objected to], there is disparagement of sense-evidence. Having pondered this, he himself [not leaving it to a commentator,] explains what was asserted in the fourth aphorism:[1]

निमित्तत्वमविवेकस्य न दृष्टहानिः ॥ ७४ ॥

An objection met.

Aph. 74. Non-discrimination is the cause [not the thing itself]; [so that] there is no disparagement of sense-evidence.

a. What was asserted before was this, that Non-discrimination is only the *occasion* of Bondage and Liberation in souls, and not that Non-discrimination itself is these two; therefore 'there is no disparagement of sense-evidence;' [for, though we see that Pain and Pleasure cannot be directly assumed or quitted, yet we also see that causes of them *can* be assumed or quitted]: such is the meaning.[2]

---

[1] ननु बन्धमुक्ती अविवेकादिति यदुक्तं तदयुक्तमविवेकस्याहेयानुपादेयत्वाल्लोके दुःखस्य तदभावसुखादेरेव च स्वतो हेयोपादेयत्वादन्यथा दृष्टहानिरित्याशङ्क्य चतुर्थसूत्रोक्तं स्वयं विवृणोति ॥

[2] अविवेकस्य पुरुषेषु बन्धमोक्षनिमित्तत्वमेव पुरोक्तं न त्वविवेक एव ताविति नातो दृष्टहानिरित्यर्थः ॥

b. He mentions, among the means conducive to Discrimination, Study, which is the essence of them :[1]

तत्त्वाभ्यासान्नेति नेतीति त्यागाद्विवेकसिद्धिः ॥ ७५ ॥

Means of Discrimination.

Aph. 75. Discrimination is perfected through abandonment [of everything], expressed by a 'No, No,' through study of the [twenty-five] Principles.

a. Discrimination is effected through study of the Principles, in the shape of abandoning, by a 'No, No,' in regard to things unintelligent, ending with Nature, the conceit [that Nature, or any of her products, is Soul]. All the others [enumerated in the list of means] are only supplemental to Study : such is the meaning.[2]

b. He states a speciality in regard to the perfecting of Discrimination :[3]

अधिकारिप्रभेदान्न[4] नियमः ॥ ७६ ॥

---

[1] विवेकस्य निष्पत्त्युपायेषु सारभूतमभ्यासमाह ॥

[2] प्रकृतिपर्यन्तेषु जडेषु नेति नेतीत्यभिमानत्यागरूपात्तत्त्वाभ्यासाद्विवेकनिष्पत्तिर्भवति । इतरत्सर्वमभ्यासस्याङ्गमात्रमित्यर्थः ॥

[3] विवेकसिद्धौ विशेषमाह ॥

[4] Vedánti Mahádeva has अधिकारप्रभेदान्न. *Ed.*

The means not efficacious everywhere.

Aph. 76. Through the difference of those competent [to engage in the matter at all], there is no necessity [that each and every one should at once be successful].

a. Since there is a division, among those competent, into the sluggish, &c., though study be made, there is no certainty that, in this very birth, Discrimination will be accomplished: such is the meaning. Therefore, every one should, by strenuousness in study, acquire for himself the *highest* degree of competency: such is the import.[1]

b. He states that Liberation takes place solely through the effecting of Discrimination, and not otherwise:[2]

[3]बाधितानुवृत्त्या मध्यविवेकतोऽप्युपभोगः ॥ ७७ ॥

Imperfect Discrimination inefficacious.

Aph. 77. Since what [Pain] has been repelled returns again, there comes, even from medium [but imperfect,] Discrimination, experience, [which it is desired to get entirely rid of].

a. But sluggish Discrimination [lower even than the

---

[1] मन्दाद्यधिकारिभेदसत्त्वादभ्यासे क्रियमाणेऽप्यस्मिन्नेव जन्मनि विवेकनिष्पत्तिर्भवतीति नियमो नास्तीत्यर्थः। अत उत्तमाधिकारमभ्यासपाटवेनात्मनः संपादयेदिति भावः॥

[2] विवेकनिष्पत्त्यैव निस्तारो नान्यथेत्याह॥

[3] The reading of Aniruddha is बाधितानुवृत्तेर्मध्य°. *Ed.*

middling variety], antecedently to direct intuition, consists only of Hearing, Pondering, and Meditating: such is the division[1] [of Discrimination].

जीवन्मुक्तश्च[2] ॥ ७८ ॥

Of Liberation during life.

Aph. 78. And he who, living, is liberated.

a. That is to say: he, also, who, while living, is liberated is just in the condition of medium Discrimination.[3]

b. He adduces evidence for there being some one liberated, though still living:[4]

उपदेश्योपदेष्टृत्वात्तत्सिद्धिः ॥ ७९ ॥

Proof that this may be.

Aph. 79. It is proved by the fact of instructed and instructor.

a. That is to say: it is proved that there are such as are liberated during life, by the mention, in the Institutes, on the subject of Discrimination,[5] of the relation of preceptor

---

[1] मन्दविवेकस्तु साक्षात्कारात्पूर्वं श्रवणमनन-ध्यानमात्ररूप इति विभागः ॥

[2] The च is omitted by Vedánti Mahádeva. *Ed.*

[3] जीवन्मुक्तोऽपि मध्यविवेकावस्थ एव भवतीत्यर्थः ॥

[4] जीवन्मुक्ते प्रमाणमाह ॥

[5] This I have substituted for 'Liberation,' a mere oversight. *Ed.*

and pupil; i. e., because it is only one liberated during life that can be an instructor[1] [in this matter].

श्रुतिश्च[2] ॥ ८० ॥

Further proof. *Aph.* 80. And there is Scripture.

a. There is also Scripture for there being persons liberated during life.[3]

b. But then, merely through hearing, too, one might become [qualified to be] an instructor. To this he replies:[4]

इतरथान्धपरंपरा ॥ ८१ ॥

A suggestion repelled. *Aph.* 81. [And not through merely hearing is one qualified to become an instructor]: otherwise, there were blind tradition.

a. That is to say: otherwise, since even a person of sluggish Discrimination [but who, yet, had *heard*,] would be an instructor, we should have a blind handing down[5] [of doctrines which would speedily become corrupted or lost].

---

[1] शास्त्रेषु विवेकविषये गुरुशिष्यभावश्रवणाज्जीवन्मुक्तसिद्धिरित्यर्थो जीवन्मुक्तस्यैवोपदेष्टृत्वसंभवादिति ॥

[2] None of the commentators but Vijnána recognizes an Aphorism in these words; and it is very doubtful whether even he does so. *Ed.*

[3] श्रुतिरपि जीवन्मुक्तेऽस्ति ॥

[4] ननु श्रवणमात्रेणाप्युपदेष्टृत्वं स्यात्। तत्राह॥

[5] इतरथा मन्दविवेकस्याप्युपदेष्टृत्वेऽन्धपरंपरापत्तिरित्यर्थः ॥

b. But then, when, through Knowledge, one's works [which are the cause of mundane existence,] have perished, how can there [still] be life? To this he replies:[1]

चक्रभ्रमणवद्धृतशरीरः ॥ ८२ ॥

How life is compatible with Liberaton.

Aph. 82. Possessed of a body, [the emancipated sage goes on living]; like the whirling of a wheel.

a. Even on the cessation of the action of the potter, the wheel, of itself, revolves for some time, in consequence of the motal inertia resulting from the previous action. So, after knowledge, though actions do not arise, yet, through the [self-continuant] action of antecedent acts, possessing an energizing body, he remains living, yet liberated;[2] [and, if he did not, but if every one who gained true knowledge were, on gaining it, to disappear, true knowledge would cease to be handed down orally; and Kapila, probably, did not contemplate books, or did not think these a secure depository of the doctrine]: such is the meaning.[3]

---

[1] ननु ज्ञानेन कर्मक्षये सति कथं जीवनं स्यात्। तत्राह ॥

[2] For another rendering, see the *Rational Refutation*, &c., p. 31. *Ed.*

[3] कुलालकर्मनिवृत्तावपि पूर्वकर्मवेगात्स्वयमेव कियत्कालं चक्रं भ्रमति। एवं ज्ञानोत्तरं कर्मानुत्पत्तावपि प्रारब्धकर्मवेगेन चेष्टमानं शरीरं धृत्वा जीवन्मुक्तस्तिष्ठतीत्यर्थः ॥

b. But then, since the continuance[1] of experience, &c., is put an end to by that 'Meditation with distinct recognition of the object,' which [see *Yoga Aphorisms*, Book I., § 17,[2]] is the cause of knowledge, how can one retain a body? To this he replies:[3]

संस्कारलेशतस्तत्सिद्धिः ॥ ८३ ॥

Difficulty of shuffling off this mortal coil.

Aph. 83. This [retention of a body] is occasioned by the least vestige of impression.

a. That is to say: the retention of a body is caused by even the least remains of those impressions[4] of objects which are the causes of having a body.[5]

b. He recapitulates the sense of the declarations of the Institute:[6]

---

[1] *Vásaná.* *Vide supra*, p. 29, note 2. *Ed.*

[2] Which here follows, with Dr. Ballantyne's translation: वितर्कविचारानन्दास्मितानुगमात्संप्रज्ञातः । '[Meditation, of the kind called] that in which there is distinct recognition [arises, in its fourfold shape,] from the attendance of (1) argumentation (*vitarka*), (2) deliberation (*vichára*), (3) beatitude (*ánanda*), and (4) egotism (*asmitá*).' *Ed.*

[3] ननु ज्ञानहेतुसंप्रज्ञातयोगेन भोगादिवासनाक्षये कथं शरीरधारणम् । तत्राह ॥

[4] This is to render the technicality *sanskára.* *Ed.*

[5] शरीरधारणहेतवो ये विषयसंस्कारास्तेषामल्पावशेषात्तस्य शरीरधारणस्य सिद्धिरित्यर्थः ॥

[6] शास्त्रवाक्यार्थमुपसंहरति ॥

विवेकान्निःशेषदुःखनिवृत्तौ कृतकृत्यता[1] नेतरा-
न्नेतरात् ॥ ८४ ॥

Recapitulation.

Aph. 84. That which was to be done has been done, when entire Cessation of Pain has resulted from Discrimination; not otherwise, not otherwise.

a. So much for the Third Book, on Dispassion.[2]

---

[1] Vijnána, according to some copies of his work, has कृतकृत्यो, the preferable reading, and that of all the other commentators known to me. *Ed.*

[2] इति वैराग्याध्यायस्तृतीयः ॥

END OF BOOK III.

BOOK IV.

Now, by means of a collection of narratives, recognized in the Institutes, the means of discriminative knowledge are to be displayed: so, for this purpose the Fourth Book is commenced.[1]

राजपुत्रवत्तत्त्वोपदेशात् ॥ १ ॥

Soul set right by hearing the truth.

Aph. 1. As in the case of the king's son, from instruction as to the truth [comes discrimination between Soul and Nature].

a. 'Discrimination' is supplied from the concluding aphorism of the preceding section. The meaning is: as, in the case of the king's son, discrimination is produced by instruction as to the truth. The story, here, is as follows: A certain king's son, in consequence of his being born under the [unlucky] star of the tenth portion[2] [of the twenty-seven portions into which the ecliptic is divided], having been expelled from his city, and reared by a certain forester, remains under the idea, that 'I am a forester.' Having learned that he is alive, a certain minister informs him: 'Thou art not a forester; thou art a king's son.'

---

[1] शास्त्रसिद्धाख्यायिकाजातमुखेनेदानीं विवेकज्ञानसाधनानि प्रदर्शनीयानीत्येतदर्थं चतुर्थाध्याय आरभ्यते ॥

[2] The Sanskrit yields 'under the star [named] Gaṇḍa.' *Ed.*

As he, immediately, having abandoned the idea of his being an outcast, betakes himself to his true royal state, saying, 'I am a *king*,' so, too, it [the Soul], in consequence of the instruction of some kind person, to the effect that 'Thou, who didst originate from the First Soul, which manifests itself merely as pure Thought, art [thyself,] a portion thereof,' having abandoned the idea of its being Nature [or of being something material or phenomenal], rests simply upon its own nature, saying, 'Since I am the son of Brahmá, I am, myself, Brahmá, and not something mundane, different therefrom:' such is the meaning.[1]

b. He exhibits another story, to prove that even women,

---

[1] पूर्वपादशेषसूत्रस्थविवेकोऽनुवर्तते। राजपुत्रस्येव तत्त्वोपदेशाद्विवेको जायत इत्यर्थः। अत्रेयमाख्यायिका। कश्चिद्राजपुत्रो गराडर्क्षजन्मना पुरान्निःसारितः शबरेण केनचित्पोषितोऽहं शबर इत्यभिमन्यमान आस्ते। तं जीवन्तं ज्ञात्वा कश्चिदमात्यः प्रबोधयति न त्वं शबरो राजपुत्रोऽसीति। स यथा झटित्येव चाराडालाभिमानं त्यक्त्वा तात्त्विकं राजभावमेवालम्बते राजाहमस्मीत्येवमेवादिपुरुषात्परिपूर्णचिन्मात्रत्वेनाभिव्यक्तादुत्पन्नस्त्वं तस्यांश इति कारुणिकोपदेशात्प्रकृत्यभिमानं त्यक्त्वा ब्रह्मपुत्रत्वादहमपि ब्रह्मैव नतु तद्विलक्षणः संसारीत्येवं स्वस्वरूपमेवालम्बत इत्यर्थः॥

Śúdras, &c., may gain the [one desirable] end, through a Bráhman, by hearing the instructions of a Bráhman:[1]

पिशाचवदन्यार्थोपदेशेऽपि ॥ २ ॥

Even when the instruction is not addressed to the hearer.

Aph. 2. As in the case of the goblin, even when the instruction was for the sake of another, [the chance hearer may be benefited].

a. That is to say: though the instruction in regard to the truth was being delivered, by the venerable Kṛishṇa, for Arjuna's benefit, knowledge of the distinction [between Soul and Nature] was produced in the case of a goblin standing near [and overhearing the discourse]: and so it may happen in the case of others, too.[2]

b. And, if knowledge is not produced from *once* instructing, then a repetition of the instruction is to be made; to which effect he adduces another story:[3]

---

[1] स्त्रीशूद्रादयोऽपि ब्राह्मणेन ब्राह्मणस्योपदेशं श्रुत्वा कृतार्थाः स्युरित्येतदर्थमाख्यायिकान्तरं दर्शयति ॥

[2] अर्जुनार्थं श्रीकृष्णेन तत्त्वोपदेशे क्रियमाणेऽपि समीपस्थस्य पिशाचस्य विवेकज्ञानं जातमेवमन्येषामपि भवेदित्यर्थः ॥

[3] यदि च सकृदुपदेशाज्ज्ञानं न जायते तदोपदेशावृत्तिरपि कर्तव्येतीतिहासान्तरमाह ॥

आवृत्तिरसकृदुपदेशात् ॥ ३ ॥

Necessity of inculcation.

Aph. 3. Repetition [is to be made], if not, from once instructing, [the end be gained].

a. That is to say: a repetition of instruction, also, is to be made; because, in the *Chhándogya* [*Upanishad*],[1] and the like, there is mention of Áruṇi, and others, as having more than once instructed Śwetaketu and others.[2]

b. With a view to the removal of desire, he sets forth, with an illustration, the fragility, &c., of Soul's accompaniments:[3]

पितापुत्रवदुभयोर्दृष्टत्वात् ॥ ४ ॥

Transitoriness of mundane things.

Aph. 4. As in the case of father and son; since both are seen; [the one, to die, and the other, to be born].

a. That is to say: Discrimination takes place, through dispassion, in consequence of its being inferred, in respect of one's own self, also, that there is death and birth; since these are seen in the case of father and son. This has

---

[1] VI., i., &c. *Ed.*

[2] उपदेशावृत्तिरपि कर्तव्या छान्दोग्यादौ श्वेतकेत्वादिकं प्रत्यारुणिप्रभृतीनामसकृदुपदेशेतिहासादित्यर्थः ॥

[3] वैराग्यार्थं निदर्शनपूर्वकमात्मसंघातस्य भङ्गुरत्वादिकं प्रतिपादयति ॥

been stated as follows: 'The coming into being, and the departure, of Soul [entangled in Nature],[1] may be inferred from [the case of] father and son.[2]

b. He next explains, by illustrative stories, the subservients to the *perfecting* of knowledge in him in whom knowledge has arisen, and who is devoid of passion:[3]

श्येनवत्सुखदुःखी त्यागवियोगाभ्याम् ॥ ५ ॥

Voluntary abandonment distinguished from involuntary.

Aph. 5. One experiences pleasure or pain [alternatively], from [voluntary] abandonment or [forcible] separation; as in the case of a hawk.

a. That is to say: since people become happy by the abandonment of things, and unhappy by [forcible] separation from them, acceptance of them ought not to be made; 'as in the case of a hawk.'[4] For a hawk, when he has food [before him], if he be driven away[5] by any one, is grieved

---

[1] Read, instead of 'of Soul,' &c., 'of one's self.' *Ed.*

[2] स्वस्य पितापुत्रयोरिवात्मनोऽपि मरणोत्पत्त्योर्दृष्टत्वादनुमितत्वाद्वैराग्येण विवेको भवतीत्यर्थः । तदुक्तम् । आत्मनः पितृपुत्राभ्यामनुमेयौ भवाप्ययाविति ॥

[3] इतः परमुत्पन्नज्ञानस्य विरक्तस्य च ज्ञाननिष्पत्त्यङ्गान्याख्यायिकादृष्टान्तैर्दर्शयति ॥

[4] See the *Mahábhárata*, xii., 6648. *Ed.*

[5] Read, 'molested' (*upahatya*). Dr. Ballantyne followed an error of the press, *apahatya*, which he did not observe that I had pointed

at being separated from the food; [but] if, of his own accord, he leaves it, then he is free from grief.[1]

अहिनिर्ल्वयनीवत्[2] ॥ ६ ॥

How Soul ought to abandon Nature.

Aph. 6. As in the case of a snake and its skin.

a. That is to say: as a snake readily abandons its old skin, from knowing that it ought to be quitted, just so he who desires liberation should abandon Nature, experienced through a long period, and effete, when he knows that it ought to be quitted. Thus it has been said: 'As a snake .. its old skin,' &c.[3]

---

out in the corrigenda to my edition of the *Sánkhya-pravachana-bháshya*. *Ed.*

[1] परिग्रहो न कर्तव्यो यतो द्रव्याणां त्यागेन लोकः सुखी. वियोगेन च दुःखी भवति श्येनव-दित्यर्थः। श्येनो हि सामिषः केनाप्युपहृत्यामिषा-द्वियोज्य दुःखी क्रियते स्वयं चेत्त्यजति तदा दुःखा-द्विमुच्यते ॥

[2] Two of my MSS. have -निर्ल्वयिनी°; the rest, -नि-र्ल्वयनी°. I have restored the etymological form of the word. *Ed*

[3] यथाहिर्जीर्णां त्वचं परित्यजत्यनायासेन हेय-बुद्ध्या तथैव मुमुक्षुः प्रकृतिं बहुकालोपभुक्तां जी-र्णां हेयबुद्ध्या त्यजेदित्यर्थः। तदुक्तम्। जीर्णां त्वचमिवोरग इति ॥

b. And, when abandoned, he should not again accept Nature and the rest. So, in regard to this, he says:[1]

छिन्नहस्तवद्वा ॥ ७ ॥

Its resumption prohibited. *Aph.* 7. Or as an amputated hand.

a. As no one takes back again an amputated hand, just so this [Nature], when abandoned, he should not readmit: such is the meaning. The word 'Or' is used in the sense of 'moreover;'[2] [the import of the conjunction being superadditive, not alternative].

असाधनानुचिन्तनं बन्धाय भरतवत् ॥ ८ ॥

Duty to be sacrificed to salvation. *Aph.* 8. What is not a means [of liberation is] not to be thought about, [as this conduces only] to bondage; as in the case of Bharata.

a. That which is not an immediate cause of Discrimination, even though it may be a duty, still is 'not to be thought about;' i.e., intention of the mind towards the performance thereof is not to be made; since it tends to Bondage, from its making us forget Discrimination. 'As in the case of Bharata:' that is to say, as was the case

---

[1] त्यक्तं च प्रकृत्यादिकं पुनर्न स्वीकुर्यादित्याह ॥

[2] यथा छिन्नं हस्तं पुनः कोऽपि नादत्ते तथैवैतत्त्यक्तं पुनर्नाभिमन्येतेत्यर्थः । वाशब्दोऽप्यर्थे ॥

with the royal sage Bharata's cherishing Dínánátha's[1] fawn, though [this was] in accordance with duty.[2]

बहुभिर्योगे विरोधो[3] रागादिभिः कुमारीशङ्खवत् ॥ ९ ॥

Company to be avoided.

Aph. 9. From [association with] many there is obstruction to concentration, through passion, &c.; as in the case of a girl's shells.[4]

a. Association is not to be made with many; because, when there is association with many, there is disturbance, through the manifestation of Passion, &c., which destroys concentration; as a jingling is produced by the mutual

---

[1] The original, *dínánátha*, compounded of *dína* and *anátha*, 'miserable and having no master,' is an epithet of 'fawn.'

For the story of Bharata and the fawn, see the *Vishṇu-puráṇa*, Book ii., Chap. xiii. *Ed.*

[2] विवेकस्य यदन्तरङ्गसाधनं न भवति स चेद्धर्मोऽपि स्यात्तथापि तदनुचिन्तनं तदनुष्ठाने चित्तस्य तात्पर्यं न कर्तव्यं यतस्तद्बन्धाय भवति विवेकविस्मारकतया । भरतवत् । यथा भरतस्य राजर्षेर्धर्म्यमपि दीनानाथहरिणशावकस्य पोषणमित्यर्थः ॥

[3] बहुभिर्योगविरोधो is the reading of Aniruddha. *Ed.*

[4] See the *Mahábhárata*, xii., 6652. *Ed.*

contact of the shells on a girl's wrist: such is the meaning.[1]

द्वाभ्यामपि तथैव ॥ १० ॥

Even that of one.

Aph. 10. Just so, from [the company of] two, also.

a. Just so, even from two there is obstruction to concentration; therefore one ought to abide quite *alone*: such is the meaning.[2]

निराशः सुखी पिङ्गलावत ॥ ११ ॥

Blessedness of those who expect nothing.

Aph. 11. He who is without hope is happy; like Pingalá.[3]

a. Having abandoned hope, let a man become possessed of the happiness called contentment; 'like Pingalá;' that is to say, as the courtesan called Pingalá, desiring a lover, having found no lover, being despondent, became happy, when she had left off hoping.[4]

---

[1] बहुभिः सङ्गो न कार्यो बहुभिः सङ्गे हि रागाद्यभिव्यक्त्या कलहो भवति योगभ्रंशको यथा कुमारीहस्तशङ्खानामन्योन्यसङ्गेन झणत्कारो भवतीत्यर्थः ॥

[2] द्वाभ्यां योगेऽपि तथैव विरोधो भवत्यत एकाकिनैव स्थातव्यमित्यर्थः ॥

[3] See the *Mahábhárata*, xii., 6447. *Ed.*

[4] आशां त्यक्त्वा पुरुषः संतोषाख्यसुखवान्भुया-

b. But then, granting that Pain may cease, on the cessation of hope, yet how can there be *happiness*, in the absence of causes thereof? It is replied: That natural happiness, resulting from the predominance of Purity in the mind, which remains obscured by hope, itself resumes its influence, on the departure of hope; as is the case with the coolness of water which [supposed natural coolness] had been hindered [from manifesting itself,] by heat: there is not, in this case, any need of *means*. And it is laid down that precisely this is happiness of Soul.[1]

c. Since it is an obstructer of Concentration, exertion with a view to experience is not to be made, since this will be effected quite otherwise; as he states:[2]

त्पिङ्गलावद्यथा पिङ्गला नाम वेश्या कान्तार्थिनी कान्तमलब्ध्वा निर्विण्णा सती विहायाशां सुखिनी बभूव तद्वदित्यर्थः ॥

[1] नन्वाशानिवृत्त्या दुःखनिवृत्तिः स्यात्सुखं तु कुतः साधनाभावादिति। उच्यते। चित्तस्य सत्त्वप्राधान्येन स्वाभाविकं यत्सुखमाशया पिहितं तिष्ठति तदेवाशाविगमे लब्धवृत्तिकं भवति तेजःप्रतिबद्धजलशैत्यवदिति न तत्र साधनापेक्षा। एतदेव चात्मसुखमित्युच्यत इति ॥

[2] योगप्रतिबन्धकत्वादारम्भोऽपि भोगार्थं न कर्तव्योऽन्यथैव तदुपपत्तेरित्याह ॥

अनारम्भेऽपि परगृहे सुखी सर्पवत् ॥ १२ ॥

Exertion needless.

Aph 12. [One may be happy,] even without exertion; like a serpent happy in another's house.

a. Supply, 'he may be happy.' The rest is simple. So it has been said:[1] 'The building of a house is, assuredly, painful, and in no way pleasant. A serpent, having entered the dwelling made by another [e.g., a rat], does find comfort.'[2]

b. From Institutes, and from preceptors, only the essence is to be accepted; since, otherwise, it may be impossible to concentrate the attention, from there being, by reason of implications,[3] discussions, &c., discrepancies in declared unessential parts, and from the multiplicity of topics. So he says:[4]

बहुशास्त्रगुरूपासनेऽपि सारादानं षट्पदवत् ॥ १३ ॥

---

[1] Quoted from the *Mahábhárata*, xii., 6649. *Ed.*

[2] सुखी भवेदिति शेषः। शेषं सुगमम्। तदुक्तम्। गृहारम्भो हि दुःखाय न सुखाय कथं चन। सर्पः परकृतं वेश्म प्रविश्य सुखमेधते ॥

[3] *Abhyupagama*, 'acceptings' (of positions, &c.). *Ed.*

[4] शास्त्रेभ्यो गुरुभ्यश्च सार एव ग्राह्योऽन्यथाभ्युपगमवादादिभिरुक्तेऽसारभागेऽन्योन्यविरोधेनार्थबाहुल्येन चैकाग्रताया असंभवादित्याह ॥

A bee-like eclecticism recommended.

Aph. 13. Though he devote himself to many Institutes and teachers, a taking of the essence [is to be made]; as is the case with the bee.

a. Supply 'is to be made.' The rest is simple. Thus it has been said: 'From small Institutes, and from great, the intelligent man should take, from all quarters, the essence; as the bee does from the flowers.'[1]

b. Be the other means what they may, the direct possession of Discrimination is to be effected only by intentness, through maintaining Meditation; as he tells us:[2]

इषुकारवन्नैकचित्तस्य समाधिहानिः ॥ १४ ॥

Intentness on one object.

Aph. 14. The Meditation is not interrupted of him whose mind is intent on one object; like the maker of arrows.[3]

a. As, in the case of a maker of arrows, with his mind intent solely on the making of an arrow, the exclusion of

---

[1] कर्तव्यमिति शेषः। अन्यत्सुगमम्। तदुक्तम्। अणुभ्यश्च महद्भ्यश्च शास्त्रेभ्यः कुशलो नरः। सर्वतः सारमादद्यात्पुष्पेभ्य इव षट्पदः ॥

[2] साधनान्तरं यथा तथा भवत्वेकाग्रतयैव समाधिपालनद्वारा विवेकसाक्षात्कारो निष्पादनीय इत्याह ॥

[3] See the *Mahábhárata*, xii., 6651. *Ed.*

other thoughts is not interrupted even by a king's passing at his side, so, too, of him whose mind is intent on one point there is in no way an 'interruption of meditation,' i. e., a failure to exclude other thoughts.[1]

[2]कृतनियमलङ्घनादानर्थक्यं लोकवत् ॥ १५ ॥[3]

Rules not to be transgressed with impunity.

Aph. 15. Through transgression of the enjoined rules there is failure in the aim; as in the world.

a. Whatever rule, for the practisers of Concentration, has been laid down in the Institutes, if it be transgressed, then the end, viz., the effecting of knowledge, is not attained. 'As in the world.' That is to say: just as, in ordinary life, if the enjoined procedures, &c., in regard to a medicine, or the like, be neglected, this or that effect thereof will not be obtained.[4]

---

[1] यथा शरनिर्माणायैकचित्तस्येषुकारस्य पार्श्वे राज्ञो गमनेनापि न वृत्त्यन्तरनिरोधो हीयत एवमेकाग्रचित्तस्य सर्वथापि न समाधिहानिर्वृत्त्यन्तरनिरोधक्षतिर्भवति ॥

[2] Aniruddha reads व्रतनियम॰. *Ed.*

[3] Nágeśa is singular in here, apparently, adding, as an aphorism: अशक्त्या ज्ञानरक्षार्थं वा लङ्घने तु न ज्ञानप्रतिबन्धः। These words occur in the midst of Vijnána's comment, and there introduce a quotation from the *Mahábhárata*. *Ed.*

[4] यः शास्त्रेषु कृतो योगिनां नियमस्तस्योल्लङ्घने

b. He states, further, that, if the rules be *forgotten*, the end will not be gained:[1]

तद्विस्मरणेऽपि भेकीवत् ॥ १६ ॥

Rules must not be forgotten.

Aph. 16. Moreover, if they be forgotten; as in the case of the female frog.

a. This is plain. And the story of the female frog is this: A certain king, having gone to hunt, saw a beautiful damsel in the forest. And she, being solicited in marriage by the king, made this stipulation: 'When water shall be shown to me by thee, then I must depart.' But, on one occasion, when wearied with sport, she asked the king, 'Where is water?' The king, too, forgetting his agreement, showed her the water. Then she, having become the she-frog *Kámarúpiṇí*,[2] daughter of the king of the frogs, entered the water. And then the king, though he sought her with nets, &c., did not regain her.[3]

ज्ञाननिष्पत्त्याख्योऽर्थो न भवति। लोकवत्। यथा लोके भैषज्यादौ विहितपथ्यादीनां लङ्घने तत्तत्सिद्धिर्न भवति तद्वदित्यर्थः॥

[1] नियमविस्मरणेऽप्यानर्थक्यमाह॥

[2] Probably this is an epithet, 'changing one's form at will,' not a proper name. *Ed.*

[3] सुगमम्। भेक्याश्चेयमाख्यायिका। कश्चिद्राजा मृगयां गतो विपिने सुन्दरीं कन्यां ददर्श। सा च राज्ञा भार्याभावाय प्रार्थिता नियमं चक्रे यदा मह्यं त्वया जलं प्रदर्श्यते तदा मया गतव्य-

b. He mentions a story with reference to the necessity of reflecting on the words of the teacher, as well as hearing them:[1]

नोपदेशश्रवणेऽपि[2] कृतकृत्यता[3] परामर्शादृते विरोचनवत् ॥ १७ ॥

Reflexion necessary, as well as hearing.

Aph. 17. Not even though instruction be heard is the end gained, without reflexion; as in the case of Virochana.[4]

a. By 'reflexion' is meant such consideration as determines the import of the teacher's words. Without this, though the instruction be heard, knowledge of the truth does not necessarily follow; for it is written, that, though hearing the instruction of Prajápati, Virochana, as

---

मिति। एकदा तु क्रीडया परिश्रान्ता राजानं पप्रच्छ कुत्र जलमिति। राजापि समयं विस्मृत्य जलमदर्शयत्। ततः सा भेकराजदुहिता कामरूपिणी भेकी भूत्वा जलं विवेश। ततश्च राजा जालादिभिरन्विष्यापि न तामविन्ददिति ॥

[1] श्रवणवद्गुरुवाक्यमीमांसाया अप्यावश्यकत्व इतिहासमाह ॥

[2] Vedánti Mahádeva has simply नोपदेशेऽपि. *Ed.*

[3] The reading of Aniruddha is कृतकृत्यः. *Ed.*

[4] See the *Chhándogya Upanishad*, viii., viii., 4. *Ed.*

between Indra and Virochana, wanted discrimination, from want of reflexion:[1]

दृष्टस्तयोरिन्द्रस्य ॥ १८ ॥

Of this further. *Aph.* 18. Of those two, it [reflexion,] was seen in the case of Indra [only].

a. Of those two who are mentioned, [indicated] by the expression 'of those two,' reflexion [was seen, &c.]. And, as between those two, viz., Indra and Virochana, reflexion was seen in the case of Indra: such is the meaning.[2]

b. And he tells us, that, by him who desires to understand thoroughly, attendance on the teacher should be practised for a long time:[3]

प्रणतिब्रह्मचर्योपसर्पणानि कृत्वा सिद्धिर्बहुकालात्तद्वत् ॥ १९ ॥

---

[1] परामर्शो गुरुवाक्यतात्पर्यनिर्णायको विचारः। तं विनोपदेशवाक्यश्रवणेऽपि तत्त्वज्ञाननियमो नास्ति प्रजापतेरुपदेशश्रवणेऽपीन्द्रविरोचनयोर्मध्ये विरोचनस्य परामर्शाभावेन विवेकाभावश्रुतेरित्यर्थः ॥

[2] तच्छब्देनोच्यमानयोः परामर्शः। तयोरिन्द्रविरोचनयोर्मध्ये परामर्श इन्द्रस्य दृष्टश्चेत्यर्थः ॥

[3] सम्यग्ज्ञानार्थिना च गुरुसेवा बहुकालं कर्तव्येत्याह ॥

The process requires time.

Aph. 19. Having performed reverence, the duties of a student, and attendance, one has success after a long time; as in his case.

a. 'As in his case.' That is to say: as in the case of Indra, so in the case of another, too, only after having practised, under a preceptor, reverence, study of the *Vedas*, service, &c., is there 'success,' i. e., the revelation of truth; not otherwise.[1]

न कालनियमो वामदेववत् ॥ २० ॥[2]

The time for the process may embrace successive states of being.

Aph. 20. There is no determination of the time; as in the case of Vámadeva.[3]

a. In the arising of knowledge, there is 'no determination of the time,' as, for instance, in its taking place only from causes dependent on the senses. 'As in the case of Vámadeva.' That is to say: as, in consequence of causes pertaining to a previous life, knowledge arose, in the case of Vámadeva, even when in embryo, so it may in the case of another.[4]

---

[1] तद्वत् । इन्द्रस्येवान्यस्यापि गुरौ प्रणतिवेदाध्ययनसेवादीन्कृत्वैव सिद्धिस्तत्त्वार्थस्फूर्तिर्भवति नान्यथेत्यर्थः ॥

[2] Aniruddha seems to intend, as an aphorism, after No. 20, these words: वामदेवस्य तत्त्वज्ञानात्क्षिप्रं मुक्तिदर्शनात् ।. But perhaps there has been tampering with the text, on the part of copyists. *Ed.*

[3] See the *Aitareya Upanishad*, ii., iv., 5. *Ed.*

[4] ऐन्द्रियकसाधनादेव भवतीत्यादिर्ज्ञानोदये का-

b. But then, since it is written, that the means of knowledge need be nothing other than devotion to those [viz., Brahmá, &c.,] who [unlike the Absolute,] have Qualities, knowledge may result from *this*. Why, then, a hard and subtle process of Concentration? To this he replies:[1]

अध्यस्तरूपोपासनात्पारम्पर्येण[2] यज्ञोपासकाना-
मिव ॥ २१ ॥

Inferior means not altogether unprofitable.

Aph. 21. Through devotion to something under a superinduced form, [attainment to, or approach towards, knowledge takes place] *by degrees*; as in the case of those who devote themselves to sacrifices.

a. Supply 'there is attainment.' Through devotion to Souls, e.g., Brahmá, Vishnu, Śiva, under the forms superinduced on them, the effecting of knowledge takes place 'by degrees,' i.e., by the successive attainment of

---

त्नियमो नास्ति। वामदेववत्। वामदेवस्य ज-न्मान्तरीयसाधनेभ्यो गर्भेऽपि यथा ज्ञानोदयस्त-थान्यस्यापीत्यर्थः ॥

[1] ननु सगुणोपासनाया अपि ज्ञानहेतुत्वश्रवणात्तत एव ज्ञानं भविष्यति किमर्थं दुष्करसूक्ष्मयोगचर्येति। तत्राह ॥

[2] Here the aphorism ends, in my copies of Nágeśa's commentary, and also in some copies of Vijnána's commentary which I examined in India. *Ed.*

the worlds of Brahmá, &c., or else through the purification of the Good principle, &c., but not *directly;* as is the case with sacrificers [whose slaughter of animals, requiring to be expiated, throws them back, so far, in the road to emancipation]: such is the meaning.[1]

b. He tells us, that, moreover, there is no certainty that successive rise to the worlds of Brahmá, &c., would effect knowledge:[2]

[3]इतरलाभेऽप्यावृत्तिः पञ्चाग्नियोगतो जन्मश्रुतेः ॥ २२ ॥

Scriptural proof that heaven gives not liberation.

Aph. 22. Moreover, after the attainment of what [like the world of Brahmá,] is other [than the state of emancipated soul], there is return [to mundane existence]; because it is written [in the 5th *Prapáṭhaka* of the *Chhándogya Upanishad*[4]]: 'From conjunction with the five fires there is birth,' &c.

---

[1] सिद्धिरित्यनुषज्यते । अध्यस्तरूपैः पुरुषाणां ब्रह्मविष्णुहरादीनामुपासनात्पारम्पर्येण ब्रह्मादिलोकप्राप्तिक्रमेण सत्त्वशुद्धिद्वारा वा ज्ञाननिष्पत्तिर्न साक्षाद्यथा याज्ञिकानामित्यर्थः ॥

[2] ब्रह्मादिलोकपरंपरयापि ज्ञाननिष्पत्तौ नास्ति नियम इत्याह ॥

[3] One of my copies of Aniruddha omits अपि after इतरलाभे. *Ed.*

[4] This reference is taken from Vijnána, who, however, does not

a. He exhibits an illustration, to the effect that the effecting of knowledge takes place only in the case of him who is free from passion:[1]

विरक्तस्य हेयहानमुपादेयोपादानं[2] हंसक्षीरवत्
॥ २३ ॥

Discrimination illustrated.

Aph. 23. By him who is free from passion what is to be left is left, and what is to be taken is taken; as in the case of the swan and the milk.

a. That is to say: only by him who is free from passion is there a quitting 'of what is to be left,' i. e., of Nature, &c., and a taking 'of what is to be taken,' i. e., of Soul; as it is only the swan,—and not the crow, or the like,—that, out of milk and water mingled, by means of leaving the unimportant water, takes the valuable milk,[3] [as the Hindus insist that it does].

---

represent that the original of the words 'From conjunction,' &c., is found, literally, in the *Chhándogya Upanishad.* *Ed.*

[1] ज्ञाननिष्पत्तिर्विरक्तस्यैवेत्यत्र निदर्शनमाह ॥

[2] Vijnána, according to some MSS., has, peculiarly, हेयहानमुपादेयादानं; and his comment, in those MSS., follows this reading. *Ed.*

[3] विरक्तस्यैव हेयानां प्रकृत्यादीनां हानमुपादेयस्य चात्मन उपादानं भवतिर्यथा दुग्धजलयोरेकीभावापन्नयोर्मध्येऽसारजलत्यागेन सारभूतक्षीरोपादानं हंसस्यैव नतु काकादेरित्यर्थः ॥

b. He tells us that both of these also take place in consequence of association with a perfect[1] man :[2]

लब्धातिशययोगाद्वा[3] तद्वत् ॥ २४ ॥

Benefit of good society. *Aph.* 24. Or through association with one who has obtained excellence ;[4] as in the case thereof.

a. That is to say: moreover, from association with him by whom 'excellence,' i.e., excellence in knowledge, has been obtained, the aforesaid [discrimination] takes place; just as in the case of the swan, [§ 23]; as, in the case of Alarka,[4] Discrimination manifested itself spontaneously, merely through simple association with Dattátreya.[5]

b. He tells us that we ought not to associate with those who are infected with desire :[6]

न कामचारित्वं रागोपहते शुकवत्[7] ॥ २५ ॥

---

[1] *Siddha. Vide supra*, p. 115, note 3. For the cognate *siddhi*, *vide infra*, p. 310, note 4. *Ed.*

[2] सिद्धपुरुषसङ्गादप्येतदुभयं भवतीत्याह ॥

[3] Nágeśa omits वा. *Ed.*

[4] See the *Márkaṇḍeya-puráṇa*, ch. xvi. *Ed.*

[5] लब्धोऽतिशयो ज्ञानकाष्ठा येन तत्सङ्गादप्युक्तं भवति हंसवदेवेत्यर्थो यथालर्कस्य दत्तात्रेयसङ्गम-मात्रादेव स्वयं विवेकः प्रादुरभूदिति ॥

[6] रागिसङ्गो न कार्य इत्याह ॥

[7] Aniruddha has न शुकवत्कामचारित्वं रागोपहतेः । *Ed.*

Danger of unsuitable society.

Aph. 25. Not of his own accord should he go near one who is infected with desire; like the parrot.

a. Association is not to be made, voluntarily, with a person infected with desire. 'Like the parrot.' That is to say: just as the bird [called a] parrot, by reason of its being exceedingly beautiful, does not [by going near people,] act in a rash manner, through fear of being imprisoned by those who covet it for its beauty.[1]

b. And he states the harm of association with those who labour under desire:[2]

गुणयोगाद्बद्धः[3] शुकवत् ॥ २६ ॥

Of this further.

Aph. 26. [Else he may become] bound, by conjunction with the cords; as in the case of the parrot.

a. And, in the case of associating with those persons, he may become bound, 'by conjunction with the cords,' i. e., by conjunction with their Desire, &c., [the Qualities, punningly compared to cords]; just 'as in the case of the

---

[1] रागोपहते पुरुषे कामतः सङ्गो न कर्तव्यः। शुकवत्। यथा शुकपक्षी प्रकृष्टरूप इति कृत्वा कामचारं न करोति रूपलोलुपैर्बन्धनभयात्तद्वदित्यर्थः ॥

[2] रागिसङ्गे तु दोषमाह ॥

[3] All the commentators but Vijnána read बन्धः, instead of बद्धः. *Ed.*

parrot;' that is to say, just as the bird [called a] parrot becomes bound by the cords, i. e., the ropes, of the hunter.[1]

b. He determines, by two [aphorisms], the means of [effecting] dispassion:[2]

न भोगाद्रागशान्तिर्मुनिवत् ॥ २७ ॥

Means of dispassion. *Aph.* 27. Not by enjoyment is desire appeased; as in the case of the saint.

a. That is to say: as, in the case of the saint, Saubhari,[3] desire was not appeased by enjoyment, so, also in the case of others, it is not.[4]

b. But, further:[5]

दोषदर्शनादुभयोः ॥ २८ ॥

Of this further. *Aph.* 28. From seeing the fault of both.

---

[1] तेषां सङ्गे तु गुणयोगात्तदीयरागादियोगाद्बन्धः स्याच्छुकवदेव यथा शुकपक्षी व्याधस्य गुणै रज्जुभिर्बद्धो भवति तद्वदित्यर्थः ॥

[2] वैराग्यस्याप्युपायमवधारयति द्वाभ्याम् ॥

[3] See the *Vishṇu-puráṇa*, Book iv., Ch. ii. and iii. *Ed.*

[4] यथा मुनेः सौभरेर्भोगान्न रागशान्तिरभूदेवमन्येषामपि न भवतीत्यर्थः ॥

[5] अपि तु ॥

a. That is to say: only 'from seeing the fault,' e. g., of being changeable, of consisting of pain, &c., 'of both,' i. e., of Nature and her productions, does the appeasing of desire take place; just as in the case of the saint [§ 27]. For it is written, that Saubhari, just from seeing the evil of society, was afterwards dispassionate.[1]

b. He tells us that incompetency even to accept instruction attaches to him who is infected with the fault of desire, &c:[2]

न [3]मलिनचेतस्युपदेशबीजप्ररोहोऽजवत् ॥ २९ ॥

Agitation excludes instruction.

Aph. 29. Not in the case of him whose mind is disturbed does the seed of instruction sprout; as in the case of Aja.

a. In him whose mind is disturbed by desire, &c., not even does a sprout spring up from that seed of the tree of knowledge which is in the shape of instruction. 'As in the case of Aja.' That is to say: as not a sprout from

---

[1] उभयोः प्रकृतितत्कार्ययोः परिणामित्वदुःखात्मकत्वादिदोषदर्शनादेव रागशान्तिर्भवति मुनिवदेवेत्यर्थः। सौभरेर्हि सङ्गदोषदर्शनादेव पश्चाद्वैराग्यं श्रूयते ॥

[2] रागादिदोषोपहतस्योपदेशग्रहणेऽप्यनधिकारमाह ॥

[3] Vijnána, agreeably to some MSS., has मलिनचेतनस्याप्युपदेश°. One of my MSS. of Aniruddha has मलिने. *Ed.*

the seed of instruction, though delivered to him by Vasishṭha, sprang up in the king named Aja, whose mind was disturbed by grief for his wife.[1] [2]

b. What need of more?[3]

नाभासमात्रमपि मलिनदर्पणवत् ॥ ३० ॥

Of this further. *Aph.* 30. Not even a mere semblance [of this true knowledge arises in him whose mind is disturbed]; as in the case of a foul mirror.

a. Even superficial knowledge does not arise, from instruction, in one whose mind is disturbed, through the obstruction caused by its wandering away, e.g., to other objects; as an object is not reflected in a foul mirror, through the obstruction caused by the impurities: such is the meaning.[4]

---

[1] उपदेशरूपं यज्ज्ञानवृक्षस्य बीजं तस्याङ्कुरोऽपि रागादिमलिनचित्ते नोत्पद्यते । अजवत् । यथाजनाम्नि नृपे भार्याशोकमलिनचित्ते वसिष्ठेनोक्तस्याप्युपदेशबीजस्य नाङ्कुर उत्पन्न इत्यर्थः ॥

[2] See Kálidása's *Raghuvanśa*, Book viii. *Ed.*

[3] किं बहुना ॥

[4] आपातज्ञानमपि मलिनचेतस्युपदेशान्न जायते विषयान्तरसंचारादिभिः प्रतिबन्धाद्यथा मलैः प्रतिबन्धान्मलिनदर्पणेऽर्थो न प्रतिबिम्बति तद्वदित्यर्थः ॥

b. Or, if knowledge should spring up in any kind of way, still it may not, he tells us, be in accordance with the instruction :[1]

न तज्जस्यापि[2] तद्रूपता पङ्कजवत्[3] ॥ ३१ ॥

Knowledge not necessarily perfect knowledge.

Aph. 31. Nor, even though sprung therefrom, is that [knowledge, necessarily,] in accordance therewith; like the lotus.

a. Though sprung 'therefrom,' i.e., from instruction, knowledge is not [necessarily,] in accordance with the instruction, in case this has not been entirely understood. 'Like the lotus.' That is to say: just as the lotus, though the seed be of the best, is not in accordance with the seed, when the mud is faulty. The mind of the student is compared to the mud[4] [in which the lotus-seed was sown].

---

[1] यदि वा यथाकथंचिज्ज्ञानं जायेत तथाप्युपदेशानुरूपं न भवेदित्याह ॥

[2] Vedánti Mahádeva reads तज्जन्यस्यापि. *Ed.*

[3] Aniruddha has पङ्कजादिवत्. *Ed.*

[4] तस्मादुपदेशाज्जातस्यापि ज्ञानस्योपदेशानुरूपता न भवति सामग्र्येणानवबोधात् । पङ्कजवत् । यथा बीजस्योत्तमत्वेऽपि पङ्कदोषाद्बीजानुरूपतापङ्कजस्य न भवति तद्वदित्यर्थः । पङ्कस्थानीयं शिष्यचित्तम् ॥

b. But then, since the Soul's end is, indeed, gained by [the attainment of] supernatural power in the worlds [§ 21. *a.*] of Brahmá, &c., to what purpose is the effecting of knowledge, with so much toil, for liberation? To this he replies:[1]

न [2]भूतियोगेऽपि[3] कृतकृत्यतोपास्यसिद्धिवदुपास्यसिद्धिवत् ॥ ३२ ॥

Heaven not perfect bliss.

Aph. 32. Not even on the attainment of glorification has that been done which was to be done; as is the case with the perfection[4] of the objects worshipped, as is the case with the perfection of the objects worshipped.

a. Even though one attain to supernatural power, 'that has not been done which was to be done,' i. e., the end has not been gained; because it is attended by the grief of deficiency and excess. 'As is the case with the perfection of the objects worshipped.' That is to say: as, though the possession of perfection [so called,] belongs to 'the objects

---

[1] ननु ब्रह्मलोकादिष्वैश्वर्येणैव पुरुषार्थसिद्धा किमर्थमेतावता प्रयासेन मोक्षाय ज्ञाननिष्पादनम् । तत्राह ॥

[2] According to Nágeśa and Vedánti Mahádeva, भूत°; and this *bhúta*, a synonym of *bhúti*, the former explains by *aiśwarya*. See note 4, below. *Ed.*

[3] One of my MSS. of Aniruddha omits अपि. *Ed.*

[4] Nágeśa, commenting on this aphorism, explains *siddhi*, here rendered 'perfection,' by *aiśwarya*, 'supernatural power.' *Ed.*

worshipped,' i. e., to Brahmá, &c., [still] that has not been done which was to be done; since it is written, that even *these*, while in the sleep of Concentration, &c., [still] *practise* Concentration, [from fear of losing what they have attained to]. Just in like manner is the case with him who, by the worship of these, has attained to their supernatural power. Such is the meaning.[1]

b. So much for the Fourth Book, that of Tales, in the Commentary, composed by Vijnána Bhikshu, on Kapila's Declaration of the Sánkhya.[2]

---

[1] ऐश्वर्ययोगेऽपि कृतकृत्यता कृतार्थता नास्ति क्षयातिशयदुःखैरनुगमात् । उपास्यसिद्धिवत् । यथोपास्यानां ब्रह्मादीनां सिद्धियोगेऽपि न कृतकृत्यता तेषामपि योगनिद्रादौ योगाभ्यासश्रवणात् । तथैव तदुपासनया प्राप्ततदैश्वर्यस्यापीत्यर्थः ॥

[2] इति विज्ञानभिक्षुनिर्मिते कापिलसाङ्ख्यप्रवचनस्य भाष्य आख्यायिकाध्यायश्चतुर्थः ॥

END OF BOOK IV.

BOOK V.

a. The tenets of his Institute are completed. Next is begun a Fifth Book, in order to set aside the primâ facie notions of others in regard to his Institute. Among those, in the first place he disposes of the objection that the Benediction implied by the expression 'Well,' in the first Aphorism [of Book I.], is purposeless:[1]

मङ्गलाचरणं शिष्टाचारात्फलदर्शनाच्छ्रुतितश्चेति[2] ॥ १ ॥

Reasons for a Benedictory Opening.

Aph. 1. The [use of a] Benediction [is justified] by the practice of the good, by our seeing its fruit, and by Scripture.

a. The [use of a] Benediction, which we made, is proved to be proper to be made, by these proofs: such is the

---

[1] स्वशास्त्रसिद्धान्तः पर्याप्तः। इतः परं स्वशास्त्रे परेषां पूर्वपक्षानपाकर्तुं पञ्चमाध्याय आरभ्यते। तत्रादावादिसूत्रेऽथशब्देन यन्मङ्गलं कृतं तद्व्यर्थमित्याक्षेपं समाधत्ते ॥

[2] Aniruddha has, instead of श्रुति°, भूति°. *Vide supra,* p. 310, note 2, for *bhúti. Ed.*

meaning. The word *iti* is intended to preclude the expectation of any other reasons.[1]

b. He repels those who entertain the primâ facie view, that what was asserted in the expression, 'because it is not proved that there *is* a Lord' [see Book I., Aph. 92], is not made out; because [forsooth,] his existence is proved by his being the giver of the fruits of works:[2] [3]

नेश्वराधिष्ठिते फलनिष्पत्तिः[4] कर्मणा तत्सिद्धेः॥२॥

Needlessness of a Lord.

Aph. 2. Not from its [the world's,] being governed by a Lord is there the effectuation of fruit; for it is by works [i.e., by merit and demerit,] that this is accomplished.

a. That is to say: it is not proper [to suppose] the effectuation of the change [of the elements] into the shape of the [appropriate] fruit of works, on the ground that the cause is 'governed by a Lord;' because it is possible for

---

[1] मङ्गलाचरणं यत्कृतं तस्यैतैः प्रमाणैः कर्तव्यतासिद्धिरित्यर्थः। इतिशब्दो हेत्वन्तराकाङ्क्षानिरासार्थः॥

[2] ईश्वरासिद्धेरिति यदुक्तं तन्नोपपद्यते कर्मफलदातृतया तत्सिद्धेरिति ये पूर्वपक्षिणस्तान्निराकरोति॥

[3] For another rendering, see the *Rational Refutation*, &c., p. 78. *Ed.*

[4] Aniruddha's reading is फलसंपत्तिः, and Vedánti Mahádeva has सदाफलसंपत्तिः. *Ed.*

the fruit to be effected by the works [i.e., the merit and demerit,] alone, which are indispensable; [and, if we *do* make the additional and cumbrous supposition of a Lord, he cannot reward a man otherwise than according to his works].[1] [2]

b. He declares, further, in [several] aphorisms, that it is not the case that the Lord is the giver of fruit: [3]

स्वोपकारादधिष्ठानं लोकवत् ॥ ३ ॥

The supposed Lord would be selfish.

Aph. 3. [If a Lord were governor, then,] from intending his own benefit, his government [would be selfish], as is the case [with ordinary governors] in the world.

a. If the Lord were the governor, then his government would be only for his own benefit; as is the case [with ordinary rulers] in the world: such is the meaning.[4]

---

[1] ईश्वराधिष्ठिते कारणे कर्मफलरूपपरिणामस्य निष्पत्तिर्न युक्तावश्यकेन कर्मणैव फलनिष्पत्तिसंभवादित्यर्थः ॥

[2] See, for a somewhat different translation, the *Rational Refutation*, &c., p. 78. *Ed.*

[3] ईश्वरस्य फलदातृत्वं न घटतेऽपीत्याह सूत्रैः ॥

[4] ईश्वरस्याधिष्ठातृत्वे स्वोपकारार्थमेव लोकवदधिष्ठानं स्यादित्यर्थः ॥

b. In reply to the doubt, 'grant that the Lord, also, be benefited: what harm?' he says:[1]

लौकिकेश्वरवदितरथा ॥ ४ ॥

And, therefore, not the Lord spoken of.

Aph. 4. [He must, then, be] just like a worldly lord, [and] otherwise [than you desire that we should conceive of him].

a. If we agree that the Lord, also, is benefited, he, also, must be something mundane, 'just like a worldly lord;' because, since his desires are [on that supposition,] not [previously] satisfied, he must be liable to grief, &c.: such is the meaning.[2]

b. In reply to the doubt, 'be it even so,' he says:[3]

पारिभाषिको वा ॥ ५ ॥

The difficulty perhaps originates in a mistaken expression.

Aph. 5. Or [let the name of Lord be] technical.

a. If, whilst there exists also a world, there be a Lord, then let yours, like ours, be merely a technical term for

---

[1] भवत्वीश्वरस्याप्युपकारः का क्षतिरित्याशङ्क्याह ॥

[2] ईश्वरस्याप्युपकारस्वीकारे लौकिकेश्वरवदेव सोऽपि संसारी स्यादपूर्णकामतया दुःखादिप्रसङ्गादित्यर्थः ॥

[3] तथैव भवत्वित्याशङ्क्याह ॥

that soul which emerged at the commencement of the creation; since there cannot be an eternal lordship, because of the contradiction between mundaneness and the having an unobstructed will: such is the meaning.[1]

b. He states another objection to the Lord's being the governor:[2]

न रागादृते [3]तत्सिद्धिः प्रतिनियतकारणत्वात्
॥ ६ ॥

Objection to there being a Lord.

Aph. 6. This [position, viz., that there is a Lord,] cannot be established without [assuming that he is affected by] Passion; because that is the determinate cause [of all energizing].

a. That is to say: moreover, it cannot be proved that he is a *governor*, unless there be Passion; because Passion is the determinate cause of activity.[4]

---

[1] संसारसत्त्वेऽपि चेदीश्वरस्तर्हि सर्गाद्युत्पन्नपुरुषे परिभाषामात्रमस्माकमिव भवतामपि स्यात्संसारित्वाप्रतिहतेच्छत्वयोर्विरोधान्नित्यैश्वर्यानुपपत्तेरित्यर्थः ॥

[2] ईश्वरस्याधिष्ठातृत्वे बाधकान्तरमाह ॥

[3] जगत्सिद्धिः is the lection of Vedánti Mahádeva, in the text, and also in the comment. *Ed.*

[4] किं च रागं विना नाधिष्ठातृत्वे सिध्यति प्रवृत्तौ रागस्य प्रतिनियतकारणत्वादित्यर्थः ॥

b. But then, be it so, that there is Passion in the Lord, even. To this he replies :[1]

तद्योगेऽपि न नित्यमुक्तः ॥ ७ ॥

This objection, further.

Aph. 7. Moreover, were that [Passion] conjoined with him, he could not be eternally free.

a. That is to say: moreover, if it be agreed that there is conjunction [of the Lord] with Passion, he cannot be eternally free; and, therefore, thy tenet [of his eternal freedom] is invalidated.[2]

b. Pray [let us ask], does lordship arise from the immediate union, with Soul, of the wishes, &c., which we hold to be properties of Nature, [not properties of Soul]? Or from an influence by reason of the mere existence of proximity, as in the case of the magnet? Of these he condemns the former alternative:[3]

---

[1] नन्वेवमस्तु रागोऽपीश्वरे। तत्राह॥

[2] रागयोगेऽपि स्वीक्रियमाणे स नित्यमुक्तो न स्यात्ततश्च ते सिद्धान्तहानिरित्यर्थः॥

[3] ऐश्वर्यं किं प्रधानधर्मत्वेनास्मदभिमतानामिच्छादीनां साक्षादेव चेतनसंबन्धात्। किं वायस्कान्तमणिवत्संनिधिसत्तामात्रेण प्रेरकत्वादिति। तत्राद्यं पक्षं दूषयति॥

प्रधानशक्तियोगाच्चेत्सङ्गापत्तिः[1] ॥ ८ ॥

Objection, on one branch of an alternative.

Aph. 8. If it were from the conjunction of the properties of Nature, it would turn out that there is association, [which Scripture denies of Soul].

a. From the conjunction, with Soul, of 'the properties of Nature,' i.e., Desire, &c., Soul, also, would turn out [contrary to Scripture,] to be associated with properties.[2]

b. But, in regard to the latter [alternative], he says:[3]

[4]सत्तामाचाच्चेत्सर्वैश्वर्यम् ॥ ९ ॥

Objection, on the other branch.

Aph. 9. If it were from the mere existence [of Nature, not in association, but simply in proximity], then lordship would belong to every one.

---

[1] -योगाच्चेद्धर्मसङ्गापत्तिः is the reading of Vijnána, in some MSS., and, in some, that of Nágeśa, who, however, in others, omits चेत्. *Ed.*

[2] प्रधानशक्तेरिच्छादेः पुरुषे योगात्पुरुषस्यापि धर्मसङ्गापत्तिः ॥

[3] अन्ये त्वाह ॥

[4] Some MSS. of Vijnána exhibit, instead of सत्तामाचात्, सत्तामाचेण. *Ed.*

a. That is to say: if lordship is by reason of the mere existence of proximity, as in the case of the magnet [which becomes affected by the simple proximity of iron], then it is settled, as we quite intend it should be, that even all men, indifferently, experiencers in this or that [cycle of] creation, [may] have lordship; because it is only by conjunction with all experiencers, that Nature produces Mind, &c. And, therefore, your tenet of there being only one Lord is invalidated.[1]

b. Be it as you allege; yet these are false reasonings; because they contradict the evidence which establishes [the existence of] a Lord. Otherwise, Nature, also, could be disproved by thousands of false reasonings of the like sort. He therefore says:[2]

प्रमाणाभावान्न तत्सिद्धिः १० ॥

Denial that there is any evidence of a Lord.

Aph. 10. It is not established [that there is an eternal Lord]; because there is no evidence of it.

---

[1] अयस्कान्तवत्संनिधिसत्तामात्रेण चेदैश्वर्यं तर्हि सर्वेषामेव तत्तत्सर्गेषु भोक्तॄणां पुंसामविशेषेणैश्वर्यमस्मदभिप्रेतमेव सिद्धमखिलभोक्तृसंयोगादेव प्रधानेन महदादिसर्जनादिति। ततश्चैक एवेश्वर इति भवत्सिद्धान्तहानिरित्यर्थः ॥

[2] स्यादेतदीश्वरसाधकप्रमाणविरोधेनैतेऽसत्तर्का एव। अन्यथैवंविधासत्तर्कसहस्रैः प्रधानमपि बाधितुं शक्यत इत्यत आह ॥

a. Its establishment, i.e., the establishing that there is an eternal Lord. Of the Lord, in the first place, there is not *sense*-evidence; so that only the evidences of inference and of testimony can be offered; and these are inapplicable: such is the meaning.[1]

b. The inapplicability he sets forth in two aphorisms:[2]

संबन्धाभावान्नानुमानम् ॥११॥

Denial that it can be established by inference.

Aph. 11. There is no inferential proof [of there being a Lord]; because there is [here] no [case of invariable] association [between a sign and that which it might betoken].

a. 'Association,' i.e., invariable concomitancy. 'There is none;' i.e., none exists, [in this case]. And so there is no inferential proof of there being a Lord; because, in such arguments as, 'Mind, or the like, has a maker, because it is a product,' [the fact of] invariable concomitancy[3] is not established; since there is no compulsion [that every product should have had an intelligent maker]. Such is the meaning.[4]

---

[1] तत्सिद्धिर्नित्येश्वरसिद्धिः। ईश्वरे तावत्प्रत्यक्षं नास्तीत्यनुमानशब्दावेव प्रमाणे वक्तव्ये ते च न संभवत इत्यर्थः॥

[2] असंभवमेव प्रतिपादयति सूत्राभ्याम्॥

[3] *Vyápyatwa*, here rendered, is regarded as a synonym of *vyápti*, by which *sambandha*, 'association,' is interpreted just above. Hence I have bracketed the words 'the fact of.' *Ed.*

[4] संबन्धो व्याप्तिः। अभावोऽसिद्धिः। तथा च

b. Nor, moreover, he tells us, is there [the evidence of] Testimony[1] [to there being a Lord]:

श्रुतिरपि प्रधानकार्यत्वस्य ॥ १२ ॥

Denial that there is Scripture for it.

Aph. 12. Moreover, there is Scripture for [this world's] being the product of Nature, [not of a Lord].

a. Scripture asserts, exclusively, that the world is the product of Nature, not that it has Soul for its cause.[2]

b. He refutes, diffusely, by a cluster [of seven aphorisms],[3] the opinion of an opponent in regard to that which was established in the first Section,[4] viz., 'Bondage does not arise from Ignorance,' [conjoined with Soul].[5]

महदादिकं सकर्तृकं कार्यत्वादित्याद्यनुमानेष्वप्रयोजकत्वेन व्याप्यत्वासिद्ध्या नेश्वरेऽनुमानमित्यर्थः ॥

[1] नापि शब्द इत्याह ॥

[2] प्रपञ्चे प्रधानकार्यत्वस्यैव श्रुतिरस्ति न चेतनकारणत्वे ॥

[3] Read, instead of 'by a cluster,' &c., 'by enunciations.' *Vide* p. 264, note 4, *supra*. *Ed.*

[4] *Pada*, here used for *adhyáya*, which the translator renders by 'Book.' For the Aphorism referred to, and carelessly quoted in part, *vide supra*, p. 24. *Ed.*

[5] नाविद्यातो बन्ध इति यत्सिद्धान्तितं प्रथमपादे तत्र परमतं विस्तरतः प्रघट्टकेन दूषयति ॥

नाविद्याशक्तियोगो निःसङ्गस्य ॥ १३ ॥

Conjunction, in the case of the solitary, would be a contradiction.

Aph. 13. With that which is solitary there cannot be conjunction of the property of Ignorance.

a. Since Soul has no association [with anything whatever], it is plainly impossible for it to be united with the property of Ignorance.[1]

b. But then, [it may be replied,] what is to be asserted is, that the conjunction of Ignorance is simply through force of Ignorance [which is a negation, or nonentity]; and so, since this is no *reality*, there is no *association* occasioned thereby. To this he replies:[2]

तद्योगे तत्सिद्धावन्योन्याश्रयत्वम् ॥ १४ ॥

A suggestion repelled.

Aph. 14. Since the existence of this [alleged *negative* Ignorance] is established [only] on the ground of its [pretended] conjunction, there is a vicious circle.[3]

a. And, if it is by the conjunction of Ignorance that Ignorance is established, there is 'a vicious circle,' [lite-

---

[1] निःसङ्गतया चेतनस्याविद्याशक्तियोगः साक्षान्न संभवतीति ॥

[2] नन्वविद्यावशादेवाविद्यायोगो वक्तव्यस्तथा चापारमार्थिकत्वान्न तया सङ्ग इति । तत्राह ॥

[3] For a different translation of this Aphorism, and of what introduces and succeeds it, see the *Rational Refutation*, &c., p. 257. *Ed.*

rally, a resting of each on the other, alternately], a resting a thing on itself, or, in short, a *regressus in infinitum*.[1]

b. In reply to the doubt [suggested by the Naiyáyika], 'but then, as in the case of seed and sprout, the *regressus in infinitum* is no objection,' he replies:[2]

न बीजाङ्कुरवत्सादिसंसारश्रुतेः ॥ १५ ॥

The world has a beginning.

Aph. 15. It is not as in the case of seed and sprout; for Scripture teaches that the world *has* a beginning.

a. There cannot belong to it such a *regressus in infinitum* as that of seed and sprout; because there is Scripture for the fact that the mundane state of souls, consisting of all undesirable things, viz., Ignorance, &c., had a beginning. For we hear, in Scripture, that these cease to exist at the dissolution of all things, in profound sleep, &c. Such is the meaning.[3]

b. But then, [you Vedántís will say], according to us, Ignorance is technically so termed, and is not, e. g., in

---

[1] अविद्यायोगादविद्यासिद्धौ चान्योन्याश्रयत्वमात्माश्रयत्वमनवस्था वेति शेषः ॥

[2] ननु बीजाङ्कुरवदनवस्था न दोषायेत्याशङ्क्याह ॥

[3] बीजाङ्कुरवदनवस्था न संभवति पुरुषाणां संसारस्याविद्याद्यखिलानर्थरूपस्य सादित्वश्रुतेः । प्रलयसुषुप्त्यादावभावश्रवणादित्यर्थः ॥

the shape, specified by the *Yoga*, of supposing what is not soul to be soul; and so, just like your 'Nature,' since this [Ignorance] of ours has an unbroken eternity, though it be lodged in Soul, there is no disparagement of the solitariness thereof: in regard to this doubt, having deliberated on this artificial sense of the word 'Ignorance,' he objects to it:[1]

विद्यातोऽन्यत्वे[2] ब्रह्मबाधप्रसङ्गः[3] ॥ १६ ॥

Soul and knowledge not identical.

Aph. 16. Then Brahma would be found to be excluded [from existence]; because he is something else than knowledge.

a. If the meaning of the word 'Ignorance' (*avidyá*) be only 'otherness than knowledge,' then *Brahma*, soul itself, would be found to be excluded, to perish, through his being annihilable by knowledge; since *he* is other than knowledge: such is the meaning.[4] [Further]:

---

[1] नन्वस्माकमविद्या पारिभाषिकी नतु योगोक्तानात्मन्यात्मबुद्ध्यादिरूपा तथा च भवतां प्रधानवदेवास्माकमपि तस्या अखण्डानादितया पुरुषनिष्ठत्वेऽपि नासङ्गताहानिरित्याशङ्कायां परिकल्पितमविद्याशब्दार्थं विकल्प्य दूषयति ॥

[2] One of my MSS. of Nágeśa has विद्यान्यत्वे. *Ed.*

[3] -प्रसक्तेः, found in some MSS. of Vijnána, is the reading of Aniruddha and of Nágeśa. *Ed.*

[4] यदि विद्यान्यत्वमेवाविद्याशब्दार्थस्तर्हि तस्य

अबाधे नैष्फल्यम् ॥ १७ ॥

Knowledge, not excluding ignorance, would be resultless.

Aph. 17. Were there not exclusion, then there would be resultlessness.

a. But, if the existence of ignorance were really not excluded by knowledge, then there would be resultlessness of knowledge, because of its not debarring Ignorance, [which is the only result competent to knowledge]: such is the meaning.[1]

b. He censures the other alternative,[2] [viz., that knowledge *might* exclude Soul]:

विद्याबाध्यत्वे जगतोऽप्येवम् ॥ १८ ॥

On the Vedánta theory, the world ought to vanish.

Aph. 18. If it [Ignorance,] meant the being excludible by Knowledge, it would be [predicable], in like manner, of the world, also.

a. If, on the other hand, the being excludible by Knowledge, in the case of the soul, which possesses properties,

---

ज्ञाननाश्यतया ब्रह्मण आत्मनोऽपि बाधो नाशः प्रसज्यते विद्याभिन्नत्वादित्यर्थः ॥

[1] यदि त्वविद्यारूपमपि विद्यया न बाध्येत तर्हि विद्यावैफल्यमविद्यानिवर्तकत्वाभावादित्यर्थः ॥

[2] पक्षान्तरं दूषयति ॥

be, indeed, what is meant by the being Ignorance, in that case 'the world,' the whole mundane system, viz., Nature, Mind, &c., would, also, in like manner, be Ignorance. And so, the whole mundane system being merely Ignorance, since the Ignorance would be annihilated by one man's knowledge, the mundane system would become invisible to others, also. Such is the import.[1]

तद्रूपत्वे सादित्वम्[2] ॥ १९ ॥

The Vedánta theory self-contradictory.

Aph. 19. If it [Ignorance,] were of *that* nature, it would be something that had a commencement.

a. Or suppose it to be the case, that to be Ignorance means simply the being excludible by Knowledge, still such a thing could not have had an *eternal* existence in souls [as held by Vedántís (see § 15, *b.*)], but must have had a commencement. For it is proved, by such re-

---

[1] यदि पुनर्विद्यया चेतने धर्मिणि बाध्यत्वमेवाविद्यात्वमुच्यते तथा सति जगतः प्रकृतिमहदाद्यखिलप्रपञ्चस्याप्येवमविद्यात्वं स्यात् । तथा चाखिलप्रपञ्चस्यैवाविद्यात्वे सत्येकस्य ज्ञानेनाविद्यानाशादन्यैरपि प्रपञ्चो न दृश्येतेति भावः ॥

[2] Owing to a clerical defect, both my MSS. of Nágeśa's work omit this Aphorism, and also much of the comment preceding and following it. *Ed.*

cited texts as, 'Consisting of knowledge alone,'[1][2] &c., that, at the time of the universal dissolution, &c., the soul consists of Knowledge alone. Such is the meaning. Therefore, it is settled that there is no other Ignorance, annihilable by Knowledge, than that stated in the *Yoga* system; and this is a property of the understanding only, not a property of the soul.[3]

b. By a cluster of [six] aphorisms,[4] he clears up the primâ facie view of an opponent, in regard to that which was stated in the same Book [Book V., § 2], that Nature's energizing is due to Merit:[5]

---

1 *Bṛihadáraṇyaka Upanishad*, ii. 4, 12; or *Śatapatha-bráhmaṇa*, xiv., 5, 4, 12. *Ed.*

2 Professor Gough has, 'a pure indifference of thought.' *Philosophy of the Upanishads*, p. 153. *Ed.*

3 भवतु वा यथा कथंचिद्विद्याबाध्यत्वमेवाविद्यात्वं तथापि तादृशवस्तुनः सादित्वमेव पुरुषेषु नत्वनादित्वं संभवति । विज्ञानघन एवेत्याद्युक्तश्रुतिभिः प्रलयादौ पुरुषस्य चिन्मात्रत्वसिद्धेरित्यर्थः । तस्माद्योगदर्शनोक्तादन्या नास्त्यविद्या ज्ञाननाश्या सा च बुद्धिधर्म एव न पुरुषधर्म इति सिद्धम् ॥

4 Read, instead of 'by a cluster,' &c., 'by enunciations.' *Ed.*

5 अत्रैवाध्याये कर्मनिमित्ता प्रधानप्रवृत्तिरिति यदुक्तं तत्र परपूर्वपक्षं समाधत्ते प्रघट्टकेन ॥

न धर्मापलापः प्रकृतिकार्यवैचित्र्यात् ॥ २० ॥

Merit is undeniable.

Aph. 20. There is no denying Merit; because of the diversity in the operations of Nature.

a. Merit is not to be denied on the ground of its being no object of sense; because it is inferred; since, otherwise, 'the diversity in the operations of Nature' [accommodating one person, and inconveniencing another,] would be unaccounted for: such is the meaning.[1]

b. He states further proof, also:[2]

श्रुतिलिङ्गादिभिस्तत्सिद्धिः ॥ २१ ॥

Proofs of this.

Aph. 21. It [the existence of Merit,] is established by Scripture, by tokens, &c.

a. He shows to be a fallacy the argument of the opponent, that Merit exists not, because of there being no sense-evidence of it:[3]

न नियमः प्रमाणान्तरावकाशात् ॥ २२ ॥

---

[1] अप्रत्यक्षतया धर्मापलापो न संभवति प्रकृतिकार्येषु वैचित्र्यान्यथानुपपत्त्या तदनुमानादित्यर्थः ॥

[2] प्रमाणान्तरमप्याह ॥

[3] प्रत्यक्षाभावाद्धर्मासिद्धिरिति परस्य हेतुमाभासीकरोति ॥

Sense-evidence not the only kind of evidence.

Aph. 22. There is, here, no necessity; for there is room for other proofs.

a. That is to say: there is no necessity that a thing of which there is no mundane sense-evidence must be non-existent; because things are subject to *other* proofs.[1]

b. He proves that there exists Demerit, as well as Merit:[2]

उभयचाप्येयम् ॥ २३ ॥

Demerit as certain as Merit.

Aph. 23. It is thus, moreover, in both cases.

a. That is to say: the proofs apply to Demerit, just as they do to Merit.[3]

अर्थात्सिद्धिश्चेत्समानमुभयोः ॥ २४ ॥

The proof of each the same.

Aph. 24. If the existence [of Merit] be as of course, [because, otherwise, something would be unaccounted for], the same is the case in respect of both.

a. But then, *merit* is proved to exist by a natural consequence in this shape, viz., that, otherwise, an injunction

---

[1] लौकिकप्रत्यक्षाभावाद्वस्त्वभाव इति नियमो नास्ति प्रमाणान्तरेणापि वस्तूनां विषयीकरणादित्यर्थः ॥

[2] धर्मवदधर्ममपि साधयति ॥

[3] धर्मवदधर्मेऽप्येवं प्रमाणानीत्यर्थः ॥

would be unaccounted for; but there is none such in respect of *demerit*: so how can Scriptural or logical argument be extended to *demerit*? If any one says this, it is not so; since there is proof, in the shape of natural consequence, 'it is alike, in respect of both,' i. e., of both merit and demerit; because, otherwise, a *prohibitory* injunction, such as, 'He should not approach another's wife,' would be unaccounted for. Such is the meaning.[1]

b. He repels the doubt, that, if Merit, &c., be acknowledged [to exist], then, in consequence of souls' having properties, &c., they must be liable to modification, &c.:[2]

अन्तःकरणधर्मत्वं धर्मादीनाम् ॥ २५ ॥

Merit, &c., inhere in what.

Aph. 25. It is of the internal organ[3] [not of *soul*,] that Merit, &c., are the properties.

---

[1] ननु विध्यन्यथानुपपत्तिरूपयार्थापत्त्या धर्मसिद्धिः सा च नास्त्यधर्मे इति कथं श्रौतलिङ्गातिदेशोऽधर्मे इति चेन्न यतः समानमुभयोर्धर्माधर्मयोरर्थापत्तिरूपं प्रमाणमस्ति परदारान्न गच्छेदिति निषेधविध्यन्यथानुपपत्तेरित्यर्थः ॥

[2] ननु धर्मादिकं चेत्स्वीकृतं तर्हि पुरुषाणां धर्मादिमत्त्वेन परिणामाद्यापत्तिरित्याशङ्कां परिहरति ॥

[3] The 'great internal organ' (*mahat*), called also *buddhi*, is here referred to. See Book I., Aph. 64, *a*. Aniruddha's comment runs:

a. In the expression '&c.' are included all those that are stated, in the *Vaiśeshika* Institute, as peculiar qualities of soul.[1][2]

b. [To the objection, that the existence of an internal organ, as well as of the Qualities from which such might arise, is debarred by Scripture, he replies]:

गुणादीनां च नात्यन्तबाधः ॥ २६ ॥

The Qualities exist, though not in soul.

Aph. 26. And of the Qualities, &c., there is not absolute debarment.

a. The Qualities, viz., Purity, &c., and their properties, viz., happiness, &c., and their products, also, viz., Mind, &c., are not denied essentially, but are denied only adjunctively in respect of soul; just as we deny that heat [in red-hot iron,] belongs to the iron.[3]

b. In regard to the doubt, 'Why, again, do we not deny

बुद्धिधर्मत्वम् । आत्मधर्मत्वे निःसङ्गत्वश्रुतिविरोधः । *Ed.*

[1] आदिशब्देन वैशेषिकशास्त्रोक्ताः सर्व आत्मविशेषगुणा गृह्यन्ते ॥

[2] *Vide supra*, p. 71, Aph. 61, *b.* *Ed.*

[3] गुणानां सत्त्वादीनां तद्धर्माणां च सुखादीनां तत्कार्याणामपि महदादीनां स्वरूपतो नास्ति बाधः किं तु संसर्गत एव चेतने बाधोऽयस्यौष्ण्यबाधवत् ॥

them an essence, as we do to what is meant by the words *sleep*, *wish*, &c ?' he says : [1]

[2]पञ्चावयवयोगात्सुखसंवित्तिः[3] ॥ २७ ॥

The above thesis argued. *Aph.* 27. By a conjunction of the five members [of an argumentative statement] we discern [that] Happiness [exists].

a. Here, in order to get a particular subject of his assertion, he takes *happiness* alone, one portion of the matter in dispute, as a representative of the entire matter. But the better reading is, 'we discern [that] Happiness, &c., [exist].' The five members of an argumentative statement are the Proposition, Reason, Example, Synthesis [of the two premises], and Conclusion; and, by the 'conjunction,' i. e., the combination, of these, all things, viz., Happiness, &c., are proved to exist. Such is the meaning. [4]

---

[1] कुतः पुनः स्वरूपत एव बाधो न भवति स्वप्नमनोरथादिपदार्थवदित्याकाङ्क्षायामाह ॥

[2] One of my MSS. of Aniruddha has -संयोगात्. *Ed.*

[3] Nágeśa has सुखादिसंवित्तिः, the lection which, according to Vijnána, is to be preferred. *Ed.*

[4] अत्र विशिष्य पक्षीकरणाय विवादविषयैकदेशस्य सुखमात्रस्य ग्रहणं सर्वविषयोपलक्षकम् । सुखादिसंवित्तिरिति पाठस्तु समीचीनः । पञ्चावयवाश्च न्यायस्य प्रतिज्ञाहेतूदाहरणोपनयनिग-

b. And the employment [of the argument] is this:

(1) Pleasure is real;
(2) Because it produces motion in something.
(3) Whatever produces motion in anything is real, as are sentient beings;
(4) And pleasure produces motion in things, in the way of horripilation, &c.:
(5) Therefore, it is real.[1]

c. But then the *Chárváka*, next, doubts whether there be any evidence other than sense-evidence; since [he contends,] there is no truth in the assertion [of an inductive conclusion], that such and such is pervaded by such and such, &c.[2] [3]

न सकृद्ग्रहणात्संबन्धसिद्धिः ॥ २८ ॥

मनानि तेषां योगान्मेलनात्सुखाद्यखिलपदार्थसिद्धिरित्यर्थः ॥

[1] प्रयोगश्चायम् । सुखं सत् । अर्थक्रियाकारित्वात् । यद्यदर्थक्रियाकारि तत्सद्यथा चेतनाः । पुलकादिरूपार्थक्रियाकारि च सुखम् । तस्मात्सदिति ॥

[2] ननु प्रत्यक्षातिरिक्तं प्रमाणमेव न भवति व्याप्यत्वाद्यसिद्धेरिरि चार्वाकः पुनः शङ्कते ॥

[3] For the Chárvákas' rejection of the authority of inference, see pp. 5, *et seq.*, of the translation of the *Sarva-darśana-sangraha* by Professors Cowell and Gough. *Ed.*

The validity of inference questioned.

Aph. 28. Not from once apprehending is a connexion established.

a. That is to say: from *once* apprehending concomitance [of a supposed token and the thing betokened], a 'connexion,' i.e., a pervadedness [or invariable attendedness of the token by the betokened,] is not established; and *frequency* [of the same apprehension] follows[1] [the rule of the single apprehension; just as a thousand times nothing amount to nothing]. Therefore [argues the sceptic,] since the apprehending of an invariable attendedness is impossible, nothing can be established by *Inference.* [This] he clears up:[2]

[3]नियतधर्मसाहित्यमुभयोरेकतरस्य वा व्याप्तिः ॥ २९ ॥

This point cleared up.

Aph. 29. Pervadedness is a constant consociation of characters, in the case of both, or of one of them.

a. 'Consociation of characters', i.e., consociation in the fact of being characters [or properties of something]; in short, concomitancy. And so we mean, that that concomitancy is 'pervadedness,' [furnishing solid ground for infer-

---

[1] As suggestive of the correction here required, see Professor Cowell's *Aphorisms of Śáṇḍilya*, &c., p. 8, text and foot-note. *Ed.*

[2] सकृत्सहचारग्रहणात्संबन्धो व्याप्तिर्न सिध्यति भूयस्त्वं चाननुगतम् । अतो व्याप्तिग्रहासंभवान्नानुमानेनार्थसिद्धिरित्यर्थः । समाधत्ते ॥

[3] Nágeśa has, instead of नियत°, नियतं. *Ed.*

ence], which is invariably non-errant, whether in the case of 'both,' the predicate and the reason, or in the case of 'one of them,' the reason only. 'Of both' is mentioned with reference to the case of 'equal pervadedness': [e. g., every equilateral triangle is equiangular, and, conversely, every equiangular triangle is equilateral]. And the invariableness may be apprehended through an appropriate confutation [or *reductio ad absurdum* of the denial of it]; so that there is no impossibility in apprehending 'pervadedness,' [and of inferring on the strength of it]. Such is the import.[1]

b. He declares that Pervadedness is not an additional principle, consisting, e. g., of some such power as is to be mentioned[2] [in § 31]:

न तत्त्वान्तरं वस्तुकल्पनाप्रसक्तेः ॥ ३० ॥

Pervadedness not an additional principle.

Aph. 30. It [Pervadedness,] is not [as some think (see § 31),] an additional principle [over and above the twenty-five (Book I., § 61)]; for it is unsuitable to postulate entities [*praeter rationem*].

---

[1] धर्मसाहित्यं धर्मतायां साहित्यं सहचार इति यावत्। तथा चोभयोः साध्यसाधनयोरेकतरस्य साधनमात्रस्य वा नियतोऽव्यभिचरितो यः सहचारः स व्याप्तिरित्यर्थः। उभयोरिति समव्याप्तिपक्षे प्रोक्तम्। नियमश्चानुकूलतर्केण ग्राह्य इति न व्याप्तिग्रहासंभव इति भावः॥

[2] व्याप्तिर्वक्ष्यमाणशक्त्यादिरूपं पदार्थान्तरं न भवतीत्याह॥

a. 'Pervadedness' is not an entity other than a fixed consociation of characters; because it is unsuitable to suppose, further, some entity as the residence of what constitutes 'pervadedness.' But *we* consider that what constitutes 'pervadedness' belongs to extant things simply. Such is the meaning.[1]

b. He states the opinion of others:[2]

निजशक्त्युद्भवमित्याचार्याः ॥ ३१ ॥

A heterodox opinion regarding 'Pervadedness.'

Aph. 31. [But certain] teachers say that it [Pervadedness,] is [another principle, in addition to the twenty-five,] resulting from the power of the thing itself.

a. But other teachers assert that 'Pervadedness' is, positively, a separate principle, in the shape of a species of power, generated by the native power of the 'pervaded.' But [they continue,] 'Pervadedness' is not simply a power of the [pervaded] thing itself; else it would exist wherever the thing is, [which 'pervadedness' does *not* do]. For smoke, when it has gone to another place [than the point of its origination], is not attended by fire; and, by going into another place, that power is put an end to. Therefore [contend these teachers,] there is no over-extension in the

---

[1] नियतधर्मसाहित्यातिरिक्तं वस्तु व्याप्तिर्न भवति व्याप्तित्वाश्रयस्य वस्तुनोऽपि कल्पनाप्रसङ्गात् । अस्माभिस्तु सिद्धवस्तुन एव व्याप्तित्वमात्रं कल्पितमित्यर्थः ॥

[2] परमतमाह ॥

above-stated definition; for, according to our doctrine, the smoke [which betokens fire] is to be specialized as that which is at the time of origination. Such is the import.[1]

आधेयशक्तियोग इति पञ्चशिखः ॥ ३२ ॥

Opinion of Panchaśikha.

Aph. 32. Panchaśikha[2] says that it ['Pervadedness,'] is the possession of the power of the sustained.

a. That is to say: Panchaśikha holds that *pervadingness* is the power which consists in being the *sustainer*, and that 'Pervadedness'[3] is the having the power which consists in being the sustained; for Intellect, and the rest, are treated as being pervaded [or invariably attended,] by Nature, &c.;[4]

---

[1] अपरे त्वाचार्या व्याप्यस्य स्वशक्तिजन्यं शक्तिविशेषरूपं तत्त्वान्तरमेव व्याप्तिरित्याहुः । निजशक्तिमात्रं तु यावद्द्रव्यस्थायितया न व्याप्तिः । देशान्तरगतस्य धूमस्य वह्न्यव्याप्यत्वाद्देशान्तरगमनेन च सा शक्तिर्नाश्यत इति नोक्तलक्षणेऽतिव्याप्तिः स्वमते तूत्पत्तिकालावच्छिन्नत्वेन धूमो विशेषणीय इति भावः ॥

[2] The translator's 'the Panchaśikha' I have everywhere corrected. *Ed.*

[3] This is to render *vyápyatwa*, on which *vide supra*, p. 320, note 3. *Ed.*

[4] बुद्ध्यादिषु प्रकृत्यादिव्याप्यताव्यवहारादाधार-

[and this means that each product, in succession, is *sustained* by what precedes it in the series].

b. But then, why is a 'power of the sustained' postulated? Let 'Pervadedness' be simply an essential power of the *thing* pervaded. To this he [Panchaśikha,] replies:[1]

न [2]स्वरूपशक्तिर्नियमः पुनर्वादप्रसक्तेः ॥ ३३ ॥

Panchaśikha's reply to an objection.

Aph. 33. The relation is not an essential power; for we should have [in that case,] a tautology.

a. But 'the relation,' viz., 'Pervadedness,' is not an essential power; for we should [thus] have a tautology; because, just as there is no difference between 'water-jar' and 'jar for water,' so, also, there is none in the case of 'Intellect' and 'what is Pervaded' [by Nature, of which Intellect consists]. Such is the meaning.[3]

ताशक्तिर्व्यापकताधेयताशक्तिमत्त्वं च व्याप्यत्वमिति पञ्चशिख इत्यर्थः ॥

[1] नन्वाधेयशक्तिः किमर्थं कल्प्यते । व्याप्यस्य वस्तुनः स्वरूपशक्तिरेव व्याप्तिरस्तु । तत्राह ॥

[2] Aniruddha and Vedánti Mahádeva read स्वरूपशक्तिनियमः. *Ed.*

[3] स्वरूपशक्तिस्तु नियमो व्याप्तिर्न भवति पौनरुक्त्यप्रसङ्गाद्घटः कलश इतिवद्बुद्धिर्व्याप्येत्यत्राप्यर्थाभेदेनेत्यर्थः ॥

b. He himself explains the 'Tautology:'[1]

विशेषणानर्थक्यप्रसक्तेः ॥ ३४ ॥

The reason why. *Aph.* 34. Because we should find the distinction unmeaning; [as Intellect does not differ from Nature at all, except as does the sustained from the sustainer].

a. This is almost explained by the preceding aphorism.[2]

b. He [Panchaśikha,] mentions another objection:[3]

पल्लवादिष्वनुपपत्तेश्च[4] ॥ ३५ ॥

A further reason. *Aph.* 35. And because it [Pervadedness,] would not be reconcilable in shoots, &c.

a. Because shoots, &c., are invariably attended [at their origination,] by trees, &c. But this cannot be called simply an essential power [in the shoot]; because, since the essential power [that which belongs to the shoot *as being* a shoot,] does not depart, even in the case of an amputated shoot, we should, even then, find it attended [by the tree, which, however, no longer accompanies it]. Such is the sense. But the power [(see § 32), which consists in having the

---

[1] पौनरुक्त्यं स्वयमेव विवृणोति ॥

[2] पूर्वसूत्र एव व्याख्यातप्रायमिदम् ॥

[3] दूषणान्तरमाह ॥

[4] Aniruddha omits च. *Ed.*

character] of the 'sustained' is destroyed at the time of amputation; so that there is no 'Pervadedness' *then*. Such is the import.[1]

b. But then what? Panchaśikha says that 'Pervadedness' is not a result of any *essential* power. Then, since smoke is not *sustained* by fire [see § 32, where he contends that 'sustainedness' is what really expresses *pervasion*], it would turn out that it [viz., smoke,] is *not* [as token of something that is betokened,] *accompanied* by fire. To this he says:[2]

आधेयशक्तिसिद्धौ निजशक्तियोगः समानन्यायात् ॥ ३६ ॥

Reply, that this would prove too much.

Aph. 36. Were it [thus] settled that it is a power of the 'sustained,' then, by the like argument, its dependence on an essential power, [as pretended by the heterodox teachers

---

[1] पल्लवादिषु वृक्षादिव्याप्यतास्ति । स्वरूपशक्तिमात्रं तु तस्य लक्षणं न संभवति छिन्नपल्लवेऽपि स्वरूपशक्तेरनपायेन तदानीमपि व्याप्यतापत्तेरित्यर्थः । आधेयशक्तिस्तु छेदकाले विनष्टेति न तदानीं व्याप्तिरिति भावः ॥

[2] ननु किं पञ्चशिखेन निजशक्त्युद्भवो व्याप्तिरेव नोच्यते । तर्हि धूमस्य वह्न्याधेयत्वाभावाद्वह्निव्याप्यतापत्तिरिति । तत्राह ॥

referred to in § 31, might be proved, also; and thus the argument proves nothing, since it proves too much].

a. That is to say: 'were it settled' that 'a power of the sustained' constitutes the fact of 'Pervadedness,' it would be really settled 'by the like argument,' i.e., by parity of reasoning, that the fact of 'Pervadedness' results from essential power, also, [§ 31, *a.*].[1]

b. It was with a view to substantiate what was stated [in § 27], viz., that the Qualities, and the rest, are established [as realities,] by the employment of the five-membered [form of argumentative exposition], that he has repelled, by an exposition of 'Pervadedness,' the objection to Inference as evidence, [or as a means of attaining right notions].[2]

c. Now, in order to establish the fact that *words*, of which the five-membered [exposition] consists, are generators of knowledge, the objection of others to a *word's* being a means of right knowledge,[3] in the shape of [the objection

---

[1] आधेयशक्तेर्व्याप्तित्वसिद्धौ निजशक्त्युद्भवोऽपि व्याप्तित्वेन सिद्ध एव समानन्यायाद्युक्तिसाम्यादित्यर्थः ॥

[2] पञ्चावयवयोगाद्गुणादिसिद्धिरिति यदुक्तं तदुपपादनाय व्याप्तिनिर्वचनेनानुमानप्रामाण्ये बाधकमपास्तम् ॥

[3] 'Being a means of right knowledge' here renders *prámáṇya*, represented, just before, by 'as evidence.' *Ed.*

of] its being inadequate, is disposed of, by means of an exposition of the powers, &c., of words:[1]

वाच्यवाचकभावः संबन्धः[2] शब्दार्थयोः ॥ ३७ ॥

Sound and sense. *Aph.* 37. The connexion between word and meaning is the relation of expressed and expresser.

a. To the 'meaning' belongs the power termed expressibleness; to the 'word,' the power termed expression: simply this is their 'connexion;' their interrelation, as it were.[3]

---

[1] इदानीं पञ्चावयवरूपशब्दस्य ज्ञानजनकत्वोपपत्तये शब्दशक्त्यादिनिर्वचनेन तदनुपपत्तिरूपं शब्दप्रामाण्ये परेषां बाधकमपास्यते ॥

[2] वाच्यवाचकसंबन्धः is the reading of Aniruddha. *Ed.*

[3] Instead of 'simply,' &c., read, 'this itself is their connexion, such [a connexion] as [is seen] in anatheticity.'

The 'connexion' in question is the *swarúpa-sambandha*, for which see Professor Cowell's translation of the *Kusumánjali*, p. 13, note †.

A better reading than the one which Dr. Ballantyne accepted from me is, certainly, that which omits the clause rendered, 'to the word, the power termed expression.' According to Nágeśa, 'the expressibleness inherent in the meaning is the connexion [intended]': अर्थगतं वाच्यत्वमनुयोगितावत्संबन्धः ।

Anuyogin and *anuyogitá*, as Professor Cowell informs me, are the opposites of *pratiyogin* and *pratiyogitá*, which latter I would represent, provisionally, by 'antithetic' and 'antitheticity.'

Pratiyogin, a very much commoner technicality than *anuyogin*, occurs in the comment on Aph. 95 of this Book. It must suffice, here, to add, that, as I learn from Professor Cowell, the *anuyogin*,

From one's knowing this [connexion between a given word and meaning], the meaning is suggested [or raised in the mind,] by the word. Such is the import.[1]

b. He mentions what things cause one to apprehend the powers[2] [in question]:

त्रिभिः संबन्धसिद्धिः[3] ॥ ३८ ॥

Sense of words how learned.

Aph. 38. The connexion [between a word and its sense] is determined by three [means].

a. That is to say: the connexion [just] mentioned [in § 37,] is apprehended by means of these three, viz., information from one competent [to tell us the meaning], the usage of the old man [whose orders to his sons we hear, and then observe what actions ensue, in consequence (see the *Sáhitya-darpaṇa*, § 11)], and application to the same thing which has a familiar name,[4] [whence we gather the sense of the less familiar synonym].

---

or 'anathetic,' of *ghaṭábháva*, 'non-existence of a jar,' is *ghaṭábháva* itself, and the *pratiyogin*, or 'antithetic,' of *ghaṭábháva* is *ghaṭa*, 'jar.' *Ed.*

[1] अर्थे वाच्यताख्या शक्तिः शब्दे वाचकताख्या शक्तिरस्ति सैव तयोः संबन्धोऽनुयोगितावत् । तज्ज्ञानाच्छब्देनार्थोपस्थितिरित्यर्थः ॥

[2] शक्तिग्राहकाण्याह ॥

[3] Aniruddha has संबन्धसिद्धेः. *Ed.*

[4] आप्तोपदेशो वृद्धव्यवहारः प्रसिद्धपदसामानाधिकरण्यमित्येतैस्त्रिभिरुक्तसंबन्धो गृह्यत इत्यर्थः ॥

न कार्ये नियम उभयथा दर्शनात् ॥ ३९ ॥

Imperatives and predications.

Aph. 39. There is no restriction to what is to be done; because we see it both ways.

a. That is to say: and there is no necessity that this apprehension of the powers [§ 37,] should occur only in the case of 'something [directed] to be done;' because, in [the secular life and dealings of] the world, we see the usage of the old man, &c., [§ 38,] in regard to what is *not* to be done [being something already extant], also, as well as in regard to what is to be done.[1]

लोके व्युत्पन्नस्य[2] वेदार्थप्रतीतिः[3] ॥ ४० ॥

Scriptural and secular senses of words the same.

Aph. 40. He who is accomplished in the secular [connexion of words with meanings] can understand the sense of the Veda.

a. Here he entertains a doubt:[4]

---

1 स च शक्तिग्रहः कार्ये एव भवतीति नियमो नास्ति लोके कार्यवदकार्येऽपि वृद्धव्यवहारादिदर्शनादित्यर्थः ॥

2 Aniruddha reads लोकव्युत्पन्नस्य. *Ed.*

3 Vijnána is singular as regards the lection -प्रतीतिः, instead of -प्रतीतेः. *Ed.*

4 अत्र शङ्कते ॥

न त्रिभिरपौरुषेयत्वाद्वेदस्य तदर्थस्यातीन्द्रियत्वात्[1] ॥ ४१ ॥

A doubt. *Aph.* 41. Not by the three [means mentioned in § 38, objects some one, can the sense of the Veda be gathered]; because the Veda is superhuman, and what it means transcends the senses.

a. Of these he first repels the assertion, that what is meant [by the Veda] is something transcending the senses:[2]

न यज्ञादेः स्वरूपतो धर्मत्वं वैशिष्ट्यात् ॥ ४२ ॥

This cleared up. *Aph.* 42. Not so [i.e., what is meant by the Veda is not something transcending the senses]; because sacrificings, &c., are, in themselves, what constitutes merit, preeminently.

a. What is asserted [in § 41,] is not the case; since sacrificings, gifts, &c., in the shape, e.g., of the relinquishment of some thing for the sake of the gods, are really, in themselves, 'what constitutes merit,' i.e., what is enjoined by the Veda, 'preeminently,' i.e., because of their having preeminent fruit. And sacrificings, &c., since they are in the shape of wishings, &c., [of which we are perfectly conscious,] are not something transcending intuition. But 'what constitutes merit' [which the objector supposes to transcend intuition,] does not belong to something mysterious that resides in sacri-

---

[1] Aniruddha exhibits the reading तदर्थस्याप्यतीन्द्रियत्वात्. *Ed.*

[2] तत्रातीन्द्रियार्थत्वमादौ निराकरोति ॥

ficings, &c., whence what is enjoined in the Veda must be beyond intuition. Such is the meaning.[1]

b. He repels also what was asserted [in § 41], viz., that, inasmuch as it [the Veda,] is superhuman, there can be no instruction by any competent person,[2] [in regard to its import]:

निजशक्तिर्व्युत्पत्त्या व्यवच्छिद्यते ॥ ४३ ॥

Knowledge of the Veda traditional.

Aph. 43. The natural force [of the terms in the Veda] is ascertained through the conversancy [therewith of those who successively transmit the knowledge].

a. But then, still, how can there be apprehension of the sense of Vaidic terms, in the case of gods, fruits [of actions], &c., which transcend sense? To this he replies:[3]

---

[1] यदुक्तं तन्न यतो देवतोद्देश्यकद्रव्यत्यागादिरूपस्य यज्ञदानादेः स्वरूपत एव धर्मत्वं वेदविहितत्वं वैशिष्ट्यात्प्रकृष्टफलकत्वात् । यज्ञादिकं चेच्छादिरूपत्वान्नातीन्द्रियम् । ननु यज्ञादिविषयकापूर्वस्य धर्मत्वं येन वेदविहितस्यातीन्द्रियता स्यादित्यर्थः ॥

[2] यच्चोक्तमपौरुषेयत्वेनाप्तोपदेशाभाव इति तदपि निराकरोति ॥

[3] ननु तथाप्यतीन्द्रियदेवताफलादिषु कथं शक्तिग्रहो वैदिकपदानां स्यात् । तत्राह ॥

योग्यायोग्येषु प्रतीतिजनकत्वात्तत्सिद्धिः[1] ॥ ४४ ॥

Intelligibility of the Veda undeniable.

Aph. 44. This really takes place; because they [viz., the words,] give rise to knowledge, in the case both of things adapted [to sense] and of things not [so] adapted.

a. He defines the peculiarities which belong to words, just because this matter is connected with the question of the power of words to cause right knowledge:[2] [3]

न नित्यत्वं वेदानां कार्यत्वश्रुतेः[4] ॥ ४५ ॥

Eternity of the Vedas denied.

Aph. 45. The Vedas are not from eternity; for there is Scripture for their being a production.

a. Then are the Vedas the work of [the Supreme] Man? To this he replies, 'No':[5]

न पौरुषेयत्वं तत्कर्तुः पुरुषस्याभावात् ॥ ४६ ॥

---

1 Aniruddha, according to one of my MSS., has तत्सिद्धेः. *Ed.*

2 शब्दप्रामाण्यप्रसङ्गेनैव शब्दगतं विशेषमवधारयति ॥

3 'Power to cause right knowledge' is to render *prámáṇya*. *Ed.*

4 One of my MSS., of Aniruddha originally had कार्यश्रुतेः. *Ed.*

5 तर्हि किं पौरुषेया वेदाः । नेत्याह ॥

The Lord not the author.

Aph. 46. They [the Vedas,] are not the work of [the Supreme] Man; because there is no such thing as the [Supreme] Man, [whom you allude to as being, possibly,] their maker.

a. Supply, 'because we deny that there is a *Lord*.'[1] [This is] simple.[2]

b. Adverting to the anticipation that there may be some other author, he says:[3]

मुक्तामुक्तयोरयोग्यत्वात् ॥ ४७ ॥

Who are not authors of the Vedas.

Aph. 47. Since the liberated is unsuited [to the work, by his indifference], and the unliberated is so, [by his want of power, neither of these can be author of the Vedas].[4]

a. But then, in that case, since they are not the work of [the Supreme] Man, it follows that they are eternal. To this he replies:[5]

नापौरुषेयत्वान्नित्यत्वमङ्कुरादिवत् ॥ ४८ ॥

---

[1] *Vide supra*, p. 112, note 3. *Ed.*

[2] ईश्वरप्रतिषेधादिति शेषः। सुगमम् ॥

[3] अपरः कर्ता भवत्वित्याकाङ्क्षायामाह ॥

[4] See Book I., Aph. 93 and 94, at pp. 113, 114, *supra*. *Ed.*

[5] नन्वेवमपौरुषेयत्वान्नित्यत्वमेवागतम्। तत्राह ॥

An illustration. *Aph.* 48. As in the case of sprouts, &c., their eternity does not follow from their not being the work of [any Supreme] Man.

a. [This is] plain.[1]

b. But then, since sprouts, &c., also, just like jars, &c., are productions, we must infer that they are the work of [the Supreme] Man. To this he replies :[2]

तेषामपि तद्योगे दृष्टबाधादिप्रसक्तिः ४९ ॥

Plants denied to be works. *Aph.* 49. Were this the case with these, also, [i.e., if it were the case that vegetables were works], we should find a contradiction to experience, &c.

a. It is seen, in the world, as an invariable fact,[3] that whatever is the work of Man is produced by a *body*. This would be debarred, &c., were the case as you contend; [for we see no *embodied* Supreme Man to whose handiwork the sprouts of the earth can be referred]. Such is the meaning.[4]

b. But then, since they were uttered by the Primal

---

[1] स्पष्टम् ॥

[2] नन्वङ्कुरादिष्वपि कार्यत्वेन घटादिवत्पौरुषेयत्वमनुमेयम् । तत्राह ॥

[3] 'Invariable fact' is to translate *vyápti*. *Ed.*

[4] यत्पौरुषेयं तच्छरीरजन्यमिति व्याप्तिर्लोके दृष्टा । तस्या बाधादिरेवं सति स्यादित्यर्थः ॥

Man, the Vedas, moreover, are, really, the work of [the Supreme] Man. To this he replies :[1]

यस्मिन्नदृष्टेऽपि कृतबुद्धिरुपजायते तत्पौरुषेयम् ॥ ५० ॥

Only what is voluntary is a work.

Aph. 50. That [only] is Man's work, in respect of which, even be it something invisible, an effort of understanding takes place.[2]

a. As in the case of what is visible, so, too, in the case of what is invisible, in respect of what thing there takes place 'an effort of understanding,' i.e., a consciousness that Thought preceded,[3] that thing alone is spoken of as Man's work: such is the meaning. Thus it has been re-

---

[1] नन्वादिपुरुषोच्चरितत्वाद्वेदा अपि पौरुषेया एवेत्याह ॥

[2] Read: 'Even where an invisible [originator] is in question, that [thing] in respect of which there arises the idea of [its] being made is [what is meant by] a production by a person.'

Aniruddha, Nágeśa, and Vedánti Mahádeva agree in supplying *kartari* after *adṛishṭe*. *Ed.*

[3] Instead of Vijnána's expression, 'the idea of [its] being preceded by consciousness,' Nágeśa has: बुद्धिपूर्वककृतत्वबुद्धिः, 'the idea that [its] being made was preceded by consciousness,' i.e., the notion that it was produced aforethought.

Vedánti Mahádeva impliedly contrasts with a jar, as being a production of an intelligent and self-conscious maker, a sprout, which originates as a factor of a series of causes and effects alternating from the time when vegetation was first evolved. Also see the two aphorisms preceding the one commented on. *Ed.*

marked that a thing is not Man's work merely through its having been uttered by Man; for no one speaks of the respiration during profound sleep as being Man's work, [or voluntary act]. But what need to speak of antecedence of Understanding? The Vedas, just like an expiration, proceed, of themselves, from the Self-existent, through the force of fate, wholly unpreceded by thought. Therefore, they are not [a Supreme] Man's work.[1] [2]

---

[1] दृष्ट इवादृष्टेऽपि यस्मिन्वस्तुनि कृतबुद्धिर्बुद्धिपूर्वकत्वबुद्धिर्जायते तदेव पौरुषेयमिति व्यवह्रियत इत्यर्थः। एतदुक्तं भवति। न पुरुषोच्चरिततामात्रेण पौरुषेयत्वं श्वासप्रश्वासयोः सुषुप्तिकालीनयोः पौरुषेयत्वव्यवहाराभावात्। किं तु बुद्धिपूर्वकत्वेन। वेदास्तु निःश्वासवदेवादृष्टवशादबुद्धिपूर्वका एव स्वयंभुवः सकाशात्स्वयं भवन्ति। अतो न ते पौरुषेयाः॥

[2] Instead of 'a thing is not Man's work,' &c., I have translated, in the *Rational Refutation*, &c., p. 65: 'Not from the mere fact of [its] being uttered by a person [can one say there is] producedness [of a thing] by [that] person; since it is not the wont to speak of the respiration of deep sleep as the production of a person: but, by [reason of its] production consciously, [a thing is said to be produced by a person]. The Vedas, however, just like an expiration, and by virtue of desert [of souls], issue, spontaneously, from Brahmá, without ever being consciously produced [by him]. Hence they are not productions of a person.'

Dr. Ballantyne was misled by the full stop mistakenly put, in my edition of the *Sánkhya-pravachana-bháshya*, before किं तु. *Ed.*

b. But then, in that case, since they are not preceded by a correct knowledge of the sense of the sentences,[1] the Vedas, moreover, like the speech of a parrot, can convey no right knowledge.[2] To this he replies[3]:

निजशक्त्यभिव्यक्तेः[4] स्वतः प्रामाण्यम् ॥ ५१ ॥

The Vedas their own evidence.

Aph. 51. They are, spontaneously, conveyers of right knowledge, from the patentness of their own power [to instruct rightly].

a. That is to say: the authoritativeness[5] of the very whole of the Vedas is established, not by such a thing as its being based on the enouncer's knowledge of the truth, but quite 'spontaneously;' because, as for the Vedas' 'own,' i.e., natural, power of generating right knowledge, *thereof* we perceive the manifestation in the invocations[6] [which produce the result promised], and in the Medical

---

1 Read, instead of 'since they are,' &c., 'since the true sense of their sentences was not originated consciously.' *Ed.*

2 The implied 'power to convey right knowledge' represents *prámáṇya.* *Ed.*

3 नन्वेवं यथार्थवाक्यार्थज्ञानापूर्वकत्वाच्छुकवाक्यस्येव वेदानामपि प्रामाण्यं न स्यात् । तत्राह ॥

4 Vedánti Mahádeva has the reading निजशक्त्याभिव्यक्तेः, and comments accordingly: निजशक्त्यैव ज्ञानजनकनिजशक्त्यैवाभिव्यक्तेः प्रमात्वस्येति शेषः । *Ed.*

5 As in the aphorism, *prámáṇya,* which, soon after, is rendered by 'validity.' *Ed.*

6 *Mantra,* a word of various meanings. *Ed.*

Scripture, [the following of which leads to cures], &c. And so there is the aphorism of the *Nyáya* [Book II., § 68 [1]]: 'And [the fact of] its being a cause of right knowledge, like the validity of invocations, and the Medical Scripture,' &c.[2]

b. In regard to the proposition [laid down in § 26, viz.], 'And of the [existence of the] Qualities, &c., there is not absolute debarment,' there was duly alleged, and developed [under § 27], one argument, viz., by the establishing the existence of Happiness, &c. Now he states another argument in respect of that[3] [same proposition]:

नासतः ख्यानं नृशृङ्गवत् ॥ ५२ ॥

Cognition is evidence of existence.

Aph. 52. There is no Cognition of what is no entity, as a man's horn.

---

[1] The correct reading of the aphorism is मन्त्रायुर्वेदवच्च तत्प्रामाण्यमाप्तप्रामाण्यात् । *Ed.*

[2] वेदानां निजा स्वाभाविकी या यथार्थज्ञानजननशक्तिस्तस्या मन्त्रायुर्वेदादावभिव्यक्तेरुपलम्भादखिलवेदानामेव स्वत एव प्रामाण्यं सिध्यति न वक्तृयथार्थज्ञानमूलकत्वादिनेत्यर्थः । तथा च न्यायसूत्रम् । मन्त्रायुर्वेदप्रामाण्यवच्च तत्प्रामाण्यमिति ॥

[3] गुणादीनां च नात्यन्तबाध इति प्रतिज्ञायां न्यायेन सुखादिसिद्धेरित्येको हेतुरुपन्यस्तः प्रपञ्चितश्च । साम्प्रतं तस्यामेव हेत्वन्तरमाह ॥

a. Be it, moreover, that the existence of pleasure, &c., is proved by the reasoning [under § 27]; it is proved by mere consciousness, also. Of pleasure, &c., were they absolutely *nonentities,* even the *consciousness* could not be accounted for; because there is no cognition of a man's horn, and the like. Such is the meaning.[1]

b. But then, [interposes the *Naiyáyika,*] if such be the case, let the Qualities, &c., be quite absolutely *real;* and then, in the expression 'not *absolute* debarment' [in § 26], the word 'absolute' is [superfluous, and, hence,] unmeaning. To this he replies:[2]

न सतो बाधदर्शनात् ॥ ५३ ॥

The Qualities, &c., not absolutely real.

Aph. 53. It is not of the *real* [that there is here cognizance]; because exclusion *is* seen [of the Qualities].

a. It is not proper [to say], moreover, that the cognizance of the Qualities, &c., is that of the absolutely real; because we see that they are excluded [and not admitted

---

[1] आस्तां तावत्पञ्चावयवेन सुखादिसिद्धिर्ज्ञानमात्रादपि तत्सिद्धिः। अत्यन्तासत्त्वे सुखादीनां ज्ञानमेव नोपपद्यते नरशृङ्गादीनामभानादित्यर्थः॥

[2] नन्वेवं गुणादिरत्यन्तं सन्नेव भवतु तथा च नात्यन्तबाध इत्यत्यन्तपदवैयर्थ्यमिति। तत्राह॥

to exist,] at the time of destruction [of the mundane system], &c.[1]

b. But then, even on that showing, let the world be different both from real and from unreal; nevertheless, the demurring to absolute debarment [in § 26,] is untenable. To this he replies:[2]

नानिर्वचनीयस्य तदभावात् ॥ ५४ ॥

A Vedántic advance rejected.

Aph. 54. It is not of what cannot be [intelligibly] expressed [that there is cognizance]; because there exists no such thing.

a. And there takes place, moreover, no cognizance of such [a thing] as is not to be expressed as either existing or not existing; 'because there exists no such thing,' i.e., because nothing is known other than what exists or what does not exist: such is the meaning. The import is, because it is proper to form suppositions only in accordance with what is seen.[3]

---

[1] अत्यन्तसतोऽपि गुणादेर्भानं न युक्तं विनाशादिकाले बाधदर्शनात् ॥

[2] नन्वेवमपि सदसद्भ्यां भिन्नमेव जगद्भवतु तथाप्यत्यन्तबाधप्रतिषेधानुपपत्तिरिति । तत्राह ॥

[3] सत्त्वेनासत्त्वेन चानिर्वचनीयं तादृशस्यापि भानं न घटते तदभावात्सदसद्भिन्नवस्त्वप्रसिद्धेरित्यर्थः । दृष्टानुसारेणैव कल्पनाया औचित्यादिति भावः ।

b. But then, on that showing, do you really approve of [the *Nyáya* notion of] 'cognizing otherwise,' [or our fancying that nature to belong to one, which belongs to another]? He replies, 'No':[1]

नान्यथाख्यातिः[2] स्ववचोव्याघातात्[3] ॥ ५५ ॥

A *Nyáya view rejected.*

Aph. 55. There is no such thing as cognizing otherwise [or cognizing that as belonging to one, which belongs to another]; because your own proposition is self-destructive.

a. This, also, is not proper [to be said], viz., that one thing appears under the character of another thing [e.g., a rope, under the character of a serpent, for which it may be mistaken, in the dusk]; 'because your own proposition is self-destructive.'[4] Of another nature [e.g., snakehood], in a different thing [e.g., a rope], *equivalence to a man's horn*, is [what is virtually] expressed by the word 'otherwise' [than the truth; both a man's horn, and the presence of snakehood in a rope mistaken for a snake, being, alike, otherwise than real]; and [yet] its *cognition* [thus] *otherwise* is asserted, [as if *that* could be cognized which is equivalent to what can *not* be cognized]: hence your own

---

[1] नन्वेवं किमन्यथाख्यातिरेवेष्टा । नेत्याह ॥

[2] Dr. Goldstücker, in his Sanskrit Dictionary, erroneously speaks of *anyathá-khyáti* as if it were a technicality of the Sánkhya philosophy, and quotes, by way of proof, the aphorism to which this note is appended. *Ed.*

[3] In one of my MSS. of Aniruddha was, originally, -बाधात्, instead of -व्याघातात्. *Ed.*

[4] See Book III., Aphorism 66, at p. 267, *supra*. *Ed.*

proposition is self-destructive. For even those who contend for 'cognizing otherwise' [as one mode of cognition,] declare that the cognition of what *does not exist* is impossible. Such is the meaning.[1] [2]

b. Expounding what he had said above, [in § 26,] 'not absolute debarment,' he sums up his doctrine :[3]

सदसत्ख्यातिर्बाधाबाधात् ॥ ५६ ॥

Summing up.

Aph. 56. They [the Qualities,] are cognized rightly or wrongly, through their being denied and not denied [appropriately or otherwise].

a. All the Qualities, &c., 'are cognized rightly and

---

[1] अन्यद्वस्त्वन्यरूपेण भासत इत्यपि न युक्तं स्ववचोव्याघातात् । अन्यत्रान्यरूपस्य नृशृङ्गतुल्यत्वमन्यथाशब्देनोच्यतेऽन्यथा च तस्य भानमुच्यत इति स्ववच एव व्याहतम् । असतो भानासंभवस्यान्यथाख्यातिवादिभिरपि वचनादित्यर्थः ॥

[2] The text followed, in this paragraph is, throughout, very inferior; and the rendering of it also calls for some alteration. Especially, as to the original, अन्यथा च copies an error of the press, my correction of which to अथ च was not heeded. See, for the purer text, pp. 23, 24, of the Appendix to my edition of the *Sánkhya-pravachana-bháshya*. *Ed.*

[3] नात्यन्तबाध इति पूर्वोक्तं विवृण्वानः स्वसिद्धान्तमुपसंहरति ॥

wrongly.' How? 'Through their being denied and not denied.' There is *non-denial*, as far as regards their existing at all; because all things [and things are made up of the Qualities,] are eternal. But there is denial, *relatively*, in Soul, of all things; just as is the case with the imaginary silver, for example, in a pearl-oyster, &c., or with the redness, &c., in crystal, &c.,[1] [which has no redness, without its following that redness, altogether and everywhere, is non-existent].

b. This investigation is concluded. Now the consideration of Words, it having presented itself in this connexion, is taken in hand incidentally, at the end;[2] [the Sánkhya not allowing to Testimony a coordinate rank with Sense and Inference]:

प्रतीत्यप्रतीतिभ्यां न स्फोटात्मकः शब्दः ॥ ५७ ॥

The Yoga theory of speech rejected.

Aph. 57. A word does not consist of [what the *Yogas* call] the 'expresser' (*sphoṭa*); by reason both of cognizance [which would disprove the existence of such imaginary

---

[1] सदसत्ख्यातिरेव सर्वेषां गुणादीनाम् । कुतः । बाधाबाधात् । तत्र स्वरूपेणाबाधः सर्ववस्तूनां नित्यत्वात् । संसर्गतस्तु बाधः सर्ववस्तूनां चैतन्येऽस्ति यथा शुक्त्यादौ बुद्धिस्थरजतादेः स्फटिकादिषु वा लौहित्यादेस्तद्वत् ॥

[2] अयं विचारः पर्याप्तः । इदानीं शब्दविचारः प्रसङ्गागत आगन्तुकतयान्ते प्रस्तूयते ॥

thing,] and of non-cognizance, [which would, in like manner, disprove it].

a. It is held, by the followers of the *Yoga*, that there exists, in distinction from the several letters, an indivisible [unit, the] word, such as 'jar,' &c.,[which they call] the 'expression;'[1] just as there is a jar, or the like, possessing parts, which is something else than the parts, viz., the shell-shaped neck, &c.; and that particular sound, termed a word, is called the 'expresser,' because of its making apparent the meaning: such a word [we Sánkhyas assert, in opposition to the *Yogas*,] is without evidence [of its existence]. Why? 'By reason both of cognizance and of non-cognizance,' [as thus]: Pray, is that word [which you choose to call the 'expression,'] cognized, or not? On the former alternative, what need of that idle thing, [the supposed 'expression'? For,] by what collection of letters, distinguished by a particular succession, this ['expression'] is manifested, let *that* be what acquaints us with the meaning. But, on the latter alternative, [viz., that it is *not* cognized], the power of acquainting us with a meaning does not belong to an 'expression' which is *not* cognized. Therefore, the hypothesis of an 'expresser' is useless. Such is the meaning.[2]

---

[1] For *sphoṭa*, 'eternal word,' which the translator renders by 'expresser,' and also by 'expression,' see Professor Cowell's edition of Colebrooke's *Essays*, vol. i., p. 331, foot-notes 2 and 3; and the translation of the *Sarva-darśana-sangraha* by Professors Cowell and Gough, pp. 209, *et seq.*

It is likewise observable that, in what precedes and follows, *śabda* is variously rendered, besides that *śabda* and *pada* are not discriminated. *Ed.*

[2] प्रत्येकवर्णेभ्योऽतिरिक्तं कलश इत्यादिरूपमखण्डमेकपदं स्फोट इति योगैरभ्युपगम्यते कम्बुग्री-

b. The eternity of the Vedas was contradicted[1] before, [under § 45]. Now he contradicts also the eternity of *letters* :[2]

न [3]शब्दनित्यत्वं कार्यताप्रतीतेः ॥ ५८ ॥

The eternity of letters denied.

Aph. 58. Sound is not eternal; because we perceive it to be made.

a. It is not proper [to say, as the Mímánsakas say], that letters are eternal, on the strength of our recognizing, e.g., that 'This is that same G'; for they are proved to be non-eternal, by the cognition, e.g., that '[the sound of] G has been produced': such is the meaning. And the *recog-*

वाद्यवयवेभ्योऽतिरिक्तो घटाद्यवयवीव स च शब्दविशेषः पदाख्योऽर्थस्फुटीकरणात्स्फोट इत्युच्यते स शब्दोऽप्रामाणिकः। कुतः। प्रतीत्यप्रतीतिभ्याम्। स शब्दः किं प्रतीयते न वा। आद्ये येन वर्णसमुदायेनानुपूर्वीविशेषविशिष्टेन सोऽभिव्यज्यते तस्यैवार्थप्रत्यायकत्वमस्तु किमन्तर्गडुना तेन। अन्त्ये त्वज्ञातस्फोटस्य नास्त्यर्थप्रत्यायनशक्तिरिति व्यर्था स्फोटकल्पनेत्यर्थः ॥

[1] *Pratishiddha,* 'demurred to.' *Ed.*

[2] पूर्वं वेदानां नित्यत्वं प्रतिषिद्धम्। इदानीं वर्णनित्यत्वमपि प्रतिषेधति ॥

[3] Nágeśa has वर्णनित्यत्वं. *Ed.*

nition has reference to the *homogeneousness* with that [one which had been previously heard]; for, otherwise, it would turn out that a *jar*, or the like, is eternal, inasmuch as it is *recognized*.[1]

b. He ponders a doubt:[2]

पूर्वसिद्धसत्त्वस्याभिव्यक्तिर्दीपेनेव घटस्य ॥ ५९ ॥

A doubt.

Aph. 59. [Suppose that] there is [in the case of sounds,] the manifestation of something whose existence was previously settled; as [the manifestation] of a [preexistent] jar by a lamp.

a. But then [some one may say], of Sound, whose existence was 'previously settled,' the manifestation, through noise, &c., *that* alone is the object in the cognition of its *production*, [which you speak of in § 58]. An example of manifestation [of a thing previously existing] is, 'as of a jar by a lamp.'[3]

---

[1] स एवायं गकार इत्यादिप्रत्यभिज्ञाबलाद्वर्णनित्यत्वं न युक्तमुत्पन्नो गकार इत्यादिप्रत्ययेनानित्यत्वसिद्धेरित्यर्थः। प्रत्यभिज्ञा च तज्जातीयताविषयिणी। अन्यथा घटादेरपि प्रत्यभिज्ञया नित्यतापत्तेरिति ॥

[2] शङ्कते ॥

[3] ननु पूर्वसिद्धसत्ताकस्यैव शब्दस्य ध्वन्यादिभिर्याभिव्यक्तिस्तन्मात्रमुत्पत्तिप्रतीतेर्विषयः। अभिव्यक्तौ दृष्टान्तो दीपेनेव घटस्येति ॥

b. He repels this :[1]

सत्कार्यसिद्धान्तश्चेत्सिद्धसाधनम् ॥ ६० ॥

The doubt disposed of. *Aph*. 60. If the dogma of products' being real [is accepted by you], then this is a proving of the already proved.

a. If you say that 'manifestation' means the taking of a present condition by means of rejecting an unarrived [or future,] condition, then this is our dogma of the reality of products [Book I., § 115]; and *such* an eternity belongs to *all* products, [not specially to Sound]; so that you are proving the already proved [or conceded]: such is the meaning. And, if 'manifestation' is asserted to be just in the shape of the cognition of what is presently real, then we should find [on your theory,] that jars, &c., also, are eternal; because it would be proper [on that theory,] that the object in the perception of production, by the operation of the causes [the potter, &c.], should be that of *knowledge* only, as in the case of words, &c., and also in the case of jars, &c.; [for the jar is *shown* by the lamp, not made by it]. Such is the import.[2] [3]

---

[1] परिहरति ॥

[2] अभिव्यक्तिर्यद्यनागतावस्थात्यागेन वर्तमानावस्थालाभ इत्युच्यते तदा सत्कार्यसिद्धान्तस्तादृशनित्यत्वं च सर्वकार्याणामेवेति सिद्धसाधनमित्यर्थः। यदि च वर्तमानतया सत एव ज्ञानमात्ररूपिण्यभिव्यक्तिरुच्यते तदा घटादीनामपि नित्यतापत्तिः कारणव्यापारेण शब्देष्विव घटादिष्वपि ज्ञानस्यैवोत्पत्तिप्रतीतिविषयत्वौचित्यादिति भावः ॥

[3] *Vide supra*, p. 142, *c*. *Ed*.

b. An objection to the non-duality of Soul, not previously mentioned, is to be adduced; therefore the refutation of the non-duality of Soul is recommenced,[1] [having been already handled under Book I., § 149]:

[2]नाद्वैतमात्मनो लिङ्गात्तद्भेदप्रतीतेः ॥ ६१ ॥

Non-duality of Soul denied on grounds of Inference.

Aph. 61. Non-duality of Soul is not; for its distinctions are cognized through signs.

a. That is to say: because it is proved to be really different [in different persons], by the sign that *one* quits Nature [or escapes from the mundane condition], while another not does quit it, &c.[3]

b. But, he tells us, there is even sense-evidence destructive of the non-distinction of Soul from things [that are] non-Soul, asserted in the Scriptural texts, 'All this is Soul only,'[4] 'All this is Brahma only:'[5][6]

[2]नानात्मनापि प्रत्यक्षबाधात् ॥ ६२ ॥

---

[1] आत्माद्वैते पूर्वानुक्तमपि बाधकमुपन्यसनीयमित्येतदर्थमात्माद्वैतनिरासः पुनरारभ्यते ॥

[2] Nágeśa, as also some copies of Vijnána's work, has नाद्वैतमात्मनां, 'non-duality of Souls.' *Ed.*

[3] प्रकृतित्यागात्यागादिलिङ्गैर्भेदस्यैव सिद्धेरित्यर्थः ॥

[4] *Chhándogya Upanishad*, vii., xxv., 2. *Ed.*

[5] आत्मैवेदं सर्वं ब्रह्मैवेदं सर्वमिति श्रुत्यात्मनोऽनात्मभिरद्वैते तु प्रत्यक्षमपि बाधकमस्तीत्याह ॥

[6] For a very similar passage, *vide supra*, p. 243, near the foot. *Ed.*

Non-duality denied on grounds of Sense. *Aph.* 62. Moreover, there is not [non-distinction of Soul] from non-Soul; because this is disproved by sense-evidence.

a. That is to say: moreover, there is *not* a non-distinction between the non-Soul, i.e., the aggregate of the experienceable, and Soul; because this is excluded also by sense-evidence, [as well as by signs, (§ 61)]; because, if Soul were not other than the whole perceptible, it would also not be different from a jar and a web; since the jar, e.g., would not be other than the web, which [by hypothesis,] is not other than the Soul: and *this* is excluded by sense-evidence, which constrains us to apprehend a distinction[1] [between a jar and a web].

b. In order to clear the minds of learners, he illustrates this point, though already established:[2]

नोभाभ्यां तेनैव ॥ ६३ ॥

The reasons combined. *Aph.* 63. Not between the two [Soul and non-Soul, is there non-difference]; for that same [couple of reasons].

a. 'Between the two,' i.e., between Soul and non-Soul, the two together, also, there is not an absolute non-difference;

---

[1] अनात्मनापि भोग्यप्रपञ्चेनात्मनो नाद्वैतं प्रत्यक्षेणापि बाधात् । आत्मनः सर्वभोग्याभेदे घटपटयोरप्यभेदः स्यात् । घटादेः पटाद्यभिन्नात्माभेदात् । स च भेदग्राहकप्रत्यक्षबाधित इत्यर्थः ॥

[2] शिष्यबुद्धिवैशारद्याय प्राप्तमप्यर्थं विशदयति ॥

for the couple of reasons [given in § 61 and § 62]: such is the meaning.[1]

b. But then, in that case, what is the drift of such Scriptural texts as, '[All] this is Soul only?' To this he replies:[2]

अन्यपरत्वमविवेकानां तत्र ॥ ६४ ॥

Scripture accommodates itself to human frailty of understanding.

Aph. 64. There it is for the sake of something else, in respect of the undiscriminating.

a. That is to say: 'in respect of the undiscriminating,' with reference to undiscriminating persons, in the case of non-difference [between Soul and non-Soul, apparently asserted in Scripture], it is 'there for the sake of something else;' i.e., the observation[3] is [designed to be] provocative of worship. For, in the secular world, through want of discrimination, body and the embodied, the experienced and the experiencer, are regarded as indifferent;[4]

---

[1] उभाभ्यां समुच्चिताभ्यामथात्मानात्मभ्यां नात्यन्ताभेदस्तेनैव हेतुद्वयेनेत्यर्थः ॥

[2] नन्वेवमात्मैवेदमित्यादिश्रुतीनां का गतिरिति । अताह ॥

[3] To render *anuváda*, which, as defined by Professor Cowell, signifies 'the reiteration or reinculcation of an injunction, it may be with further details, but without dwelling on the purpose of the injunction itself.' *Aphorisms of Śáṇḍilya*, &c., p. 75, foot-note. At pp. 24 and 25, he translates *anuváda* by 'confirmatory repetition' and 'illustrative repetition.' *Ed.*

[4] अविवेकानामविवेकिपुरुषान्प्रति तत्राद्वैते-

[and Scripture humours the worldling's delusion, with a view to eventually getting him out of it].

b. He declares, that, according to the asserters of Non-duality [of Soul], there can be no material cause of the world, either :[1]

नात्माविद्या[2] नोभयं जगदुपादानकारणं निःसङ्गत्वात् ॥ ६५ ॥

The Vedánta system supplies no material for the world.

Aph. 65. Neither Soul, nor Ignorance, nor both, can be the material cause of the world; because of the solitariness of [Soul].

a. The soul alone, or Ignorance lodged in the soul, or both together, like a pair of jar-halves [conjoined in the formation of a jar], cannot be the material of the world; 'because of the *solitariness*' of Soul. For things undergo alteration only through that particular conjunction

---

ऽन्यपरत्वमुपासनार्थकानुवाद इत्यर्थः । लोके हि शरीरशरीरिणोर्भोग्यभोक्त्रोश्चाविवेकेनाभेदो व्यवह्रियते ॥

[1] अद्वैतवादिनां जगदुपादानकारणमपि न संभवतीत्याह ॥

[2] According to Nágeśa's reading, नात्मानाद्यविद्या, 'Ignorance' is qualified as 'beginningless,' or 'eternal *a parte ante.*' Vedánti Mahádeva reads, as do some MSS. of Vijnána, नात्मा नाविद्या. *Ed.*

which is called 'association;' hence the [ever] solitary Soul, without a second, since it is not associated, cannot serve as a material cause. Nor can it do so by means of [association with] Ignorance, either; because the conjunction of Ignorance has been already excluded by the fact of *solitariness*. Moreover, that the two together should be the material is impossible, even as it is that either, severally, should be the material; simply 'because of the solitariness.' Such is the meaning. And, if you choose that Ignorance should subsist as a substance located in the soul, as the air in the heavens, then there is an abandonment of the non-duality of Soul,[1] [for which you Vedántís contend].

b. He himself [in Book I., § 145,] decided that the soul consists of light, [or knowledge]. In regard to this, he repels the primâ facie view, founded on the text, 'Brahma

---

[1] केवल आत्मात्माश्रिता वाविद्या समुच्चितं वा कपालद्वयवदुभयं न जगदुपादानं संभवत्यात्मनोऽसङ्गत्वात्। सङ्गाख्यो हि यः संयोगविशेषस्तेनैव द्रव्याणां विकारो भवति। अतोऽसङ्गत्वात्केवलस्यात्मनोऽद्वितीयस्य नोपादानत्वम्। नाविद्याद्वारापि संभवत्यसङ्गत्वेनाविद्यायोगस्य प्रागेव निरस्तत्वात्। प्रत्येकोपादानत्ववदेवोभयोपादानत्वमप्यसङ्गत्वादेवासंभवीत्यर्थः। यदि चाविद्या द्रव्यरूपा पुरुषाश्रिता गगने वायुवदिष्यते तदात्माद्वैतहानिः॥

is reality, knowledge, and joy,'[1] that the essence of the soul is *joy*, also :[2]

नैकस्यानन्दचिद्रूपत्वे द्वयोर्भेदात् ॥ ६६ ॥

Soul not joy and knowledge, both.

Aph. 66. The two natures, joy and knowledge, do not belong to *one;* because the two are different.

a. A single subject has not the nature both of joy and of intelligence; because, since pleasure is not experienced at the time of knowing pain, pleasure and knowledge are different : such is the meaning.[3]

b. But then, in that case, what becomes of the Scripture, that it [Soul,] consists of joy? To this he replies :[4]

दुःखनिवृत्तेर्गौणः ॥ ६७ ॥

---

[1] The passage thus rendered looks as if it were taken, with the addition of its opening word, from the *Bṛihadáraṇyaka Upanishad*, iii., 9, 28; or *Śatapatha-bráhmaṇa*, xiv., 6, 9, 34. *Ed.*

[2] प्रकाशस्वरूप आत्मेति स्वयं सिद्धान्तितम्। तच्च सत्यं विज्ञानमानन्दं ब्रह्मेति श्रुतेरानन्दोऽप्यात्मनः स्वरूपमिति पूर्वपक्षं निराकरोति॥

[3] एकधर्मिण आनन्दचैतन्योभयरूपत्वं न भवति दुःखज्ञानकाले सुखाननुभवेन सुखज्ञानयोर्भेदादित्यर्थः॥

[4] नन्वेवमानन्दरूपताश्रुतेः का गतिः। तत्राह।

A Vedánta term explained away.

Aph. 67. Metaphorical [is the word joy, in the sense] of the cessation of pain.

a. That is to say: the word 'joy,' in the Scriptural expression which means, really, the cessation of pain, is metaphorical. This is stated in [the maxim], 'Pleasure is the departure of both pain and pleasure.'[1]

b. He states the cause of this metaphorical employment:[2]

विमुक्तिप्रशंसा मन्दानाम् ॥ ६८ ॥

Why the term was used in a sense not literal.

Aph. 68. It is [as] a *laudation* of emancipation, for the sake of the dull.

a. That is to say: the Scripture, as an incitement to 'the dull,' i.e., the ignorant, lauds, as if it were *joy*, the emancipation, consisting in the cessation of pain, which [cessation] is the essence of the soul;[3] [4] [for the soul is such joy as consists of the absence of pain].

b. In order to manifest immediately the origin, already

---

[1] दुःखनिवृत्त्यात्मनि श्रौत आनन्दशब्दो गौण इत्यर्थः। तदुक्तं सुखं दुःखसुखात्यय इति ॥

[2] गौणप्रयोगे बीजमाह ॥

[3] मन्दानज्ञान्प्रति दुःखनिवृत्तिरूपामात्मस्वरूपमुक्तिं सुखत्वेन श्रुतिः स्तौति प्ररोचनार्थमित्यर्थः॥

[4] For another translation, beginning with the introduction to Aphorism 67, see the *Rational Refutation*, &c., p. 34. *Ed.*

declared,[1] of the internal organ, he repels the primâ facie view, that the Mind is all-pervading :[2]

न व्यापकत्वं मनसः करणत्वादिन्द्रियत्वाद्वा[3] ॥ ६९ ॥

The Mind not all-pervading.

Aph. 69. The Mind is not all-pervading; because it is an instrument, and because it is, moreover, an *organ*.

a. The Mind, meaning the totality of the internal instruments,[4] is not all-pervading; for it is an instrument, as an axe, or the like, is. The word 'and' [literally, 'or,' in the Aphorism,] implies a distributive alternative, [not an optional one]. The meaning is this, that, [while the whole of the internal instruments are *instruments*,] the particular internal instrument, the third[5] [the Mind, *manas*[6]],

---

[1] Dr. Ballantyne, under the misapprehension that 'the subtile body' was pointed to, here added, in brackets, 'in B. III., §§ 14, 15, &c.' *Ed.*

[2] अन्तःकरणोत्पत्तेः पूर्वोक्ताया आञ्जस्येनोपपत्तये मनोवैभवपूर्वपक्षमपाकरोति ॥

[3] Aniruddha and Vedánti Mahádeva seem to add the words वास्यादिवच्चक्षुरादिवच्च. See the passage immediately following the aphorism. *Ed.*

[4] The term *manas*, the translator's 'Mind,' denotes not only one of the three internal organs, but, sometimes, as here, all three taken together. See the *Rational Refutation*, &c., pp. 45, 46, text and foot-notes. *Ed.*

[5] See Book II., Aph. 30, at p. 208, *supra*. *Ed.*

[6] The words here bracketed I have substituted for 'the subtile body, mentioned under B. III., § 12, *a*.' *Ed.*

is not all-pervading; because *it* is, moreover, an *organ*.[1] But knowledge, &c., pervading the body, are demonstrable as only of medium extent,[2] [neither infinite nor atomic].

b. Here, there being a doubt whether this be convincing, he propounds an appropriate confutation:[3]

सक्रियत्वाद्गतिश्रुतेः ॥ ७० ॥

Proof of this. *Aph*. 70. [The Mind is not all-pervading]; for it is movable; since there is Scripture regarding the motion.

a. That is to say; since, inasmuch as there is Scripture regarding the *going* of the Soul [which, being all-pervading, cannot *go*] into another world, it being settled that it is its adjunct, the internal organ, that is movable, [see Book I., § 51], it cannot be all-pervading.[4]

---

[1] See Book II., Aph. 26, at p. 206, *supra*. *Ed.*

[2] मनसोऽन्तःकरणसामान्यस्य न विभुत्वं करणत्वाद्दास्यादिवत् । वाशब्दो व्यवस्थितविकल्पे । इन्द्रियत्वादप्यन्तःकरणविशेषस्य तृतीयस्य न विभुत्वमित्यर्थः । देहव्यापिज्ञानादिकं तु मध्यमपरिमाणेनैवोपपद्यत इति ॥

[3] अत्राप्रयोजकत्वशङ्कायामनुकूलतर्कमाह ॥

[4] आत्मनो लोकान्तरगमनश्रवन तदुपाधिभूतस्यान्तःकरणस्य सक्रियत्वे सिद्धे न विभुत्वं संभवतीत्यर्थः ॥

b. In order to prove that it is a product, he repels also the opinion that the Mind is without parts:[1]

न निर्भागत्वं तद्योगाद्घटवत्[2] ॥ ७१ ॥

The Mind has parts. *Aph.* 71. Like a jar, it [the Mind,] is not without parts; because it comes in contact therewith, [i. e., with several Senses, simultaneously].

a. The word 'therewith' refers to 'organ,' which occurs in a preceding aphorism, [§ 69]. The Mind is not without parts; 'because it comes in contact,' simultaneously, with several sense-organs. But, 'like a jar,' it is of medium size, [neither infinite nor atomic], and consists of parts. Such is the meaning. And it is to be understood that the internal organ, when in the state of a *cause,* [and not modified and expanded, e.g., into knowledge, which is its product,] *is,* indeed, atomic.[3]

---

[1] कार्यत्वोपपत्तये मनसो निरवयवत्वमपि निराकरोति ॥

[2] घटवत्, in both my MSS. of Aniruddha, is changed, by a later hand, to घटादिवत्, the reading of Vedánti Mahádeva. *Ed.*

[3] तच्छब्दः पूर्वसूत्रस्थेन्द्रियं परामृशति । मनसो न निरवयवत्वमनेकेन्द्रियेष्वेकदा योगात् । किं तु घटवन्मध्यमपरिमाणं सावयवमित्यर्थः । कारणावस्थं चान्तःकरणमणवेवेति बोध्यम् ॥

b. He demurs to the eternity of Mind, Time, &c.:[1]

प्रकृतिपुरुषयोरन्यत्सर्वमनित्यम् ॥ ७२ ॥

Eternity belongs to what.

Aph. 72. Everything except Nature and Soul is uneternal.

a. [This is] plain. And the Mind,[2] the Ether, &c., when in the state of *cause*, [not developed into product], are called *Nature*, and not Intellect,[3] &c., by reason of the absence of the special properties, viz., judgment,[4] &c.[5]

b. But then, according to such Scriptural texts as, 'He should know Illusion to be Nature, and him in whom is Illusion to be the great Lord, and this whole world to be pervaded by portions of him,'[6] since Soul and Nature,

---

[1] मनःकालादीनां नित्यत्वं प्रतिषेधति ॥

[2] Intended to represent *antaḱkaraṇa*, 'internal organ.' *Vide supra*, p. 370, note 4. *Ed.*

[3] The very inferior, because ambiguous, reading, in the original, *manas*, I have changed to *buddhi*, and have displaced Dr. Ballantyne's corresponding 'Mind.' *Ed.*

[4] *Vyavasáya.* For its synonym, *adhyavasáya, vide supra*, p. 209, note 1. *Ed.*

[5] सुगमम् । कारणावस्थं चान्तःकरणाकाशादिकं प्रकृतिरेवोच्यते नतु बुद्ध्यादिकं व्यवसायाद्यसाधारणधर्माभावात् ॥

[6] *Śwetáśwatara Upanishad*, iv., 10. Professor Gough translates, differently: 'Let the sage know that Prakṛiti is Máyá, and that Maheśwara is the Máyin, or arch-illusionist. All this shifting world is filled with portions of him.' A foot-note explains 'Maheśwara' as intending 'Íśwara, Rudra, Hara, or Śiva.' *Philosophy of the Upanishads*, p. 224. *Ed.*

also, are made up of parts, they must be uneternal. To this he replies :[1]

न भागलाभो भोगिनो[2] निर्भागत्वश्रुतेः ॥ ७३ ॥

---

[1] ननु । मायां तु प्रकृतिं विद्यान्मायिनं तु महेश्वरम् । तस्यावयवभूतैस्तु व्याप्तं सर्वमिदं जगत् । इत्यादिश्रुतिभिः पुंप्रकृत्योरपि सावयवत्वादनित्यत्वमिति । तत्राह ॥

[2] This reading is peculiar; many MSS. of Vijnána, with which agree Aniruddha, Nágeśa, and Vedánti Maháideva, having भागिनः. Their elucidations of the aphorism here follow. Aniruddha: न कारणलाभो भागिनो जगत्कारणस्य प्रधानस्य । निर्भागत्वश्रुतेः । मूलकारणत्वान्नास्य कारणान्तरमिति श्रुतेः । Nágeśa: पुंप्रकृतिविषये भागिनो भागलाभोऽवयवावयविभावो न युज्यते । Then follows the quotation as in Vijnána. Vedánti Maháideva: भागाः कारणानि यस्य कार्यत्वे न सन्ति तस्य प्रधानस्य न कारणलाभो निर्भागत्वश्रुतेः । Some MSS. of Vijnána have precisely the words of Nágeśa, transcribed above, barring the quite immaterial substitution of प्रकृतिपुरुषविषये at the beginning.

भागिनः is, without doubt, the correct reading. Vijnána and Nágeśa take it to denote 'Soul and Nature;' Aniruddha and Vedánti Maháideva, 'Nature' only. *Bhágin* means, literally, 'that which is made up of parts,' or 'the Whole.' Hence, 'Whole' is to take the place of Dr. Ballantyne's 'Experiencer.' It occurs again in Aph. 81 of this Book, at p. 379, *infra*. *Ed.*

Soul and Nature not made up of parts.

Aph. 73. No parts [from the presence of which in the discerptible, one might infer destructibility,] are found in the Experiencer; for there is Scripture for its being without parts.

a. Parts are not appropriate to 'the Experiencer,' i. e., to Soul, or to Nature; for there is Scripture for their being without parts; that is to say, because of such [texts] as, 'Without parts, motionless, quiescent, unobjectionable, passionless.'[1 2]

b. It has been stated [in Book I., § 1,] that Emancipation is the cessation of pain. In order to corroborate this, he then repels the doctrines of others, in regard to Emancipation:[3]

नानन्दाभिव्यक्तिर्मुक्तिर्निर्धर्मत्वात्[4] ॥ ७४ ॥

A view of Emancipation disputed.

Aph. 74. Emancipation is not a manifestation of joy; because there

---

[1] भोगिनः पुरुषस्य प्रधानस्य चावयवो न युज्यते निरवयवत्वश्रुतेः । निष्कलं निष्क्रियं शान्तं निरवद्यं निरञ्जनम् । इत्यादिनेत्यर्थः ॥

[2] *Śwetáśwatara Upanishad*, vi., 19. Professor Gough renders as follows: 'Without parts, without action, and without change; blameless and unsullied.' *Philosophy of the Upanishads*, pp. 232, 233. *Ed.*

[3] दुःखनिवृत्तिर्मोक्ष इत्युक्तम् । तदवधारणाय तत्र मोक्षे परेषां मतानि निराकरोति ॥

[4] Vedánti Mahádeva omits मुक्तिः, according to my sole MS. Most probably, however, there is, here, a mistake of the copyist. *Ed.*

are no *properties* [in Soul, as, e.g., in the shape of joy].

a. There belongs to Soul no *property* in the shape of joy, or in the shape of manifestation; and the *essence* [of Soul] is quite eternal, and, therefore, not something to be produced by means: therefore, Emancipation is not a manifestation of joy: such is the meaning.[1]

न विशेषगुणोच्छित्तिस्तद्वत् ॥ ७५ ॥

Second view disputed. *Aph.* 75. Nor, in like manner, is it [Emancipation,] the destruction of special qualities.

a. Emancipation is, moreover, not the destruction of all special qualities, 'In like manner.' Because there are absolutely *no* properties [in Soul, (see § 74)]. Such is the meaning.[2]

न विशेषगतिर्निष्क्रियस्य ॥ ७६ ॥

A third view disputed. *Aph.* 76. Nor is it [Emancipation,] any particular going of that [Soul,] which is motionless.

a. Moreover, emancipation is not a going to the world

---

[1] आत्मन्यानन्दरूपोऽभिव्यक्तिरूपश्च धर्मो नास्ति स्वरूपं च नित्यमेवेति न साधनसाध्यम् । अतो नानन्दाभिव्यक्तिर्मोक्ष इत्यर्थः ॥

[2] अशेषविशेषगुणोच्छेदोऽपि न मुक्तिः । तद्वत् । निर्धर्मत्वादेवेत्यर्थः ॥

of Brahmá;[1] because the Soul, since it is motionless, does not *go*.[2]

नाकारोपरागोच्छित्तिः क्षणिकत्वादिदोषात् ॥७७॥

A fourth view disputed. *Aph.* 77. Nor is it [Emancipation,] the destruction of the influence of [intellectual] forms, by reason of the faults of momentariness, &c.

a. The meaning is, that also the doctrine of the Nihilist, that the Soul consists merely of momentary knowledge, that Bondage is the modifying thereof by objects, and that emancipation is the destruction of the influence thereof called Memory,[3] is inadmissible; because, by reason of the faults of *momentariness*, &c., [such] emancipation is not the Soul's aim.[4]

b. He censures another [conception of] emancipation of the Nihilist's:[5]

न सर्वोच्छित्तिरपुरुषार्थत्वादिदोषात् ॥ ७८ ॥

---

[1] See Book IV., Aph. 21, *a.*, and Aph. 31, *b.*, at pp. 301 and 310, *supra*. *Ed.*

[2] ब्रह्मलोकगतिरपि न मोक्ष आत्मनो निष्क्रियत्वेन गत्यभावात् ॥

[3] *Vásaná;* for which *vide supra*, p. 29, note 2. *Ed.*

[4] क्षणिकज्ञानमेवात्मा तस्य विषयाकारता बन्धस्तद्वासनाख्योपरागस्य नाशो मोक्ष इति यन्नास्तिकमतं तदपि न क्षणिकत्वादिदोषेण मोक्षस्यापुरुषार्थत्वादित्यर्थः ॥

[5] नास्तिकस्यैव मुक्त्यन्तरं दूषयति ॥

A fifth view disputed. *Aph.* 78. Nor is it [Emancipation,] destruction of all; for this has, among other things, the fault of *not* being the Soul's aim.

a. Likewise, the entire destruction of the Soul, which consists of knowledge, is not emancipation; because, among other things, we do not see, in the world, that the annihilation of the soul is the soul's aim: such is the meaning.[1]

एवं शून्यमपि ॥ ७९ ॥

A sixth view disputed. *Aph.* 79. So, too, the Void.

a. The annihilation of the whole universe, consisting of cognition and the cognizable, is, thus, also, not emancipation; because Soul's aim is not effected by Soul's annihilation: such is the meaning.[2]

संयोगाश्च वियोगान्ता इति न देशादिलाभोऽपि ॥ ८० ॥

A seventh view disputed. *Aph.* 80. And conjunctions terminate in separations; therefore, it [Emancipation,] is not the acquisition of lands, &c., either.

---

[1] ज्ञानरूपस्यात्मनः सामग्र्येणैवोच्छित्तिरपि न मोक्ष आत्मनाशस्य लोके पुरुषार्थत्वादर्शनादिभ्य इत्यर्थः ॥

[2] ज्ञानज्ञेयात्मकाखिलप्रपञ्चनाशोऽप्येवमात्मनाशेनापुरुषार्थत्वान्न मोक्ष इत्यर्थः ॥

a. From its perishableness, possessorship is not Emancipation.[1]

न भागियोगो भागस्य ॥ ८१ ॥

An eighth view disputed. *Aph*. 81. Nor is it [Emancipation,] conjunction of a Part with the Whole.[2]

a. Emancipation is not absorption of 'a Part,' i.e., the Soul, into 'the Whole,' i.e., that of which it is [on the view in question,] a part, viz., the Supreme Soul; for the reason assigned [in § 80], viz., 'conjunctions terminate in separations,' and because we do not admit a Lord [Book I., § 92], and because, thus, self-dissolution is not Soul's aim: such is the meaning.[3]

---

[1] विनाशित्वात्स्वाम्यं न मुक्तिरिति ॥

[2] Aniruddha writes as follows, in his elucidation of the eighty-first Aphorism: न ब्रह्मणो भागो जीवात्मा ब्रह्मणो भागाभावात् । योगस्य वियोगान्तत्वात्पुनर्बन्धप्रसङ्गः । His introduction to the Aphorism runs: भागस्य जीवात्मनो भागिनि ब्रह्मणि योगो मुक्तिरिति तद्दूषयति । *Ed.*

[3] भागस्यांशस्य जीवस्य भागिन्यंशिनि परमात्मनि लयो न मोक्षः संयोगा हि वियोगान्ता इत्युक्तहेतोरीश्वरानभ्युपगमाच्च तथा स्वलयस्यापुरुषार्थत्वाच्चेत्यर्थः ॥

नाणिमादियोगोऽप्यवश्यंभावित्वात्तदुच्छित्तेरितर-योगवत्[1] ॥ ८२ ॥

A ninth view disputed.

Aph. 82. Nor is it [Emancipation], moreover, conjunction with the [power of] becoming as small as an atom, &c.; since, as is the case with other conjunctions, the destruction of this must necessarily take place.

a. Moreover, conjunction with superhuman power, e.g., the assuming the size of an atom, is not Emancipation; because, just as is the case with connexions with other superhuman powers, the destruction of this, also, follows, of necessity: such is the meaning.[2]

नेन्द्रादिपदयोगोऽपि तद्वत् ॥ ८३ ॥

A tenth view disputed.

Aph. 83. Nor, just as in that case, is it [Emancipation], moreover, conjunction with the rank of Indra, &c.

a. Nor is the attainment of the superhuman power of Indra, &c., Emancipation,—just as is the case with other superhuman powers [such as assuming atomic bulk];—by reason of perishableness: such is the meaning.[3]

---

[1] Both my MSS. of Aniruddha exhibit the questionable reading -वियोगवत्. *Ed.*

[2] अणिमाद्यैश्वर्यसंबधोऽपि न मुक्तिरैश्वर्यान्तरसंबन्धवदेव तस्याप्युच्छेदनियमादित्यर्थः ॥

[3] इन्द्राद्यैश्वर्यलाभोऽपि न मुक्तिरितरैश्वर्यवत्क्षयिष्णुत्वादित्यर्थः ॥

b. He repels the objection of an opponent to what has been stated [in Book I., § 61], that the Organs are products of Self-consciousness :[1]

न भूतप्रकृतित्वमिन्द्रियाणामाहङ्कारिकत्व-श्रुतेः[2] ॥ ८४ ॥

The organs whence. *Aph.* 84. The Organs are not formed of the Elements [as the *Naiyáyikas* assert]; because there is Scripture for their being derived from Self-consciousness.

a. With advertence to the opinion that *Power,* &c., also, are principles, he repels the determination of categories [insisted upon by the various sects] of his opponents, and the notion that Emancipation comes through a knowledge of these [categories] merely :[3]

न षट्पदार्थनियमस्तद्बोधान्मुक्तिः[4] ॥ ८५ ॥

---

[1] इन्द्रियाणामाहङ्कारिकत्वं यदुक्तं तत्र परविप्रतिपत्तिं निराकरोति ॥

[2] Vedánti Mahádeva has, instead of आहङ्कारिकत्व°, अहंकारत्व°. *Ed.*

[3] शक्त्यादिकमपि तत्त्वमस्तीत्याशयेन परेषां पदार्थप्रतिनियमं तन्मात्रज्ञानान्मुक्तिं च निराकरोति ॥

[4] Nágeśa and Vedánti Mahádeva add च, as does Vijnána, according to the best MSS. *Ed.*

The categories of the Vaiśeshika objected to.

Aph. 85. The rule of six categories is not [the correct one]; nor does Emancipation result from acquaintance therewith, [as the *Vaiśeshikas* maintain].

षोडशादिष्वप्येवम् ॥ ८६ ॥

And those of the Nyáya, &c.

Aph. 86. So, too, is it in the case of the sixteen [categories of the *Nyáya*], &c.

a. In order to establish, what has been already stated [in Book I., § 62], that the five Elements are *products*, he rejects the eternity of the Earthy and other Atoms, which is held by the *Vaiśeshikas* and others:[1]

नाणुनित्यता तत्कार्यत्वश्रुतेः ॥ ८७ ॥

The eternity of Atoms unscriptural.

Aph. 87. [The five Elements being *products*, as declared in Book I., § 61], Atoms are not eternal, [as alleged in the *Nyáya*]; for there is Scripture for their being products.

a. Although that text of Scripture is not seen by us, because it has disappeared, in the lapse of time, &c., yet it is to be inferred from the words of teachers, and from the tradition of Manu,[2] [Ch. I., v. 27].

---

[1] पञ्चभूतानां पूर्वोक्तकार्यत्वोपपत्त्यर्थं वैशेषिकाद्यभ्युपगतं पार्थिवाद्यणुनित्यत्वमपाकरोति ॥

[2] यद्यप्यस्माभिः सा श्रुतिर्न दृश्यते काललु-

b. But then, how can an Atom, which is without parts, be a product? To this he replies:[1]

न निर्भागत्वं[2] कार्यत्वात् ॥ ८८ ॥

The Scripture decisive of the question.

Aph. 88. Since it is a product, it is not without parts.

a. That is to say: since the fact, established by Scripture, of their being products, cannot be otherwise accounted for, the [so-called] Atoms of Earth, &c., are *not* without parts.[3]

b. He repels the objection of the Nihilist, that direct cognition of Nature, or of Soul, is impossible; because [forsooth,] the cause of a thing's being directly cognizable is colour:[4]

न्त्वादिना तथाप्याचार्यवाक्यान्मनुस्मरणाच्चानुमेया ॥

[1] ननु निरवयवस्य परमाणोः कथं कार्यत्वं घटते । तत्राह ॥

[2] Aniruddha reads न तन्निर्भागत्वं. *Ed.*

[3] श्रुतिसिद्धकार्यत्वान्यथानुपपत्त्या पृथिव्याद्यणूनां न निरवयवत्वमित्यर्थः ॥

[4] प्रकृतिपुरुषसाक्षात्कारो न संभवति रूपस्य द्रव्यसाक्षात्कारहेतुत्वादिति नास्तिकाक्षेपं निराकरोति ॥

[1]न रूपनिबन्धनात्प्रत्यक्षनियमः[2] ॥ ८९ ॥

A cavil disposed of.

Aph. 89. There is no necessity that direct cognition should have *colour* as its cause.

a. It is no rule, that to be directly cognizable should result from colour only, [or other object of sense], as the cause; because direct cognition may result from Merit, &c., [viz., mystical practices, and so forth], also: such is the meaning.[3]

b. Well, if that be the case, pray is the *dimension* of an Atom a reality, or not? With reference to this, he decides the question of dimension,[4] [as follows]:

न [5]परिमाणचातुर्विध्यं द्वाभ्यां तद्योगात् ॥ ९० ॥

---

[1] A marginal note in one of my MSS. of Aniruddha mentions तद्रूप° as a variant. Both my MSS. of Nágeśa have, erroneously, -निर्बन्धात्, instead of -निबन्धनात्. *Ed.*

[2] Aniruddha and Vedánti Mahádeva have प्रत्यक्षत्वनियमः. *Ed.*

[3] रूपादेव निमित्तात्प्रत्यक्षतेति नियमो नास्ति धर्मादिनापि साक्षात्कारसंभवादित्यर्थः ॥

[4] नन्वेवं किमणुपरिमाणं वस्त्वस्ति न वेत्याकाङ्क्षायां परिमाणनिर्णयं करोति ॥

[5] One of my MSS of Aniruddha has परिमाणे. *Ed.*

Dimension of what kinds.

Aph. 90. There are not four varieties of dimension; because those can be accounted for by two.

a. There are not four kinds of dimension, viz., small, great, long, and short; but there are only two sorts. 'Because those can be accounted for by two:' that is to say, the four varieties can be accounted for by merely two, the atomic [or *positively* small,] and the great. Such is the meaning. For the short and the long are merely subordinate kinds of the dimension called great; else we should have, e.g., no end of dimensions, in the shape of the crooked, &c.[1]

b. He rebuts the Nihilist's denial of genera,[2] [as follows]:

अनित्यत्वेऽपि[3] स्थिरतायोगात्प्रत्यभिज्ञानं सामान्यस्य ॥ ९१ ॥

Genus proved by recognition.

Aph. 91. Though these [individuals] be uneternal, recognition, as being associated with constancy, is of genus.

---

[1] अणु महद्दीर्घं ह्रस्वमिति परिमाणचातुर्विध्यं नास्ति द्वैविध्यं तु वर्तत एव। द्वाभ्यां तद्योगात्। द्वाभ्यामेवाणुमहत्परिमाणाभ्यां चातुर्विध्यसंभवादित्यर्थः। महत्परिमाणस्यावान्तरभेदावेव हि ह्रस्वदीर्घौ। अन्यथा वक्रादिरूपैः परिमाणानन्त्यप्रसङ्गादिभिः॥

[2] सामान्येषु नास्तिकविप्रतिपत्तिं निराकरोति॥

[3] Nágeśa, according to one of my MSS. omits अपि. *Ed.*

a. Hence, he says, it is not proper to deny [the existence of] genus:[1]

न तदपलापस्तस्मात् ॥ ९२ ॥

And not to be denied. *Aph.* 92. Therefore it [genus,] is not to be denied.

a. But then [it may be said], recognition is to be accounted for simply by a *non-existence,* in the shape of the exclusion of what is not the thing [recognized]: and let *this* be what is meant by the word 'genus.' To this he replies:[2]

नान्यनिवृत्तिरूपत्वं[3] भावप्रतीतेः ॥ ९३ ॥

Genus positive, not negative. *Aph.* 93. It [genus,] does not consist in *exclusion* of something else; because it is cognized as an entity.

a. That is to say: genus does not consist in exclusion [of something else]; because 'This is that same' is the cognition of something *positive;* for, otherwise, the only thing cognized would be, 'This is not a non-jar.'[4]

---

[1] तस्मान्न सामान्यापलापो युक्त इत्याह ॥

[2] नन्वतद्व्यावृत्तिरूपेणाभावेनैव प्रत्यभिज्ञोपपादनीया सैव च सामान्यशब्दार्थोऽस्तु । तत्राह ॥

[3] One of my MSS. of Nágeśa has, pretty obviously by mere error, नान्यवृत्तिरूपत्वं. *Ed.*

[4] स एवायमिति भावप्रत्ययान्निवृत्तिरूपत्वं न सामान्यस्येत्यर्थः। अन्यथा हि नायमघट इत्येव प्रतीयेत ॥

b. But still, recognition may be caused by *likeness*. To this he replies:[1]

न तत्वान्तरं सादृश्यं प्रत्यक्षोपलब्धेः ॥ ९४ ॥

Likeness not a distinct principle.

Aph. 94. Likeness is not a separate principle; for it is directly apprehended, [as one manifestation of Community].

a. That is to say: likeness is nothing other than sameness in many parts, &c.; for it is directly apprehended as consisting in sameness;[2] [the *likeness* of a fair face to the moon, e. g., consisting in the *sameness* of the pleasurable feeling, &c., occasioned by the sight of either].

b. The conjecture, 'But then, let likeness be really an inherent power, and not [a modified aspect of] Community,' he repels:[3]

[4]निजशक्त्यभिव्यक्तिर्वा वैशिष्ट्यात्तदुपलब्धेः ॥ ९५ ॥

---

[1] ननु सादृश्यनिबन्धना प्रत्यभिज्ञा भविष्यति। तत्राह ॥

[2] भूयोऽवयवादिसामान्यादतिरिक्तं न सादृश्यमस्ति प्रत्यक्षत एव सामान्यरूपतयोपलम्भादित्यर्थः ॥

[3] ननु स्वाभाविकी शक्तिरेव सादृश्यमस्तु नतु तत्सामान्यमित्याशङ्कामपाकरोति ॥

[4] Aniruddha has निजधर्माभि°. *Ed.*

Nor a peculiar power. *Aph.* 95. Nor is it [likeness,] a manifestation of [something's] own power; because the apprehension of it is different.

a. Moreover, likeness is not the manifestation of a particular natural power of a thing; because the apprehension of likeness is different from the apprehension of power. For the cognition of a power is not dependent on the cognition of another thing; the cognition of likeness, on the other hand, is dependent on the cognition of a correlative,[1] as is the case with the cognition of a non-existence; so that the two conceptions are heterogeneous. Such is the meaning.[2]

b. But still, let the likeness among individual jars, &c., be merely that they have [all alike,] the name, e. g., of jar. To this he replies:[3]

न संज्ञासंज्ञिसंबन्धोऽपि[4] ॥ ९६ ॥

---

[1] *Pratiyogin*; on which *vide supra*, p. 342, note 3. *Ed.*

[2] वस्तुनः स्वाभाविकशक्तिविशेषोत्पादोऽपि न सादृश्यं शक्त्युपलब्धितः सादृश्योपलब्धेर्विलक्षणत्वात् । शक्तिज्ञानं हि नान्यधर्मिज्ञानसापेक्षं सादृश्यज्ञानं पुनः प्रतियोगिज्ञानमपेक्षतेऽभावज्ञानवदिति ज्ञानयोर्वैलक्षण्यमित्यर्थः ॥

[3] ननु तथापि घटादिसंज्ञकत्वमेव घटादिव्यक्तीनां सादृश्यमस्तु । तत्राह ॥

[4] The reading of Nágeśa is न संज्ञासंज्ञिनोः संबन्धोऽपि. *Ed.*

Nor the relation between names and things.

Aph. 96. Nor, moreover, is it [likeness,] the connexion between name and named.

a. Because even he who does not know the connexion between a name and the thing named may cognize a likeness,[1] [e. g., between two jars].

b. Moreover:[2]

न संबन्धनित्यतोभयानित्यत्वात् ॥ ९७ ॥

How it cannot be so.

Aph. 97. That connexion [viz., between name and named,] is not eternal; since both [the correlatives] are uneternal.

a. Since both the name and the named are uneternal, the relation between them, also, is not eternal. How, then, can there be, through *that*, the likeness of a departed thing in a thing present? Such is the meaning.[3]

b. But then, though the correlatives be uneternal, let

---

[1] संज्ञासंज्ञिभावमजानतोऽपि सादृश्यज्ञानादिति ॥

[2] अपि च ॥

[3] संज्ञासंज्ञिनोरनित्यत्वात्तत्संबन्धस्यापि न नित्यता। अतः कथं तेनातीतवस्तुसादृश्यं वर्तमानवस्तुनि स्यादित्यर्थः ॥

the *relation* be eternal. What is to hinder *this?* To this he replies :[1]

नातः[2] संबन्धो धर्मिग्राहकमानबाधात्[3] ॥ ९८ ॥

Another suggestion repelled.

Aph. 98. The connexion is not so [not eternal], for this reason, viz., because this is debarred by the evidence which acquaints us with the thing; [i. e., the supposition is inconsistent with the definition of the term].

a. Connexion is proved only where *disjunction* incidentally subsists; because, otherwise, there is no room for the supposition of *connexion ;* the case being accounted for,—as will be explained,—simply by *the natural state of the matter.* And this incidental disjunction is impossible, if connexion be eternal. Therefore, connexion is not eternal; for this is debarred by the very evidence that acquaints us with Connexion. Such is the meaning.[4]

---

[1] ननु संबन्ध्यनित्यत्वेऽपि संबन्धो नित्यः स्यात्। किमत्र बाधकम्। तत्राह॥

[2] Read **नाजः**, 'not unoriginated,' *i.e.*, 'not eternal,' qualifying 'connexion.' 'For this reason' renders **अतः**. The reading **नातः**, the manuscript authority for which is of the slightest, is treated as if no better than a typographical error, in the corrigenda to my edition of Vijnána's work. *Ed.*

[3] Aniruddha has, instead of **-मान॰**, **-प्रमाण॰**. In the margin of one of my MSS. of his commentary is the variant **-मानाभावात्**. *Ed.*

[4] कादाचित्कविभागे सत्येव संबन्धः सिध्यति।

b. But, on this showing, there could be no such thing as the eternal [connexion called] Coinherence[1] between those two eternals, a Quality and the thing qualified; [which Coinherence, or intimate relation, is one of the categories of the *Nyáya*]. To this he replies:[2]

[3]न समवायोऽस्ति प्रमाणाभावात् ॥ ९९ ॥

The Category of Intimate Relation rejected.

Aph. 99. There is no [such thing as] Coinherence, [such as the Naiyáyikas insist upon]; for there is no evidence [for it].

a. But then [it may be said], the evidence of it is, the perception that something is qualified [or conjoined with a quality which *inheres* in it], and the unaccountableness, otherwise, of the cognition of something as qualified. To this he replies:[4]

अन्यथा वक्ष्यमाणरीत्या स्वरूपेणैवोपपत्तौ संबन्धकल्पनानवकाशात् । स च कादाचित्को विभागो न संबन्धनित्यत्वे संभवति । अतः संबन्धग्राहकप्रमाणेनैव बाधान्न नित्यः संबन्ध इत्यर्थः ॥

[1] *Samaváya;* of which the preferable rendering, proposed by Professor Cowell, is 'interpenetration.' *Ed.*

[2] नन्वेवं नित्ययोर्गुणगुणिनोर्नित्यः समवायो नोपपद्येत । तत्राह ॥

[3] The reading of Nágeśa is तत्राप्यस्ति. His gloss runs: समवाये प्रमाणाभाव इत्यर्थः । *Ed.*

[4] ननु वैशिष्ट्यप्रत्यक्षं विशिष्टबुद्ध्यन्यथानुपपत्तिश्च प्रमाणम् । तत्राह ॥

उभयत्राप्यन्यथासिद्धेर्न[1] प्रत्यक्षमनुमानं वा[2] ॥ १०० ॥

This argued.

Aph. 100. Neither perception nor inference [is evidence for the existence of Coinherence]; since, as regards both alike, the case is otherwise disposed of.[3]

a. Since, 'as regards both alike,' i. e., the perception of qualifiedness, and the inferring of it, 'the case is otherwise disposed of;'[4] viz., simply by *the natural state* [of the thing and its qualities], neither of the two is evidence for [the imaginary category called] Coinherence: such is the meaning.[5]

b. It is a tenet, that, from the agitation of Nature the conjunction of Nature and Soul takes place, and thence results creation. In regard to that, there is this objection of the atheists, that 'Nothing whatever possesses the action called agitation; everything is momentary; where

---

1 One of my MSS. of Aniruddha simply omits न; while the other has उभयथाप्यसिद्धेः *Ed.*

2 Nágeśa gives प्रत्यक्षानुमाने. *Ed.*

3 Read, instead of 'the case is otherwise disposed of,' 'the establishment [which they lead to] is otherwise.' *Ed.*

4 See the preceding note. *Ed.*

5 उभयत्रापि वैशिष्ट्यप्रत्यक्षे तदनुमाने च स्वरूपेणैवान्यथासिद्धेर्न तदुभयं समवाये प्रमाणमित्यर्थः ॥

it arises, even there it perishes; therefore, no motion is proved to be inferrible from conjunction [of anything] with another place;' [the fruit, for instance, which appears to reach the ground not being that fruit, any longer existent, which appeared to drop from the tree]. To this he replies:[1]

नानुमेयत्वमेव[2] क्रियाया नेदिष्ठस्य तत्तद्वतोरेवा-[3]
परोक्षप्रतीतेः ॥ १०१ ॥

Motion is matter of perception.

Aph. 101. Motion is not a matter of inference; for he who stands very near has, indeed, direct cognition both of it and of what it belongs to.

a. In Book Second the different opinions were merely mentioned, that the Body is formed of five elements, and so forth; but no particular one was considered. In regard to this question, he denies the view of an opponent:[4]

---

[1] प्रकृतेः क्षोभात्प्रकृतिपुरुषसंयोगस्तस्मात्सृष्टिरिति सिद्धान्तः। तत्रायं नास्तिकानामाक्षेपो नास्ति क्षोभाख्या कस्यापि क्रिया सर्वं वस्तु क्षणिकं यत्रोत्पद्यते तत्रैव विनश्यतीत्यतो न देशान्तरसंयोगोन्नेया क्रिया सिध्यतीति। तत्राह॥

[2] Some MSS. of Vijnána omit एव, as does Nágesa. *Ed.*

[3] Nágesa omits एव. *Ed.*

[4] द्वितीयाध्याये शरीरस्य पाञ्चभौतिकत्वादिरूपैर्मतभेदा एवोक्ता नतु विशेषोऽवधृतः। अत्रापरपक्षं प्रतिषेधति॥

न पाञ्चभौतिकं शरीरं बहूनामुपादानायोगात् ॥ १०२ ॥

The Body is of earth only.

Aph. 102. The Body does not consist of *five* elements; because many [heterogeneous things] are unsuitable as the material.

a. He will mention, that, whilst there is but one material, the material of every Body is earth :[1]

न स्थूलमिति नियम आतिवाहिकस्यापि विद्यमानत्वात् ॥ १०३ ॥

There is a Subtile as well as a Gross, Body.

Aph. 103. It [the Body,] is not, necessarily, the Gross one; for there is, also, the vehicular [transmigrating or Subtile] one.

a. Senses, [the organ of vision, for example,] distinct from the eye-balls, have been already mentioned. In order to substantiate this [point], he refutes the opinion, that the senses reveal what they do not reach to :[2]

नाप्राप्तप्रकाशकत्वमिन्द्रियाणामप्राप्तेः सर्वप्राप्तेर्वा ॥ १०४ ॥

---

[1] एकोपादानकत्वेऽपि पृथिव्येवोपादानं सर्वशरीरस्येति वक्ष्यति ॥

[2] गोलकेभ्योऽतिरिक्तानीन्द्रियाणि प्रागुक्तानि। तदुपपादनायेन्द्रियाणामप्राप्तप्रकाशकत्वं निराकरोति ॥

Connexion between sense and object.

Aph. 104. The senses do not reveal what they do not reach to; because of their not reaching, or because [else,] they might reach everything.

a. The senses do not reveal things unconnected with them. 'Because of their not reaching.' For we do not see that lamps, or the like, reveal what they do not reach to; and because, if they were to reveal what they do *not* reach to, we should find them revealing *all* things, viz., those intercepted, and the like. Such is the meaning. Therefore there is an organ, other than the eye-ball, for the sake of connexion with the distant sun, &c. Such is the import. And the instruments reveal the objects simply by delivering the object to the soul,—for they are, themselves, unintelligent;—as a mirror reveals the face. Or [in other words], their revealing an object is simply their taking up an image of the object.[1]

b. He repels the conjecture: But then, in that case, the opinion [of the Naiyáyikas,] that the sight is luminous

---

[1] स्वासंबद्धार्थानीन्द्रियाणि न प्रकाशयन्ति । अप्राप्तेः । प्रदीपादीनामप्राप्तप्रकाशकत्वादर्शनादप्राप्तप्रकाशकत्वे व्यवहितादिसर्ववस्तुप्रकाशकत्वप्रसङ्गाच्चेत्यर्थः । अतो दूरस्थसूर्यादिसंबन्धार्थं गोलकातिरिक्तमिन्द्रियमिति भावः । करणानां चार्थप्रकाशकत्वं पुरुषेऽर्थसमर्पणद्वारैव स्वतो जडत्वाद्दर्पणस्य मुखप्रकाशकत्ववत् । अथ वार्थप्रतिबिम्बोद्ग्रहणमेवार्थप्रकाशकत्वमिति ॥

is quite right; for we see Light alone glide rapidly to a distance, in the form of rays:[1]

न तेजोऽपसर्पणात्तैजसं चक्षुर्वृत्तितस्त-
त्सिद्धेः ॥ १०५ ॥

The Sight not formed of Light.

Aph. 105. Not because Light glides [and the Sight does so, too,] is the Sight luminous [or formed of Light]; because the thing is accounted for by [the theory of] modifications, [to be now explained].

a. The Sight is not to be asserted to be luminous, on the ground that light is seen to glide. Why? Because, just as in the case of the vital air, where there is no luminosity, the gliding forth can be accounted for through a kind of modification. Such is the meaning. For, as the vital air, without having at all parted from the body, glides out ever so far from the end of the nose, under the modification called breathing, [and thus smells a distant flower], just so the Sight, though a non-luminous substance, without, indeed, quitting [connexion with] the body, all in a moment will dart off [like the protruded feeler of a polyp,] to a distant object, such as the sun, by means of the species of change called modification.[2]

---

[1] नन्वेवं चक्षुषस्तैजसत्वमेव युक्तं तेजस एव किरणरूपेणाशुदूरापसर्पणदर्शनादिति शङ्कां निराकरोति ॥

[2] तेजसोऽपसर्पणं दृष्टमिति कृत्वा तैजसं चक्षुर्न वाच्यम् । कुतः । अतैजसत्वेऽपि प्राणवदेव वृत्ति-

b. But what is the proof that there is any such modification? To this he replies:[1]

प्राप्तार्थप्रकाशलिङ्गाद्वृत्तिसिद्धिः ॥ १०६ ॥

Proof of his theory of vision, that it accounts for the phenomena.

Aph. 106. By the sign of the display of the attained object the [existence of the] modification [which could alone account for that display,] is proved.

a. He shows [us] the nature of the modification, to account for the going, though without parting from the Body:[2]

भागगुणाभ्यां तत्त्वान्तरं वृत्तिः संबन्धार्थं सर्पतीति ॥ १०७ ॥

Of the theory, further.

Aph. 107. The 'modification' is another principle than a fragment, or

---

भेदेनापसर्पणोपपत्तेरित्यर्थः । यथा हि प्राणः शरीरमसंत्यज्यैव नासाग्राद्बहिः कियद्दूरं प्राणनाख्यवृत्त्यापसरत्येवमेवातैजसद्रव्यमपि चक्षुर्देहमसंत्यज्यापि वृत्त्याख्यपरिणामविशेषेण झटित्येव दूरस्थं सूर्यादिकं प्रत्यपसरेदिति ॥

¹ नन्वेवंभूतवृत्तौ किं प्रमाणम् । तत्राह ॥

² देहमपरित्यज्यापि गमनोपपत्तये वृत्तेः स्वरूपं दर्शयति ॥

a quality, [of the Sight, or other sense]; because it is for the sake of *connexion* that it glides forth.

a. The modification is not a *fragment* of the Sight, or other sense, [serving as] the cause of the revealing of objects,—a part disjoined like a spark,—or a *quality*, like, e.g., Colour; but the modification, whilst a portion thereof, is something else than a fragment, or a quality. For, if there were disruption, connexion of the sun, &c., with the Sight would not, through it, take place; and, if it were a quality, the motion called 'gliding forth' would be unaccountable; [for a quality cannot move by itself]. Such is the meaning.[1]

b. But, if, thus, the 'modifications' are *substances*, how is [the term] 'modification' applied to the *qualities* of intellect, in the shape of Desire, &c.? To this he replies:[2]

न [3]द्रव्यनियमस्तद्योगात् ॥ १०८ ॥

---

[1] अर्थप्रकाशहेतोश्चक्षुरादेर्भागो विस्फुलिङ्गवद्विभक्तांशो रूपादिवद्गुणश्च न वृत्तिः किं तु तदेकदेशभूता भागगुणाभ्यां भिन्ना वृत्तिः। विभागे हि सति तद्द्वारा चक्षुषः सूर्यादिसंबन्धो न घटते गुणत्वे च सर्पणाख्यक्रियानुपपत्तेरित्यर्थः ॥

[2] नन्वेवं वृत्तीनां द्रव्यत्वे कथमिच्छादिरूपबुद्धिगुणेषु वृत्तिव्यवहारः। तत्राह ॥

[3] Aniruddha and Vedánti Mahádeva have the reading द्रव्ये. *Ed.*

'Modifications' may be qualities, as well as substances.

Aph. 108. It [the term 'modification,'] is not confined to substances; because it is etymological, [not technical, and applies, etymologically, to a quality, as well].

a. Since it is also stated, in Scripture, that the sense-organs are formed of the Elements, the doubt may occur, whether the Scriptural texts are, perhaps, to be applied distributively, according to the difference of particular worlds. In regard to this, he says:[1]

न देशभेदेऽप्यन्योपादानतास्मदादिवन्नियमः[2] ॥ १०९ ॥

The materials of the organs everywhere the same.

Aph. 109. Not though there be a difference of locality, is there a difference in the material [of which the organs are formed]: the rule is as with the like of us.

a. Not through 'difference of locality,' as the world of Brahmá, and the like, is it, again, the fact, that the organs have any other material than self-consciousness; but the rule is, that those of all alike are formed of self-consciousness; as is the case, e. g., with us who live in this terrestrial world. For we hear, in Scripture, of only one Subtile Body

---

[1] इन्द्रियाणां भौतिकत्वस्यापि श्रवणात्कदाचिल्लोकविशेषभेदेन श्रुतिव्यवस्था शङ्क्येत। तत्राह ॥

[2] Some MSS. of Vijnána exhibit अस्मदादाविव नियमः, the lection of Nágeśa. *Ed.*

[made up of the organs], transmigrating generally through the different localities. Such is the meaning.[1]

b. But then, in that case, how is the Scripture relating to the materiality [of the organs] to be accounted for? To this he replies:[2]

निमित्तव्यपदेशात्तद्व्यपदेशः[3] ॥ ११० ॥

A non-literal text accounted for.

Aph. 110. The mention thereof [viz., of materiality, as if it belonged to the organs,] is because there is [intended to be made, thereby, a more emphatic] mention of the concomitant cause.[4]

a. There is designation as the material cause, in the case even where the cause is [but] concomitant, with a

---

[1] न ब्रह्मलोकादिदेशभेदतोऽपीन्द्रियाणामहंकारातिरिक्तोपादानकत्वं किं त्वस्मदादीनां भूर्लोकस्थानामिव सर्वेषामेवाहङ्कारिकत्वनियमः। देशभेदेनैकस्यैव लिङ्गशरीरस्य संचारमात्रश्रवणादित्यर्थः॥

[2] नन्वेवं भौतिकत्वश्रुतिः कथमुपपद्यताम्। तत्राह॥

[3] Probably from mere oversight, my MS. of Vedánti Mahádeva's work omits तद्°. *Ed.*

[4] *Nimitta*, 'instrumental cause.' *Nimitta-kárana* is rendered 'occasional cause' at p. 194, *supra*. Colebrooke's representatives are 'chief or especial cause' and 'efficient cause.' *Ed.*

view to indicating its *importance;* just as fire is [spoken of as arising] from fuel, [which fuel is a necessary concomitant of, though not really the substance of, the fire]. Hence are they [the organs,] spoken of as being formed of the Elements. Such is the meaning. For, only in reliance on the support of Light, or other Element, do the Organs, viz., the Sight, &c., [formed] from the accompanying Self-consciousness, come to exist; as fire, in reliance on the support of earthly fuel, results from the attendant Light,[1] [or Heat, which cannot manifest itself alone].

b. As the subject presents itself, he determines the variety that belongs to Gross Body:[2]

ऊष्मजाण्डजजरायुजोद्भिज्जसाङ्कल्पिकसांसिद्धिकं चेति न नियमः ॥ १११ ॥

Varieties of Gross Bodies.

Aph. 111. The heat-born, egg-born, womb-born, vegetable, thought-born, and spell-born; such is not an exhaustive division [of Gross Body, though a rough and customary one].

---

[1] निमित्तेऽपि प्राधान्यविवक्षयोपादानत्वव्यपदेशो भवति यथेन्धनादग्निरिति । अतो भूतोपादानत्वव्यपदेश इत्यर्थः । तेजआदिभूतोपष्टम्भेनैव हि तदनुगताहंकाराच्चक्षुरादीन्द्रियाणि भवन्ति यथा पार्थिवेन्धनोपष्टम्भेन तदनुगतात्तेजसोऽग्निर्भवतीति ॥

[2] स्थूलशरीरगतं विशेषं प्रसङ्गादवधारयति ॥

a. It was stated, before, that Body has only one Element as its material. In this same connexion, he observes discriminatively, as follows :[1]

सर्वेषु पृथिव्युपादानमसाधारण्यात्तद्व्यपदेशः पूर्ववत् ॥ ११२ ॥

The material of Bodies. *Aph.* 112. In all [Bodies] Earth is the material: in consideration [however,] of some speciality, there is designation as this [or that other element than earth, as entering into the constitution of some given body], as in the preceding case [treated under § 110].

a. In all Bodies the material is Earth only. 'In consideration of some speciality;' i.e., in consequence of intensity through excess, &c., in the case of Body, as before [in the case of the Organs], there is, however, designation as consisting of Elements, five, or four, &c., on the ground only of there being a *support,* as in the case of the materiality of the Organs. Such is the meaning.[2]

b. But then, since the vital air is the principal thing in

---

[1] शरीरस्यैकमात्रभूतोपादानकत्वं पूर्वोक्तम् । अनेनैव प्रसङ्गेन विशिष्याह ॥

[2] सर्वेषु शरीरेषु पृथिव्येवोपादानम् । असाधारण्यात् । आधिक्यादिभिरुत्कर्षाच्छरीरे पञ्चचतुरादिभौतिकत्वव्यपदेशस्तु पूर्ववदिन्द्रियाणां भौतिकत्ववदुपष्टम्भकत्वमात्रेणेत्यर्थः ॥

the Body, let the vital air itself be the originant of the Body. To this he replies :[1]

न देहारम्भकस्य प्राणत्वमिन्द्रियशक्तितस्तत्सिद्धेः[2] ॥ ११३ ॥

The vital air not the source of the Body.

Aph. 113. The vital air is not [on the allegation that it is the principal thing in the Body, to be considered] the originant of the Body; because it [the vital air, or spirit,] subsists through the power of the organs.

a. The vital air, consisting in the function of the organs, does not subsist in the absence of the organs. Therefore, since, in a *dead* Body, in consequence of the absence of the organs, there is the absence of the vital air, the vital air is not the originant of the Body.[3]

b. But then, in that case, since the vital air is not the cause of the Body, the Body might come into existence even without the vital air. To this he replies :[4]

---

[1] ननु प्राणस्य शरीरे प्राधान्यात्प्राण एव देहारम्भकोऽस्तु । तत्राह ॥

[2] Instead of तत्सिद्धेः, Vedánti Mahádeva has तत्सिद्धिः. *Ed.*

[3] करणवृत्तिरूपः प्राणः करणवियोगे न तिष्ठति । अतो मृतदेहे करणाभावेन प्राणाभावान्न प्राणो देहारम्भक इति ॥

[4] नन्वेवं प्राणस्य देहाकारणत्वे प्राणं विनापि देह उत्पद्येत । तत्राह ॥

भोक्तुरधिष्ठानाद्भोगायतननिर्माणमन्यथा पूतिभावप्रसङ्गात्[1] ॥ ११४ ॥

Soul essential to a living Body.

Aph. 114. The site of experience [viz., the Body,] is constructed [only] through the superintendence of the experiencer [Soul]: otherwise, we should find putrefaction.

a. 'Through the superintendence,' i. e., only through the operation, 'of the experiencer,' i. e., Soul [literally, that which has the vital airs], is 'the construction of the site of experience,' i. e., the Body; because, 'otherwise,' i. e., if the operation of the vital airs were absent, we should find putrefaction in the semen and blood, just as in a dead body. Such is the meaning. And thus, by the several operations of circulating the juices, &c., the vital air is a *concomitant* cause[2] of the Body, through the sustaining of it: such is the import.[3]

b. But then [it may be said], it is only the vital air, itself, that can be the superintender; because it is this which

---

[1] Aniruddha reads -प्रसक्तेः; Vedánti Mahádeva, -प्रसङ्गः. *Ed.*

[2] *Nimitta-kárana. Vide supra*, p. 400, note 4. *Ed.*

[3] भोक्तुः प्राणिनोऽधिष्ठानाद्व्यापारादेव भोगायतनस्य शरीरस्य निर्माणं भवति । अन्यथा प्राणव्यापाराभावे शुक्रशोणितयोः पूतिभावप्रसङ्गान्मृतदेहवदित्यर्थः । तथा च रससंचारादिव्यापारविशेषैः प्राणो देहस्य निमित्तकारणं धारकत्वादिति भावः ॥

operates, not the Soul, since *it* is motionless, and since there is no use in the superintendence of what does not operate. To this he replies:[1]

भृत्यद्वारा[2] स्वाम्यधिष्ठितिर्नैकान्तात् ॥ ११५ ॥

The Soul 'acting by another's actions.'

Aph. 115. Through a servant, not directly, is superintendence [exercised] by the master.

a. In the construction of the Body, 'superintendence,' in the shape of energizing, is not 'directly,' i. e., immediately, [exercised] 'by the master,' i. e., by Soul, but 'through its servant,' in the shape of the vital airs; as in the case of a king's building a city: such is the meaning.[3]

b. It was stated before [Book II., § 1,] that Nature's [agency] is 'for the emancipation of what is [really, though not apparently,] emancipated.' In reference to the objection of opponents in regard to this, viz., 'How can the

---

[1] ननु प्राणस्यैवाधिष्ठानत्वं संभवति व्यापारवत्त्वान्न प्राणिनः कूटस्थत्वान्निर्व्यापारस्याधिष्ठाने प्रयोजनाभावाच्चेति । तत्राह ॥

[2] According to one of my MSS., the lection of Aniruddha is भृत्यवर्गद्वारा. *Ed.*

[3] देहनिर्माणे व्यापाररूपमधिष्ठानं स्वामिनश्चेतनस्यैकान्तात्साक्षान्नास्ति किं तु प्राणरूपभृत्यद्वारा यथा राज्ञः परनिर्माण इत्यर्थः ॥

soul be eternally free, when we see it bound?' with a view to demonstrating its eternal freedom, he says:[1]

समाधिसुषुप्तिमोक्षेषु ब्रह्मरूपता ॥ ११६ ॥

Soul ever free.

Aph. 116. In Concentration, profound sleep, and emancipation, it [Soul,] consists of Brahma.[2]

a. Then what is the difference of emancipation from profound sleep and concentration? To this he replies:[3]

द्वयोः सबीजमन्यत्र[4] तद्धतिः ॥ ११७ ॥

Perfect and imperfect emancipation.

Aph. 117. In the case of the two, it is with a seed; in the case of the other, this is wanting.

a. 'In the case of the two,' viz., concentration and profound sleep, the identity with Brahma[5] is 'with a seed,' i. e., associated with some cause of Bondage, [or reappearance in the mundane state]; 'in the case of the other,' i. e.,

---

[1] विमुक्तमोक्षार्थं प्रधानस्येत्युक्तं प्राक्। तत्र कथमात्मा नित्यमुक्तो बन्धदर्शनादिति परेषामाक्षेपे नित्यमुक्तिमुपपादयितुमाह ॥

[2] See the *Rational Refutation*, &c., p. 33. *Ed.*

[3] तर्हि कः सुषुप्तिसमाधिभ्यां मोक्षस्य विशेषः। तत्राह ॥

[4] Aniruddha has सबीजत्वमन्यस्य; and so has Vedánti Mahádeva, according to some copies. *Ed.*

[5] *Brahmatwa*, the abstract of *Brahma*. *Ed.*

in emancipation, this cause is absent: this is the distinction. Such is the meaning.[1]

b. But then, Concentration and profound sleep are *evident;* but what evidence is there of *Emancipation?* This objection of the atheist he repels:[2]

द्वयोरिव त्रयस्यापि[3] दृष्टत्वान्नतु द्वौ ॥ ११८ ॥

The reality of Emancipation.

Aph. 118. But there are not the two [only]; because the triad, also [Emancipation inclusive], is evident; as are the two.

a. The meaning is, that, since Emancipation, also, is 'evident,' i.e., is inferrible, through the example of Concentration and profound sleep, there are not the two, viz., profound sleep and Concentration, only; but Emancipation, also, really is. And the argument is thus. The quitting of that identity with Brahma[4] which [identity] exists during profound sleep, &c., takes place only through a fault, viz., Desire, or the like, lodged in the mind; and, if this fault be annihilated by knowledge, then there results

---

[1] द्वयोः समाधिसुषुप्त्योः सबीजं बन्धबीजसहितं ब्रह्मत्वमन्यच्च मोक्षे बीजस्याभाव इति विशेष इत्यर्थः ॥

[2] ननु समाधिसुषुप्ती दृष्टे स्तो मोक्षे तु किं प्रमाणमिति नास्तिकाक्षेपं परिहरति ॥

[3] Vedánti Mahádeva omits अपि. *Ed.*

[4] *Brahma-bháva,* the same as *brahmatwa.* *Ed.*

a *permanent* condition, quite similar to profound sleep, &c.; and it is precisely *this* that is Emancipation.[1] [2]

b. But then [suggests some one, with reference to § 117], granting, that, even notwithstanding the existence of the 'seed' [or source of return to the mundane state,] called Memory,[3] a mental modification after the form of any object does not arise during *concentration*, inasmuch as Memory is [then] dulled [or deadened] by apathy, &c., yet, in the case of a person in *profound sleep*, since Memory prevails, there will really be cognition of objects; consequently, it is not proper to say that there is identity with Brahma during profound sleep. To this he replies:[4]

---

[1] समाधिसुषुप्तिदृष्टान्तेन मोक्षस्यापि दृष्टत्वादनुमितत्वान्नतु द्वौ सुषुप्तिसमाधी एव किं तु मोक्षोऽप्यस्तीत्यर्थः। अनुमानं चेत्थम्। सुषुप्त्यादौ यो ब्रह्मभावस्तत्त्यागश्चित्तगताद्रागादिदोषादेव भवति स चेद्दोषो ज्ञानेन नाशितस्तर्हि सुषुप्त्यादिसदृश्येवावस्था स्थिरा भवति सैव मोक्ष इति॥

[2] See the *Rational Refutation*, &c., p. 33. *Ed.*

[3] Here and below, this renders *vásaná*, on which *vide supra*, p. 29, note 2. *Ed.*

[4] ननु वासनाख्यबीजसत्त्वेऽपि वैराग्यादिना वासनाकौण्ठ्यादर्थाकारा वृत्तिः समाधौ मा भवतु सुषुप्ते तु वासनाप्राबल्यादर्थज्ञानं भविष्यत्येवेति न सुषुप्तौ ब्रह्मरूपता युक्तेति। तत्राह॥

वासनया नार्थख्यापनं[1] दोषयोगेऽपि न निमित्तस्य प्रधानबाधकत्वम् ॥ ११९ ॥

Memory inactive during profound sleep.

Aph. 119. There is not the revelation, by memory, of an object likewise during the conjunction of a [more potent] fault [such as sleep]: the secondary cause does not debar the principal.[2]

a. As in the case of apathy, so, also when there is the conjunction of the fault of sleep, Memory does not reveal its own objects, does not remind us of its objects; for the 'secondary,' the subordinate, Memory,[3] cannot defeat the

---

[1] This I find nowhere; and I believe it to be without warrant. I have printed, agreeably to the reading of Aniruddha, Vedánti Mahádeva, and the best MSS. of Vijnána, वासनयानर्थख्यापनं, and have noticed, in some copies of the last-named commentator, the variant वासनया न स्वार्थख्यापनं. Nágeśa has the latter reading, followed by दोषयोगात्, with omission of अपि. The Serampore edition of the *Sánkhya-pravachana-bháshya* has वासनाया न स्वार्थख्यापनं, for which I find no authority. *Ed.*

[2] The rendering given above is susceptible of improvement; and so, very probably, is that which follows: 'Where, moreover, there is influence from an obstruction [like that offered by sleep], mental impression does not inform one of objects [and, hence, one is then exempt from desires, &c., and in a state identical with that of emancipation]: a cause [of desires, &c.; and such is mental impression,] does not countervail what is predominant, [*e.g.*, sleep, which is, as it were, temporary Brahmahood or emancipation].'

Aniruddha's interpretation of this obscure aphorism, possibly by reason of his elliptical mode of expression, is far from clear. His view of its sense is, certainly, peculiar. *Ed.*

[3] *Sanskára*, here used as synonymous with *vásaná*. *Ed.*

more potent fault of Sleep: such is the meaning. For the really more potent fault makes the memory powerless, incompetent to produce its effects; [and so there is nothing, in this, to prevent identification of Soul with Brahma, during profound sleep, any more than during apathetic Concentration]: such is the import.[1]

b. It was stated, in the Third Book [§ 83], that the retention of a Body by him who is emancipated while still living, is 'in consequence of a mere vestige of impression.'[2] To this it is objected as follows. Experience is observed, in the case of the [alleged person] emancipated during life, just as in the case of the like of us, [and this experience continuous,] even though it may be constantly in respect of a single object: now, this is unaccountable [on the hypothesis of his really *being* emancipated]; because the antecedent *impression* is annihilated, exactly on its having produced the first [instant of] experience, and because no subsequent impression arises, inasmuch as *knowledge* debars it; just as is the case with Merit. To this he replies:[3]

---

[1] यथा वैराग्ये तथा निद्रादोषयोगेऽपि सति वासनया न स्वार्थख्यापनं स्वविषयस्मारणं भवति यतो न निमित्तस्य गुणीभूतस्य संस्कारस्य बलवत्तरनिद्रादोषबाधकत्वं संभवतीत्यर्थः। बलवत्तर एव हि दोषो वासनां दुर्बलां स्वकार्यकुण्ठां करोतीति भावः॥

[2] Here, and often below, 'impression' is to render *sanskára*. *Ed.*

[3] संस्कारलेशतो जीवन्मुक्तस्य शरीरधारणमिति तृतीयाध्याये प्रोक्तम्। तत्रायमाक्षेपः।

एकः संस्कारः क्रियानिर्वर्तको[1] नतु प्रतिक्रियं संस्कारभेदा बहुकल्पनाप्रसक्तेः ॥ १२० ॥

An objection met to the possibility of emancipation in one still living.

Aph. 120. A single impression [suffices to generate, and] lasts out[2] the experience: but there are not different impressions, one to each [instant of] experience; else, we should have a postulation of many, [where a single one may suffice].

a. In like manner, in the case of the whirling of the potter's wheel, the self-continuant principle,[3] called motal inertia, is to be regarded as only one, continuing till the completion of the whirling.[4]

b. It has been stated [§ 111,] that there are vegetable Bodies. He repels the objection of the atheist, that, in the case in question, there is not a *Body*, inasmuch as there is no knowledge of the external:[5]

जीवन्मुक्तस्य शश्वदेकस्मिन्नप्यर्थेऽस्मदादीनामिव भोगो दृश्यते सोऽनुपपन्नः प्रथमं भोगमुत्पाद्यैव पूर्वसंस्कारनाशात्संस्कारान्तरस्य च ज्ञानप्रतिबन्धेन कर्मवदनुदयादिति। तत्राह ॥

1 The reading -निवर्त°, found in several MSS., is a gross error. *Ed.*

2 Read, instead of 'lasts out,' 'brings about.' *Ed.*

3 This phrase is meant to translate *sanskára*. *Ed.*

4 कुलालचक्रभ्रमणस्थलेऽप्येवं वेगाख्यः संस्कार एक एव भ्रमणसमाप्तिपर्यन्तस्थायी बोध्यः ॥

5 उद्भिज्जं शरीरमस्तीत्युक्तम्। तत्र बाह्यबु-

न बाह्यबुद्धिनियमो[1] वृक्षगुल्मलतौषधिवनस्पतितृणवीरुधादीनामपि भोक्तृभोगायतनत्वं पूर्ववत् ॥ १२१ ॥

The Vegetable organism really a Body.

Aph. 121. Knowledge of the external is not indispensable [to constitute a Body]: trees, shrubs, climbers, annuals, trees with invisible flowers, grasses, creepers, &c., [which have internal consciousness], are, also, sites of experiencer and experience; as in the former case.

a. There is no necessity that that only should be a Body, in which there is knowledge of the external; but it is to be held that the being a Body, in the form of being the site of experiencer and experience, belongs also to trees, &c., which have internal consciousness; because, 'as in the former case,' meaning the putrescence already mentioned [see § 114], of the Bodies of men, &c., [which takes place] in the absence of the superintendence of an experiencer [the living soul], even in the same way do withering, &c., take place in the Bodies of trees, &c., also: such is the meaning. And to this effect there is Scripture.[2]

ग्भावाच्छरीरत्वं नास्तीति नास्तिकाक्षेपमपाकरोति ॥

[1] Aniruddha and Vedánti Mahádeva here end one aphorism, and treat what follows as a second. Vijnána formally defends the reading to which he gives the preference. *Ed.*

[2] न बाह्यज्ञानं यत्रास्ति तदेव शरीरमिति नियमः किं तु वृक्षादीनामन्तःसंज्ञानामपि भो-

स्मृतेश्च[1] ॥ १२२ ॥

Law, as well as Scripture, is authority for this.

Aph. 122. And from the Legal Institutes [the same fact may be inferred, viz., that vegetables have bodies and are conscious].

a. But then, from the fact that trees, &c., also, are thus conscious, we should find merit and demerit accruing to them. To this he replies:[2]

न देहमात्रतः कर्माधिकारित्वं वैशिष्ट्यश्रुतेः॥१२३॥

Vegetables not moral agents.

Aph. 123. Not merely through a Body is there susceptibility of Merit and Demerit; for Scripture tells us the distinction.

a. The vital spirit is not liable to the production of Merit and Demerit through a *Body* merely. Why? 'For Scripture tells us the distinction:' because we are told, in Scripture, that the liability results just from the being

---

क्तृभोगायतनत्वरूपं शरीरत्वं मन्तव्यं यतः पूर्ववत्पूर्वोक्तो यो भोक्त्रधिष्ठानं विना मनुष्यादिशरीरस्य पूतिभावस्तद्वदेव वृक्षादिशरीरेष्वपि शुष्कतादिकमित्यर्थः। तथा च श्रुतिः॥

1 Nágeśa pretty evidently does not regard these words as an aphorism. *Ed.*

2 ननु वृक्षादिष्वप्येवं चेतनत्वेन धर्माधर्मोत्पत्तिप्रसङ्गः। तत्राह॥

distinguished by a Brahmanical Body, or the like [animal body, not vegetable]. Such is the meaning.[1]

b. Showing that the liability to Merit and Demerit is solely through the *kind* of Body, he mentions how Body is of three kinds :[2]

त्रिधा[3] त्रयाणां व्यवस्था कर्मदेहोपभोगदेहोभय-
देहाः ॥ १२४ ॥

Body of three principal kinds.

Aph. 124. Among the three there is a threefold distribution; the Body of merit, the Body of experience, and the Body of both.

a. There is a threefold distribution of Body 'among the three,' i. e., among those highest, lowest, and intermediate,—all living beings,—viz., the Body of merit, the Body of experience, and the Body of both: such is the meaning. Of these, a Body of merit belongs to the preeminent sages; a Body of experience, to Indra and others, and to things immovable, &c.; and a Body of both, to the royal sages. Here the division is [not exhaustive, but] into three, because of the preeminence [of these]; for,

---

[1] न देहमात्रेण धर्माधर्मोत्पत्तियोग्यत्वं जीवस्य। कुतः। वैशिष्ट्यश्रुतेः। ब्राह्मणादिदेहविशिष्टत्वेनैवाधिकारश्रवणादित्यर्थः ॥

[2] देहभेदेनैव कर्माधिकारं दर्शयन्देहत्रैविध्यमाह ॥

[3] Vedánti Mahádeva, if my single copy of his work may be relied on, omits this word. *Ed.*

otherwise, we should have all alike possessed of a Body of experience,[1] [like Indra].

b. He mentions also a fourth Body :[2]

न किंचिदप्यनुशयिनः ॥ १२५ ॥

A fourth kind of Body.

Aph. 125. Not any one [of these], moreover, is that of the apathetic.

a. That is to say: the Body which belongs to the ascetics is different from all these three; such as was that of Dattátreya, Jaḍabharata, and others; for they possessed bodies consisting of mere knowledge.[3]

b. In order to establish the non-existence of a Lord, which was stated before, he disproves the eternity of

---

[1] त्रयाणामुत्तमाधममध्यमानां सर्वप्राणिनां त्रिप्रकारो देहविभागः कर्मदेहभोगदेहोभयदेहा इतीत्यर्थः। तत्र कर्मदेहः परमर्षीणां भोगदेह इन्द्रादीनां स्थावरादीनां चोभयदेहश्च राजर्षीणामिति। अत्र प्राधान्येन त्रिधा विभागोऽन्यथा सर्वस्यैव भोगदेहत्वापत्तेः ॥

[2] चतुर्थमपि शरीरमाह ॥

[3] विरक्तानां शरीरमेतत्त्रयविलक्षणमित्यर्थः। यथा दत्तात्रेयजडभरतादीनां तेषां ज्ञानमात्रप्रधानदेहत्वादिति ॥

knowledge, desire, action, &c., which is accepted by others[1] [as existing in the case of the Lord]:

न बुद्ध्यादिनित्यत्वमाश्रयविशेषेऽपि वह्नि-
वत् ॥ १२६ ॥

Argument against the existence of a Lord.

Aph. 126. Eternity does not [as is alleged by those who wish to establish the existence of a Lord,] belong to knowledge,[2] &c., even in the case of the particular site, [viz., that of the supposed Lord]; as is the case with fire.

a. That is to say: just as we infer, from the example of ordinary fire, that the empyrean fire,[3] also, is not eternal.[4]

आश्रयासिद्धेश्च ॥ १२७ ॥

---

[1] उक्तस्येश्वराभावस्य स्थापनाय पराभ्युपगतं ज्ञानेच्छाकृत्यादिनित्यत्वं प्रतिषेधति ॥

[2] *Buddhi,* rendered 'intellect' at pp. 196, &c., *supra.* Much as at p. 209, *supra,* Vijnána hereupon remarks: बुद्धिरत्राध्यवसायाख्या वृत्तिः । *Ed.*

[3] The world, viewed as Brahmá's egg, is fabled to be surrounded by seven envelopes. One of these is the *ávaraṇa-tejas,* Dr. Ballantyne's 'empyrean fire.' See Professor Wilson's translation of the *Vishṇu-puráṇa* (ed. 1864, &c.), vol. i., p. 40. I have to thank Prof. Cowell for this reference. *Ed.*

[4] यथा लौकिकवह्निदृष्टान्तेनावरणतेजसोऽप्यनित्यत्वानुमानमित्यर्थः ॥

The argument really ex abundantiâ.

Aph. 127. And, because the site [viz., the supposed Lord,] is unreal, [it matters not, in the present instance, whether knowledge, &c., may be eternal, or not].

a. But then, in that case, how can it, indeed, be possible that there should arise Omniscience, &c., adequate to the creation of the universe; since we do not behold, in mundane life, *such* superhuman powers [though we do see some,] arising from penance and the rest [of the alleged means of acquiring superhuman powers]? To this he replies:[1]

योगसिद्धयोऽप्यौषधादिसिद्धिवन्नापलपनीयाः ॥ १२८ ॥

The height to which asceticism may elevate.

Aph. 128. The superhuman powers[2] of concentration, just like the effects of drugs, &c., are not to be gainsaid.

a. That is to say: by the example of the effects of drugs, &c., even the superhuman powers of assuming atomic magnitude, &c., which result from concentration, and are adapted to the work of creation, &c., are established.[3]

---

[1] नन्वेवं ब्रह्माण्डादिसर्जनसमर्थं सर्वज्ञत्वादिकं कथं जन्यं संभाव्येतापि लोके तपआदिभिरेवमैश्वर्यादर्शनादिति । तत्राह ॥

[2] *Vide supra*, p. 310, note 4. *Ed.*

[3] औषधादिसिद्धिदृष्टान्तेन योगजा अप्यणिमादिसिद्धयः सृष्ट्याद्युपयोगिन्यः सिध्यन्तीत्यर्थः ॥

b. He refutes him who asserts that Thought belongs to the Elements; since this is hostile to the establishment [of the existence] of Soul:[1]

न भूतचैतन्यं प्रत्येकादृष्टेः[2] सांहत्येऽपि च [3]सांहत्येऽपि च ॥ १२९ ॥

Argument against Materialism.

Aph. 129. Thought does not belong to the Elements; for it is not found in them separately, or, moreover, in the state of combination,—or, moreover, in the state of combination.

a. That is to say: Thought does not exist in the five Elements, even when in the state of combination; because we do not find Thought in them, severally, at the time of disjunction;[4] [and there can be nothing in the product which does not preexist in the cause].

---

[1] पुरुषसिद्धिप्रतिकूलतया भूतचैतन्यवादिनं प्रत्याचष्टे ॥

[2] Aniruddha has प्रत्येकानुपलब्धेः; Nágeśa, प्रत्येकादृष्टे. *Ed.*

[3] Both here and just before, Nágeśa reads स्वसां°, as does Vijnána, also, according to some MSS. *Ed.*

[4] संहतभावावस्थायामपि पञ्चभूतेषु चैतन्यं नास्ति विभागकाले प्रत्येकं चैतन्यादृष्टेरित्यर्थः ॥

END OF BOOK V.

BOOK VI.

Having explained, in four Books, all the matter of the Institute, and having, in the Fifth Book, thoroughly established it, by refuting the opinions of opponents, now, in a Sixth Book, he recapitulates the same matter, which is the essence of the Institute, while condensing it. For, in addition [to what has preceded], an enumeration of the matters before mentioned, namely, a summary, having been composed, learners acquire an undoubting, accurate, and more solid knowledge; so that, therefore, reiteration is not here to be imputed as a fault; because the method is that of fixing a stake, [viz., by repeated blows], and because arguments, &c., not previously stated, are adduced.[1]

अस्त्यात्मा [2]नास्तित्वसाधनाभावात्[3] ॥ १ ॥

---

[1] अध्यायचतुष्केण समस्तशास्त्रार्थं प्रतिज्ञाय पञ्चमाध्याये परपक्षनिराकरणेन प्रसाध्येदानीं तमेव सारभूतशास्त्रार्थं षष्ठाध्यायेन संकलयन्नुपसंहरति। उक्तार्थानां हि पुनस्तन्त्राख्ये विस्तरे कृते शिष्याणामसंदिग्धाविपर्यस्तो दृढतरो बोध उत्पद्यत इत्यतः स्थूणानिखननन्यायादनुक्तयुक्त्याद्युपन्यासाच्च नात्र पौनरुक्त्यं दोषाय ॥

[2] Vedánti Mahádeva, in my single accessible MS., reads नास्तित्वे. *Ed.*

[3] -साधकाभावात्, agreeably to Nágeśa. *Ed.*

The existence of Soul.

Aph. 1. Soul is; for there is no proof that it is not.

a. Soul really is existent, generically; since we are aware of this, that 'I think;' because there is no evidence to defeat this. Therefore, all that is to be done is to *discriminate* it [from things in general]. Such is the meaning.[1]

b. The discrimination of it he establishes by means of two proofs:[2]

देहादिव्यतिरिक्तोऽसौ[3] वैचित्र्यात् ॥ २ ॥

Soul is not Body, &c.

Aph. 2. This [Soul,] is different from the Body, &c.; because of heterogeneousness, [or complete difference between the two].

षष्ठीव्यपदेशादपि ॥ ३ ॥

The usage of language is evidence for this.

Aph. 3. Also because it [Soul,] is expressed by means of the sixth [or possessive,] case.

a. That is to say: Soul is different from Body, &c., also because the learned express it by the possessive case, in

---

[1] जानामीत्येवं प्रतीयमानतया पुरुषः सामान्यतः सिद्ध एवास्ति बाधकप्रमाणाभावात् । अतस्तद्विवेकमात्रं कर्तव्यमित्यर्थः ॥

[2] तत्र विवेकं हेतुद्वयेन साधयति ॥

[3] Some copies of Vedánti Mahádeva's work omit असौ. *Ed.*

such examples as, 'This [is] my body,' 'This [is] my understanding;' for the possessive case would be unaccountable, if there were absolute non-difference[1] [between the Body, or the like, and the Soul, to which it is thus attributed as a possession].

b. But then, suppose that this, also, is like the expressions, 'The Soul's Thought' [Soul and Thought being identical], 'Ráhu's head' [the trunkless Ráhu being *all* head], 'The statue's body,' &c. To this he replies:[2]

न [3]शिलापुत्रवद्धर्मिग्राहकमानबाधात् ॥ ४ ॥

An objection disposed of.

Aph. 4. It is not as in the case of the statue;[4] because there is [there] a contradiction to the evidence which acquaints us with the thing.

a. This expression by means of the possessive case,

---

[1] ममेदं शरीरं ममेयं बुद्धिरित्यादेर्विदुषां षष्ठीव्यपदेशादपि देहादिभ्य आत्मा भिन्नोऽत्यन्ताभेदे षष्ठ्यनुपपत्तेरित्यर्थः ॥

[2] ननु पुरुषस्य चैतन्यं राहोः शिरः शिलापुत्रस्य शरीरमित्यादिव्यपदेशवदयमपि भवतु । तत्राह ॥

[3] Aniruddha and Vedánti Mahádeva have शिलापुत्रक॰.

Śiláputra is 'grindstone,' according to the dictionaries; *śiláputraka*, in the few places where I have seen it, may well signify 'torso.' *Ed.*

[4] With reference to the word thus rendered, see the preceding note. *Ed.*

[viz., 'My body' (§ 3)] is not like 'The statue's body,' &c. In such a case as 'The statue's body,' there is a mere fiction; 'for it is contradicted by the evidence which acquaints us with the thing;' [sense being the evidence that there is here no body other than the statue]. But, in such an expression as 'My body,' there is no contradiction by evidence; for the contradiction, by Scripture and other evidences, is only in supposing the Body to be the Soul. Such is the meaning.[1]

b. Having settled that Soul is different from Body, &c., he settles its emancipation:[2]

अत्यन्तदुःखनिवृत्त्या कृतकृत्यता ॥ ५ ॥

Soul's aim how accomplished.

Aph. 5. Through the entire cessation of pain, there is done what was to be done.

a. But then, since there is an equality of gain and loss, inasmuch as, through the cessation of Pain there is the

---

[1] शिलापुत्रस्य शरीरमित्यादिवदयं षष्ठीव्यपदेशो न भवति। शिलापुत्रादिस्थले धर्मिग्राहकप्रमाणेन बाधाद्विकल्पमात्रम्। मम शरीरमिति व्यपदेशे तु प्रमाणबाधो नास्ति देहात्मताया एव श्रुत्यादिप्रमाणैर्बाधादित्यर्थः॥

[2] देहादिव्यतिरिक्ततया पुरुषमवधार्य तन्मुक्तिमवधारयति॥

ceasing of Pleasure, also, *that* cannot be Soul's aim. To this he replies :[1]

यथा दुःखात्क्लेशः[2] पुरुषस्य न तथा सुखादभिलाषः ॥ ६ ॥

Pleasure no compensation for Pain.

Aph. 6. Not such desire for pleasure is there to Soul, as there is annoyance from Pain.

a. And so the aversion to Pain, having excluded also the desire for Pleasure, gives rise to a wish for the cessation of Pain simply; so that there is not an equality of gain and loss,[3] [but a clear gain, in the desired release].

b. He declares that Soul's aim is simply the cessation of Pain; because Pain is, indeed, abundant, in comparison of Pleasure :[4]

---

[1] ननु दुःखनिवृत्त्या सुखस्यापि निवर्तनात्तुल्यायव्ययत्वेन न सा पुरुषार्थ इति । तत्राह ॥

[2] Instead of क्लेशः, some MSS. of Vijnána's commentary, as also Nágeśa and Vedánti Mahádeva, have द्वेषः; and a marginal note in one of my copies of Aniruddha states this to be the true reading. *Ed.*

[3] तथा च सुखाभिलाषं बाधित्वापि दुःखद्वेषो दुःखनिवृत्तावेवेच्छां जनयतीति न तुल्यायव्ययत्वमिति ॥

[4] सुखापेक्षया दुःखस्य बहुलत्वादपि दुःखनिवृत्तिरेव पुरुषार्थ इत्याह ॥

[1]कुत्रापि कोऽपि सुखीति ॥ ७ ॥

Pleasure sparingly dispensed.

Aph. 7. For [only] some one, somewhere, is happy.

a. Among innumerable grasses, trees, brutes, birds, men, &c., very few,—a man, a god, or the like,—are happy: such is the meaning.[2]

तदपि दुःखशबलमिति दुःखपक्षे निःक्षिपन्ते विवेचकाः ॥ ८ ॥

Pleasure undeserving of the name.

Aph. 8. It [Pleasure,] is also mixed with Pain; therefore the discriminating throw it to the side of [and reckon it as so much,] Pain.

a. He rejects the opinion that Soul's aim is not the simple cessation of Pain, but this [cessation] tinctured with Pleasure:[3]

सुखलाभाभावादपुरुषार्थत्वमिति चेन्न[4] द्वैविध्यात्[5] ॥ ९ ॥

---

[1] Vedánti Mahádeva prefixes न. *Ed.*

[2] अनन्ततृणवृक्षपशुपक्षिमनुष्यादिमध्ये स्वल्पो मनुष्यदेवादिरेव सुखी भवतीत्यर्थः ॥

[3] केवला दुःखनिवृत्तिर्न पुरुषार्थः किं तु सुखोपरक्तेति मतमपाकरोति ॥

[4] Aniruddha has चेन्नैवं. *Ed.*

[5] One of my MSS. of Aniruddha has वैचित्र्यात्. *Ed.*

Cessation of suffering is a joy.

Aph. 9. If you say that this [cessation of Pain] is not Soul's aim, inasmuch as there is no acquisition of Pleasure, then it is not as you say; for there are two kinds [of things desired].

a. For we see, amongst men, quite a distinct aspiration: [the first,] 'May I be happy;' [the second,] 'May I not be miserable;' [and the latter is *our* conception of beatitude].[1]

b. He ponders a doubt:[2]

निर्गुणत्वमात्मनोऽसङ्गत्वादिश्रुतेः[3] ॥ १० ॥

A doubt.

Aph. 10. The Soul [some one may suggest,] has *no* quality; for there is Scripture for its being unaccompanied, &c.

a. Therefore the cessation of Pain, indeed, [a property which does not belong to it,] cannot be Soul's aim: such is the meaning.[4]

b. He clears up this[5] [doubt]:

---

1 सुखी स्यां दुःखी न स्यामिति हि पृथगेव लोकानां प्रार्थना दृश्यत इति ॥

2 शङ्कते ॥

3 Aniruddha has असङ्गादिश्रुतेः; Nágeśa, असङ्गत्वश्रुतेः. *Ed.*

4 अतो न दुःखनिवृत्तिरपि पुरुषार्थो घटत इत्यर्थः ॥

5 तमाधत्ते ॥

परधर्मत्वेऽपि तत्सिद्धिरविवेकात् ॥ ११ ॥

This cleared up.

Aph. 11. Though it [the Pain,] be the property of something else, yet it exists in it [the Soul,] through non-discrimination.

a. Though qualities, viz., pleasure, pain, &c., belong [only] to the *Mind*, they exist, i.e., they abide, in the shape of a *reflexion*, in it, viz., in Soul, 'through non-discrimination,' as the cause, owing to the conjunction of Nature with Soul: such is the meaning. And this has been set forth in the First Book.[1]

b. The binding of Soul by the qualities [or fetters,] arises from non-discrimination: but from what does non-discrimination arise? With reference to this, he says:[2]

अनादिरविवेकोऽन्यथा दोषद्वयप्रसक्तेः ॥ १२ ॥

Two reasons why non-discrimination must have been from eternity.

Aph. 12. Non-discrimination [of Soul from Nature] is beginningless; because, otherwise, two objections would present themselves.

a. For, had it a beginning, then, if [first,] it arose quite spontaneously, bondage might befall even the liberated;

---

[1] सुखदुःखादिगुणानां चित्तधर्मत्वेऽपि तचात्मनि सिद्धिः प्रतिबिम्बरूपेणावस्थितिरविवेकान्निमित्ता-त्प्रकृतिपुरुषसंयोगद्वारेत्यर्थः। एतच्च प्रथमाध्याये प्रतिपादितम् ॥

[2] अविवेकमूलः पुरुषे गुणबन्धोऽविवेकस्तु किंमूलक इत्याकाङ्क्षायामाह ॥

and, if [secondly,] it were produced by Desert, &c., there would be a *regressus in infinitum*, inasmuch as we should have to search for another [previous instance of] non-discrimination, to stand as the cause of [that] Desert, &c., also: such is the meaning.[1]

b. And then, if it be without beginning, it must be everlasting. To this he replies:[2]

न नित्यः स्यादात्मवदन्यथानुच्छित्तिः[3] ॥ १३ ॥

Non-discrimination, though from eternity, may be cut short.

Aph. 13. It [non-discrimination,] cannot be everlasting [in the same manner] as the soul is; else, it could not be cut short, [as we affirm that it can be].

a. It is not everlasting, indivisible, and beginningless, in the same way as the soul is; but it is beginningless, in the shape of an *on-flow* [which may be stopped]. For, otherwise, the cutting short of a beginningless *entity* would, as is established by Scripture, be unfeasible, [though the beginningless antecedent *non-entity* of a given jar may be readily understood to terminate, on the production of the jar]. Such is the meaning.[4]

---

[1] सादित्वे हि स्वत एवोत्पादे मुक्तस्यापि बन्धापत्तिः कर्मादिजन्यत्वे च कर्मादिकं प्रत्यपि कारणत्वेनाविवेकान्तरान्वेषणेऽनवस्थेत्यर्थः ॥

[2] ननु चेदनादिस्तर्हि नित्यः स्यादिति। तत्राह ॥

[3] Nágeśa has स्यादात्मवदुच्छित्तेः. *Ed.*

[4] आत्मवन्नित्योऽखण्डानादिर्न भवति किं तु

b. Having stated the cause of [Soul's] Bondage, he states the cause of Liberation:[1]

प्रतिनियतकारणनाश्यत्वमस्य ध्वान्तवत् ॥ १४ ॥

Bondage how destructible.

Aph. 14. It [Bondage,] is annihilable by the allotted cause, [viz., discrimination of Soul from Nature]; as darkness is [annihilable by the allotted cause, viz., Light].

अत्रापि प्रतिनियमोऽन्वयव्यतिरेकात् ॥ १५ ॥

This enforced.

Aph. 15. Here, also, [viz., in the case of Bondage and Discrimination, as in the case of Darkness and Light,] there is allotment, [as is proved] both by positive and negative consociation;[2] [Liberation taking place where Discrimination is, and not where it is not].

a. He reminds [us] of what was mentioned in the first Book,[3] viz., that Bondage cannot be innate, &c:[4]

प्रवाहरूपेणानादिः। अन्यथानादिभावस्य श्रुतिसिद्धोच्छेदानुपपत्तेरित्यर्थः॥

[1] बन्धकारणमुक्त्वा मोक्षकारणमाह ॥

[2] *Vide supra*, p. 43, note 2, and p. 194, note 3. Prof. Cowell defines *anwaya-vyatireka* as 'affirmative and negative induction,' in his edition of Colebrooke's *Essays*, vol. i., p. 315, note 3. See also his translation of the *Kusumánjali*, pp. 7 and 23. *Ed.*

[3] *Vide supra*, p. 8. *Ed.*

[4] बन्धस्य स्वाभाविकत्वादिकं न संभवतीति प्रथमाध्यायोक्तं स्मारयति ॥

[1]प्रकारान्तरासंभवादविवेक एव बन्धः ॥ १६ ॥

Bondage not innate.

Aph. 16. Since it cannot be [accounted for] in any other way, it is non-discrimination alone that is [the *cause* of] Bondage, [which cannot be innate].

a. 'Bondage' here means the *cause* of Bondage, named the conjunction of pain. The rest is plain.[2]

b. But then, since liberation, also, from its being a product, is liable to destruction, Bondage should take place over again. To this he replies:[3]

न मुक्तस्य पुनर्बन्धयोगोऽप्यनावृत्तिश्रुतेः ॥ १७ ॥

Bondage does not recur.

Aph. 17. Further, Bondage does not again attach to the liberated; because there is Scripture[4] for its non-recurrence.

---

1 Vedánti Mahádeva has प्रकारान्तराभावाद्°. *Ed.*

2 बन्धोऽत्र दुःखयोगाख्यबन्धकारणम् । शेषं सुगमम् ॥

3 ननु मुक्तेरपि कार्यतया विनाशापत्त्या पुनर्बन्धः स्यादिति । तत्राह ॥

4 Vijnána and Nágeśa quote the text: न स पुनरावर्तते । Aniruddha and Vedánti Mahádeva cite the longer passage: आत्मा ज्ञातव्यः प्रकृतितो विवेक्तव्यो न पुनरावर्तते । See note 4, at p. 182, *supra*. Since that note was written, I have observed the words आत्मा वा अरे द्रष्टव्यः in the *Bṛihadá-*

अपुरुषार्थत्वमन्यथा[1] ॥ १८ ॥

Evidence of this.

Aph. 18. Else, it [liberation,] would not be Soul's aim, [which it is].

a. He states the reason why this is not Soul's aim: [2]

अविशेषापत्तिरुभयोः ॥ १९ ॥

Force of the evidence.

Aph. 19. What happened to both would be alike, [if liberation were perishable].

a. That is to say: there would be no difference between the two, the liberated and the bound; because of their being alike liable to future bondage; and, therefore, such [perishable emancipation] is not Soul's aim,[3] [but emancipation final and complete].

b. But then, in that case, if you acknowledge that there is a *distinction* between the bond and the free, how is it

---

ranyaka Upanishad, ii., 4, 5, and *Śatapatha-bráhmaṇa*, xiv., 5, 4, 5. Aniruddha, in his comment on an Aphorism which soon follows, the twenty-third, quotes them correctly, with their ensuing context; a fact which suggests that my criticism on Váchaspati Miśra's quotation, ventured in the note above referred to, may be hasty. *Ed.*

1 Aniruddha, in one of my MSS., and Vedánti Mahádeva have अन्यथापुरुषार्थत्वम् । *Ed.*

2 अपुरुषार्थत्वे हेतुमाह ॥

3 भाविबन्धत्वसाम्येनोभयोर्मुक्तबद्धयोर्विशेषो न स्यात्ततश्चापुरुषार्थत्वमित्यर्थः ॥

that you have asserted [Book I., § 19,] the *eternal* freedom [of *all* souls alike]? To this he replies:[1]

मुक्तिरन्तरायध्वस्तेर्न परः[2] ॥ २० ॥

The nature of liberation.

Aph. 20. Liberation is nothing other than the removal[3] of the obstacle [to the Soul's recognition of itself as free].

a. But then, in that case, since Bondage and Liberation are *unreal*, Liberation must be contradictory to the texts, &c., which set forth what is Soul's aim, [as some positive and real acquisition, not merely the removal of a screen]; to which he replies:[4]

तत्राप्यविरोधः ॥ २१ ॥

An objection repelled.

Aph. 21. Even in that case, there is no contradiction.

a. That is to say: 'even in that case,' i.e., even if Liberation consists [only] in the removal of an obstacle, there is no contradiction in its being Soul's aim.[5]

---

[1] नन्वेवं बद्धमुक्तयोर्विशेषाभ्युपगमे नित्यमुक्तत्वं कथमुच्यते । तत्राह ॥

[2] Nágeśa reads परा. *Ed.*

[3] The rare word *dhwasti*, thus rendered, Vijnána and Vedánti Mahádeva explain by *dhwansa*. *Ed.*

[4] नन्वेवं बन्धमोक्षयोर्मिथ्यात्वे मोक्षस्य पुरुषार्थताप्रतिपादकश्रुत्यादिविरोध इत्याह ॥

[5] तत्राप्यन्तरायध्वंसस्य मोक्षत्वेऽपि पुरुषार्थत्वाविरोध इत्यर्थः ॥

b. But then, if Liberation be merely the removal of an obstacle, then it should be accomplished through mere *hearing* [of the error which stands in the way]; just as a piece of gold on one's neck, [which one has sought for in vain, while it was] withheld from one by ignorance [of the fact that it has been tied round one's neck with a string], is attained, [on one's hearing where it is]. To this he replies:[1]

[2]अधिकारित्रैविध्यान्न नियमः[3] ॥ २२ ॥

Another objection repelled.

Aph. 22. This [attainment of Liberation, on the mere *hearing* of the truth,] is no necessity; for there are three sorts of those competent [to apprehend the truth; but not all are qualified to appropriate it, on merely hearing it].

a. He mentions that not mere *hearing* alone is seen to be the cause of knowledge, but that there are others, also:[4]

दार्ढ्यार्थमुत्तरेषाम् ॥ २३ ॥

---

[1] नन्वन्तरायध्वंसमात्रं चेन्मुक्तिस्तर्हि श्रवणमात्रेणैव तत्सिद्धिः स्याद्ज्ञानप्रतिबद्धकण्ठचामीकरसिद्धिवदिति । तत्राह ॥

[2] Nágeśa, in some copies, and, according to some copies, Vijnána read अधिकार॰. *Ed.*

[3] This Aphorism, as given, is a literal repetition of Book I., 70, at p. 87, *supra*. *Ed.*

[4] न केवलं श्रवणमात्रं ज्ञाने दृष्टकारणमन्यदपीत्याह ॥

Utility of other means besides hearing.

Aph. 23. Of others [viz., other means besides hearing], for the sake of confirmation, [there is need].

a. He speaks of these same other means:[1]

स्थिरसुखमासनमिति न नियमः ॥ २४ ॥

Formality in postures not imperative.

Aph. 24. There is no [absolute] necessity that what is steady and promoting ease should be a [*particular*] posture, [such as any of those referred to in Book III., § 34].

a. That is to say: there is no necessity that a 'posture' should be the 'lotus-posture,' or the like; because whatever is steady and promotes ease is a [suitable] 'posture.'[2]

b. He states the principal means[3] [of Concentration]:

ध्यानं निर्विषयं मनः ॥ २५ ॥

The efficient means of Concentration.

Aph. 25. Mind without an object is Meditation.

a. That is to say: what Internal Organ is void of any modification, *that* is 'Meditation,' i.e., Concentration, in the shape of exclusion of the modifications of Intellect: by reason of the identity [here,] of effect and cause, the word 'cause' is employed for 'effect.' For it will be

---

[1] उत्तराण्येव साधनान्याह ॥

[2] आसने पद्मासनादिनियमो नास्ति यतः स्थिरं सुखं च यत्तदेवासनमित्यर्थः ॥

[3] मुख्यं साधनमाह ॥

declared how Meditation effects this[1] [exclusion of the modifications of Intellect].

b. But then, since Soul is alike, whether there be Concentration or Non-concentration, what have we to do with Concentration? Having pondered this doubt, he clears it up:[2]

उभयथाप्यविशेषश्चेन्नैवमुपरागनिरोधाद्विशेषः ॥ २६ ॥

A distinction not without a difference.

Aph. 26. If you say that even both ways there is no difference, it is not so: there is a difference, through the exclusion [in the one case,] of the tinge [of reflected pain which exists in the other case].

a. But how can there exist a *tinge* in that which is unassociated [with anything whatever, as Soul is alleged to be]? To this he replies:[3]

निःसङ्गेऽप्युपरागोऽविवेकात् ॥ २७ ॥

---

[1] वृत्तिशून्यं यदन्तःकरणं भवति तदेव ध्यानं योगश्चित्तवृत्तिनिरोधरूप इत्यर्थः । कार्यकारणाभेदेन कारणशब्दः कार्ये प्रयुक्तः । एतत्साधनत्वेन ध्यानस्य वक्ष्यमाणत्वादिति ॥

[2] ननु योगायोगयोः पुरुषस्यैकरूप्यात्किं योगेनेत्याशङ्क्य समाधत्ते ॥

[3] ननु निःसङ्गे कथमुपरागः । तत्राह ॥

Soul tinged by what does not belong to it.

Aph. 27. Though it [Soul,] be unassociated, still there is a tingeing [reflexionally,] through Non-discrimination.

a. That is to say: though there is not a *real* tinge in that which is unassociated [with tincture, or anything else], still there is, *as it were*, a tinge; hence the tinge is treated as simply a *reflexion*, by those who discriminate the tinge[1] [from the Soul, which it delusively seems to belong to].

b. He explains this same:[2]

जपास्फटिकयोरिव नोपरागः किं त्वभिमानः ॥ २८ ॥

Its seeming presence explained.

Aph. 28. As is the case with the Hibiscus and the crystal [Book I., § 19, *c.*], there is not a tinge, but a fancy [that there is such].

a. He states the means of excluding the aforesaid tinge:[3]

ध्यानधारणाभ्यासवैराग्यादिभिस्तन्निरोधः ॥ २९ ॥

How to be got rid of.

Aph. 29. It [viz., the aforesaid tinge,] is debarred by Meditation, Restraint, Practice, Apathy, &c.

---

[1] निःसङ्गे यद्यपि पारमार्थिक उपरागो नास्ति तथाप्युपराग इव भवतीति कृत्वा प्रतिबिम्ब एवोपराग इति व्यवह्रियत उपरागविवेकिभिरित्यर्थः ॥

[2] एतदेव विवृणोति ॥

[3] यथोक्तोपरागस्य निरोधोपायमाह ॥

a. He shows the means settled by the ancient teachers, in regard to the exclusion—through Meditation, &c., lodged in the Mind,—of the tingeing of Soul:[1]

लयविक्षेपयोर्व्यावृत्त्येत्याचार्याः ॥ ३० ॥

The ancient dogma on this point.

Aph. 30. It is by the exclusion of dissolution[2] and distraction, say the teachers.

a. That is to say: through the removal, by means of Meditation, &c., of the Mind's condition of [being dissolved in] Sleep, and condition of [waking] Certainty, &c., there takes place also the exclusion of the tingeing of Soul by the condition; because, on the exclusion of any [real] object, there is the exclusion also of its reflexion: so say the ancient teachers.[3]

b. He states that there is no compulsion that Meditation, &c., should take place in caves and such places:[4]

न स्थाननियमश्चित्तप्रसादात्[5] ॥ ३१ ॥

---

[1] चित्तनिष्ठध्यानादिना पुरुषस्योपरागनिरोधे पूर्वाचार्यसिद्धं द्वारं दर्शयति ॥

[2] 'Inertness [of mind]' is a better rendering of *laya*. *Ed.*

[3] ध्यानादिना चित्तस्य निद्रावृत्तेः प्रमाणादिवृत्तेश्च निवृत्त्या पुरुषस्यापि वृत्त्युपरागनिरोधो भवति बिम्बनिरोधे प्रतिबिम्बस्यापि निरोधादिति पूर्वाचार्या आहुरित्यर्थः ॥

[4] ध्यानादौ गुहादिस्थाननियमो नास्तीत्याह ॥

[5] Aniruddha has, to a very different effect, -प्रसादाभावात्.

Meditation may take place anywhere.

Aph. 31. There is no rule about localities; for it is from tranquillity of Mind.

a. That is to say: Meditation, or the like, results simply 'from tranquillity of Mind.' Therefore, such a place as a cave is not indispensable for it.[1]

b. The discussion of Liberation is completed. Now, with an eye to the unchangeableness of Soul, he handles compendiously the cause of the world:[2]

प्रकृतेराद्योपादानतान्येषां कार्यत्वश्रुतेः ॥ ३२ ॥

Nature the material of the world.

Aph. 32. Nature is the primal material; for there is Scripture [to the effect] that the others are products.

a. That is to say: since we learn, from Scripture, that Mind, &c., are products, Nature is established under the character of the radical cause of these.[3]

b. But then, let *Soul* be the material. To this he replies:[4]

His comment runs: यत्र चित्तप्रसादो न भवति तत्र न कर्तव्यमनुष्ठानम् ॥ *Ed.*

[1] चित्तप्रसादादेव ध्यानादिकम् । अतस्तत्र न गुहादिस्थाननियम इत्यर्थः ॥

[2] समाप्तो मोक्षविचारः । इदानीं पुरुषापरिणामित्वाय जगत्कारणमुपसंहरति ॥

[3] महदादीनां कार्यत्वश्रवणात्तेषां मूलकारणतया प्रकृतिः सिध्यतीत्यर्थः ॥

[4] ननु पुरुष एवोपादानं भवतु । तत्राह ॥

नित्यत्वेऽपि नात्मनो योग्यत्वाभावात् ॥ ३३ ॥

Soul not the material of the world.

Aph. 33. Not to Soul does this [viz., to be the material of the world,] belong, though it be eternal; because of its want of suitableness.

a. That is to say: suitableness to act as material implies the possession of qualities, and the being associable: [and,] by reason of the absence of both of these, Soul, though eternal, [and, therefore, no product,] cannot serve as material.[1]

b. But then, since, from such Scriptural texts as, 'Many creatures have been produced from Soul,'[2] we may gather the fact that Soul is a cause, the assertions of an illusory creation, &c., ought to be accepted. Having pondered this adverse suggestion, he replies:[3]

श्रुतिविरोधान्न कुतर्कापसदस्यात्मलाभः ॥ ३४ ॥

The opposite view unscriptural.

Aph. 34. The despicable sophist[4] does not gain [a correct apprehension of] Soul; because of the contradictoriness [of his notions] to Scripture.

---

[1] गुणवत्त्वं सङ्गित्वं चोपादानयोग्यता तयोरभावात्पुरुषस्य नित्यत्वेऽपि नोपादानत्वमित्यर्थः ॥

[2] *Muṇḍaka Upanishad*, ii., i., 5. *Ed.*

[3] ननु बह्वीः प्रजाः पुरुषात्संप्रसूता इत्यादिश्रुतेः पुरुषस्य कारणत्वावगमाद्विवर्तादिवादा आश्रयणीया इत्याशङ्क्याह ॥

[4] Here I have offered a substitute for 'illogical outcaste.' *Ed.*

a. That is to say: the various views, in regard to Soul's being a cause, which are conceivable are, all, opposed to Scripture; therefore, the lowest of the bad reasoners, and others, who are accepters thereof,[1] have no knowledge of the nature of Soul. Hence it is to be understood that those, also, [e.g., the *Naiyáyikas*,] who assert that Soul is the substance of the qualities Pleasure, Pain, &c., are quite illogical; these, also, have no correct knowledge of Soul. And, if it be asserted that Soul is a cause [of the world], just as the sky is the *recipient* cause of the clouds, &c., [and stands, towards it, in the relation of a cause, in so far as, without the room afforded by it, these could not exist], then we do not object to *that;* for, what we deny is only that there is transformation[2] [of Soul, as material, into the world, as product].

b. Since we see, that, in the case of things motionless, locomotive, &c., the material cause is nothing else than

---

1 'Lowest . . . . thereof' I have put instead of 'base illogical holders of these.' *Ed.*

2 पुरुषकारणतायां ये ये पक्षाः संभावितास्ते सर्वे श्रुतिविरुद्धा इत्यतस्तदभ्युपगन्तॄणां कुतार्किकाद्यधमानामात्मस्वरूपज्ञानं न भवतीत्यर्थः । एतेनात्मनि सुखदुःखादिगुणोपादानत्ववादिनोऽपि कुतार्किका एव तेषामप्यात्मयथार्थज्ञानं नास्तीत्यवगन्तव्यम् । यदि चाकाशस्याभ्राद्यधिष्ठानकारणतावदात्मनः कारणत्वमुच्यते तदा तन्न निराकुर्मः परिणामस्यैव प्रतिषेधादिति ॥

earth, &c., how can *Nature* be the material of all? To this he replies:[1]

पारम्पर्येऽपि प्रधानानुवृत्तिरणुवत् ॥ ३५ ॥

Nature the ultimate material cause.

Aph. 35. Though but mediately [the cause of products], Nature is inferred [as the ultimate cause of the intermediate causes,]; just as are Atoms, [by the *Vaiśeshikas*].

सर्वत्र कार्यदर्शनाद्विभुत्वम् ॥ ३६ ॥

Nature all-pervading.

Aph. 36. It [Nature,] is all-pervading; because [its] products are seen everywhere.

a. But then, only if it be *limited*, can it be said that, 'Wherever a product arises, there does it [Nature,] go [or act];' [for what is unlimited, and fills all space, can find no other space to *move* into]. To this he replies:[2]

गतियोगेऽप्याद्यकारणताहानिरणुवत् ॥ ३७ ॥

An objection parried.

Aph. 37. Though motion may attach to it, this does not destroy its character as ultimate cause; just as is the case with Atoms.

a. 'Motion' means action. Though it be present, this does not prevent its [Nature's,] being the radical cause; just as is the case with the earthy and other

---

[1] स्थावरजङ्गमादिषु पृथिव्यादीनामेव कारणत्वदर्शनात्कथं प्रकृतेः सर्वोपादानत्वम् । तत्राह ॥

[2] ननु परिच्छिन्नत्वेऽपि यत्र कार्यमुत्पद्यते तत्र गच्छतीति वक्तव्यम् । तत्राह ॥

Atoms, according to the opinion of the *Vaiśeshikas*: such is the meaning.[1]

प्रसिद्धाधिक्यं प्रधानस्य न नियमः ॥ ३८ ॥

Nature the proper substitute for eight of the substances in the Nyáya list.

Aph. 38. Nature is something in addition to the notorious [nine Substances of the *Naiyáyikas*]: it is no matter of necessity [that there should be precisely nine].

a. And the argument, here, is the Scriptural declaration, that *eight* [of the pretended primitive substances] are *products*: such is the import.[2]

सत्त्वादीनामतद्धर्मत्वं तद्रूपत्वात् ॥ ३९ ॥

Nature consists of the three Qualities.

Aph. 39. Purity and the others are not *properties* of it [viz., Nature]; because they are its *essence*.

a. That is to say: Purity and the other Qualities are not *properties* of Nature; because they are what *constitutes* Nature.[3]

b. He determines the motive of Nature's energizing;

---

[1] गतिः क्रिया। तत्सत्त्वेऽपि मूलकारणताया अहानिर्यथा वैशेषिकमते पार्थिवाद्यणूनामित्यर्थः ॥

[2] अष्टानामेव कार्यत्वश्रवणं चात्र तर्क इति भावः ॥

[3] सत्त्वादिगुणानां प्रकृतिधर्मत्वं नास्ति प्रकृतिस्वरूपत्वादित्यर्थः ॥

since, if we held the energizing to be without a motive, Emancipation would be inexplicable:[1]

अनुपभोगेऽपि पुमर्थं सृष्टिः प्रधानस्योष्ट्रकुङ्कुमवहनवत्[2] ॥ ४० ॥

Nature's disinterestedness.

Aph. 40. Nature, though it does not enjoy [the results of its own energizing], creates for the sake of Soul; like a cart's carrying saffron, [for the use of its master. See Book III., § 58].

a. He states the concomitant[3] cause of diversified creation:[4]

कर्मवैचित्र्यात्सृष्टिवैचित्र्यम् ॥ ४१ ॥

Nature treats every one according to his deserts.

Aph. 41. The diversity of creation is in consequence of the diversity of Desert.

---

[1] प्रधानप्रवृत्तेः प्रयोजनमवधारयति निष्प्रयोजनप्रवृत्त्यभ्युपगमे मोक्षानुपपत्तेरिति ॥

[2] Nágeśa is peculiar in giving, as an Aphorism, in substitution for these words, the clause from the introduction to it, printed just above, viz., निष्प्र°, &c., but ending with the nominative case -अनुपपत्तिः. The Serampore edition of the *Sánkhya-pravachana-bháshya* has, as the Aphorism, very corruptly, in part: प्रयोजनप्रवृत्त्यभ्युपगमे मोक्षानुपपत्तेः ॥ *Ed.*

[3] *Nimitta*, on which *vide supra*, p. 400, note 4. *Ed.*

[4] विचित्रसृष्टौ निमित्तकारणमाह ॥

a. But then, granting that *creation* is due to Nature, yet whence is *destruction?* For a couple of opposite results cannot belong to one and the same cause. To this he replies:[1]

साम्यवैषम्याभ्यां कार्यद्वयम् ॥ ४२ ॥

Contrary results from Nature how.

Aph. 42. The two results are through equipoise and the reverse of equipoise.

a. Nature is the triad of Qualities, viz., Purity, &c.; and their 'reverse of equipoise' is their aggregation in excess or defect; the absence of this [reverse of equipoise] is 'equipoise:'[2] through these two causes two opposite results, in the shape of creation and destruction, arise from one and the same: such is the meaning.[3]

b. But then, since it is Nature's attribute to create, there should be the mundane state, even after [the discriminative] knowledge, [which, it is alleged, puts an end to it]. To this he replies:[4]

---

[1] ननु भवतु प्रधानात्सृष्टिः प्रलयस्तु कस्मात् । न ह्येकस्मात्कारणाद्विरुद्धकार्यद्वयं घटते । तचाह ॥

[2] Compare Book I., Aph. 61, *a*, at p. 71, *supra*. *Ed.*

[3] सत्त्वादिगुणत्रयं प्रधानं तेषां च वैषम्यं न्यूनातिरिक्तभावेन संहननं तदभावः साम्यं ताभ्यां हेतुभ्यामेकस्मादेव सृष्टिप्रलयरूपं विरुद्धकार्यद्वयं भवतीत्यर्थः ॥

[4] ननु प्रधानस्य सृष्टिस्वाभाव्याज्ज्ञानोत्तरमपि संसारः स्यात् । तचाह ॥

विमुक्तबोधान्न सृष्टिः प्रधानस्य लोकवत् ॥ ४३ ॥

Nature's energy does not debar emancipation.

Aph. 43. Since [or when,] the emancipated has understood [that he never was really otherwise], Nature does not create; just as, in the world, [a minister does not toil, when the king's purpose has been accomplished].[1]

a. But then, Nature does not rest from creating; for we see the mundane condition of the ignorant: and so, since Nature goes on creating, to the emancipated, also, Bondage may come again. To this he replies:[2]

नान्योपसर्पणेऽपि मुक्तोपभोगो[3] निमित्ताभा-
वात् ॥ ४४ ॥

No reason why Nature should invade the emancipated.

Aph. 44. Even though it [Nature,] may invade others [with its creative influences], the *emancipated* does not experience, in consequence of the absence of a concurrent cause,[4] [e.g., Non-discrimination, in the absence of which there is no reason why the emancipated should be subjected to Nature's invasion].

---

[1] Compare Aph. 66 of Book III., at p. 267, *supra*. *Ed.*

[2] ननु प्रधानस्य सृष्ट्युपरमो नास्त्यज्ञानां संसारदर्शनात्तथा च प्रधानसृष्ट्या मुक्तस्यापि पुनर्बन्धः स्यात् । तत्राह ॥

[3] Some copies of Vijnána here introduce भवति; and Nágeśa has the lection विमुक्तभोगो भवति. *Ed.*

[4] *Nimitta*, on which *vide supra*, p. 400, note 4. *Ed.*

a. But then, *this* arrangement could be possible then, [only] if there were a *multiplicity* of souls: but *that* is quite excluded by the text of the non-duality of Soul. Having pondered this doubt, he says:[1]

पुरुषबहुत्वं व्यवस्थातः ॥ ४५ ॥

Multeity of Soul proved from the Veda.

Aph. 45. The multeity of Soul [is proved] by the distribution [announced by the *Veda* itself].

a. That is to say: the multeity of Soul is proved, absolutely, by the distribution of Bondage and Emancipation mentioned in such Scriptural texts as, 'Whoso understand this, these are immortal, while others experience only sorrow.'[2] [3]

b. But then, the distribution of Bondage and Liberation may be through the difference of adjunct. To this he replies:[4]

---

[1] नन्वियं व्यवस्था तदा घटेत यदि पुरुषबहुत्वं स्यात्। तदेव त्वात्माद्वैतश्रुतिबाधितमित्याशङ्क्याह ॥

[2] ये तद्विदुरमृतास्ते भवन्त्यथेतरे दुःखमेवोपयन्तीत्यादिश्रुत्युक्तबन्धमोक्षव्यवस्थात एव पुरुषबहुत्वं सिध्यतीत्यर्थः ॥

[3] *Śatapatha-bráhmaṇa*, xiv., 7, 2, 15. *Ed.*

[4] ननूपाधिभेदाद्बन्धमोक्षव्यवस्था स्यात्। तत्राह ॥

उपाधिश्चेत्तत्सिद्धौ[1] पुनर्द्वैतम् ॥ ४६ ॥

Unity excluded by the supposition of Souls.

Aph. 46. If [you acknowledge] an adjunct [of Soul], then, on *its* being established, there is *duality*, [upsetting the dogma founded on in § 44].

a. But then, the adjuncts, moreover, consist of 'Ignorance,' [which, according to the Vedánta, is no reality]; so that by these there is no detriment to [the Vedántic dogma of] non-duality. With reference to this doubt, he says:[2]

द्वाभ्यामपि प्रमाणविरोधः ॥ ४७ ॥

The Vedánta cannot evade non-duality.

Aph. 47. Even by the two the authority is contradicted.

a. That is to say: even by acknowledging the two, viz., Soul and Ignorance, a contradiction is constituted to the text, [which is alleged as] the authority for non-duality.[3]

b. He states another couple of objections, also:[4]

द्वाभ्यामप्यविरोधान्न पूर्वमुत्तरं च साधकाभावात् ॥ ४८ ॥

---

[1] Nágesa has उपाधिसिद्धिश्चेत्तत्सिद्धौ. *Ed.*

[2] ननूपाधयोऽप्यविद्यका इति न तैरद्वैतभङ्ग इत्याशङ्कायामाह ॥

[3] पुरुषोऽविद्येति द्वाभ्यामप्यङ्गीकृताभ्यामद्वैतप्रमाणस्य श्रुतेर्विरोधस्तदवस्थ एवेत्यर्थः ॥

[4] अपरमपि दूषणद्वयमाह ॥

The establishment of the Vedánta tenet implies a contradiction.

Aph. 48. The primâ facie view [of the Vedánta] is not [to be allowed any force, as an objection]; because, by [admitting] two, [viz., Soul and Ignorance], there is no opposition [to our own dualistic theory of Soul and Nature]: and the subsequent [dogma, viz., that one single Soul is the only reality, is not to be allowed]; because of the non-existence of a proof, [which, if it *did* exist, would, along with Soul, constitute a duality].

a. But then, Soul will be demonstrated by its self-manifestation. To this he replies:[1]

प्रकाशतस्तत्सिद्धौ कर्मकर्तृविरोधः[2] ॥ ४९ ॥

Self-manifestation contradictory.

Aph. 49. [And,] in its [Soul's,] being demonstrated by the light [of itself, as you Vedántís say it is], there is the [unreconciled] opposition of patient and agent [in one, which is a contradiction].

a. That is to say: if Soul be demonstrated by the light which Soul consists of, there is the 'opposition of patient and agent'[3] [in one].

b. But then, there is no contradiction [here,] between patient and agent; because it [the Soul], through the property of light which is lodged in it, can, itself, furnish

---

1 ननु स्वप्रकाशतयात्मा सेत्स्यति। तत्राह ॥

2 Aniruddha has कर्मकर्तृत्वविरोधः; Nágeśa, कर्तृकर्मविरोधः. *Ed.*

3 चैतन्यरूपप्रकाशतश्चैतन्यसिद्धौ कर्मकर्तृविरोध इत्यर्थः ॥

the relation to itself; just as the *Vaiśeshikas* declare, that, through the intelligence lodged in it, it is, itself, an *object* to itself. To this he replies:[1]

जडव्यावृत्तो[2] जडं प्रकाशयति[3] चिद्रूपः ॥ ५० ॥

Illuminating function of Soul.

Aph. 50. This [Soul], in the shape of Thought, discrepant from the non-intelligent, reveals the non-intelligent.

a. But then, in that case, if duality be established in accordance with proofs, &c., what becomes of the Scriptural text declaring non-duality? To this he replies:[4]

न श्रुतिविरोधो रागिणां वैराग्याय तत्सिद्धेः ॥ ५१ ॥

A salvo for the Vaidic view.

Aph. 51. There is no contradiction to Scripture [in our view]; because that [text of Scripture which seems to

---

[1] ननु नास्ति कर्मकर्तृविरोधः स्वनिष्ठप्रकाशधर्मद्वारा स्वस्य स्वसंबन्धसंभवात्। यथा वैशेषिकानां स्वनिष्ठज्ञानद्वारा स्वस्य स्वयं विषय इति। तत्राह॥

[2] Aniruddha has -वृत्तौ. *Ed.*

[3] From this point, Vedánti Mahádeva, according to my one poor MS. of his work, has a very different reading, which, however, owing to the carelessness of the copyist, I am unable to reproduce. *Ed.*

[4] नन्वेवं प्रमाणाद्यनुरोधेन द्वैतसिद्धावद्वैतश्रुतेः का गतिः। तत्राह॥

assert absolute non-duality] is [intended] to produce apathy in those who have desires, [and who would be better for believing in 'the *nothingness* of the things of time'].

a. He tells us that the assertors of non-duality are to be shunned, not only for the reason above mentioned, but, also, because of the non-existence of evidence to convince us that the world is unreal:[1]

जगत्सत्यत्वमदुष्टकारणजन्यत्वाद्बाधकाभावात्
॥ ५२ ॥

The world's reality irrefragable.

Aph. 52. The world is real; because it results from an unobjectionable cause, and because there is [in Scripture,] no debarrer [of this view of the matter].

a. We see, in the world, that no reality belongs to dream-objects, or to the [fancied] yellowness of [invariably white] conch-shells, and the like; inasmuch as these are results of the internal organ, &c., when [not normal, but] injured by [i.e., under the injurious influence of] Sleep,[2] &c.: and this is not [the state of things] in the [waking] Universe, in which Mind is the first,[3] [4] [according to Book I., § 71].

---

[1] न केवलमुक्तयुक्त्यैवाद्वैतवादिनो हेया अपि तु जगदसत्यताग्राहकप्रमाणाभावेनापीत्याह ॥

[2] For 'injured,' &c., read, 'impeded by the obstruction [offered] by Sleep.' *Ed.*

[3] Instead of 'in which,' &c., read, '[consisting of] the Great One, &c.' *Ed.*

[4] निद्रादिदोषदुष्टान्तःकरणादिजन्यत्वेन स्वाप्नविषयशङ्खपीतिमादीनामसत्यत्वं लोके दृष्टं तच्च महदादिप्रपञ्चे नास्ति ॥

b. He declares that the Universe is real, not merely in its existent state [at any given instant], but, also, always:[1]

प्रकारान्तरासंभवात्सदुत्पत्तिः ॥ ५३ ॥

Creation excluded.

Aph. 53. Since it cannot be [accounted for] in any other way, manifestation [of whatever is manifested] is of what is real, [i.e., of what previously existed].

a. That is to say: since, through the aforesaid reasons, it is impossible that the unreal should come into existence, what does come into existence, or is manifested, is what really existed [previously,] in a subtile form.[2]

b. Though [it is declared that] the being the agent and the being the experiencer belong to diverse subjects, he asserts the distribution [of agency to Self-consciousness, and of experience to Soul,] by two aphorisms:[3]

अहंकारः कर्ता न पुरुषः ॥ ५४ ॥

The real agent who.

Aph. 54. Self-consciousness, not Soul, is the agent.

---

[1] न केवलं वर्तमानदशायामेव प्रपञ्चः सन्नपि तु सदैवेत्याह ॥

[2] पूर्वोक्तयुक्तिभिरसदुत्पादासंभवात्सूक्ष्मरूपेण सदेवोत्पद्यतेऽभिव्यक्तं भवतीत्यर्थः ॥

[3] कर्तृत्वभोक्तृत्वयोर्वैयधिकरण्येऽपि व्यवस्थामुपपादयति सूत्राभ्याम् ॥

चिदवसाना भुक्तिस्तत्कर्मार्जितत्वात् ॥ ५५ ॥

Experience is got rid of when.

Aph. 55. Experience ceases at [discrimination of] Soul, [as being quite distinct from Nature]; since it arises from its [Soul's,] Desert, [which is not, *really*, Soul's, but which, while Non-discrimination lasts, is made over to Soul; just as the fruits of the acts of a king's ministers are made over to the king].

a. He shows the reason for what was stated before, viz., that cessation of action does not result from enterings into the world of Brahmá:[1]

चन्द्रादिलोकेऽप्यावृत्तिर्निमित्तसद्भावात्[2] ॥ ५६ ॥

Paradise no security against transmigration.

Aph. 56. Even in the world of the moon, &c., there is return [to mundane existence]; because of there really being a cause [of such return].

a. 'A cause,' viz., Non-discrimination, Desert, &c.[3]

b. But then, through the counsels of the persons dwelling in these various [supermundane] worlds, there ought to be no return [to mundane existence]. To this he replies:[4]

---

[1] ब्रह्मलोकान्तर्गतिभिर्नास्ति निष्कृतिरिति पूर्वोक्ते कारणं दर्शयति ॥

[2] Instead of -सद्भावात्, Aniruddha has -संभवात्. *Ed.*

[3] निमित्तमविवेककर्मादिकम् ॥

[4] ननु तत्तल्लोकवासिजनोपदेशादनावृत्तिः स्यात् । तत्राह ॥

लोकस्य नोपदेशात्सिद्धिः[1] पूर्ववत् ॥ ५७ ॥

This point enforced. *Aph.* 57. Not by the counsel of [supermundane] people is there effectuation [of Emancipation]; just as in the former case, [the case, viz., of counsel given by mundane instructors].

a. But, in that case, what becomes of the text that there is no return from the world of Brahmá? To this he replies:[2]

पारम्पर्येण तत्सिद्धौ विमुक्तिश्रुतिः ॥ ५८ ॥

A salvo for a Scriptural text. *Aph.* 58. There is Scripture [declaratory] of Emancipation, [on going to the world of Brahmá]; this [Emancipation] being effected [more readily in that world than in this, but only] by intermediacy [of the appropriate means].

a. He alleges the Scriptural text of Soul's *going* [to the locality where it is to experience], even though it be all-filling,[3] [and can, therefore, have no place into which to move]:

गतिश्रुतेश्च व्यापकत्वेऽप्युपाधियोगाद्भोगदेशका-
ललाभो व्योमवत् ॥ ५९ ॥

Another. *Aph.* 59. And, in accordance with the text of its 'going,' though it [Soul,]

---

1 Aniruddha has, instead of सिद्धिः, तत्सिद्धिः. *Ed.*

2 नन्वेवं ब्रह्मलोकादनावृत्तिश्रुतेः का गतिः। तत्राह ॥

3 परिपूर्णत्वेऽप्यात्मनो गतिश्रुतिमुपपादयति ॥

is all-pervading, yet, in time, it reaches its place of experience [or body], through conjunction with an adjunct; as in the case of Space.

a. For, as Space, though it is all-pervading, is spoken of as moving to some particular place, in consequence of its conjunction with an adjunct, such as a jar, [when we say 'the space occupied by the jar is moved to the place to which the jar is carried'], just so is it[1] [here].

b. He expounds the statement, that the site of experience [the body,] is formed through the superintendence of the experiencer,[2] [Soul]:

अनधिष्ठितस्य पूतिभावप्रसङ्गान्न[3] तत्सिद्धिः ॥ ६० ॥

The Body's existence dependent on Soul.

Aph. 60. This [constitution of a body] is not accomplished in the case of what is [organic matter] not superintended [by Soul]; because we find putrefaction [in organic matter where Soul is absent].

a. But then, let the construction of a site of experience [or a body,] for Experiencers [i.e., Souls,] take place

---

[1] यथा ह्याकाशस्य पूर्णत्वेऽपि देशविशेषगतिर्घटाद्युपाधियोगाद्व्यवह्रियते तथैवेति ॥

[2] भोक्तुरधिष्ठानाद्भोगायतननिर्माणमिति यदुक्तं तत्प्रपञ्चयति ॥

[3] The reading of Aniruddha is पूतिभावयोगान्न. *Ed.*

without any superintendence at all, through Desert. To this he replies:[1]

अदृष्टद्वारा चेदसंबद्धस्य[2] तदसंभवाज्जलादिव-
दङ्कुरे ॥ ६१ ॥

Desert not the maker of the Body.

Aph. 61. If you say that [independently of any superintendence,] it is through Desert [that a Body is formed, it is not so]; since what is unconnected [with the matter to be operated upon] is incompetent thereto; as is the case with [unapplied] water, &c., in respect of a plant.

a. That is to say: because it is impossible that Desert, which is not directly conjoined with the semen and other [elements of the Body], should operate *through Soul,* in the construction of the Body, &c.; just as it is for water, &c., *unconnected* with the seed, to operate *through tillage,* &c., in the production of a plant.[3]

b. According to the system of the *Vaiśeshikas* and others, it is settled that Soul is the superintendent, [in the construction of the Body], *in virtue of its being conjoined with Desert.* But he tells us, that, in his own doc-

---

[1] नन्वधिष्ठानं विनैवादृष्टद्वारा भोक्तृभ्यो भोगायतननिर्माणं भवतु । तचाह ॥

[2] Nágeśa reads चेदसंबद्ध°. *Ed.*

[3] शुक्रादौ साक्षादसंबद्धस्यादृष्टस्य शरीरादिनिर्माणे भोक्तृद्वारत्वासंभवाद्बीजासंबद्धानां जलादीनामङ्कुरोत्पत्तौ कर्षादिद्वारत्ववदित्यर्थः ॥

trine, since Desert, &c., are not properties of Soul, the Soul cannot, *through these*, be the cause[1] [of the Body]:

निर्गुणत्वात्तदसंभवादहंकारधर्मा ह्येते ॥ ६२ ॥

Reason for this. *Aph.* 62. For this is impossible [viz., that the Soul should, *through its Desert, &c.*, be the cause of Body]; because it has *no* qualities for these [viz., Desert, &c.,] are properties of Self-consciousness, [not of Soul].

a. And so, in *our* opinion, it is settled that Soul superintends [in the causing of the Body,] quite directly, by conjunction simply, without reference to anything intermediate: such is the import.[2]

b. But, if Soul be all-pervading, then the limitedness of the living soul, which is set forth in Scripture, is unfounded. To repel this doubt, he says:[3]

---

[1] वैशेषिकादिनयेनादृष्टस्य संबन्धघटकतयात्मनोऽधिष्ठातृत्वं स्थापितम् । स्वसिद्धान्ते त्वदृष्टादीनामात्मधर्मत्वाभावात्तद्द्वारा भोक्तुर्हेतुत्वमेव न संभवतीत्याह ॥

[2] तथा चास्मन्मते द्वारनैरपेक्ष्येण संयोगमात्रेण साक्षादेव भोक्तुरधिष्ठानं सिध्यतीति भावः ॥

[3] ननु चेत्पुरुषो व्यापकस्तर्हि श्रुतिप्रतिपादितं जीवपरिच्छिन्नत्वमनुपपन्नम् । तामिमामाशङ्कां परिहर्तुमाह ॥

विशिष्टस्य जीवत्वमन्वयव्यतिरेकात् ॥ ६३ ॥

Soul how limited and unlimited.

Aph. 63. The nature of a living soul belongs to that which is qualified, [not to Soul devoid of qualities, as is proved] by direct and indirect arguments.[1]

a. To be a living soul is the being possessed of the vital airs; and this is the character of the soul distinguished by personality, not of pure Soul,[2] [which is unlimited].

b. Desiring, now, to set forth the difference between the products of Mind [or the Great Principle,] and of Self-consciousness, he first states the products of Self-consciousness:[3]

अहंकारकर्त्रधीना कार्यसिद्धिर्नेश्वराधीना प्रमाणाभावात् ॥ ६४ ॥

The real agent what.

Aph. 64. The effectuation of works is dependent on the agent Self-consciousness, not dependent on a Lord, [such as is feigned by the *Vaiśeshikas*]; because there is no proof [of the reality of such].[4]

a. By this aphorism are set forth, as are also established

---

[1] On *anwaya-vyatireka*, *vide supra*, p. 428, note 2. *Ed.*

[2] जीवत्वं प्राणित्वं तच्चाहंकारविशिष्टपुरुषस्य धर्मो नतु केवलपुरुषस्य ॥

[3] इदानीं महदहंकारयोः कार्यभेदं प्रतिपिपादयिषुरादावहंकारकार्यमाह ॥

[4] See Book I., Aph. 92, at p. 112, *supra*. *Ed.*

by Scripture and the Legal Institutes, the creative and the destructive agencies of Brahmá and Rudra[1] [respectively], owing to their adjunct, Self-consciousness,[2] [or personality].

b. But then, grant that Self-consciousness is the maker of the others, still who is the maker of Self-consciousness? To this he replies :[3]

अदृष्टोद्भूतिवत्समानत्वम् ॥ ६५ ॥

The real agent whence.

Aph. 65. It is the same as in the arising of Desert.

a. Just as, at the creations, &c., the manifestation of Desert, which sets Nature energizing, results solely from the particular *time*,—since, if we were to suppose other Desert as the instigator of this, we should have an infinite regress,—just so Self-consciousness arises from *time* alone, as the cause; but there is not another maker thereof, also : thus, the two [cases] are alike : such is the meaning.[4]

---

1 This is an appellation of Śiva. *Ed.*

2 अनेन सूत्रेणाहंकारोपाधिकं ब्रह्मरुद्रयोः सृष्टिसंहारकर्तृत्वं श्रुतिस्मृतिसिद्धमपि प्रतिपादितम् ॥

3 ननु भवत्वहंकारोऽन्येषां कर्ताहंकारस्य तु कः कर्ता । तत्राह ॥

4 यथा सर्गादिषु प्रकृतिक्षोभककर्माभिव्यक्तिः कालविशेषमात्राद्भवति तदुद्बोधककर्मान्तरस्य क-

महतोऽन्यत् ॥ ६६ ॥

Orthodox recognition of Brahmá, Śiva, and Vishṇu, put forward.

Aph. 66. The rest is from Mind, [the Great Principle].

a. What is other than the products of Self-consciousness [or personality], viz., Creation, &c., that, viz., Preservation, &c., results from the Great Principle alone; because, inasmuch as it consists of pure Goodness, having no Conceit, Passion, &c., it is moved solely by benevolence towards others: such is the meaning. And by this aphorism is established the character, as Preserver, of Vishṇu, owing to the Great Principle, as adjunct[1 2] [of the soul, which, without adjunct, would neither create, preserve, nor destroy (see § 64)].

b. It has been stated, before, that the relation of Nature and Soul, as experienced and experiencer, is caused by Non-discrimination [of the one from the other]. Here, what is Non-discrimination, itself, caused by?

स्पनेऽनवस्थाप्रसङ्गात्तथैवाहंकारः कालमात्रानिमित्तादेव जायते न तु तस्यापि कर्चन्तरमस्तीति समानत्वमावयोरित्यर्थः ॥

[1] अहंकारकार्यात्सृष्ट्यादेर्यदन्यत्पालनादिकं तन्महत्तत्त्वादेव भवति विशुद्धसत्त्वतयाभिमानरागाद्यभावेन परानुग्रहमात्रप्रयोजनकत्वादित्यर्थः । अनेन च सूत्रेण महत्तत्त्वोपाधिकं विष्णोः पालकत्वमुपपादितम् ॥

[2] The text here followed is very inferior. *Ed.*

With reference to this doubt, he states that all philosophers reject, in common, the doubt whether we should have an infinite regress, on the supposition of a *stream* of Non-discrimination; because *this* [regress] is *valid*;[1] [since an infinite regress which is in conformity with the truth is no sound cause of objection]:

कर्मनिमित्तः प्रकृतेः स्वस्वामिभावोऽप्यनादिर्बीजाङ्कुरवत् ॥ ६७ ॥

A theory which may be acquiesced in without detriment to the argument.

Aph. 67. The relation of possession and possessor, also, if attributed [as it is by some,] to Desert, in the case of Nature [and Soul], like [the relation of] seed and plant, [which takes the shape of an infinite regress of alternants], is beginningless.

अविवेकनिमित्तो[2] वा पञ्चशिखः ॥ ६८ ॥

A second.

Aph 68. Or [the case is, likewise, one of an infinite regress,] if it [the relation between Nature and Soul,] be attributed to Non-discrimination [of Soul from Nature], as Panchaśikha [holds].

---

[1] अविवेकनिमित्तकः प्रकृतिपुरुषयोर्भोग्यभोक्तृभाव इति प्रागुक्तम् । तत्राविवेक एव किंनिमित्तक इत्याकाङ्क्षायामविवेकधाराकल्पनेऽनवस्थापत्तिरित्याशङ्कायाः प्रामाणिकत्वेन परिहारः सर्ववादिसाधारण इत्याह ॥

[2] -निमित्तकः is the reading of Aniruddha. *Ed.*

लिङ्गशरीरनिमित्तक इति सनन्दनाचार्यः ॥ ६९ ॥

A third.

Aph. 69. [The case is the same,] if, as the teacher Sanandana does, we attribute it [the relation between Nature and Soul,] to the Subtile Body, [which, in the shape of its elemental causes, attends Soul, even during the periodical annihilations of the world].

a. He sums up the import of the declarations of the Institute :[1]

यद्वा तद्वा तदुच्छित्तिः पुरुषार्थस्तदुच्छित्तिः पुरुषार्थः ॥ ७० ॥

The summing up.

Aph. 70. Be that the one way, or the other, the cutting short thereof [viz., of the relation between Nature and Soul,] is Soul's aim ; the cutting short thereof is Soul's aim.

---

[1] शास्त्रवाक्यार्थमुपसंहरति ॥

THE END.

CORRECTIONS AND ADDITIONS.

IN THE BODY OF THE PAGE.

P. 12, l. 19. Instead of 'indestructible,' read 'impracticable.'

P. 23, l. 7. 'That is to say,' &c. See, for a more correct rendering, the *Rational Refutation*, &c., p. 63.

P. 25, l. 2. Read, instead of 'your own implied dogma,' 'the dogma which you accept.'

P. 32, l. 8. The reference to the second note is omitted.

P. 35, l. 14. एक आत्मा is the reading of Aniruddha and Nágesa; एकात्मा, that of Vijnána and Vedánti Mahádeva.

P. 44, l. 3. Aniruddha has पूर्वभाविमात्रे.

P. 46, l. 14. Read, instead of तत्वं, तत्त्वं.

P. 52, l. 10. 'That is to say,' &c. For another version, see the *Rational Refutation*, &c., p. 119.

P. 56, l. 7. Read निर्गुणा°.

P. 58, l, 13. Almost certainly, this interpolation was taken from the Serampore edition of the *Sánkhya-pravachana-bháshya*. My copy of that work was lent, in 1851, to Pandit Híránanda Chaube, who prepared, for Dr. Ballantyne, the Sanskrit portion of what corresponds to pp. 1—183, *supra*, in which, additions, compressions, interpolations, and other alterations lawlessly made by him, and scholia of his own devising, were introduced with regrettable frequency.

P. 59, l. 15—p. 61, l. 13. For another rendering, from a text here and there somewhat different, see the *Rational Refutation*, &c. pp. 12, 13.

P. 69, l. 10. Read वह्नेः.

P. 85, l. 13. 'This Ignorance,' &c. The original of this is i., v., 4, of the *Vishṇu-puráṇa*.

P. 143, l. 4. Read -ङ्कुरवत्.

P. 149, l. 1. Read 'is meant.'

P. 199, l. 5. 'An internal' is better.

P. 216, l. 8. Instead of 'it is one with the internal organ,' read 'the internal organ is really one.' The implication is, that *buddhi*, *ahankára*, and *manas* really make one whole, called *manas*, in the wider sense of that term.

P. 233, l. 8. Read मूर्तत्वेऽपि.

P. 246, l. 12. Remove the brackets which enclose 'promoting.' Compare p. 433, l. 7.

P. 272, l. 16. Read 'family;' i.e., as.'

P. 292, l. 9. Read पिङ्गलावत्.

P. 437, l. 10. Read कार्यत्वश्रुतेः.

IN THE NOTES.

P. 13, l. 1. Read स्वाभाविकायापायो°, and remove, in p. 12, *a.*, the brackets enclosing the words 'the positive destruction of.' Dr. Ballantyne's maimed expression I find nowhere but in the Serampore edition of the *Sánkhya-pravachana-bháshya.*

P. 18, l. 2. Read चित्तस्यैवास्तु.

P. 30, l. 1. Nágeśa has -निमित्ततः, which Vijnána and Vedánti Mahádeva recognize as a reading.

P. 35, l. 5. Read 'Aniruddha and Nágeśa have.'

P. 39, ll. 5, 6. See, for the true reading of what is here given corruptly, the *Chhándogya Upanishad*, vi., ii., 1, 2.

P. 47, l. 5. Read बध्येतेत्याशयः.

P. 54, l. 3. In the Serampore edition of the *Sánkhya-pravachana-bháshya*, the reading is घटसंवृत आकाशे, which obviates the anacoluthism spoken of in p. 53, note 4.

P. 54, l. 4. From the *Indische Studien*, where referred to at the foot of p. 53, it appears that Professor Weber found, in the *Amṛita-bindu Upanishad*, v. 13, here quoted, घटोपमः, instead of नभोपमः. Compare, further, Gauḍapáda's *Máṇḍúkyopanishat-káriká*, iii., 4, *et seq.*

P. 55, l. 4. Read, instead of 'Vedánti Mahádeva,' 'Nágeśa.'

P. 63, l. 4. Read सिध्यति, and so in p. 70, l. 5, and p. 107, l. 6.

P. 64, l. 1. Read *vásaná*.

P. 64, l. 4. The verses in question also occur as ii., 32, of Gaudapáda's *Mánḍúkyopanishat-káriká*. They are quoted and translated in the *Rational Refutation*, &c., pp. 189, 190, where they are professedly taken, I cannot now say how tenably, from the *Viveka-chúḍámaṇi*, which is credulously affiliated on Śankara Áchárya.

P. 68, l. 6. Read साक्षात्का-.

P. 77, l. 1. Read अथ वा.

P. 102, l. 4. Read -श्रुतिज्ञानार्थं.

P. 118, l. 3. The quotation in question is xvi., 3, 4, of the *Yoga-vásishṭha*. For a more correct translation of it, see the *Rational Refutation*, &c., p. 214.

P. 182, l. 7. For emendations of sundry matters in note 4, see p. 429, note 4.

P. 204, ll. 2, 3. The Serampore edition of the *Sánkhya-pravachana-bháshya* has त्वधिष्ठाने, answering to its अधिष्ठाने in the Aphorism; also, अधिष्ठानमित्येव वा पाठः.

P. 326, l. 6. Read 'clerical.'

In the foregoing pages, reference has been made, again and again, to the Serampore edition of the *Sánkhya-pravachana-bháshya* published in 1821. Of the imperfections of that edition some notion may be formed from the facts, that it gives, as if they were commentary, no fewer than twenty-six of the Aphorisms, that it wholly omits six others, repeats two, curtails or mangles several, and, more than once, represents, as Aphorisms, fragments of Vijnána's exposition. Still, if great liberties have not been taken with his materials by the pandit who prepared it for the press, it may be considered as possessing the value of an inferior manuscript. Hence it has been thought worth while to extract from it, as below, its principal peculiar readings of the Aphorisms, over and above those already remarked on. The pages and notes referred to are those of the present work.

Book I. Aph. 2. निवृत्तेः. Aph. 24. तावदप॰. Aph. 41. पूर्वभावमात्रेणानियमः। Aph. 43. तर्हि is omitted. Aph. 67. As in the MSS. spoken of in p. 82, note 3. Aph. 73. अन्येषां. Aph. 81. न कर्मोपादानायोगात्। Aph. 97. विशेषकार्यमिति.

Book II. Aph. 3. Only न श्रवणमात्रात्तत्सिद्धिः। Aph. 6. As in Aniruddha. See p. 190, note 3. Aph. 26. च is inserted. See p. 206, note 1.

Book III. Aph. 12. स्वातन्त्र्यं तद्वृते. Aph. 15. च is omitted. See p. 235, note 3. Aph. 63. विरक्तबो॰. Aph. 66. विरमतेऽ. See p. 267, note 3.

Book IV. Aph. 26. बन्धः. See p. 305, note 3.

Book V. Aph. 4. एव, instead of इतरथा. Aph. 6. तु is added at the end. Aph. 33. As in Aniruddha and Vedánti Mahádeva. See p. 338, note 2. Aph. 39. कार्यनियमः. Aph. 40. -प्रतीतेः. See p. 344, note 3. Aph. 51. As in Vedánti Mahádeva. See p. 352, note 4. Aph. 57. स्फोटशब्दः, instead of स्फोटात्मकः शब्दः. Aph. 80. तद्वति, instead of इति. Aph. 89. तद्रूप॰. See p. 384, note 1. Aph. 98. -मानाभावात्. See p. 390, note 3. Aph. 120. क्रियानिमित्तको. Aph. 123. वैशिष्ट्योक्तः, instead of वैशिष्ट्यश्रुतेः.

Book VI. Aph. 11. परधर्मापि. Aph. 13. अन्यथात्वमिति, instead of अन्यथानुच्छित्तिः. Aph. 26. उभयोऽप्य॰.

Published by

Facsimile Publisher
Ashok Vihar, Delhi-110052 (India)
Website: www.facsimilepublisher.com

Distributed by

Gyan Books Pvt. Ltd.
5, Ansari Road, Daryaganj, New Delhi-110002 (India)
E-mail: books@gyanbooks.com, Website: www.gyanbooks.com

2 222000 012052